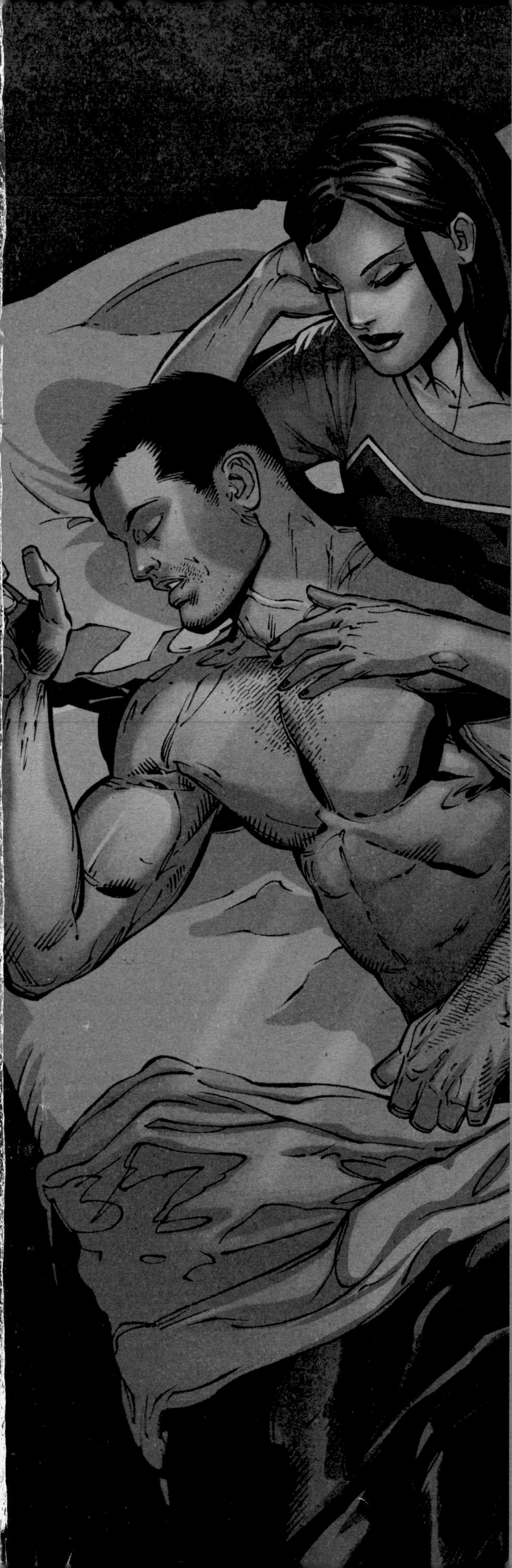

VOLUME 5
A SAVAGE END

SUPERMAN/WONDER WOMAN

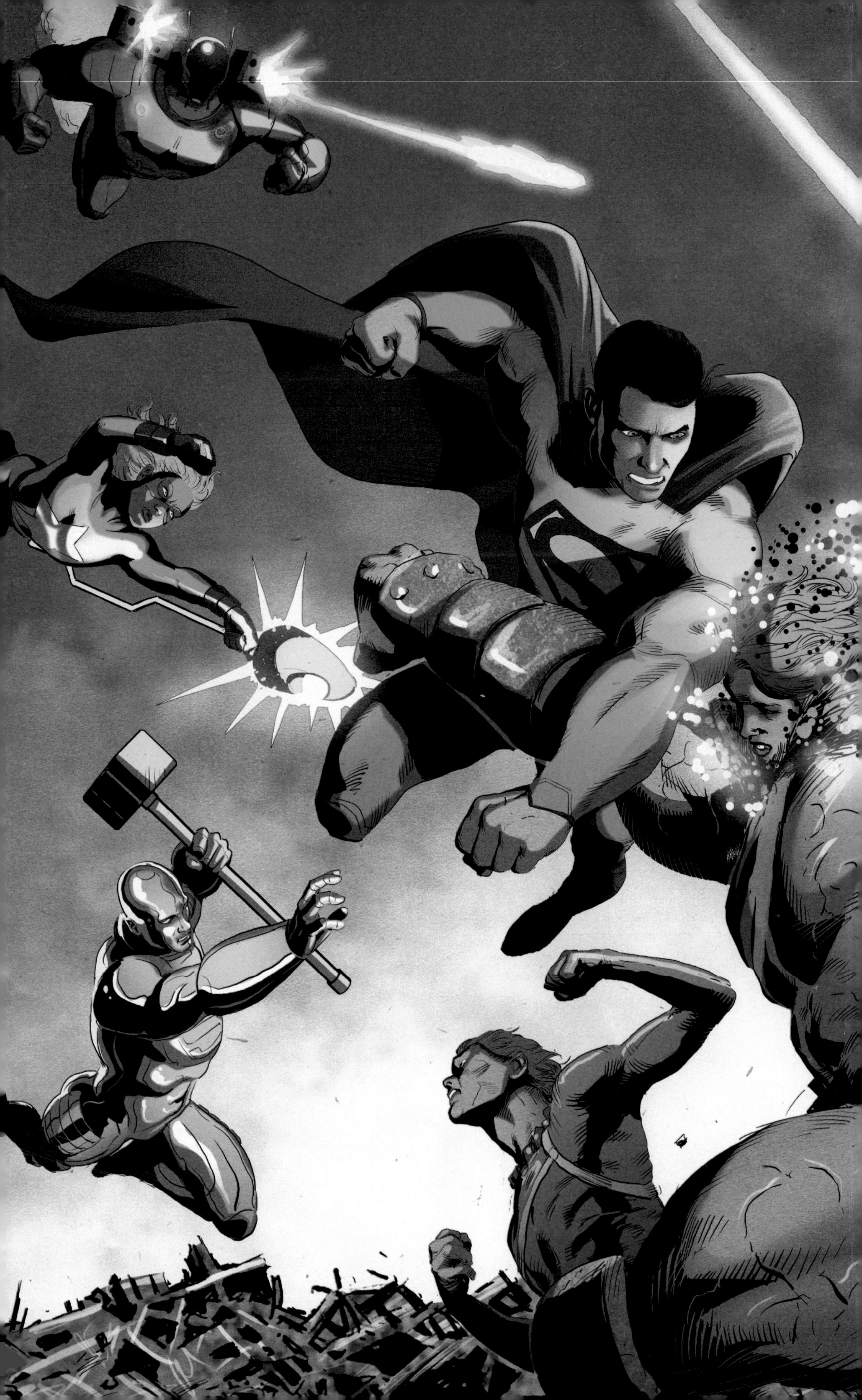

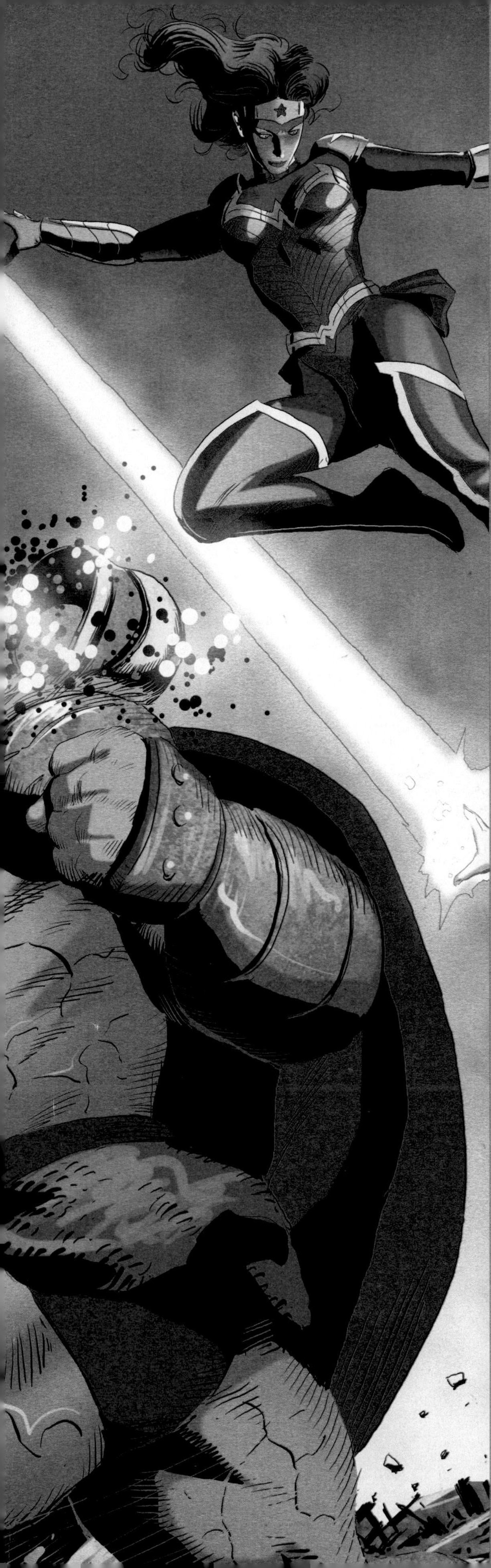

SUPERMAN/WONDER WOMAN

VOLUME 5
A SAVAGE END

WRITTEN BY
BRIAN BUCCELLATO
KEITH CHAMPAGNE
PETER J. TOMASI

PENCILS BY
ED BENES
GIUSEPPE CAFARO
CHRISCROSS
JORGE JIMÉNEZ
DOUG MAHNKE
POP MHAN
CLIFF RICHARDS
MARCO SANTUCCI

INKS BY
ED BENES
GIUSEPPE CAFARO
CHRISCROSS
JONATHAN GLAPION
SCOTT HANNA
JORGE JIMÉNEZ
MICHEL LACOMBE
DOUG MAHNKE
JAIME MENDOZA
POP MHAN
CLIFF RICHARDS

COLOR BY
HI-FI
LEE LOUGHRIDGE
LEONARDO OLEA
WIL QUINTANA
ALEJANDRO SÁNCHEZ
ALEX SINCLAIR
BETH SOTELO

LETTERS BY
MARILYN PATRIZIO
TRAVIS LANHAM
ROB LEIGH
DAVID SHARPE

COLLECTION COVER ART BY
JOHN ROMITA JR.
SCOTT HANNA AND LAURA MARTIN

SUPERGIRL BASED ON CHARACTERS CREATED BY
JERRY SIEGEL & JOE SHUSTER
SUPERMAN CREATED BY
JERRY SIEGEL & JOE SHUSTER
BY SPECIAL ARRANGEMENT
WITH THE JERRY SIEGEL FAMILY

WONDER WOMAN CREATED BY
WILLIAM MOULTON MARSTON

ANDREW MARINO Assistant Editor – Original Series
EDDIE BERGANZA Group Editor – Original Series
JEB WOODARD Group Editor – Collected Editions
SUZANNAH ROWNTREE Editor – Collected Edition
STEVE COOK Design Director – Books
DAMIAN RYLAND Publication Design

BOB HARRAS Senior VP – Editor-in-Chief, DC Comics

DIANE NELSON President
DAN DiDIO Publisher
JIM LEE Publisher
GEOFF JOHNS President & Chief Creative Officer
AMIT DESAI Executive VP – Business & Marketing Strategy, Direct to Consumer & Global Franchise Management
SAM ADES Senior VP – Direct to Consumer
BOBBIE CHASE VP – Talent Development
MARK CHIARELLO Senior VP – Art, Design & Collected Editions
JOHN CUNNINGHAM Senior VP – Sales & Trade Marketing
ANNE DePIES Senior VP – Business Strategy, Finance & Administration
DON FALLETTI VP – Manufacturing Operations
LAWRENCE GANEM VP – Editorial Administration & Talent Relations
ALISON GILL Senior VP – Manufacturing & Operations
HANK KANALZ Senior VP – Editorial Strategy & Administration
JAY KOGAN VP – Legal Affairs
THOMAS LOFTUS VP – Business Affairs
JACK MAHAN VP – Business Affairs
NICK J. NAPOLITANO VP – Manufacturing Administration
EDDIE SCANNELL VP – Consumer Marketing
COURTNEY SIMMONS Senior VP – Publicity & Communications
JIM (SKI) SOKOLOWSKI VP – Comic Book Specialty Sales & Trade Marketing
NANCY SPEARS VP – Mass, Book, Digital Sales & Trade Marketing

SUPERMAN/WONDER WOMAN VOLUME 5: A SAVAGE END

DC Comics, 2900 West Alameda Ave., Burbank, CA 91505
Printed by LSC Communications, Salem, VA, USA. 11/18/16. First Printing.
ISBN: 978-1-4012-6545-8

Library of Congress Cataloging-in-Publication Data is available.

PEFC Certified

Printed on paper from
sustainably managed
forests, controlled
sources

PEFC/29-31-337   www.pefc.org

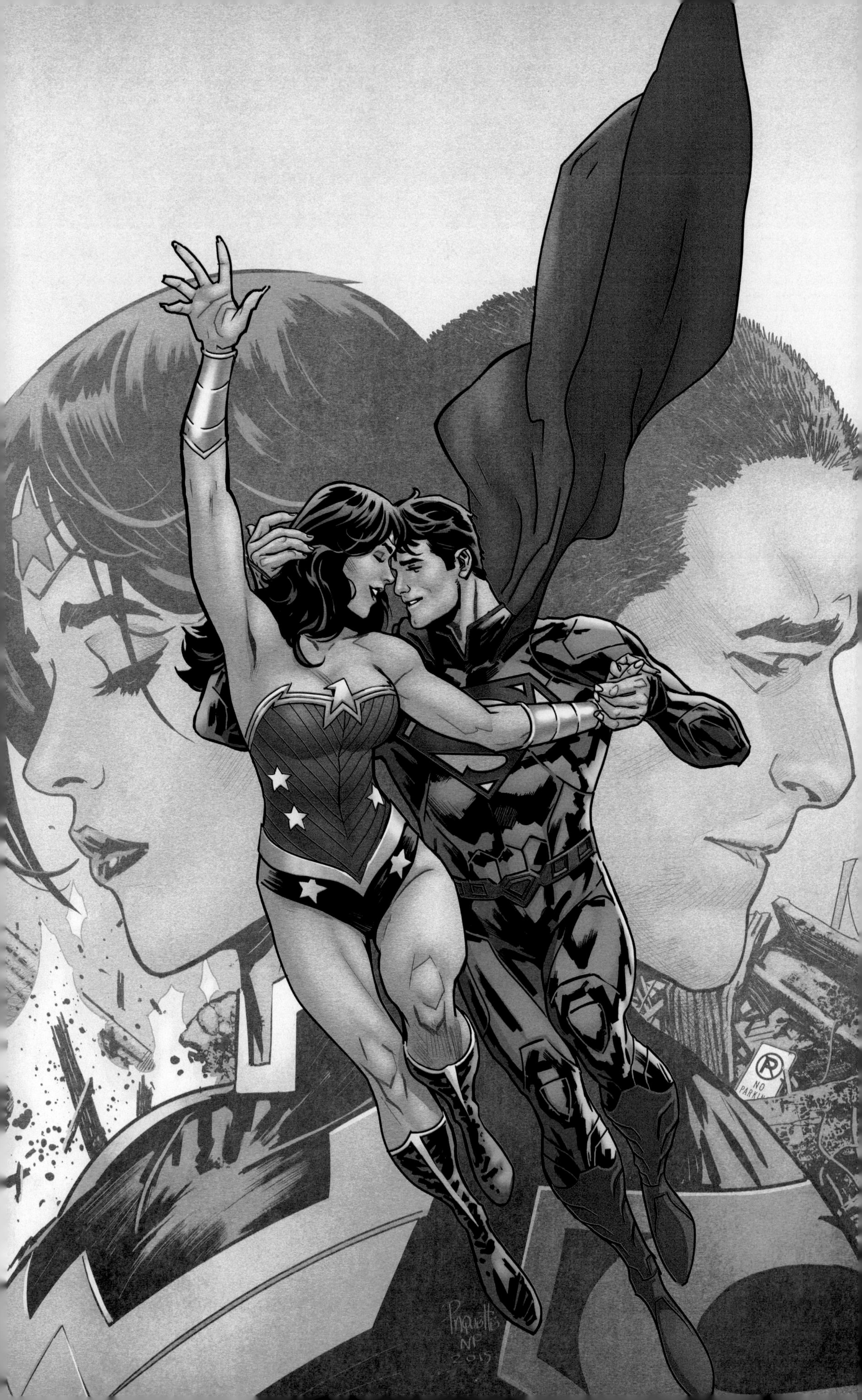
NO
PARKIN

BEGINNINGS AND ENDS PETER J. TOMASI writer MARCO SANTUCCI penciller MICHEL LACOMBE inker BETH SOTELO colorist
TAKING A BREATH KEITH CHAMPAGNE writer CHRISCROSS artist LEONARDO OLEA colorist

MARILYN PATRIZIO letterer cover by YANICK PAQUETTE & NATHAN FAIRBAIRN

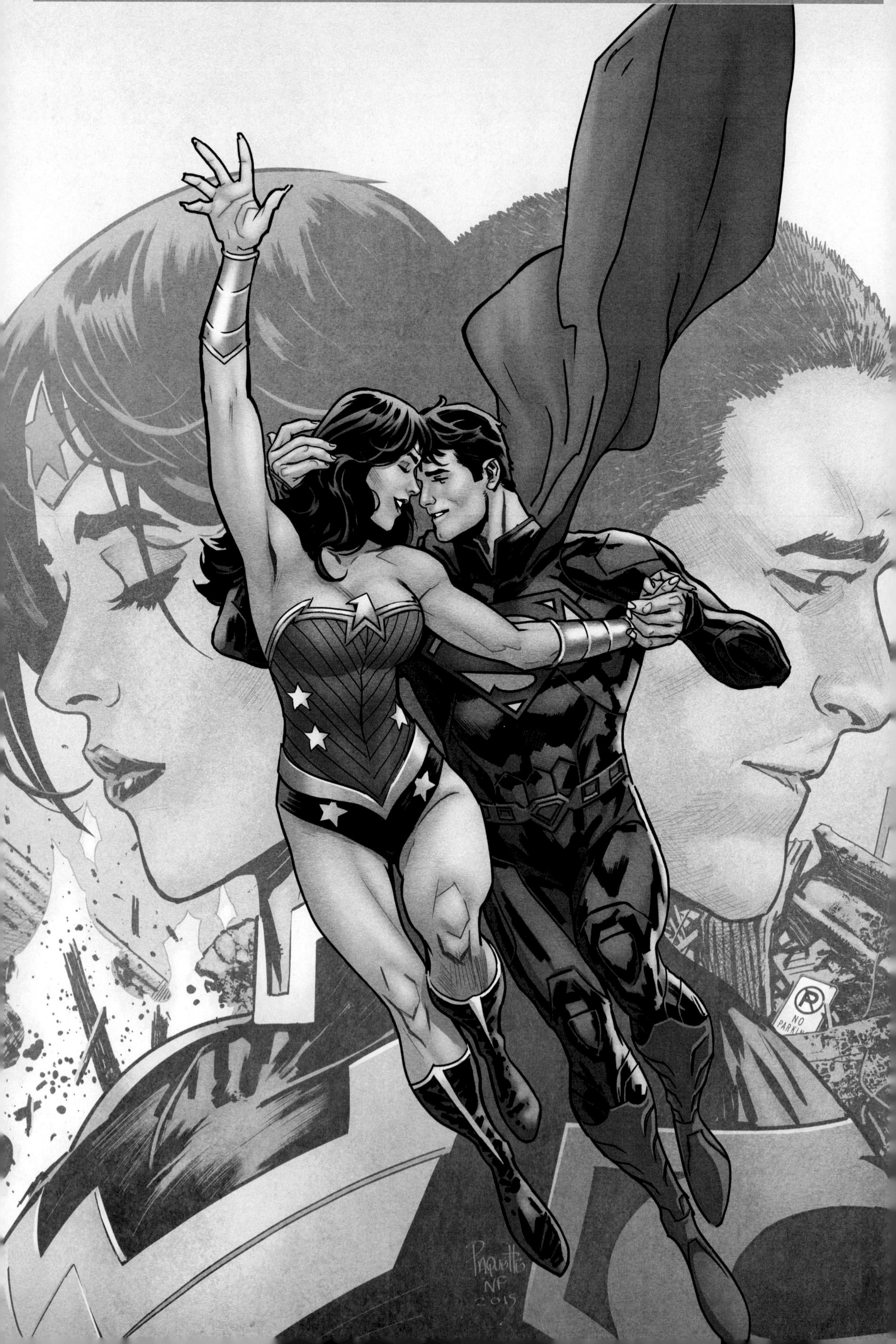

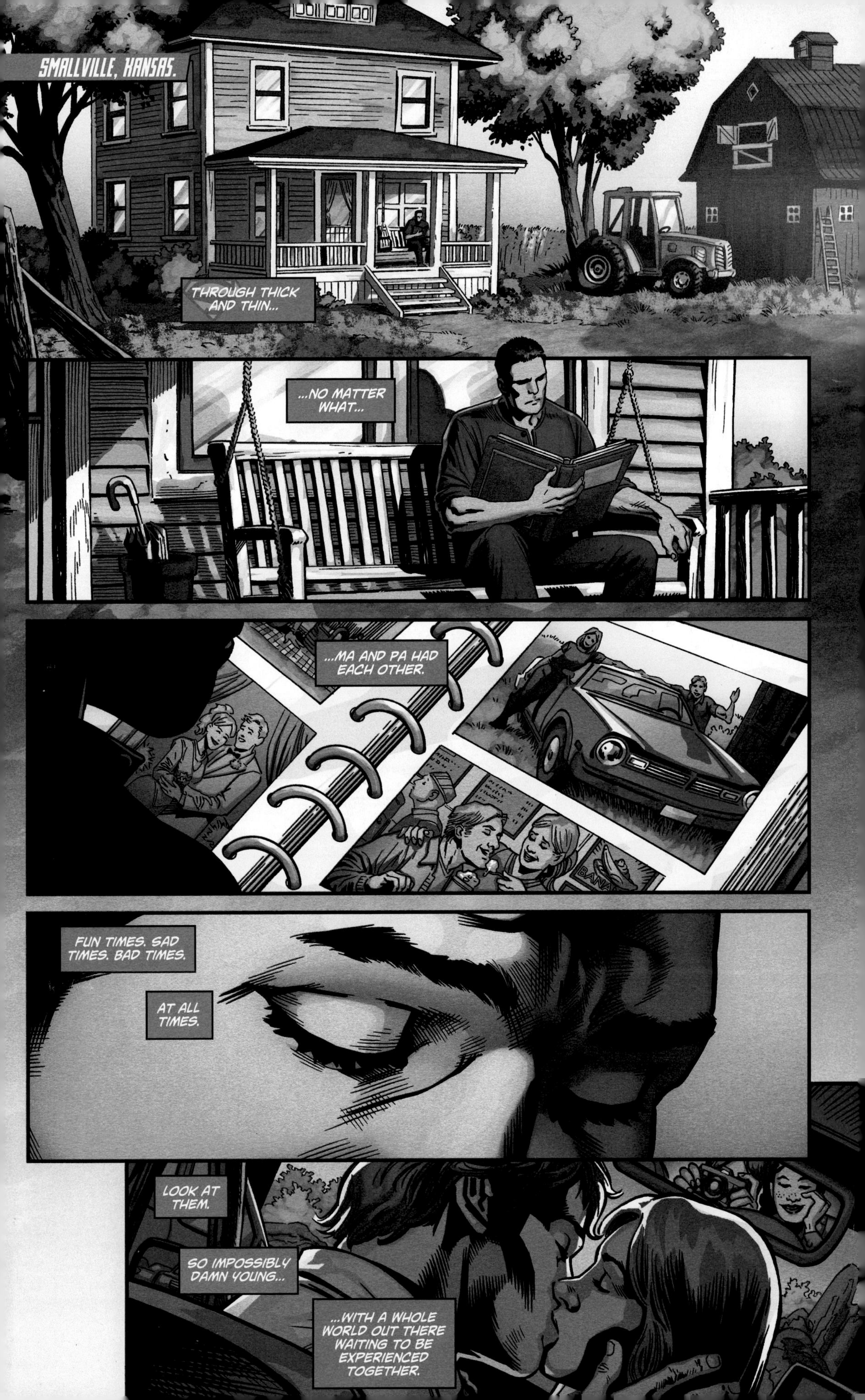
SMALLVILLE, KANSAS.
THROUGH THICK AND THIN...
...NO MATTER WHAT...
...MA AND PA HAD EACH OTHER.
FUN TIMES. SAD TIMES. BAD TIMES.
AT ALL TIMES.
LOOK AT THEM.
SO IMPOSSIBLY DAMN YOUNG...
...WITH A WHOLE WORLD OUT THERE WAITING TO BE EXPERIENCED TOGETHER.

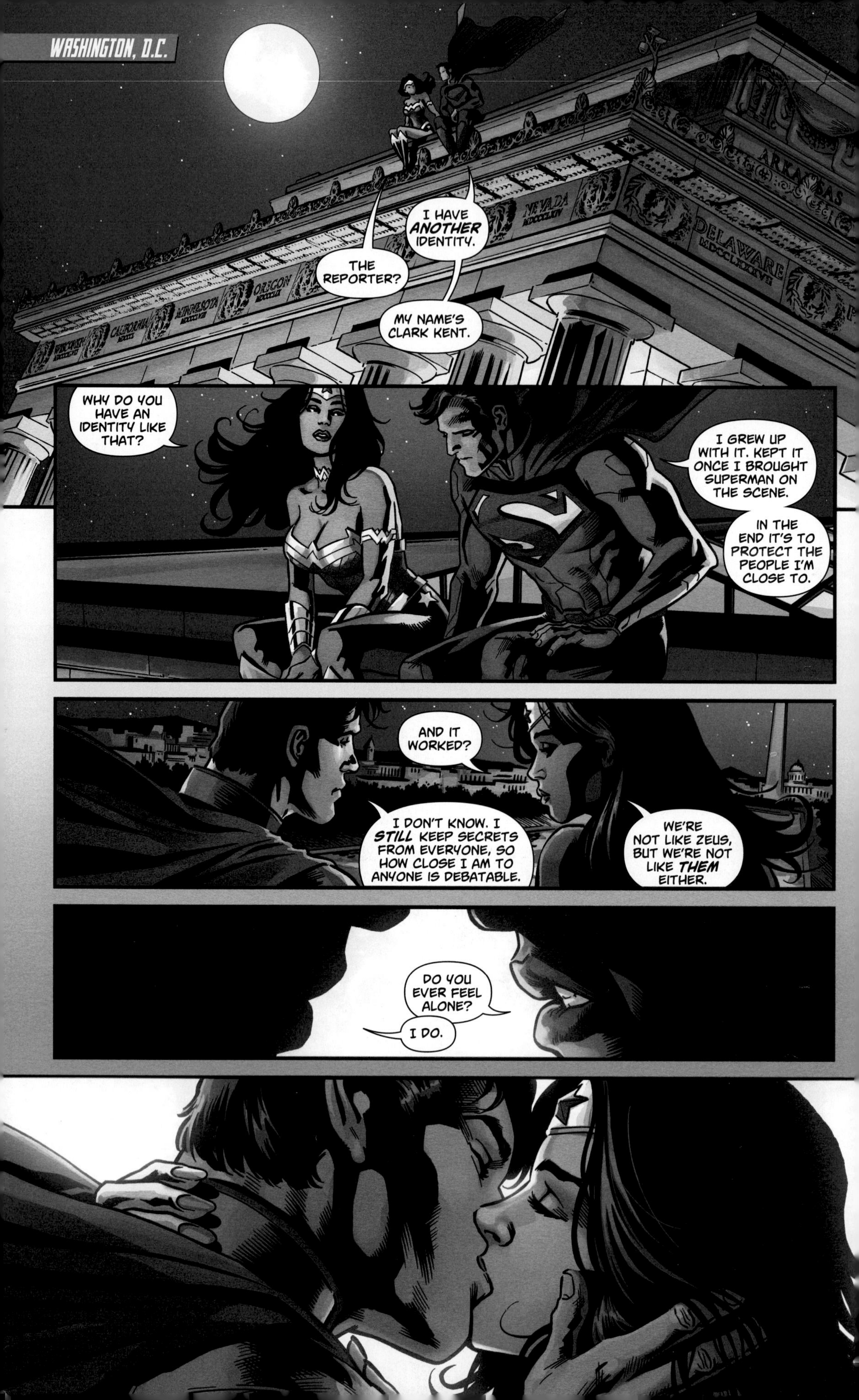
WASHINGTON, D.C.
I HAVE ANOTHER IDENTITY.
THE REPORTER?
MY NAME'S CLARK KENT.
WHY DO YOU HAVE AN IDENTITY LIKE THAT?
I GREW UP WITH IT. KEPT IT ONCE I BROUGHT SUPERMAN ON THE SCENE.
IN THE END IT'S TO PROTECT THE PEOPLE I'M CLOSE TO.
AND IT WORKED?
I DON'T KNOW. I STILL KEEP SECRETS FROM EVERYONE, SO HOW CLOSE I AM TO ANYONE IS DEBATABLE.
WE'RE NOT LIKE ZEUS, BUT WE'RE NOT LIKE THEM EITHER.
DO YOU EVER FEEL ALONE?
I DO.

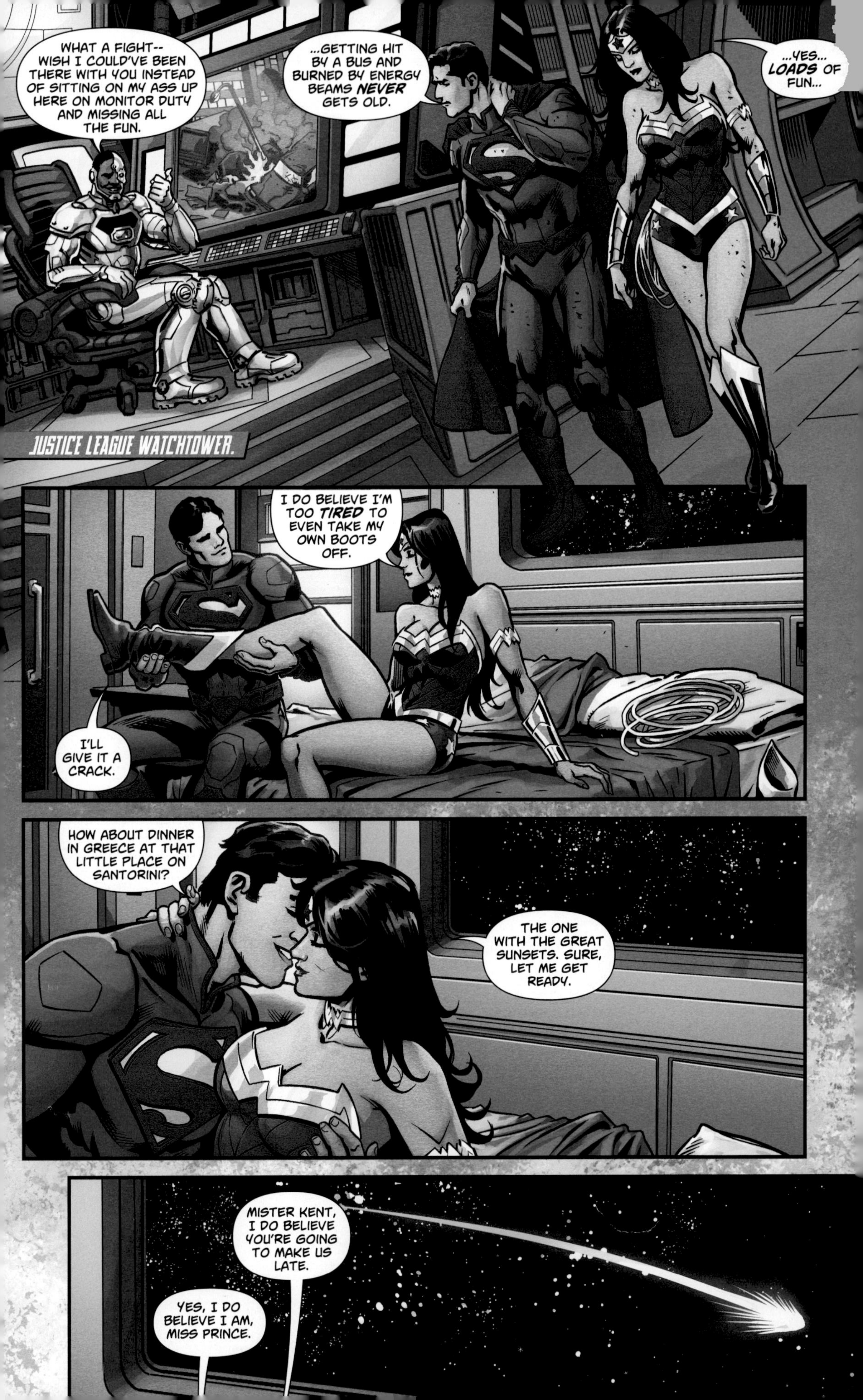
WHAT A FIGHT-- WISH I COULD'VE BEEN THERE WITH YOU INSTEAD OF SITTING ON MY ASS UP HERE ON MONITOR DUTY AND MISSING ALL THE FUN.
...GETTING HIT BY A BUS AND BURNED BY ENERGY BEAMS NEVER GETS OLD.
...YES... LOADS OF FUN...
JUSTICE LEAGUE WATCHTOWER.
I DO BELIEVE I'M TOO TIRED TO EVEN TAKE MY OWN BOOTS OFF.
I'LL GIVE IT A CRACK.
HOW ABOUT DINNER IN GREECE AT THAT LITTLE PLACE ON SANTORINI?
THE ONE WITH THE GREAT SUNSETS. SURE, LET ME GET READY.
MISTER KENT, I DO BELIEVE YOU'RE GOING TO MAKE US LATE.
YES, I DO BELIEVE I AM, MISS PRINCE.

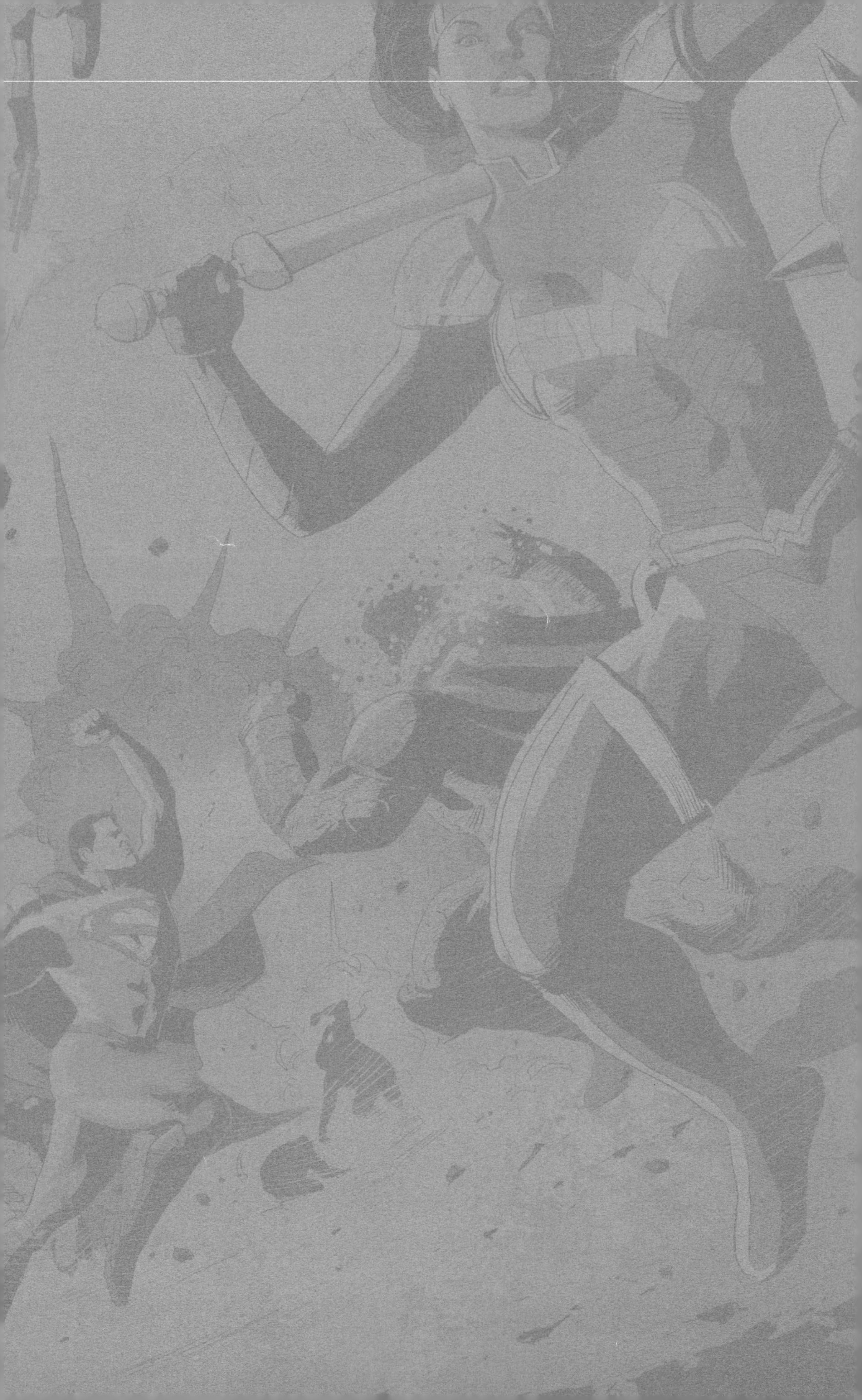

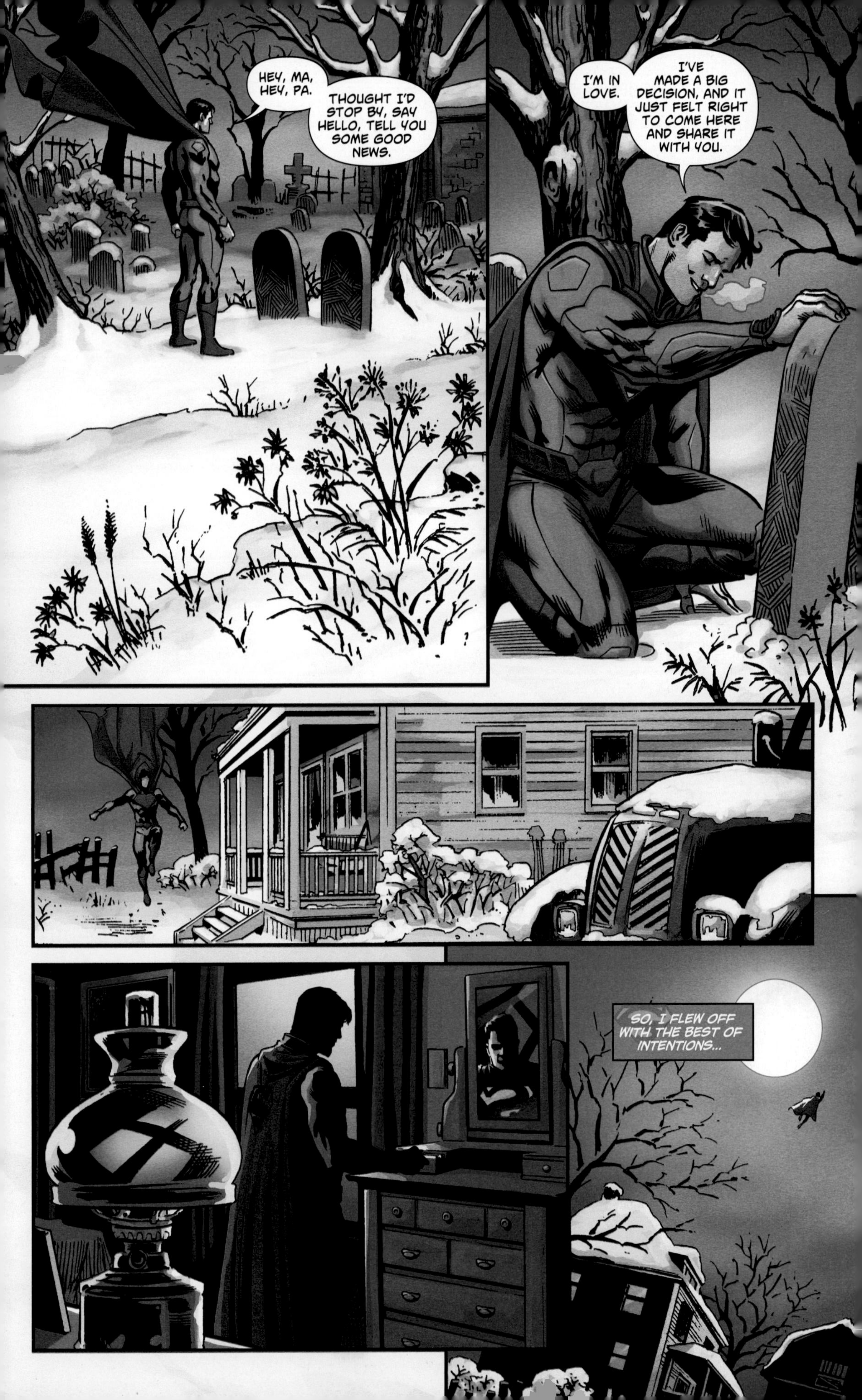
HEY, MA, HEY, PA.
THOUGHT I'D STOP BY, SAY HELLO, TELL YOU SOME GOOD NEWS.
I'M IN LOVE.
I'VE MADE A BIG DECISION, AND IT JUST FELT RIGHT TO COME HERE AND SHARE IT WITH YOU.
SO, I FLEW OFF WITH THE BEST OF INTENTIONS...

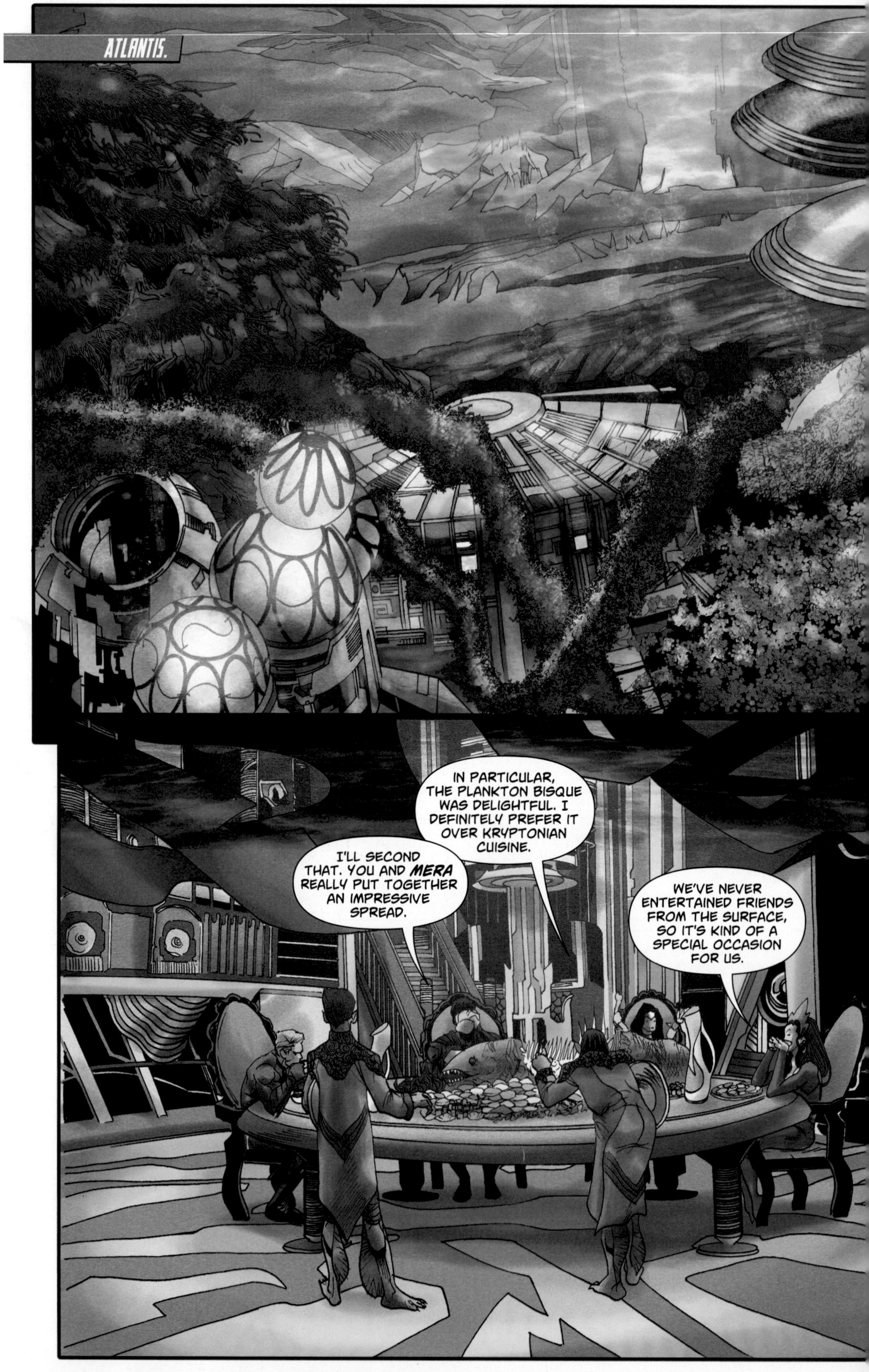
ATLANTIS.
IN PARTICULAR, THE PLANKTON BISQUE WAS DELIGHTFUL. I DEFINITELY PREFER IT OVER KRYPTONIAN CUISINE.
I'LL SECOND THAT. YOU AND MERA REALLY PUT TOGETHER AN IMPRESSIVE SPREAD.
WE'VE NEVER ENTERTAINED FRIENDS FROM THE SURFACE, SO IT'S KIND OF A SPECIAL OCCASION FOR US.

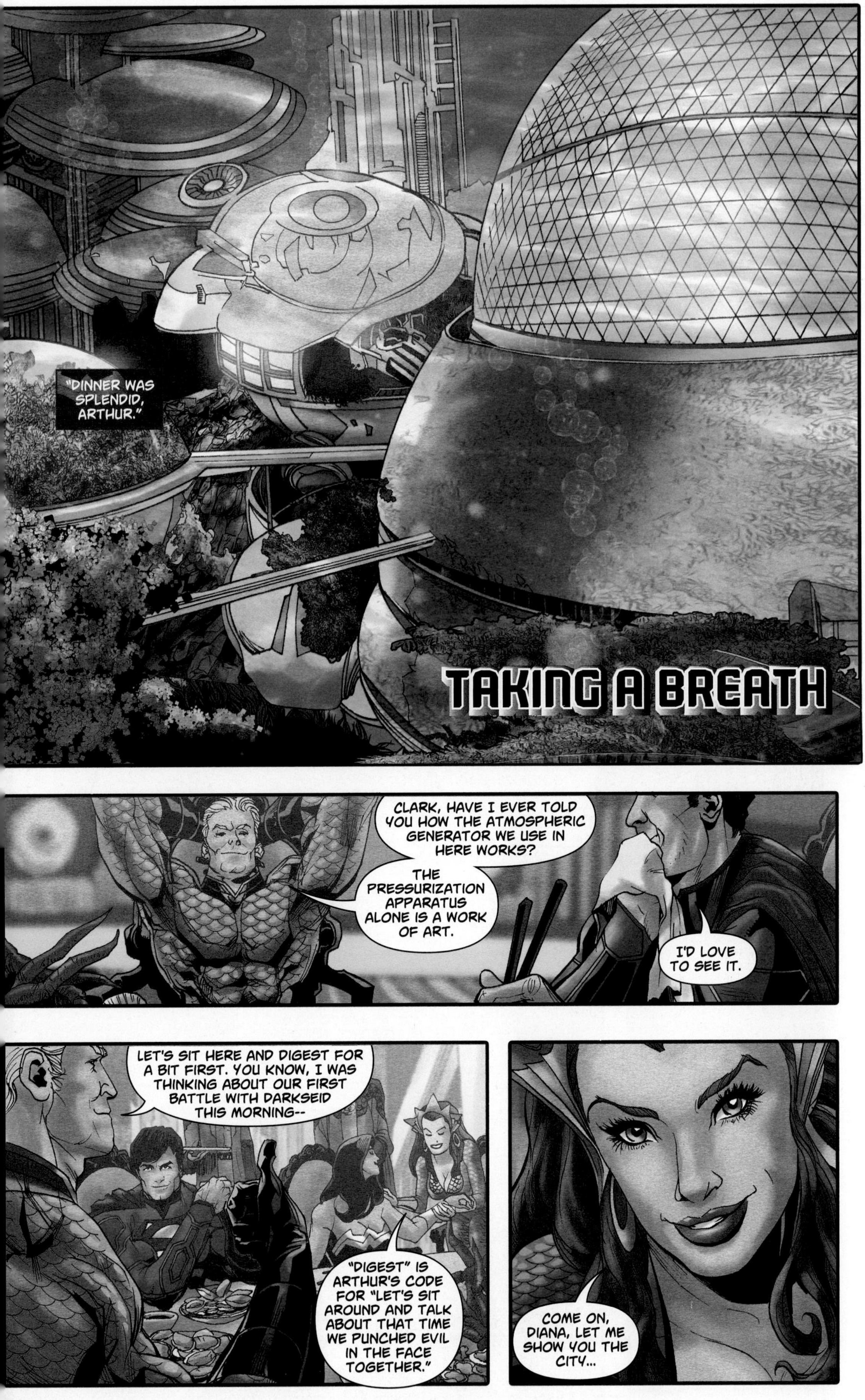
"DINNER WAS SPLENDID, ARTHUR."
TAKING A BREATH
CLARK, HAVE I EVER TOLD YOU HOW THE ATMOSPHERIC GENERATOR WE USE IN HERE WORKS?
THE PRESSURIZATION APPARATUS ALONE IS A WORK OF ART.
I'D LOVE TO SEE IT.
LET'S SIT HERE AND DIGEST FOR A BIT FIRST. YOU KNOW, I WAS THINKING ABOUT OUR FIRST BATTLE WITH DARKSEID THIS MORNING--
"DIGEST" IS ARTHUR'S CODE FOR "LET'S SIT AROUND AND TALK ABOUT THAT TIME WE PUNCHED EVIL IN THE FACE TOGETHER."
COME ON, DIANA, LET ME SHOW YOU THE CITY...

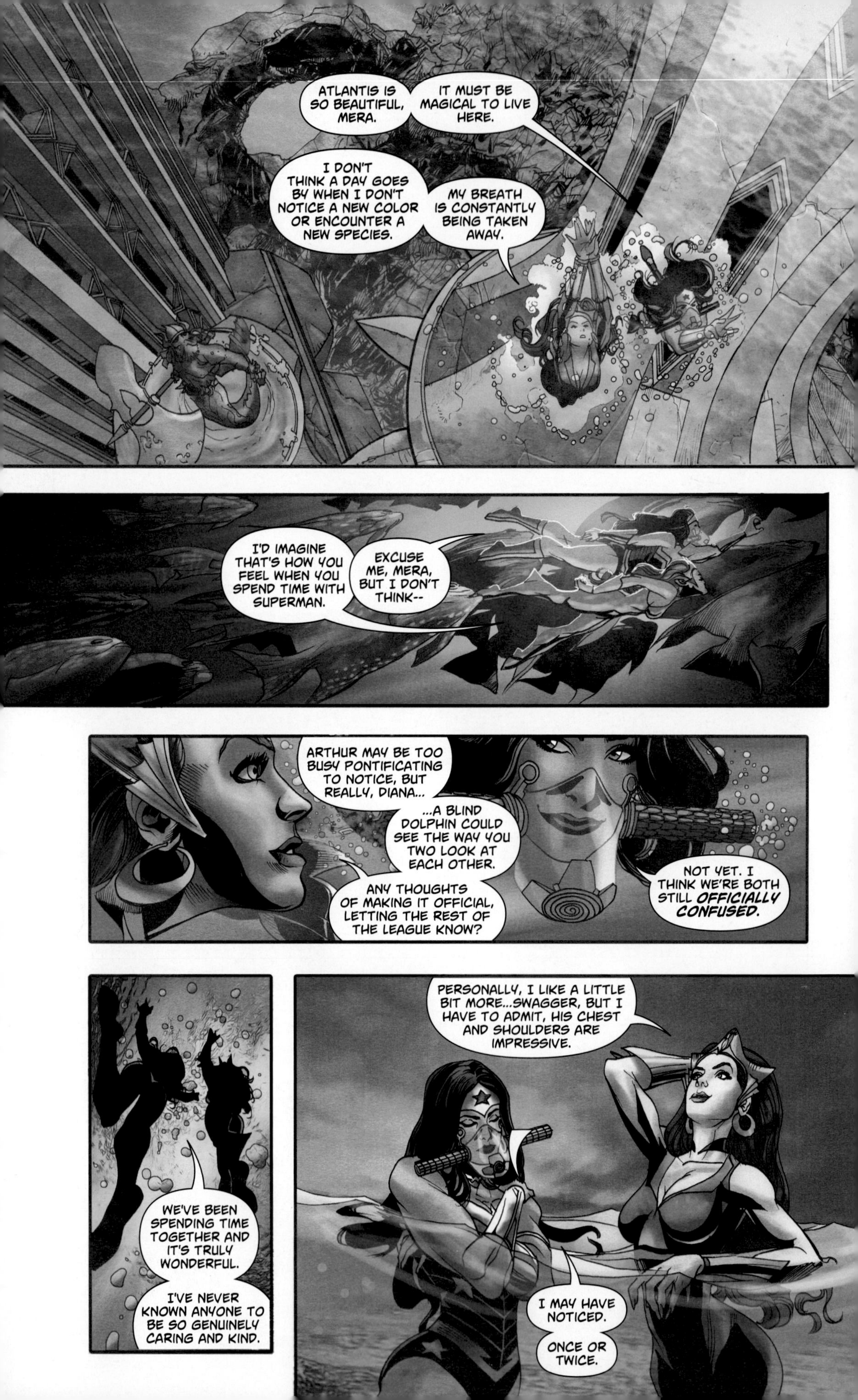
ATLANTIS IS SO BEAUTIFUL, MERA.
IT MUST BE MAGICAL TO LIVE HERE.
I DON'T THINK A DAY GOES BY WHEN I DON'T NOTICE A NEW COLOR OR ENCOUNTER A NEW SPECIES.
MY BREATH IS CONSTANTLY BEING TAKEN AWAY.
I'D IMAGINE THAT'S HOW YOU FEEL WHEN YOU SPEND TIME WITH SUPERMAN.
EXCUSE ME, MERA, BUT I DON'T THINK--
ARTHUR MAY BE TOO BUSY PONTIFICATING TO NOTICE, BUT REALLY, DIANA...
...A BLIND DOLPHIN COULD SEE THE WAY YOU TWO LOOK AT EACH OTHER.
ANY THOUGHTS OF MAKING IT OFFICIAL, LETTING THE REST OF THE LEAGUE KNOW?
NOT YET. I THINK WE'RE BOTH STILL ***OFFICIALLY CONFUSED.***
WE'VE BEEN SPENDING TIME TOGETHER AND IT'S TRULY WONDERFUL.
I'VE NEVER KNOWN ANYONE TO BE SO GENUINELY CARING AND KIND.
PERSONALLY, I LIKE A LITTLE BIT MORE...SWAGGER, BUT I HAVE TO ADMIT, HIS CHEST AND SHOULDERS ARE IMPRESSIVE.
I MAY HAVE NOTICED.
ONCE OR TWICE.

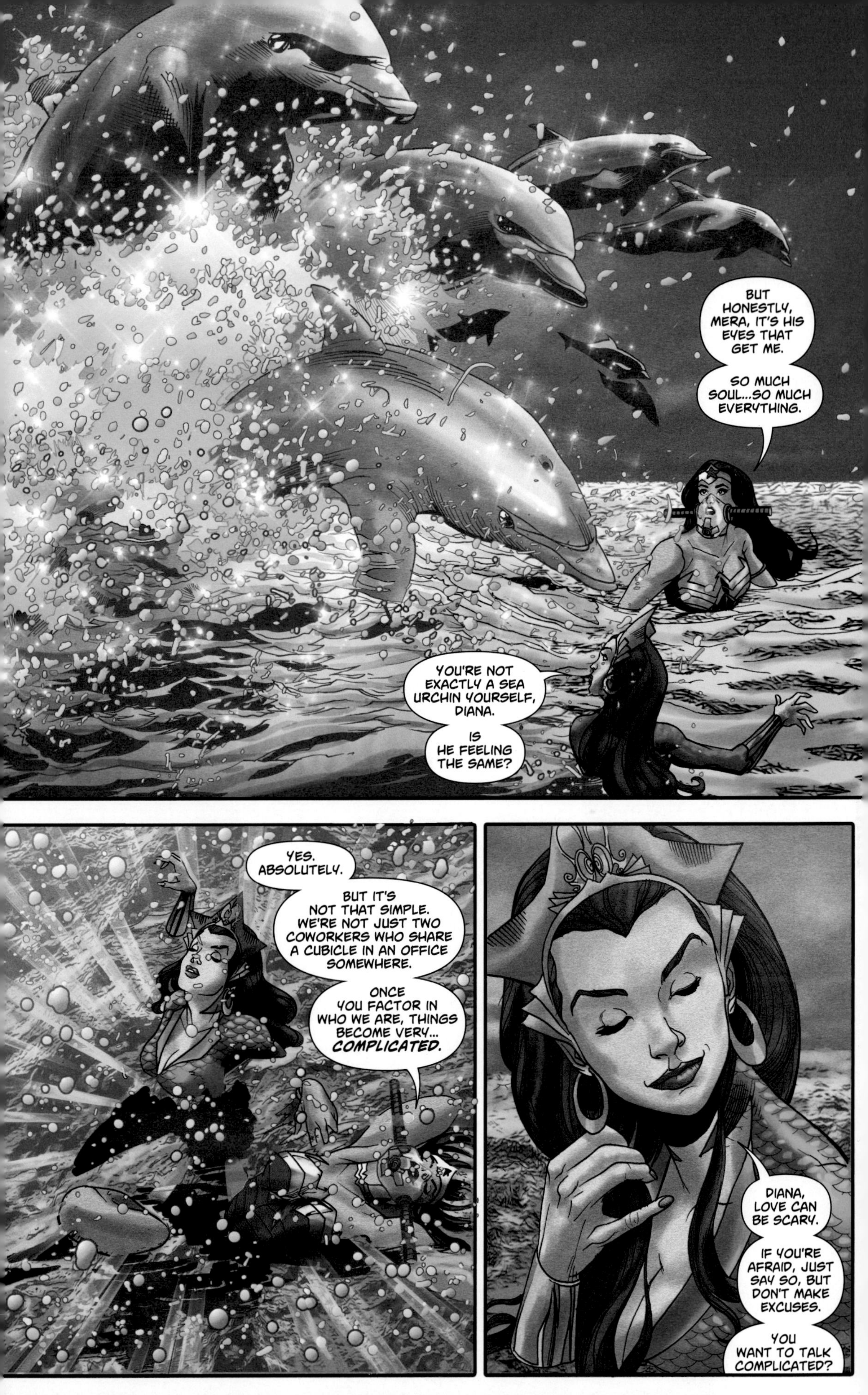
BUT HONESTLY, MERA, IT'S HIS EYES THAT GET ME.
SO MUCH SOUL...SO MUCH EVERYTHING.
YOU'RE NOT EXACTLY A SEA URCHIN YOURSELF, DIANA.
IS HE FEELING THE SAME?
YES. ABSOLUTELY.
BUT IT'S NOT THAT SIMPLE. WE'RE NOT JUST TWO COWORKERS WHO SHARE A CUBICLE IN AN OFFICE SOMEWHERE.
ONCE YOU FACTOR IN WHO WE ARE, THINGS BECOME VERY... COMPLICATED.
DIANA, LOVE CAN BE SCARY.
IF YOU'RE AFRAID, JUST SAY SO, BUT DON'T MAKE EXCUSES.
YOU WANT TO TALK COMPLICATED?

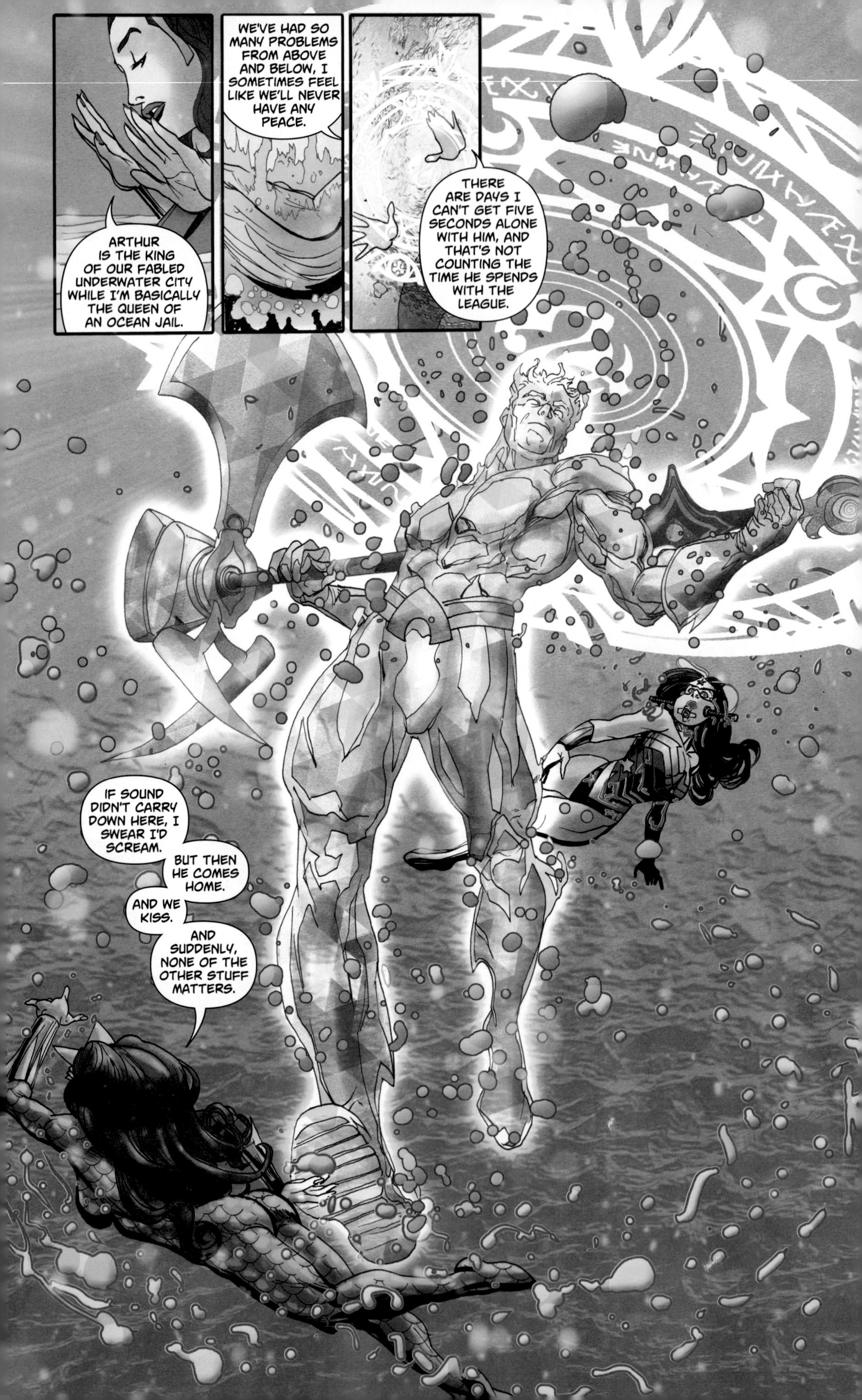
ARTHUR IS THE KING OF OUR FABLED UNDERWATER CITY WHILE I'M BASICALLY THE QUEEN OF AN OCEAN JAIL.
WE'VE HAD SO MANY PROBLEMS FROM ABOVE AND BELOW, I SOMETIMES FEEL LIKE WE'LL NEVER HAVE ANY PEACE.
THERE ARE DAYS I CAN'T GET FIVE SECONDS ALONE WITH HIM, AND THAT'S NOT COUNTING THE TIME HE SPENDS WITH THE LEAGUE.
IF SOUND DIDN'T CARRY DOWN HERE, I SWEAR I'D SCREAM.
BUT THEN HE COMES HOME.
AND WE KISS.
AND SUDDENLY, NONE OF THE OTHER STUFF MATTERS.

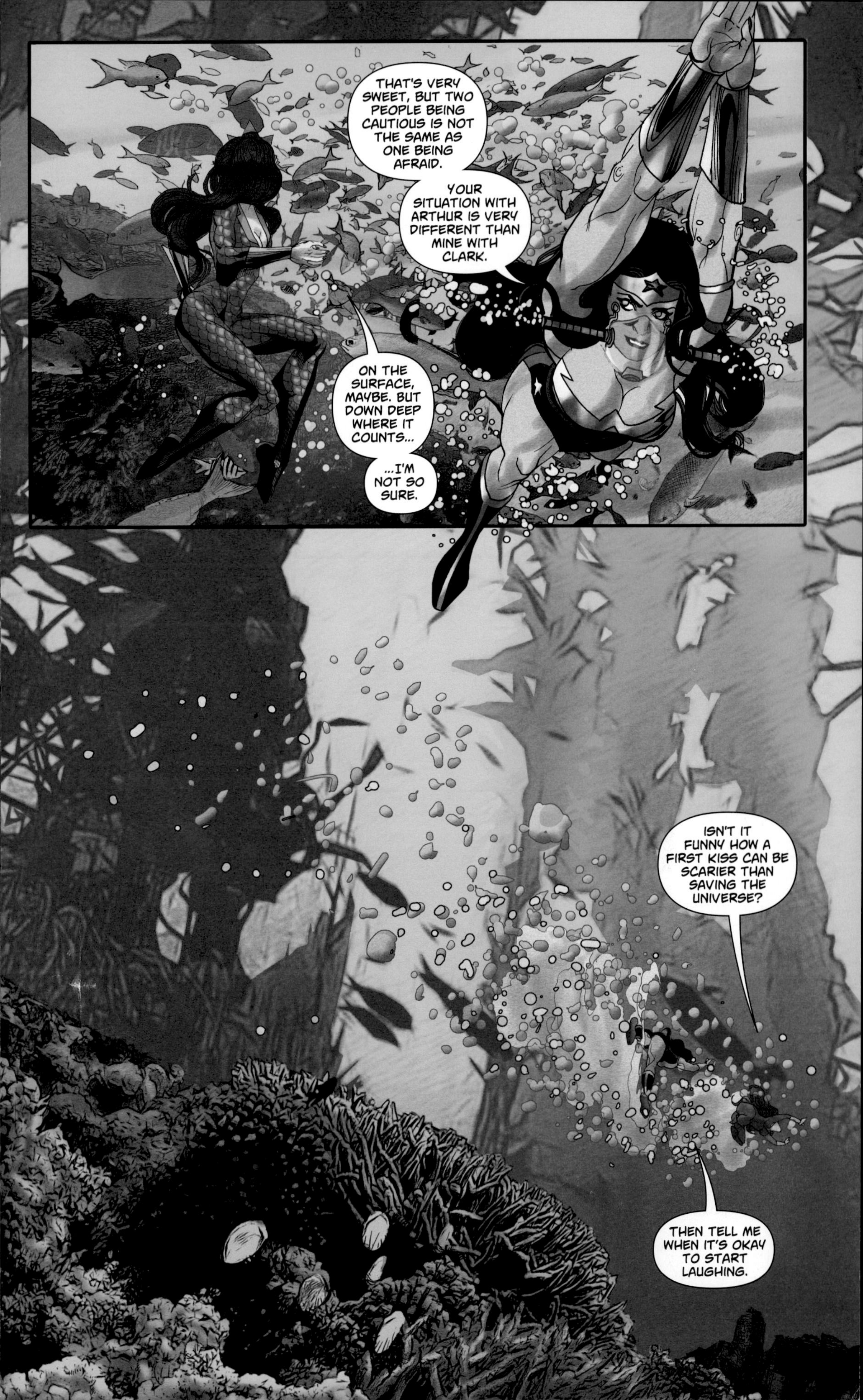
THAT'S VERY SWEET, BUT TWO PEOPLE BEING CAUTIOUS IS NOT THE SAME AS ONE BEING AFRAID.
YOUR SITUATION WITH ARTHUR IS VERY DIFFERENT THAN MINE WITH CLARK.
ON THE SURFACE, MAYBE. BUT DOWN DEEP WHERE IT COUNTS...
...I'M NOT SO SURE.
ISN'T IT FUNNY HOW A FIRST KISS CAN BE SCARIER THAN SAVING THE UNIVERSE?
THEN TELL ME WHEN IT'S OKAY TO START LAUGHING.

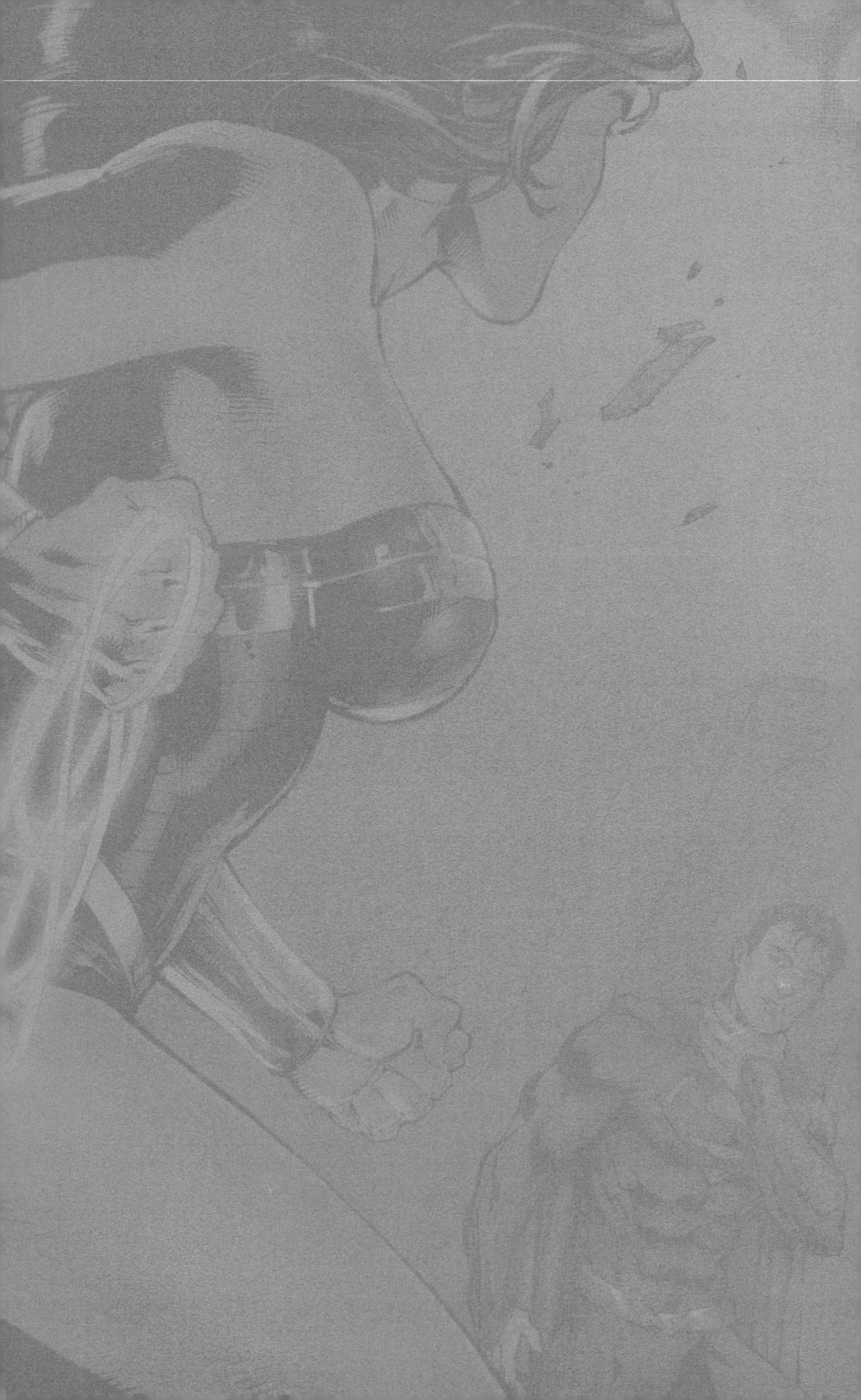

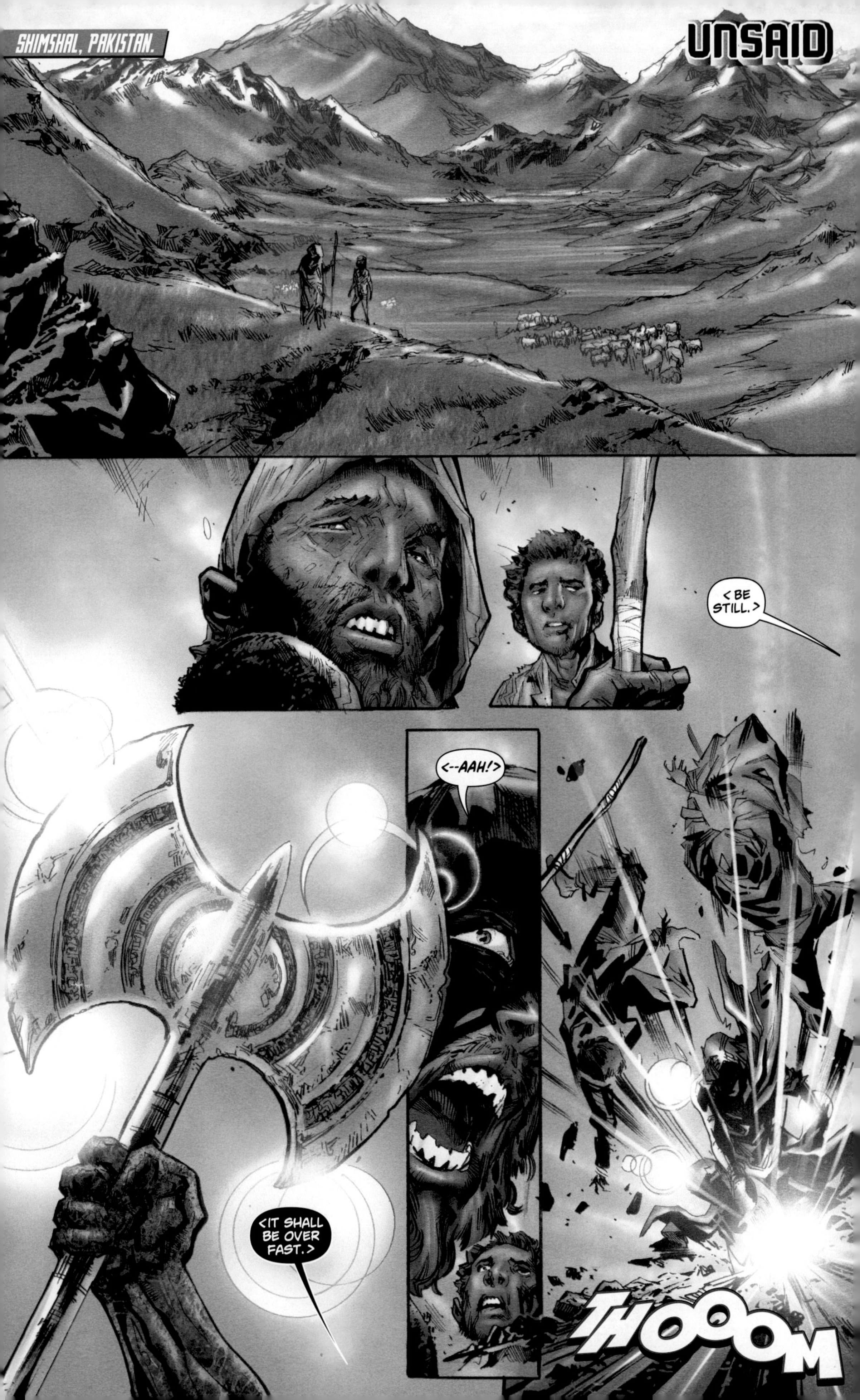
SHIMSHAL, PAKISTAN.
UNSAID
< BE STILL. >
<IT SHALL BE OVER FAST.>
<--AAH!>
THOOOM

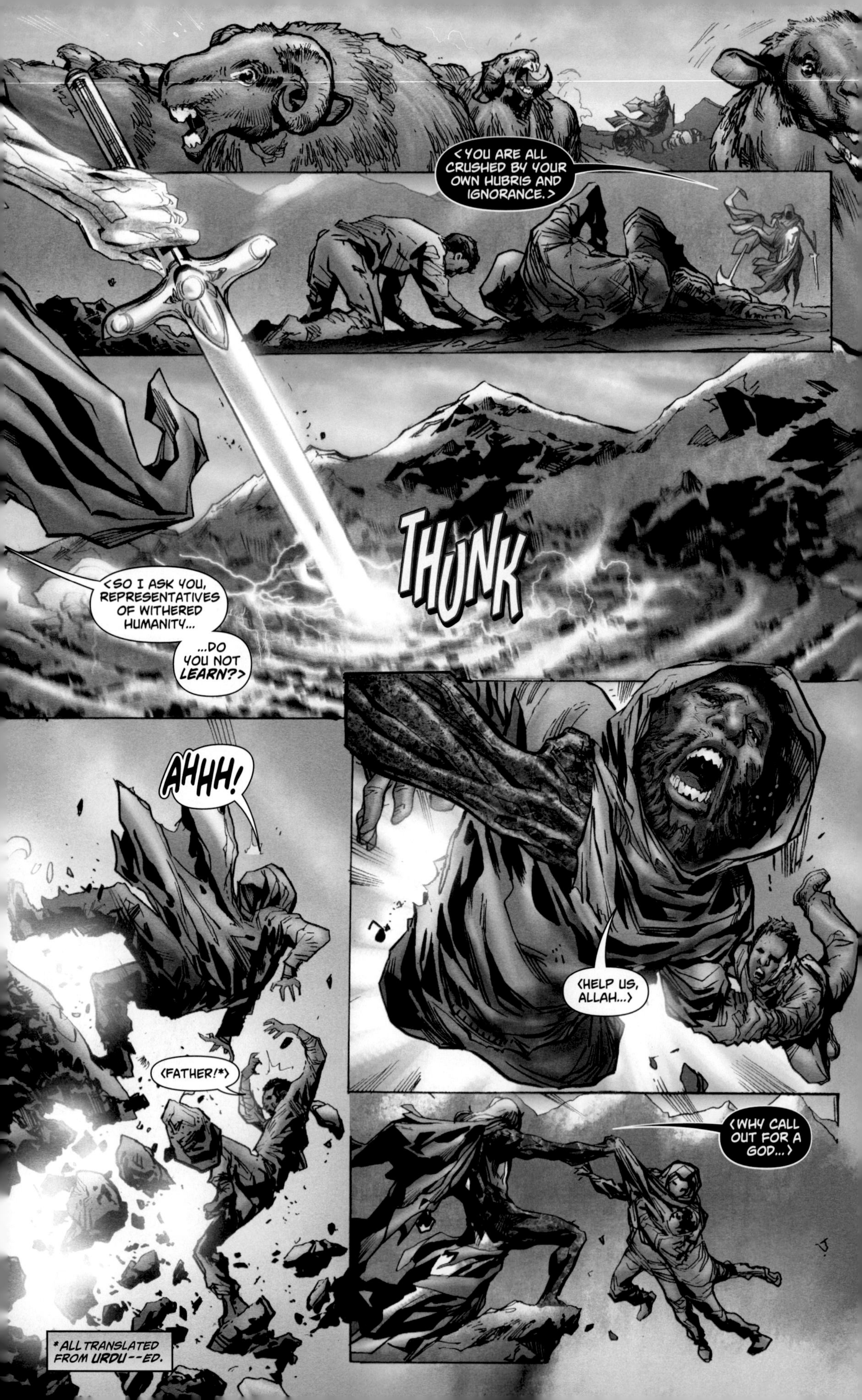

<YOU ARE ALL CRUSHED BY YOUR OWN HUBRIS AND IGNORANCE.>
THUNK
<SO I ASK YOU, REPRESENTATIVES OF WITHERED HUMANITY...
...DO YOU NOT LEARN?>
AHHH!
<FATHER!*>
<HELP US, ALLAH...>
<WHY CALL OUT FOR A GOD...>
*ALL TRANSLATED FROM URDU--ED.

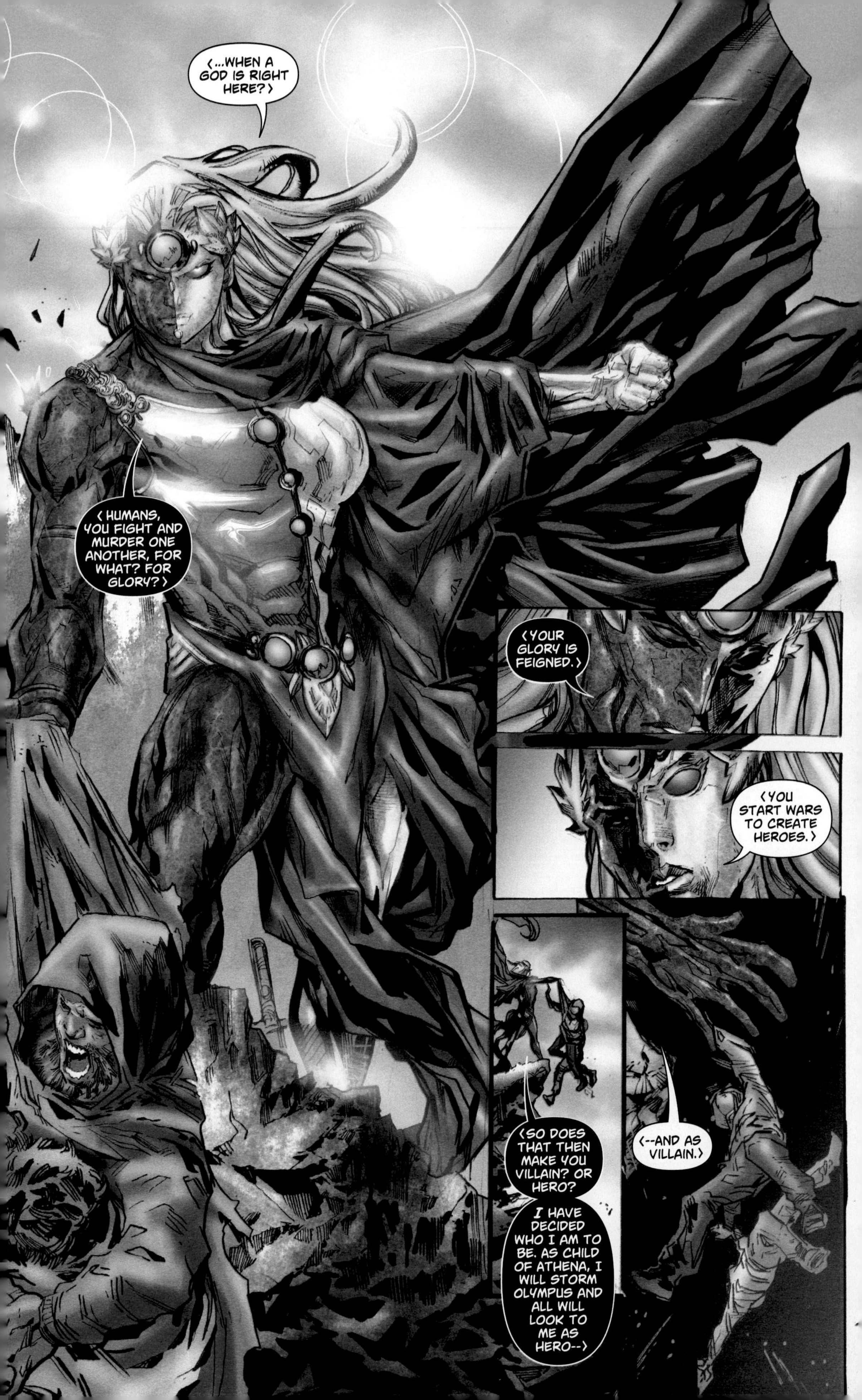
‹...WHEN A GOD IS RIGHT HERE?›
‹HUMANS, YOU FIGHT AND MURDER ONE ANOTHER, FOR WHAT? FOR GLORY?›
‹YOUR GLORY IS FEIGNED.›
‹YOU START WARS TO CREATE HEROES.›
‹SO DOES THAT THEN MAKE YOU VILLAIN? OR HERO?
I HAVE DECIDED WHO I AM TO BE. AS CHILD OF ATHENA, I WILL STORM OLYMPUS AND ALL WILL LOOK TO ME AS HERO--›
‹--AND AS VILLAIN.›

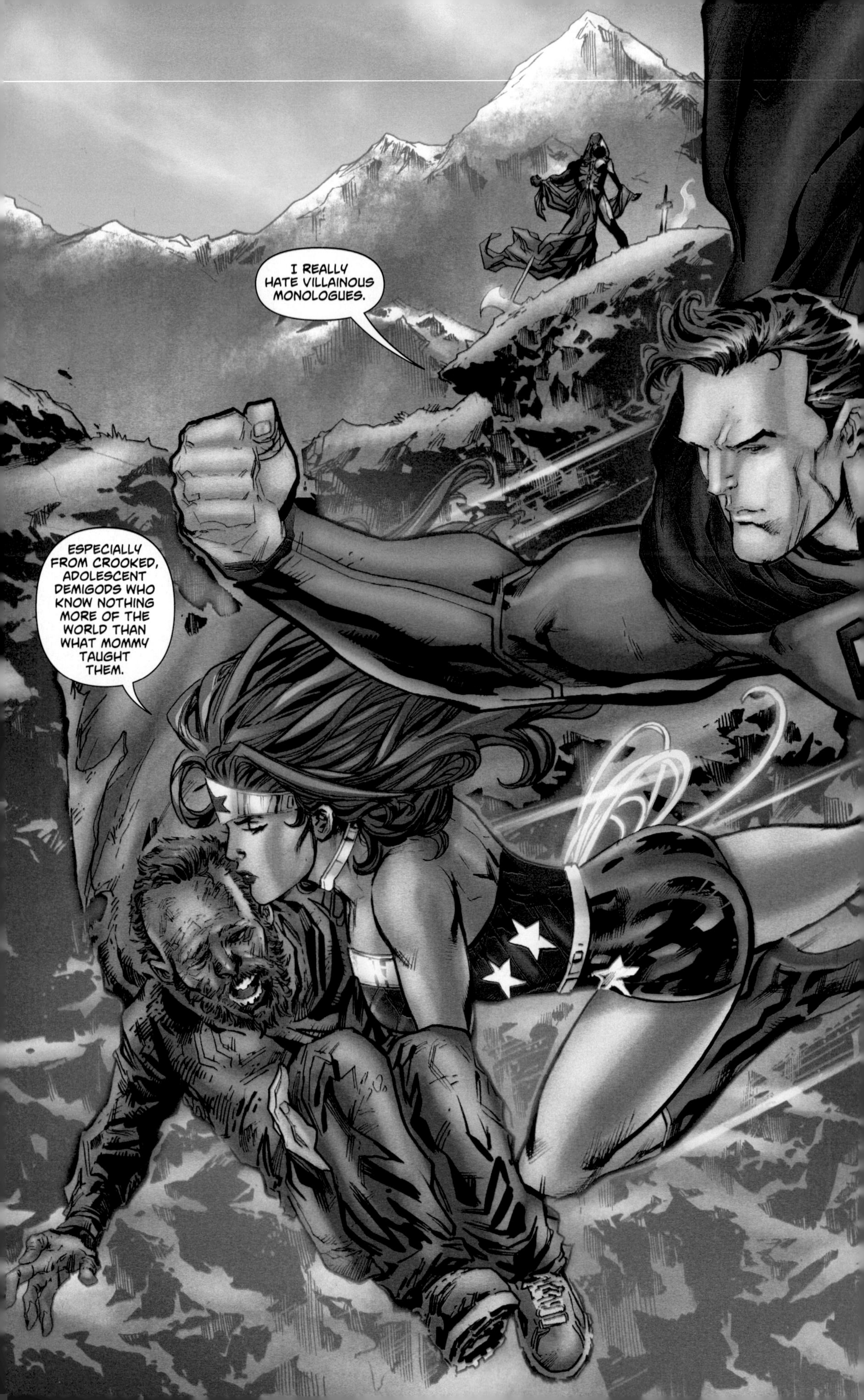
I REALLY HATE VILLAINOUS MONOLOGUES.
ESPECIALLY FROM CROOKED, ADOLESCENT DEMIGODS WHO KNOW NOTHING MORE OF THE WORLD THAN WHAT MOMMY TAUGHT THEM.

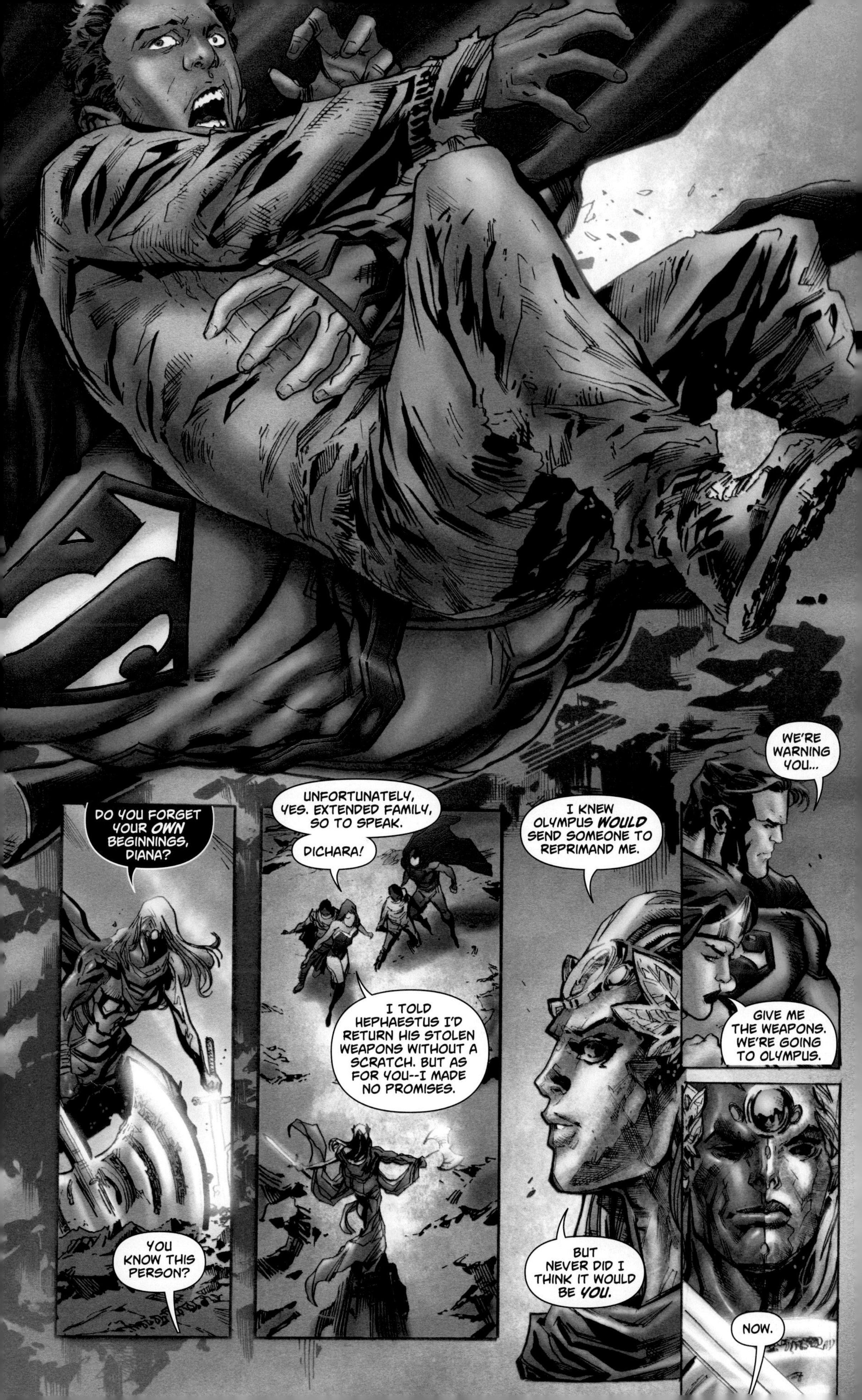
DO YOU FORGET YOUR OWN BEGINNINGS, DIANA?
YOU KNOW THIS PERSON?
UNFORTUNATELY, YES. EXTENDED FAMILY, SO TO SPEAK.
DICHARA!
I TOLD HEPHAESTUS I'D RETURN HIS STOLEN WEAPONS WITHOUT A SCRATCH. BUT AS FOR YOU--I MADE NO PROMISES.
I KNEW OLYMPUS WOULD SEND SOMEONE TO REPRIMAND ME.
BUT NEVER DID I THINK IT WOULD BE YOU.
WE'RE WARNING YOU...
GIVE ME THE WEAPONS. WE'RE GOING TO OLYMPUS.
NOW.

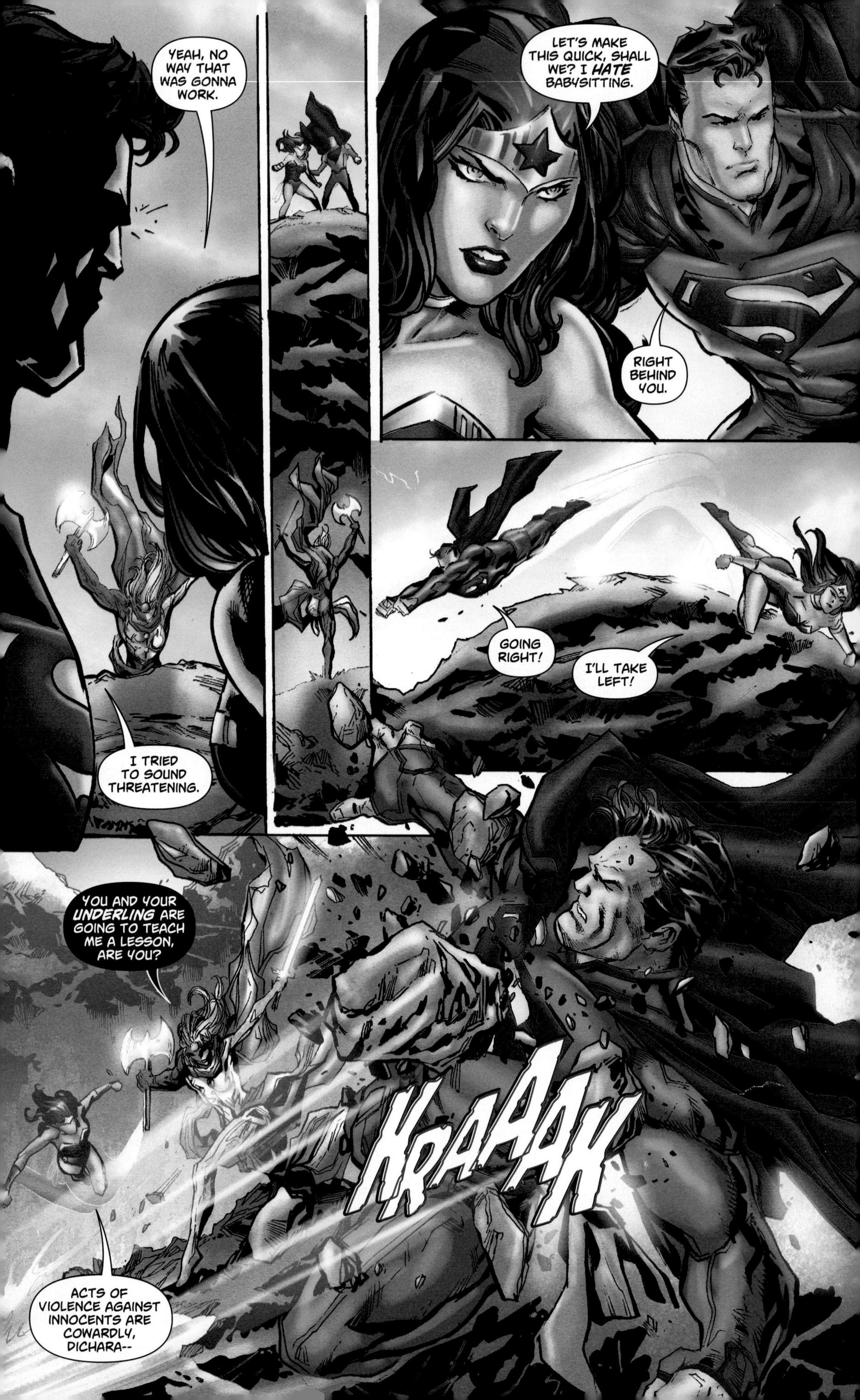
YEAH, NO WAY THAT WAS GONNA WORK.
I TRIED TO SOUND THREATENING.
LET'S MAKE THIS QUICK, SHALL WE? I HATE BABYSITTING.
RIGHT BEHIND YOU.
GOING RIGHT!
I'LL TAKE LEFT!
YOU AND YOUR UNDERLING ARE GOING TO TEACH ME A LESSON, ARE YOU?
KRAAAK
ACTS OF VIOLENCE AGAINST INNOCENTS ARE COWARDLY, DICHARA--

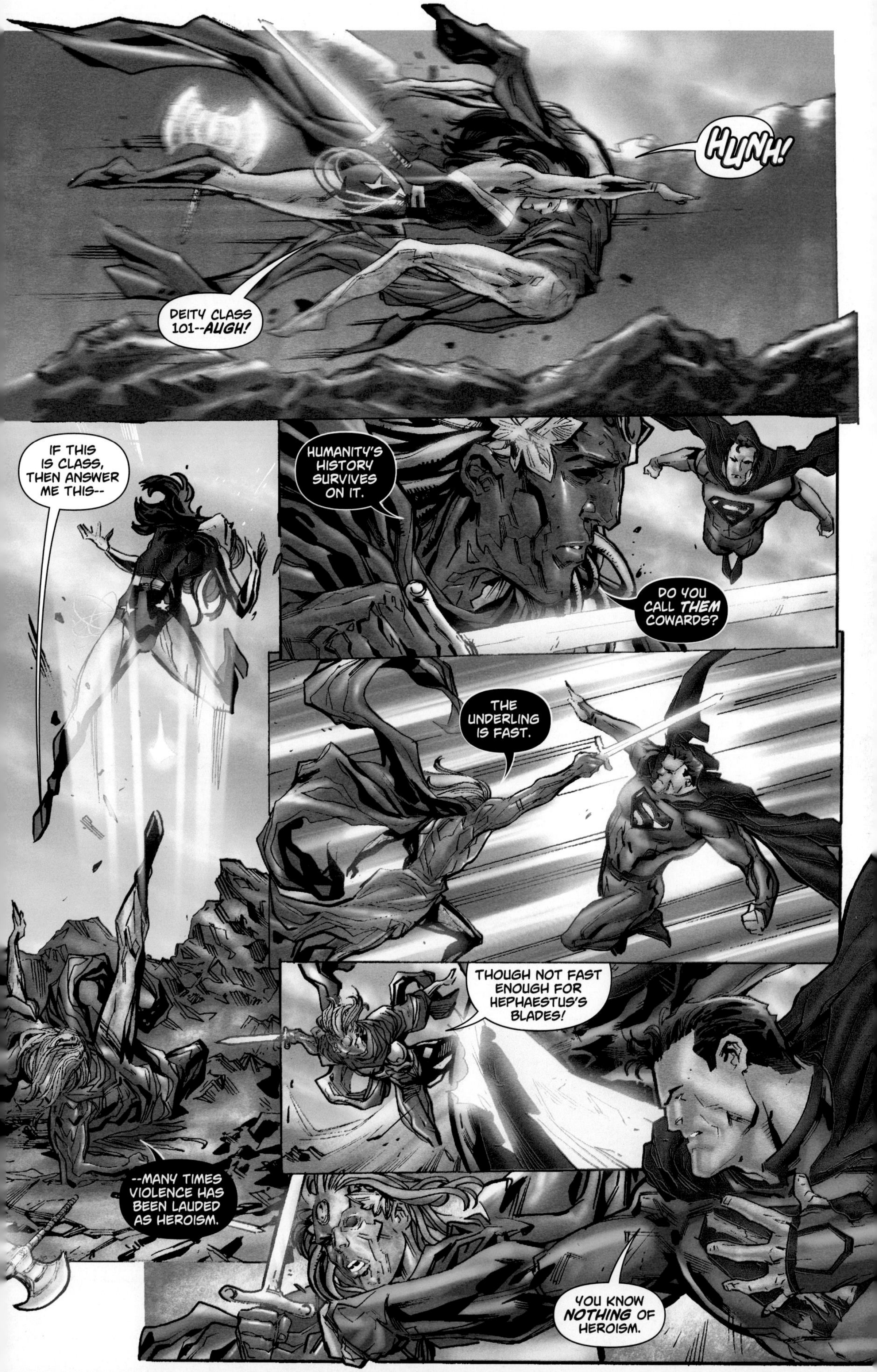
HUNH!
DEITY CLASS 101--AUGH!
IF THIS IS CLASS, THEN ANSWER ME THIS--
HUMANITY'S HISTORY SURVIVES ON IT.
DO YOU CALL THEM COWARDS?
THE UNDERLING IS FAST.
THOUGH NOT FAST ENOUGH FOR HEPHAESTUS'S BLADES!
--MANY TIMES VIOLENCE HAS BEEN LAUDED AS HEROISM.
YOU KNOW NOTHING OF HEROISM.

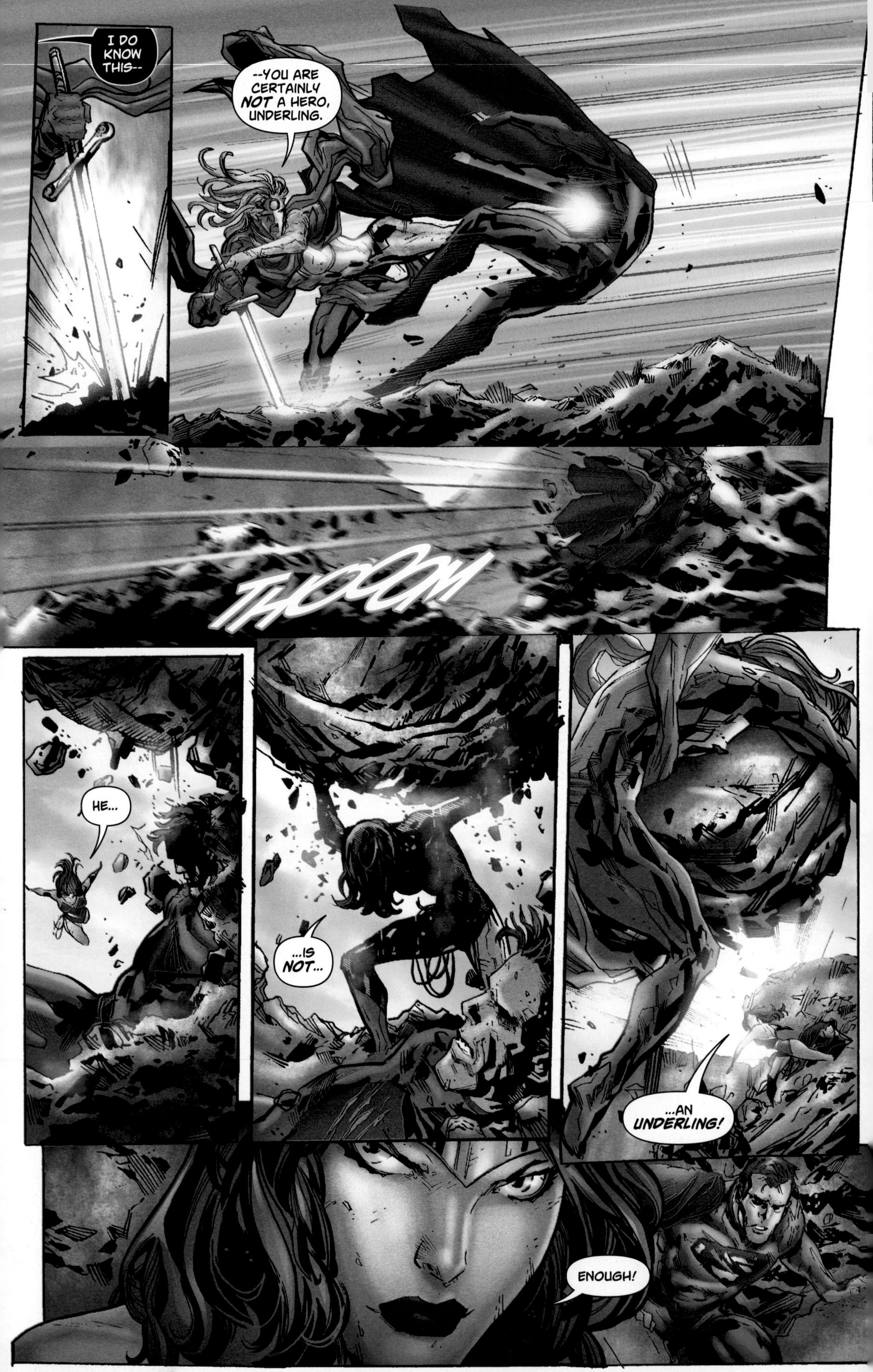
I DO KNOW THIS--
--YOU ARE CERTAINLY NOT A HERO, UNDERLING.
THOOOM
HE...
...IS NOT...
...AN UNDERLING!
ENOUGH!

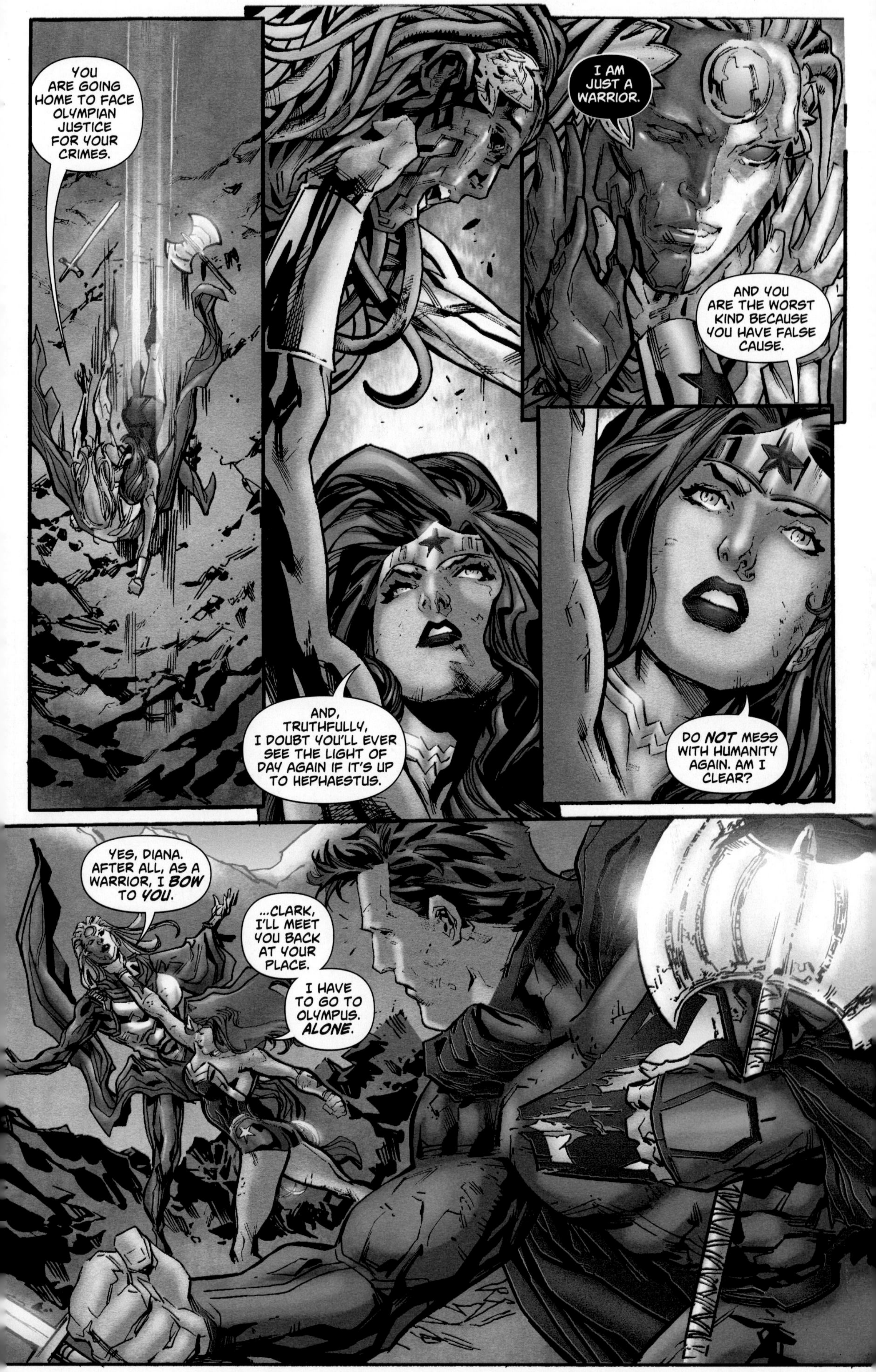

YOU ARE GOING HOME TO FACE OLYMPIAN JUSTICE FOR YOUR CRIMES.
I AM JUST A WARRIOR.
AND YOU ARE THE WORST KIND BECAUSE YOU HAVE FALSE CAUSE.
AND, TRUTHFULLY, I DOUBT YOU'LL EVER SEE THE LIGHT OF DAY AGAIN IF IT'S UP TO HEPHAESTUS.
DO NOT MESS WITH HUMANITY AGAIN. AM I CLEAR?
YES, DIANA. AFTER ALL, AS A WARRIOR, I BOW TO YOU.
...CLARK, I'LL MEET YOU BACK AT YOUR PLACE.
I HAVE TO GO TO OLYMPUS. ALONE.

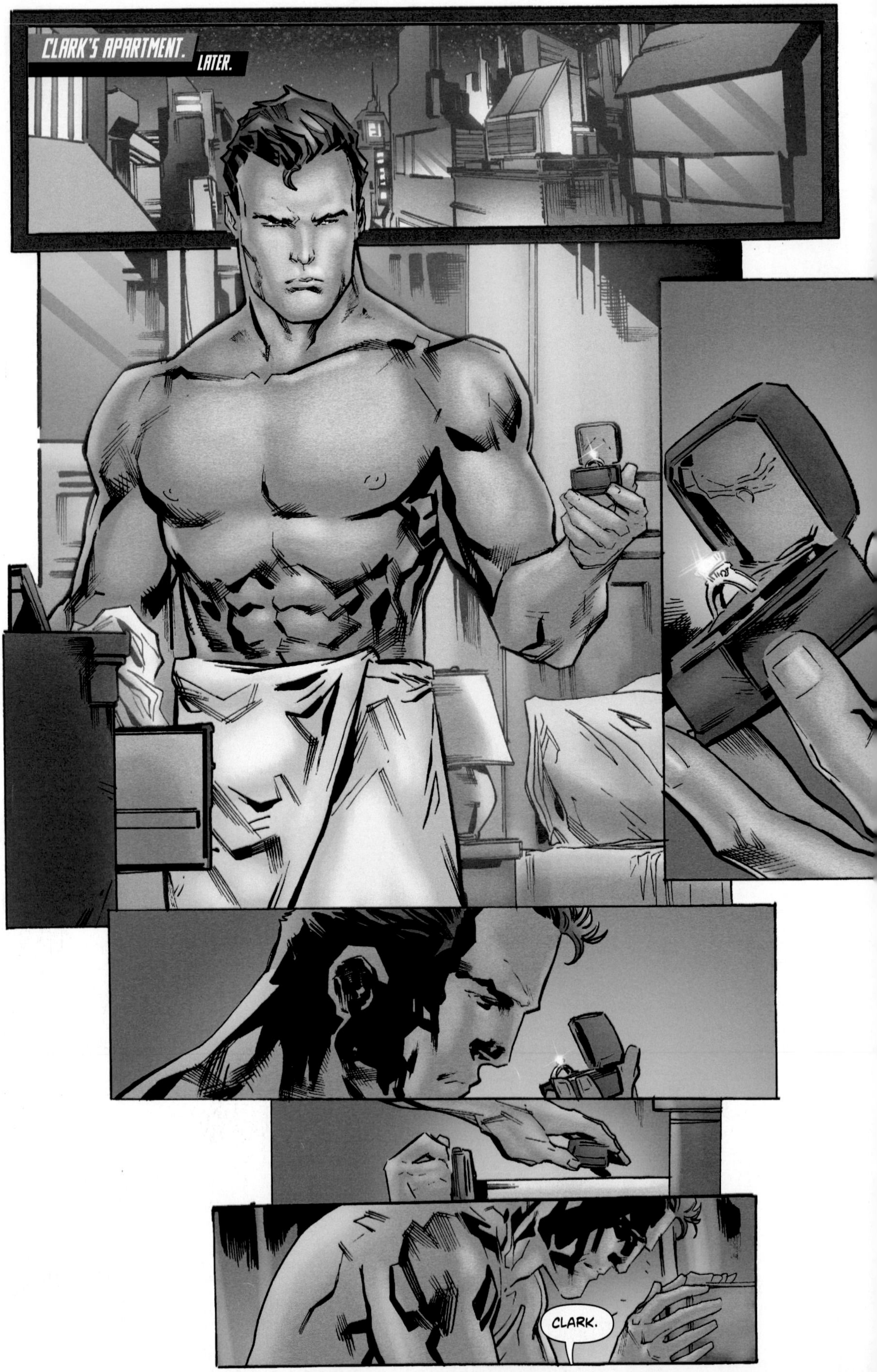
CLARK'S APARTMENT.
LATER.
CLARK.

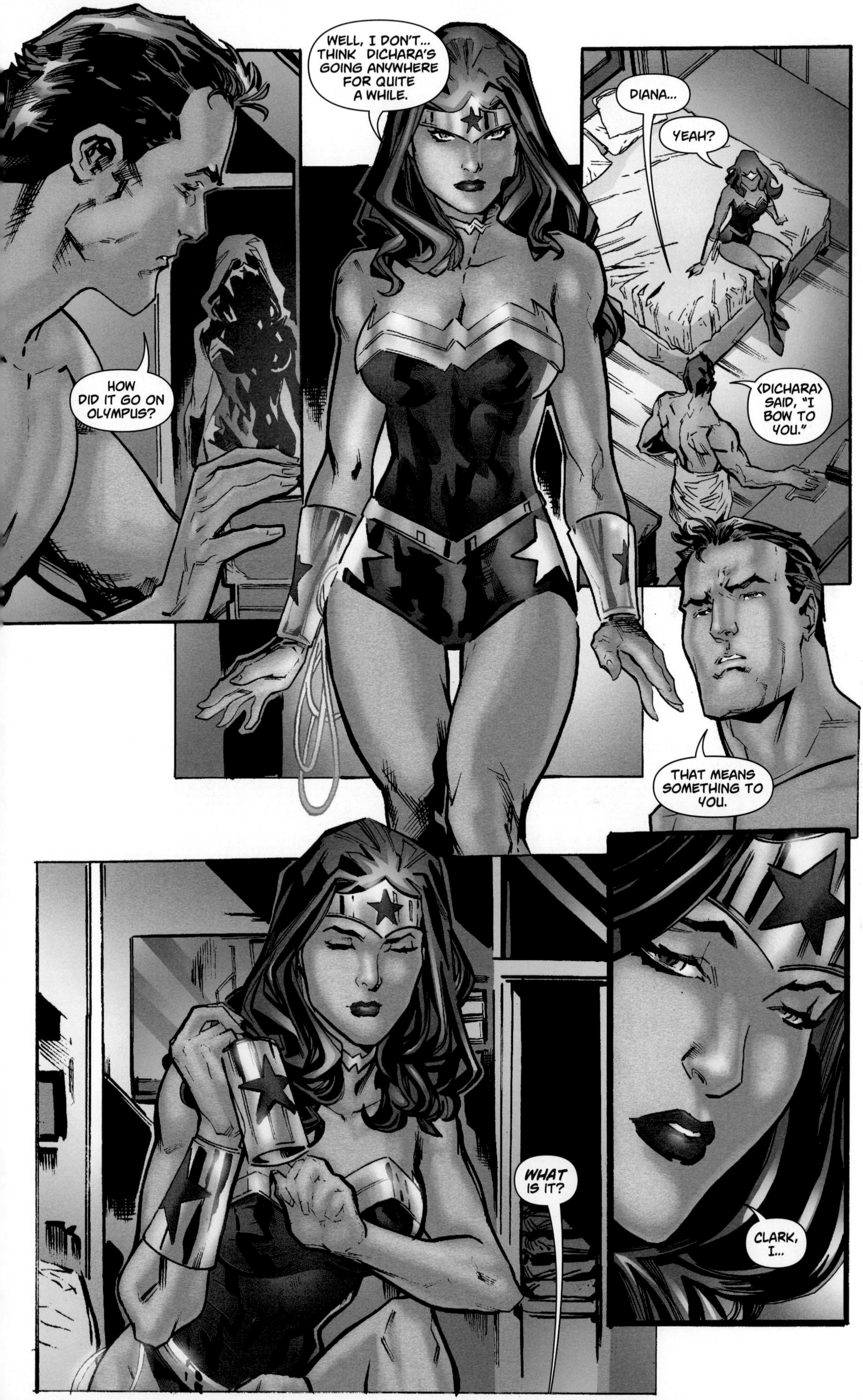
HOW DID IT GO ON OLYMPUS?
WELL, I DON'T... THINK DICHARA'S GOING ANYWHERE FOR QUITE A WHILE.
DIANA...
YEAH?
<DICHARA> SAID, "I BOW TO YOU."
THAT MEANS SOMETHING TO YOU.
WHAT IS IT?
CLARK, I...

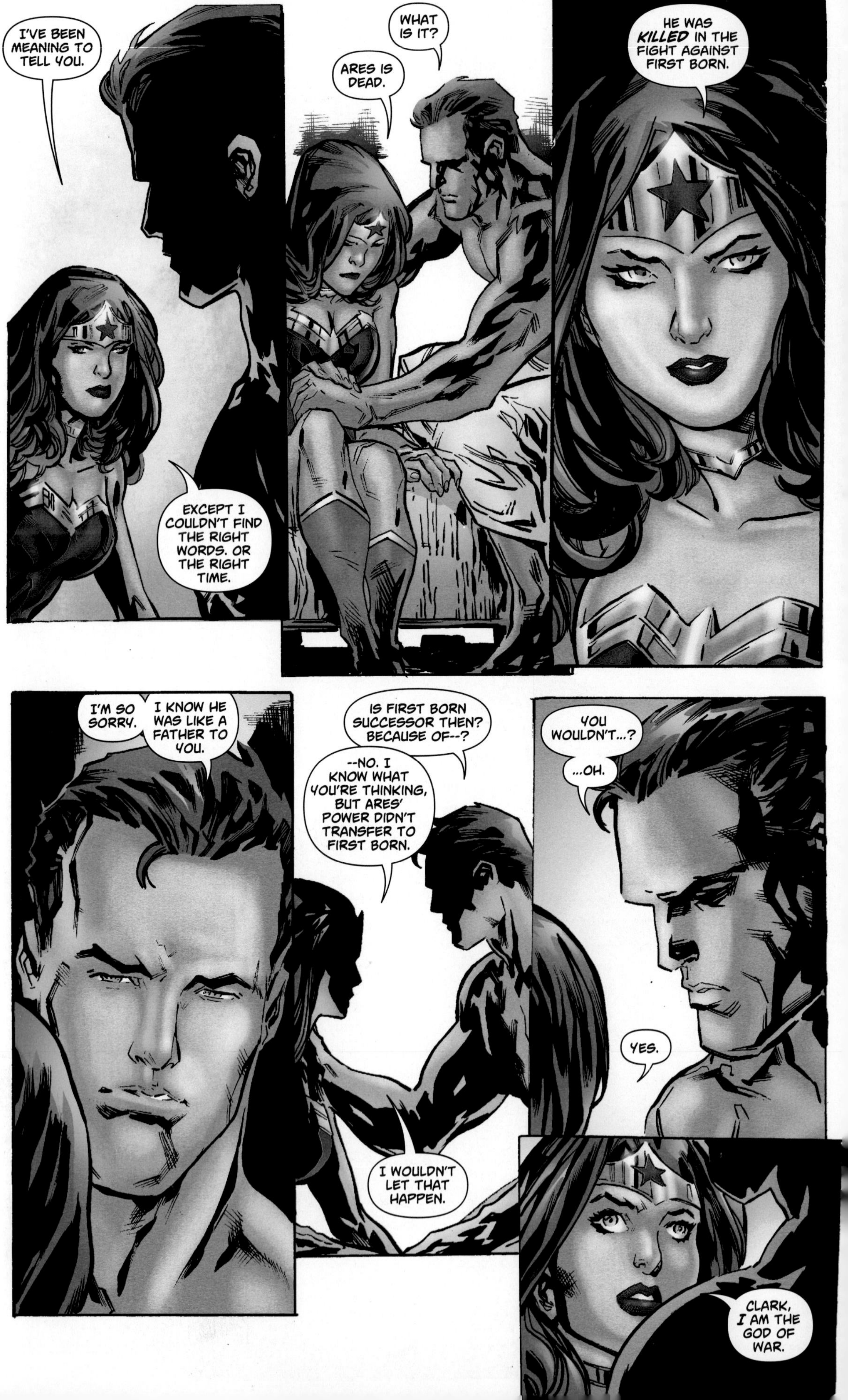
I'VE BEEN MEANING TO TELL YOU.
EXCEPT I COULDN'T FIND THE RIGHT WORDS. OR THE RIGHT TIME.
WHAT IS IT?
ARES IS DEAD.
HE WAS KILLED IN THE FIGHT AGAINST FIRST BORN.
I'M SO SORRY.
I KNOW HE WAS LIKE A FATHER TO YOU.
IS FIRST BORN SUCCESSOR THEN? BECAUSE OF--?
--NO. I KNOW WHAT YOU'RE THINKING, BUT ARES' POWER DIDN'T TRANSFER TO FIRST BORN.
I WOULDN'T LET THAT HAPPEN.
YOU WOULDN'T...?
...OH.
YES.
CLARK, I AM THE GOD OF WAR.

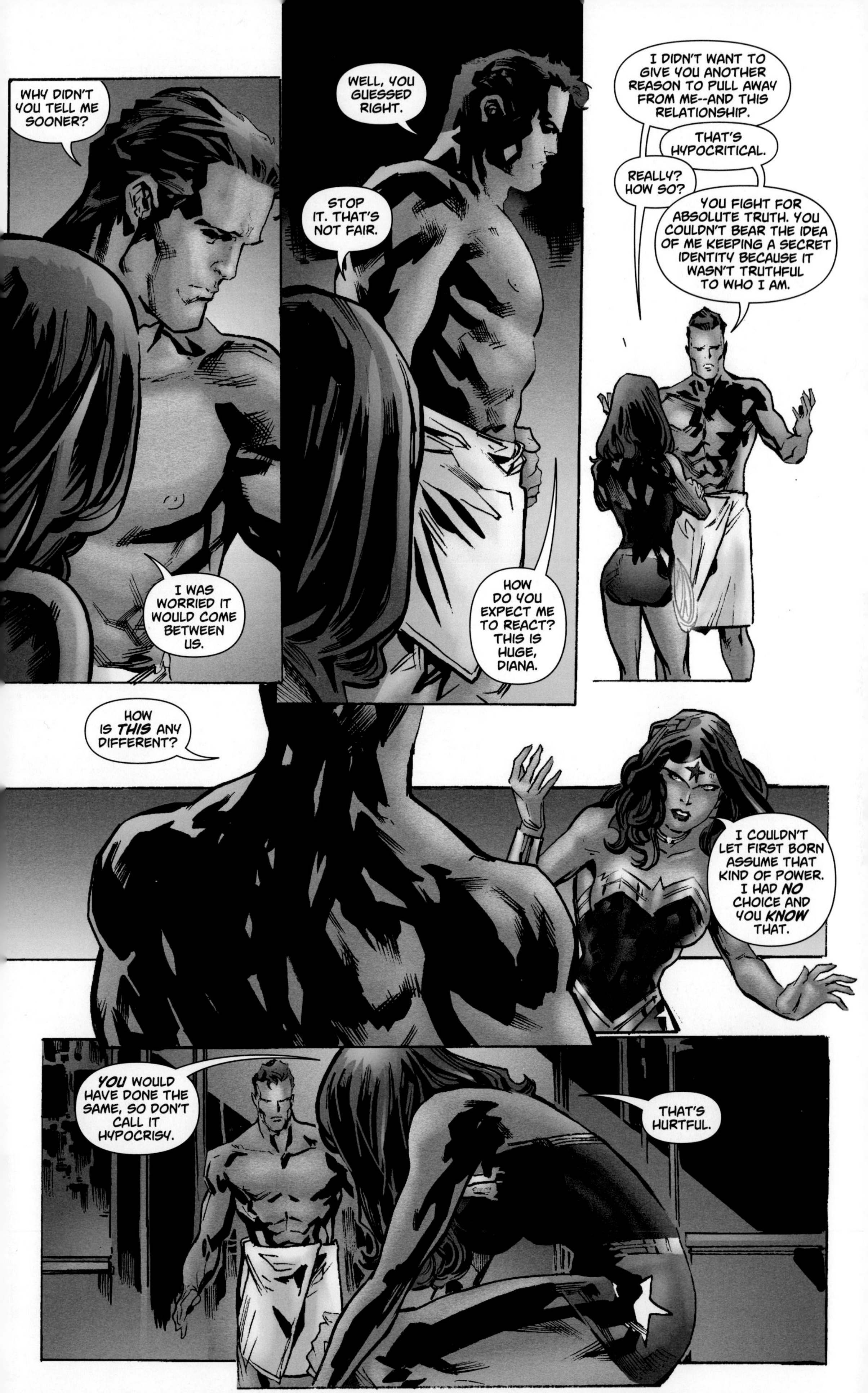
WHY DIDN'T YOU TELL ME SOONER?
I WAS WORRIED IT WOULD COME BETWEEN US.
WELL, YOU GUESSED RIGHT.
STOP IT. THAT'S NOT FAIR.
HOW DO YOU EXPECT ME TO REACT? THIS IS HUGE, DIANA.
I DIDN'T WANT TO GIVE YOU ANOTHER REASON TO PULL AWAY FROM ME--AND THIS RELATIONSHIP.
THAT'S HYPOCRITICAL.
REALLY? HOW SO?
YOU FIGHT FOR ABSOLUTE TRUTH. YOU COULDN'T BEAR THE IDEA OF ME KEEPING A SECRET IDENTITY BECAUSE IT WASN'T TRUTHFUL TO WHO I AM.
HOW IS THIS ANY DIFFERENT?
I COULDN'T LET FIRST BORN ASSUME THAT KIND OF POWER. I HAD NO CHOICE AND YOU KNOW THAT.
YOU WOULD HAVE DONE THE SAME, SO DON'T CALL IT HYPOCRISY.
THAT'S HURTFUL.

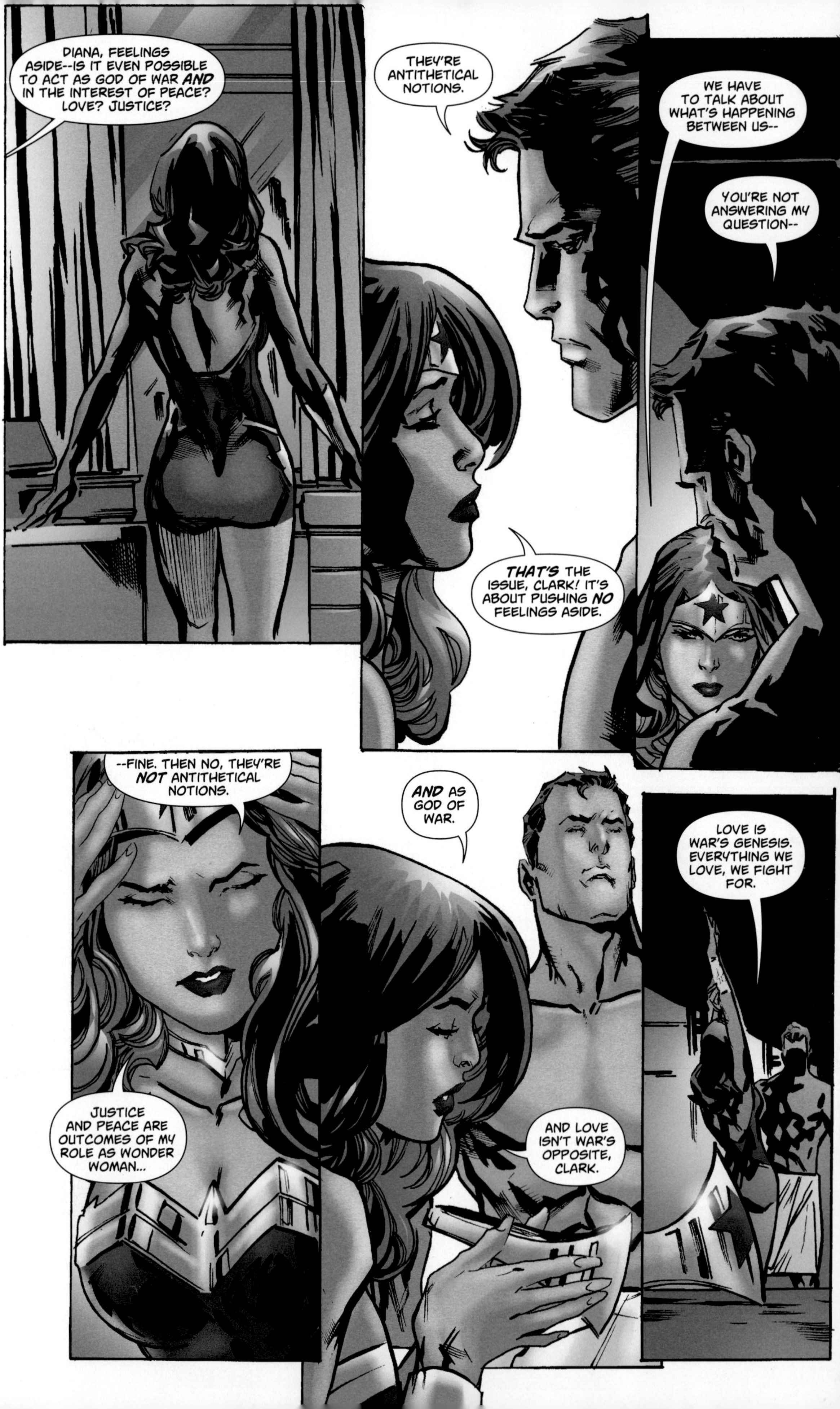
DIANA, FEELINGS ASIDE--IS IT EVEN POSSIBLE TO ACT AS GOD OF WAR AND IN THE INTEREST OF PEACE? LOVE? JUSTICE?
THEY'RE ANTITHETICAL NOTIONS.
THAT'S THE ISSUE, CLARK! IT'S ABOUT PUSHING NO FEELINGS ASIDE.
WE HAVE TO TALK ABOUT WHAT'S HAPPENING BETWEEN US--
YOU'RE NOT ANSWERING MY QUESTION--
--FINE. THEN NO, THEY'RE NOT ANTITHETICAL NOTIONS.
JUSTICE AND PEACE ARE OUTCOMES OF MY ROLE AS WONDER WOMAN...
AND AS GOD OF WAR.
AND LOVE ISN'T WAR'S OPPOSITE, CLARK.
LOVE IS WAR'S GENESIS. EVERYTHING WE LOVE, WE FIGHT FOR.

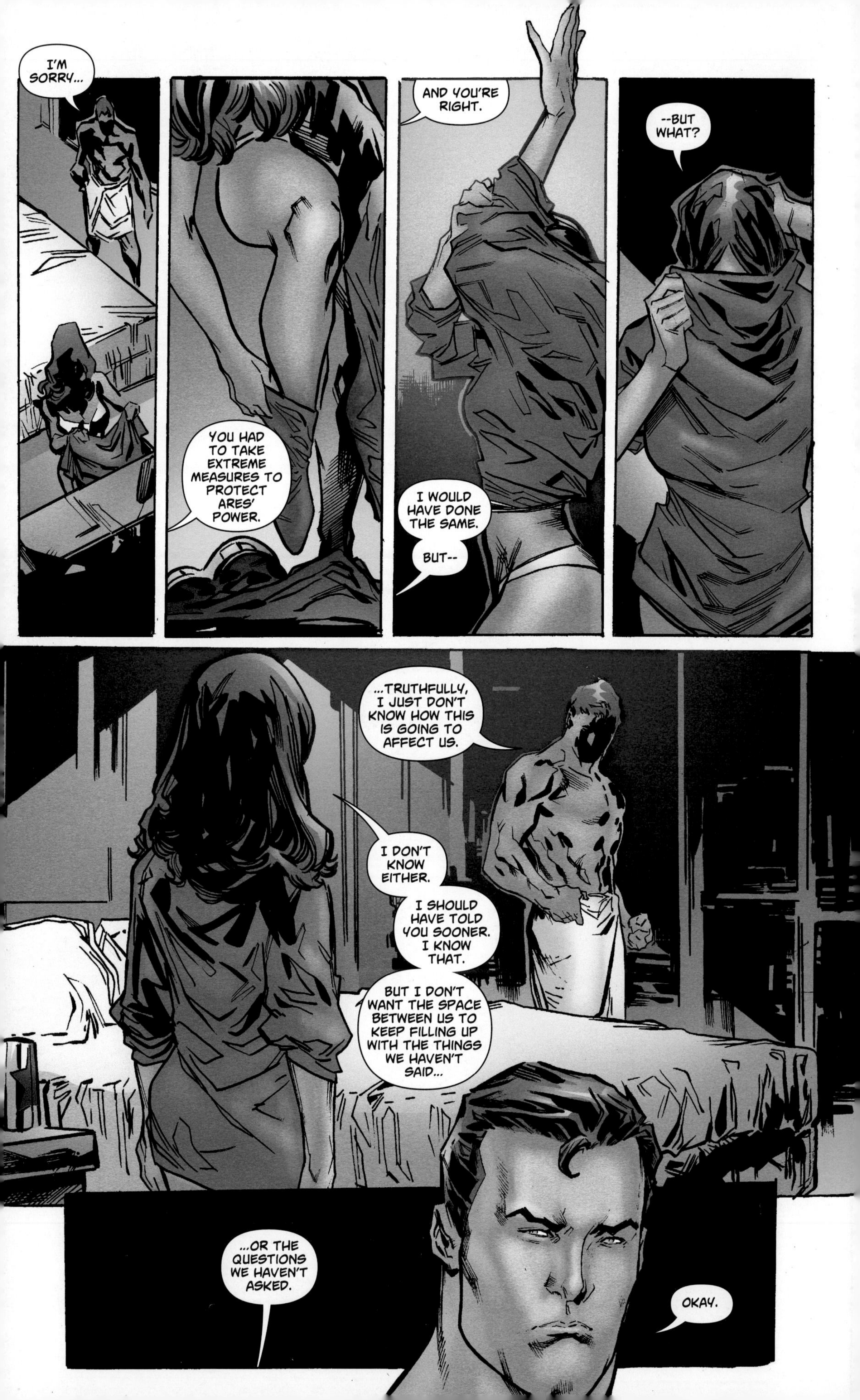
I'M SORRY...
YOU HAD TO TAKE EXTREME MEASURES TO PROTECT ARES' POWER.
AND YOU'RE RIGHT.
I WOULD HAVE DONE THE SAME.
BUT--
--BUT WHAT?
...TRUTHFULLY, I JUST DON'T KNOW HOW THIS IS GOING TO AFFECT US.
I DON'T KNOW EITHER.
I SHOULD HAVE TOLD YOU SOONER. I KNOW THAT.
BUT I DON'T WANT THE SPACE BETWEEN US TO KEEP FILLING UP WITH THE THINGS WE HAVEN'T SAID...
...OR THE QUESTIONS WE HAVEN'T ASKED.
OKAY.

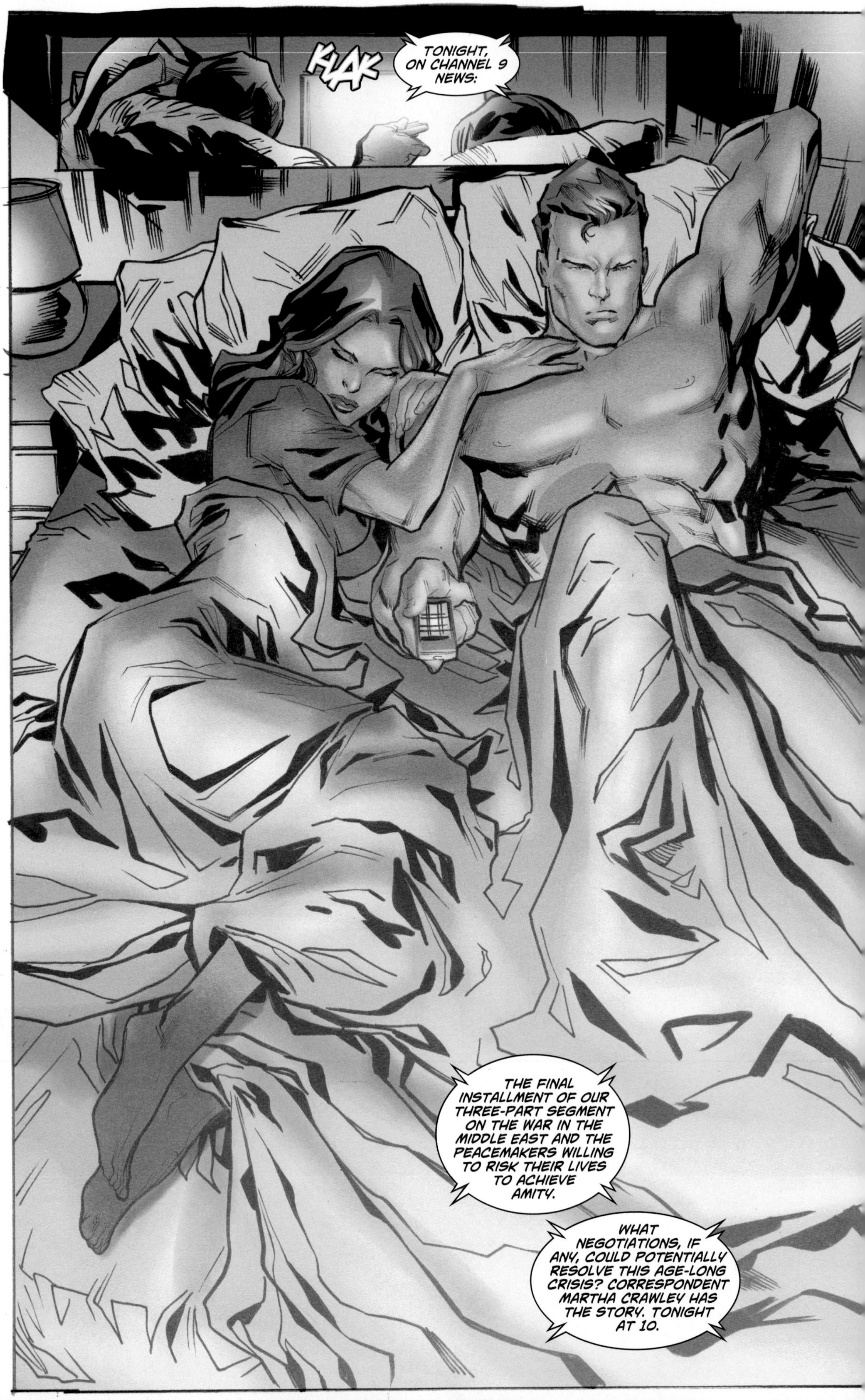
KLAK
TONIGHT, ON CHANNEL 9 NEWS:
THE FINAL INSTALLMENT OF OUR THREE-PART SEGMENT ON THE WAR IN THE MIDDLE EAST AND THE PEACEMAKERS WILLING TO RISK THEIR LIVES TO ACHIEVE AMITY.
WHAT NEGOTIATIONS, IF ANY, COULD POTENTIALLY RESOLVE THIS AGE-LONG CRISIS? CORRESPONDENT MARTHA CRAWLEY HAS THE STORY. TONIGHT AT 10.

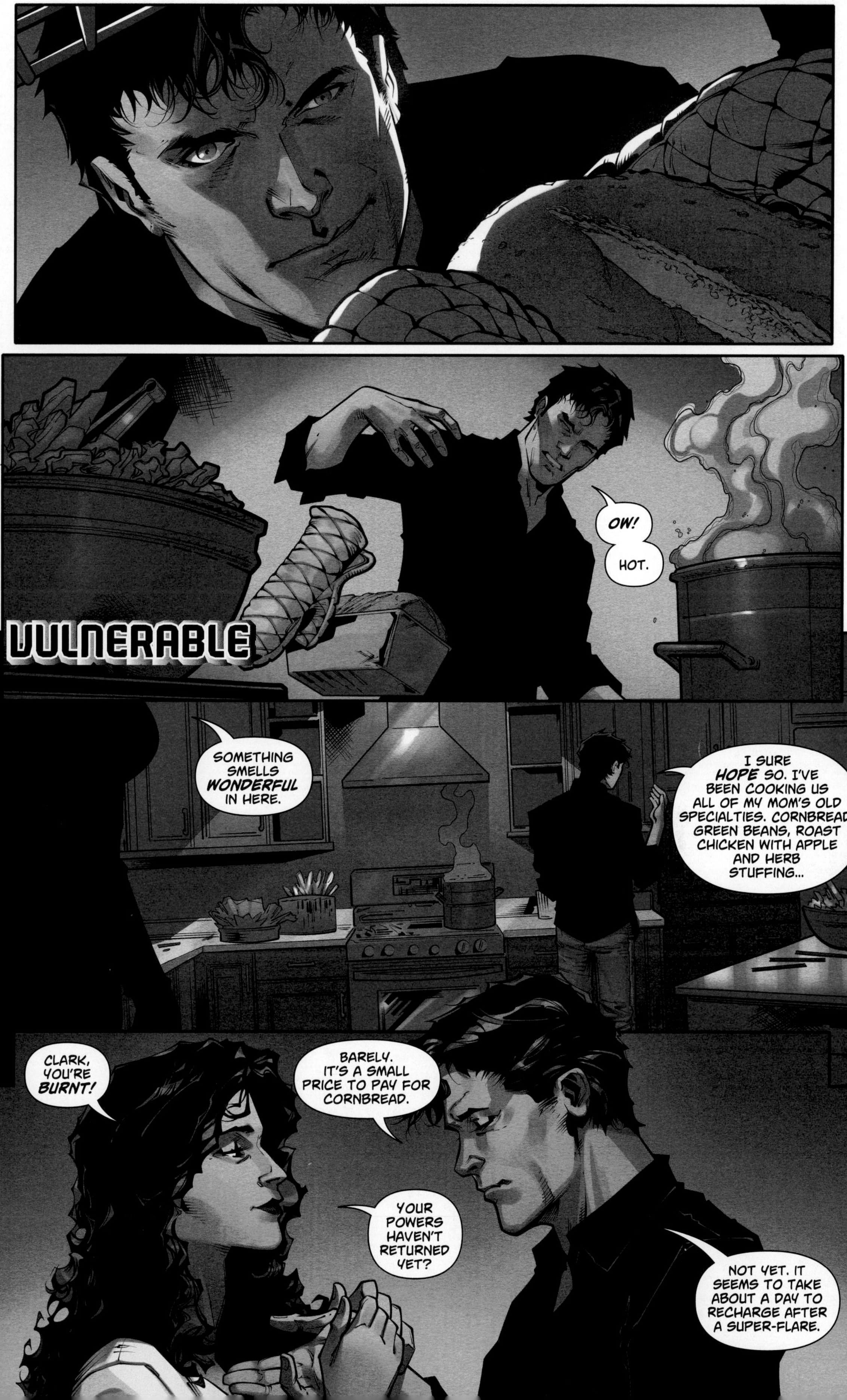
OW!
HOT.
VULNERABLE
SOMETHING SMELLS WONDERFUL IN HERE.
I SURE HOPE SO. I'VE BEEN COOKING US ALL OF MY MOM'S OLD SPECIALTIES. CORNBREAD, GREEN BEANS, ROAST CHICKEN WITH APPLE AND HERB STUFFING...
CLARK, YOU'RE BURNT!
BARELY. IT'S A SMALL PRICE TO PAY FOR CORNBREAD.
YOUR POWERS HAVEN'T RETURNED YET?
NOT YET. IT SEEMS TO TAKE ABOUT A DAY TO RECHARGE AFTER A SUPER-FLARE.

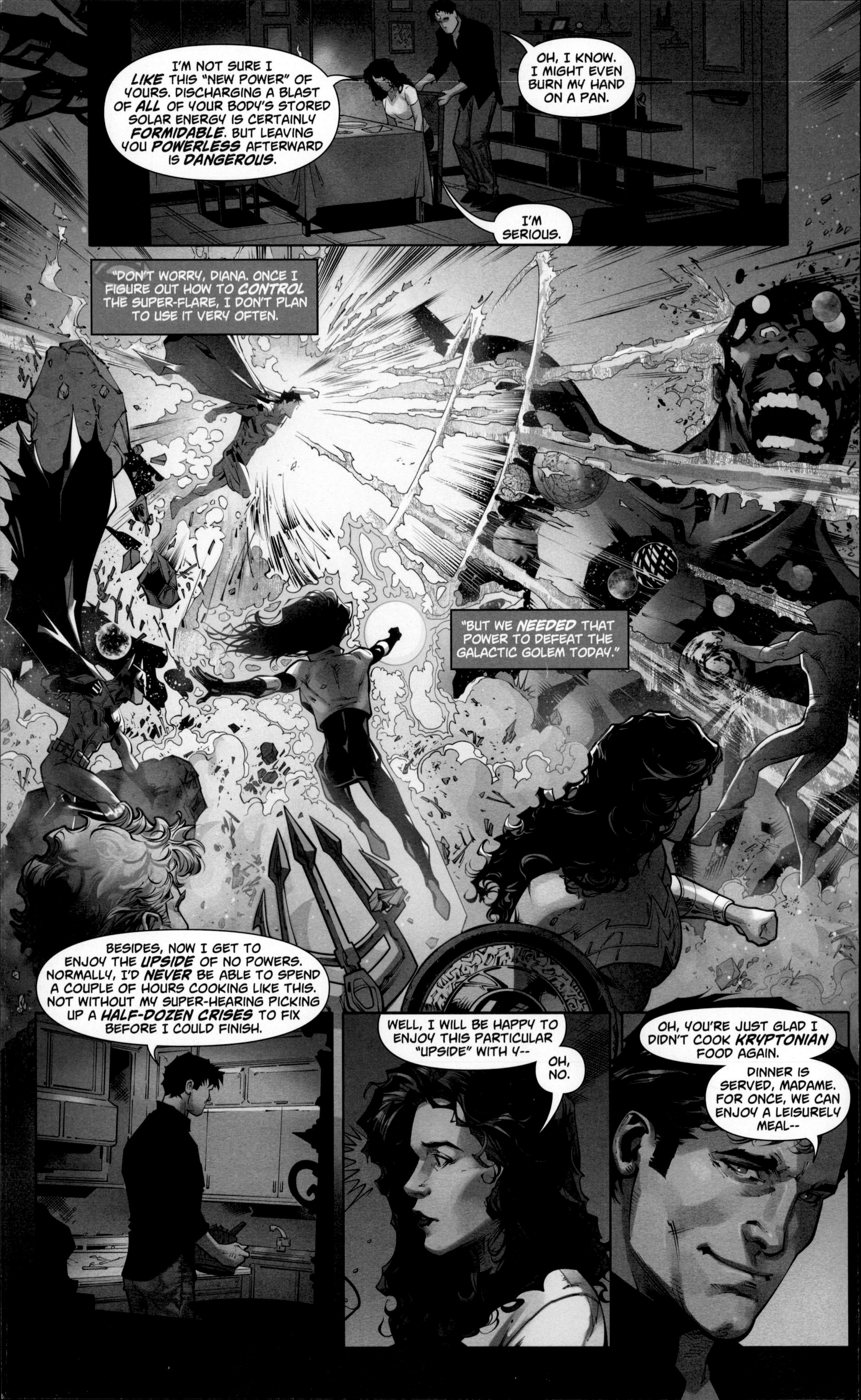
I'M NOT SURE I LIKE THIS "NEW POWER" OF YOURS. DISCHARGING A BLAST OF ALL OF YOUR BODY'S STORED SOLAR ENERGY IS CERTAINLY FORMIDABLE. BUT LEAVING YOU POWERLESS AFTERWARD IS DANGEROUS.
OH, I KNOW. I MIGHT EVEN BURN MY HAND ON A PAN.
I'M SERIOUS.
"DON'T WORRY, DIANA. ONCE I FIGURE OUT HOW TO CONTROL THE SUPER-FLARE, I DON'T PLAN TO USE IT VERY OFTEN.
"BUT WE NEEDED THAT POWER TO DEFEAT THE GALACTIC GOLEM TODAY."
BESIDES, NOW I GET TO ENJOY THE UPSIDE OF NO POWERS. NORMALLY, I'D NEVER BE ABLE TO SPEND A COUPLE OF HOURS COOKING LIKE THIS. NOT WITHOUT MY SUPER-HEARING PICKING UP A HALF-DOZEN CRISES TO FIX BEFORE I COULD FINISH.
WELL, I WILL BE HAPPY TO ENJOY THIS PARTICULAR "UPSIDE" WITH Y--
OH, NO.
OH, YOU'RE JUST GLAD I DIDN'T COOK KRYPTONIAN FOOD AGAIN.
DINNER IS SERVED, MADAME. FOR ONCE, WE CAN ENJOY A LEISURELY MEAL--

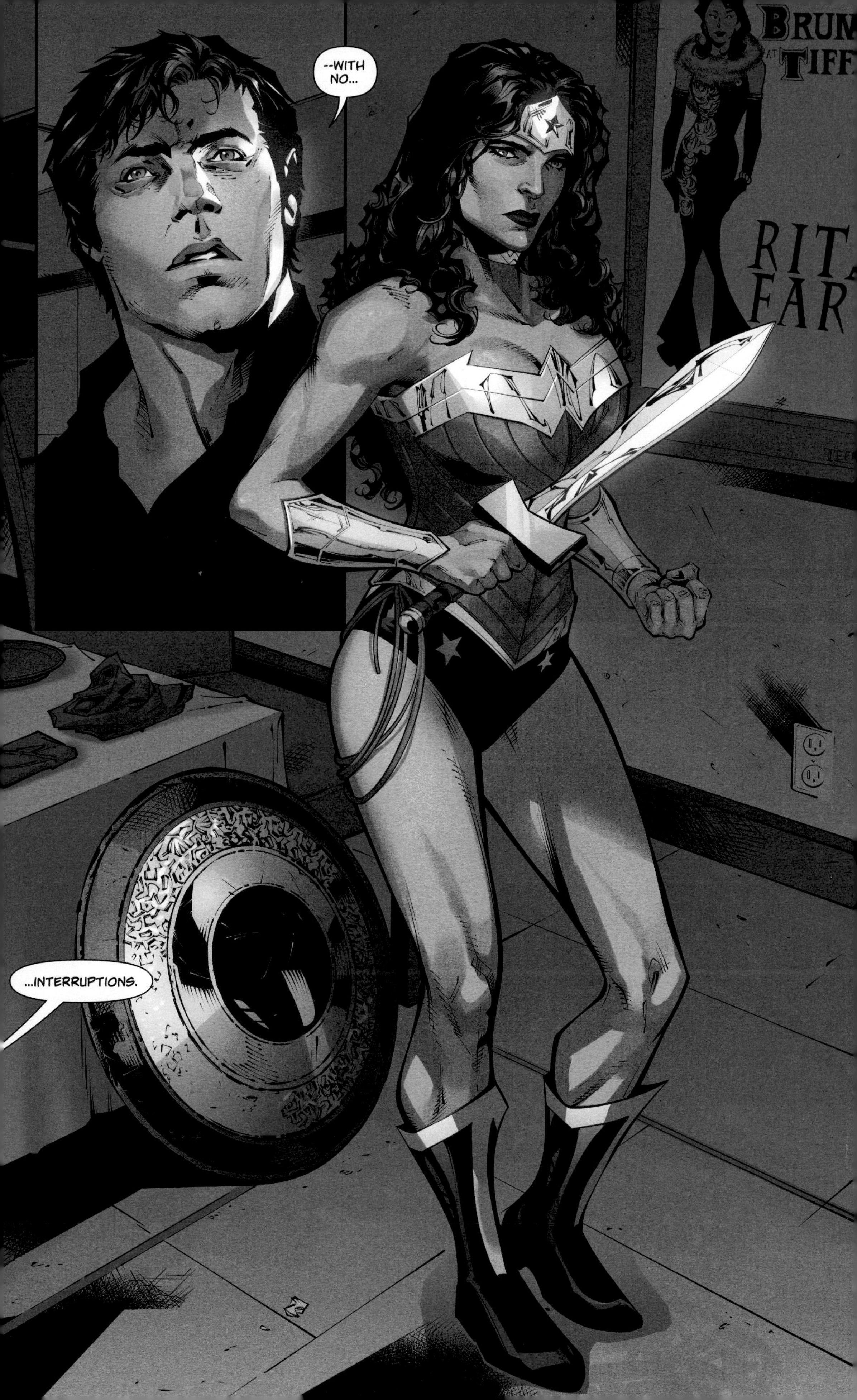
--WITH NO...
...INTERRUPTIONS.

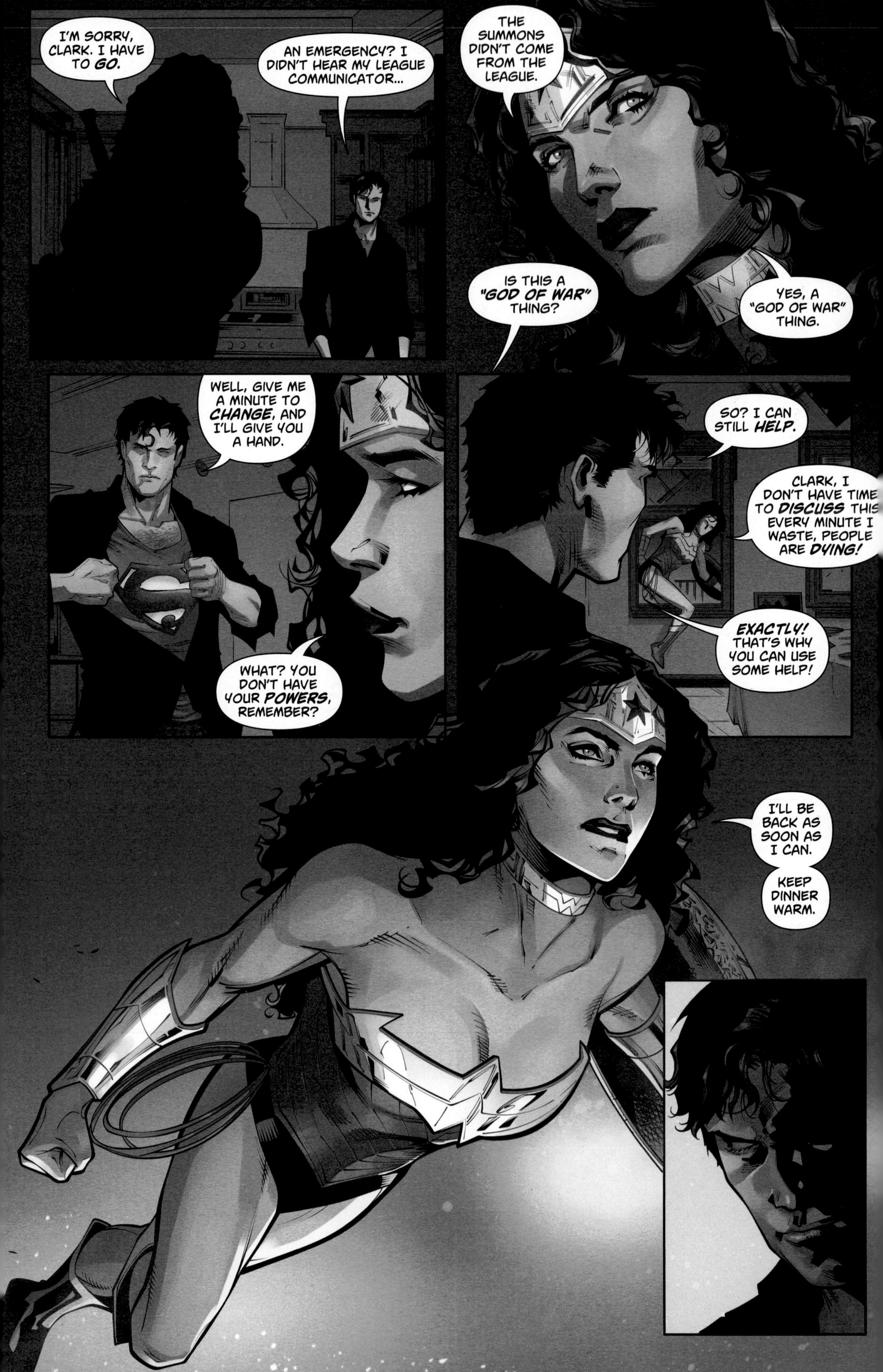
I'M SORRY, CLARK. I HAVE TO GO.
AN EMERGENCY? I DIDN'T HEAR MY LEAGUE COMMUNICATOR...
THE SUMMONS DIDN'T COME FROM THE LEAGUE.
IS THIS A "GOD OF WAR" THING?
YES, A "GOD OF WAR" THING.
WELL, GIVE ME A MINUTE TO CHANGE, AND I'LL GIVE YOU A HAND.
WHAT? YOU DON'T HAVE YOUR POWERS, REMEMBER?
SO? I CAN STILL HELP.
CLARK, I DON'T HAVE TIME TO DISCUSS THIS EVERY MINUTE I WASTE, PEOPLE ARE DYING!
EXACTLY! THAT'S WHY YOU CAN USE SOME HELP!
I'LL BE BACK AS SOON AS I CAN.
KEEP DINNER WARM.

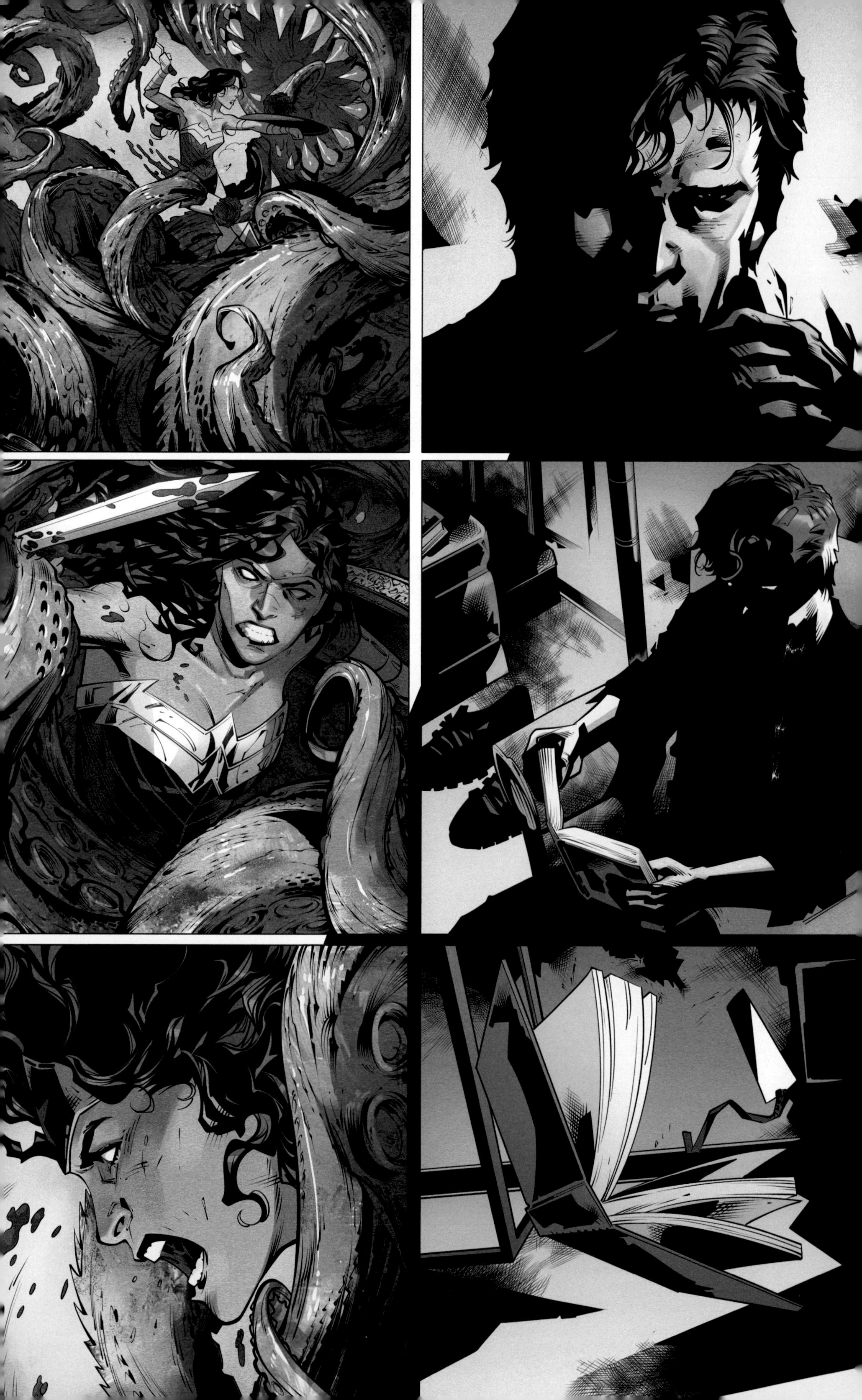

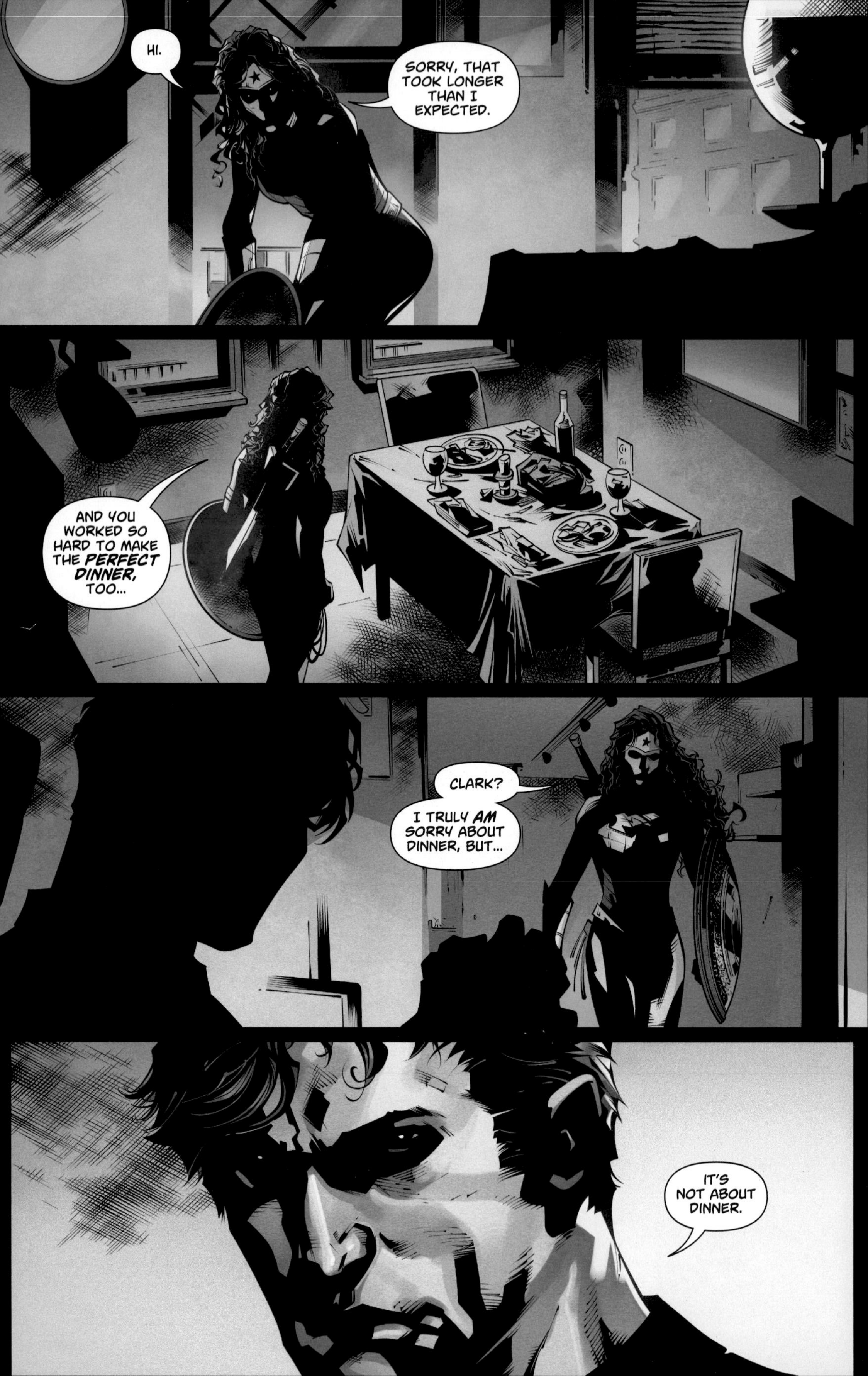
HI.
SORRY, THAT TOOK LONGER THAN I EXPECTED.
AND YOU WORKED SO HARD TO MAKE THE *PERFECT DINNER,* TOO...
CLARK?
I TRULY *AM* SORRY ABOUT DINNER, BUT...
IT'S NOT ABOUT DINNER.

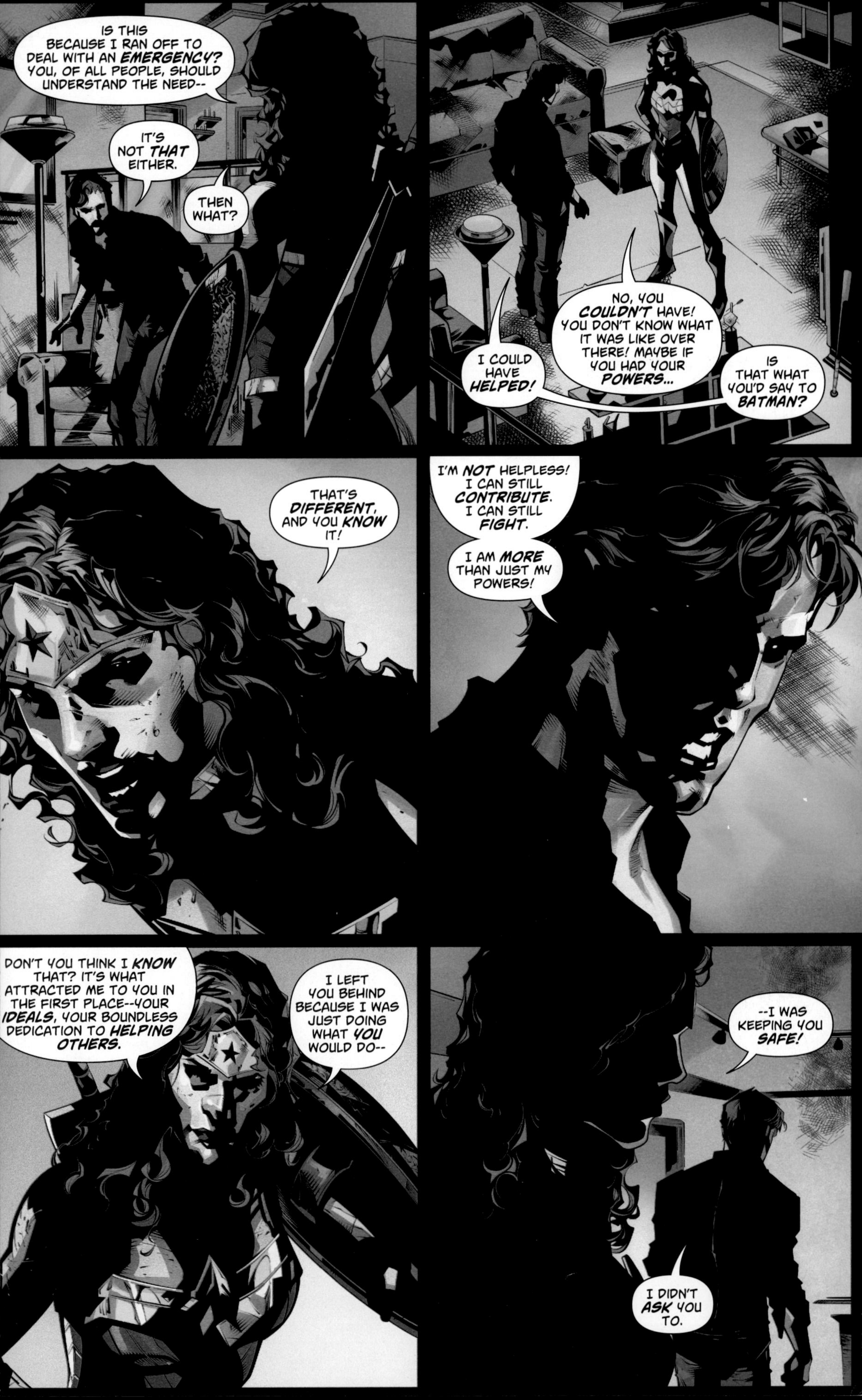
IS THIS BECAUSE I RAN OFF TO DEAL WITH AN ***EMERGENCY?*** YOU, OF ALL PEOPLE, SHOULD UNDERSTAND THE NEED--
IT'S NOT ***THAT*** EITHER.
THEN WHAT?
I COULD HAVE ***HELPED!***
NO, YOU ***COULDN'T*** HAVE! YOU DON'T KNOW WHAT IT WAS LIKE OVER THERE! MAYBE IF YOU HAD YOUR ***POWERS...***
IS THAT WHAT YOU'D SAY TO ***BATMAN?***
THAT'S ***DIFFERENT***, AND YOU ***KNOW*** IT!
I'M ***NOT*** HELPLESS! I CAN STILL ***CONTRIBUTE***. I CAN STILL ***FIGHT***.
I AM ***MORE*** THAN JUST MY POWERS!
DON'T YOU THINK I ***KNOW*** THAT? IT'S WHAT ATTRACTED ME TO YOU IN THE FIRST PLACE--YOUR ***IDEALS***, YOUR BOUNDLESS DEDICATION TO ***HELPING OTHERS***.
I LEFT YOU BEHIND BECAUSE I WAS JUST DOING WHAT ***YOU*** WOULD DO--
--I WAS KEEPING YOU ***SAFE!***
I DIDN'T ***ASK*** YOU TO.

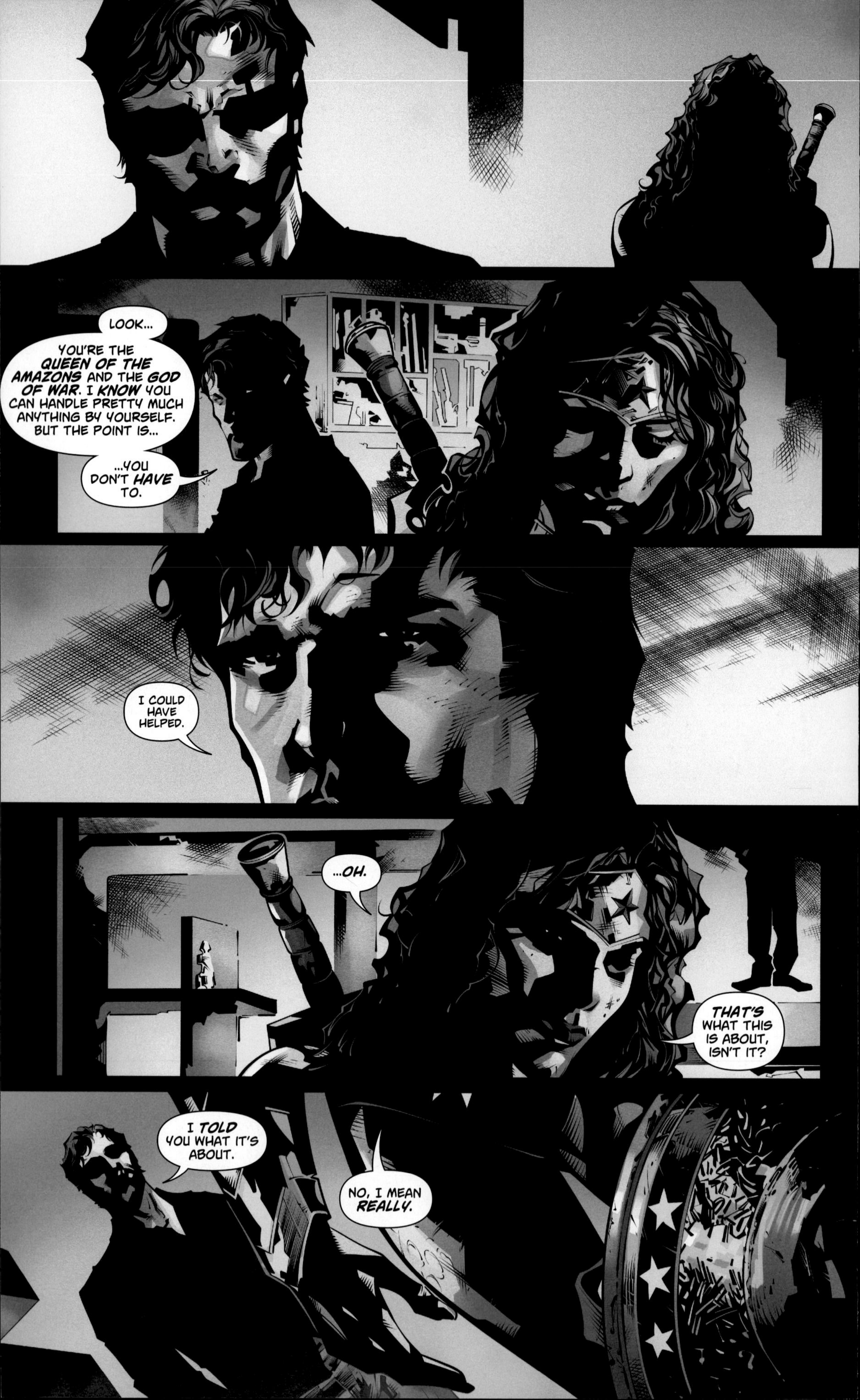
LOOK...
YOU'RE THE QUEEN OF THE AMAZONS AND THE GOD OF WAR. I KNOW YOU CAN HANDLE PRETTY MUCH ANYTHING BY YOURSELF. BUT THE POINT IS...
...YOU DON'T HAVE TO.
I COULD HAVE HELPED.
...OH.
THAT'S WHAT THIS IS ABOUT, ISN'T IT?
I TOLD YOU WHAT IT'S ABOUT.
NO, I MEAN REALLY.

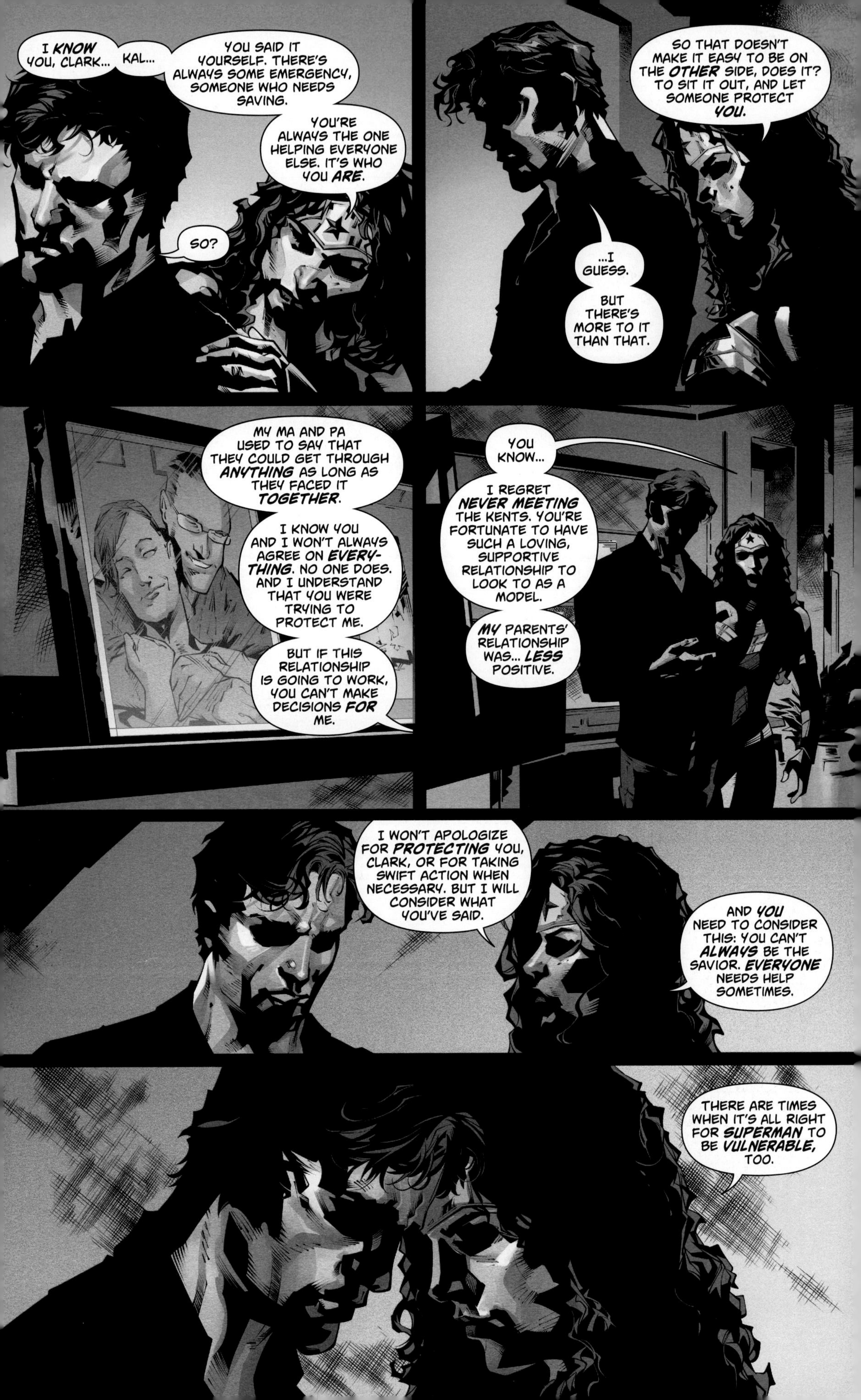

I KNOW YOU, CLARK...
KAL...
YOU SAID IT YOURSELF. THERE'S ALWAYS SOME EMERGENCY, SOMEONE WHO NEEDS SAVING.
YOU'RE ALWAYS THE ONE HELPING EVERYONE ELSE. IT'S WHO YOU ARE.
SO?
SO THAT DOESN'T MAKE IT EASY TO BE ON THE OTHER SIDE, DOES IT? TO SIT IT OUT, AND LET SOMEONE PROTECT YOU.
...I GUESS.
BUT THERE'S MORE TO IT THAN THAT.
MY MA AND PA USED TO SAY THAT THEY COULD GET THROUGH ANYTHING AS LONG AS THEY FACED IT TOGETHER.
I KNOW YOU AND I WON'T ALWAYS AGREE ON EVERY-THING. NO ONE DOES. AND I UNDERSTAND THAT YOU WERE TRYING TO PROTECT ME.
BUT IF THIS RELATIONSHIP IS GOING TO WORK, YOU CAN'T MAKE DECISIONS FOR ME.
YOU KNOW...
I REGRET NEVER MEETING THE KENTS. YOU'RE FORTUNATE TO HAVE SUCH A LOVING, SUPPORTIVE RELATIONSHIP TO LOOK TO AS A MODEL.
MY PARENTS' RELATIONSHIP WAS... LESS POSITIVE.
I WON'T APOLOGIZE FOR PROTECTING YOU, CLARK, OR FOR TAKING SWIFT ACTION WHEN NECESSARY. BUT I WILL CONSIDER WHAT YOU'VE SAID.
AND YOU NEED TO CONSIDER THIS: YOU CAN'T ALWAYS BE THE SAVIOR. EVERYONE NEEDS HELP SOMETIMES.
THERE ARE TIMES WHEN IT'S ALL RIGHT FOR SUPERMAN TO BE VULNERABLE, TOO.

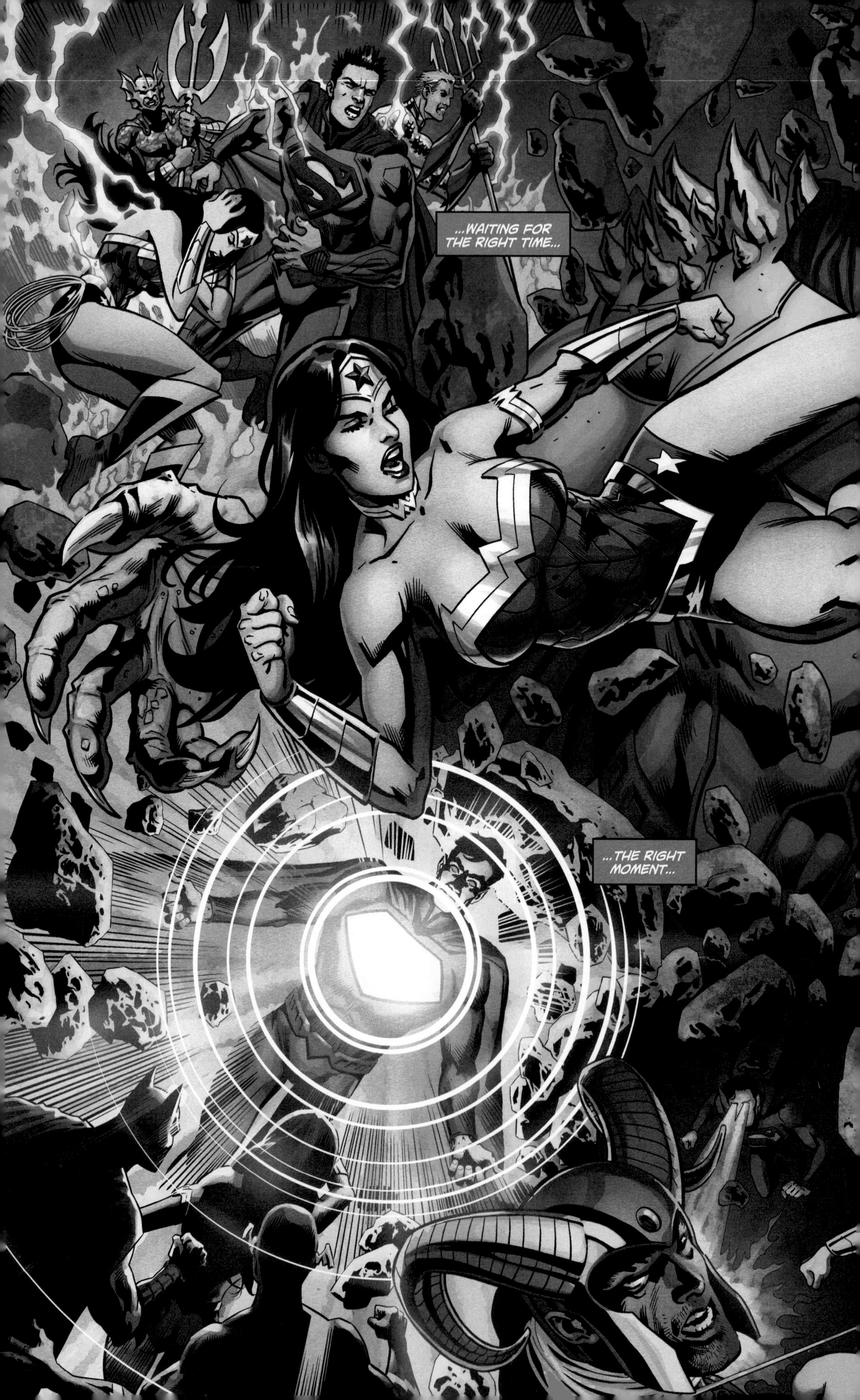
...WAITING FOR THE RIGHT TIME...
...THE RIGHT MOMENT...

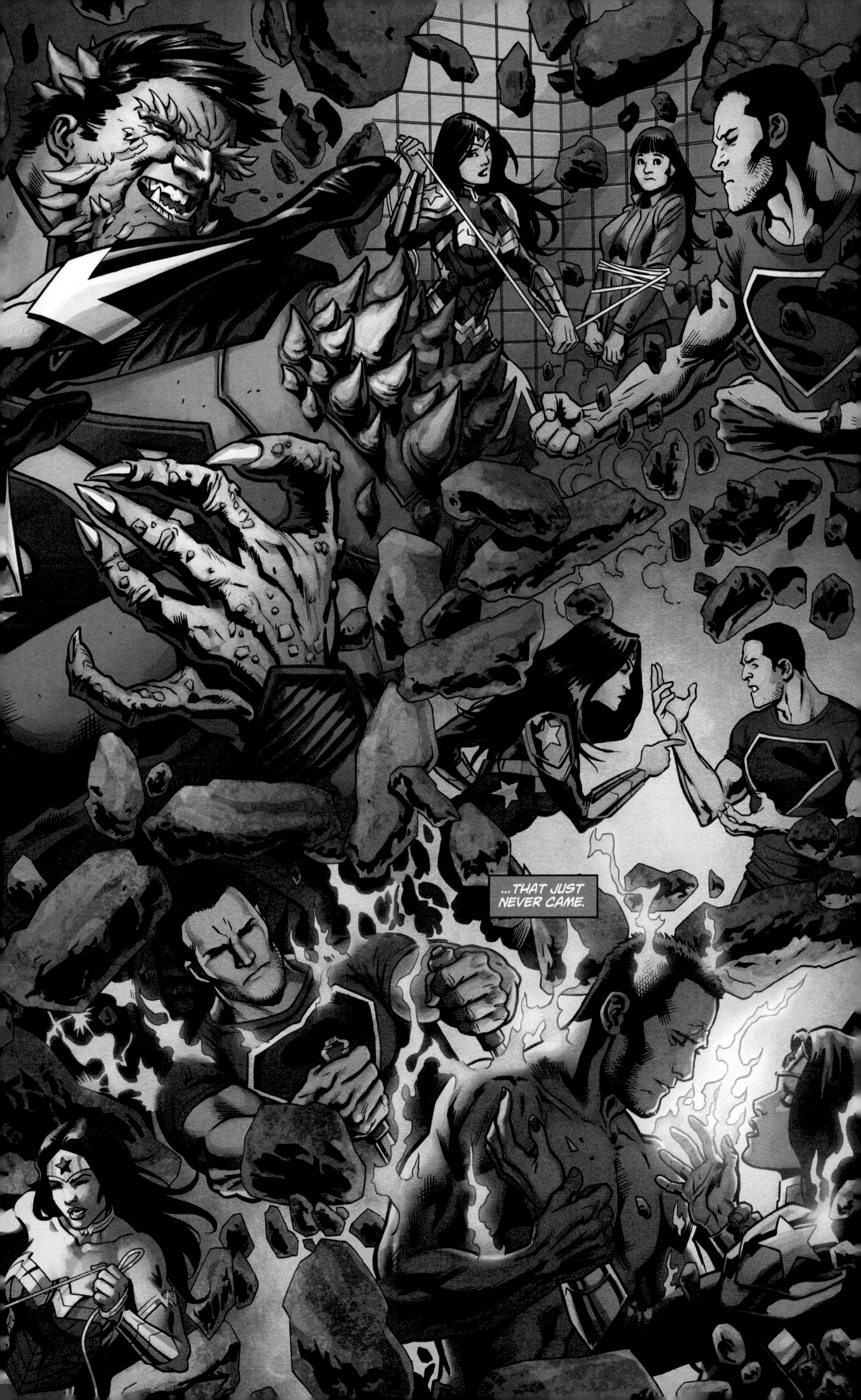
...THAT JUST NEVER CAME.

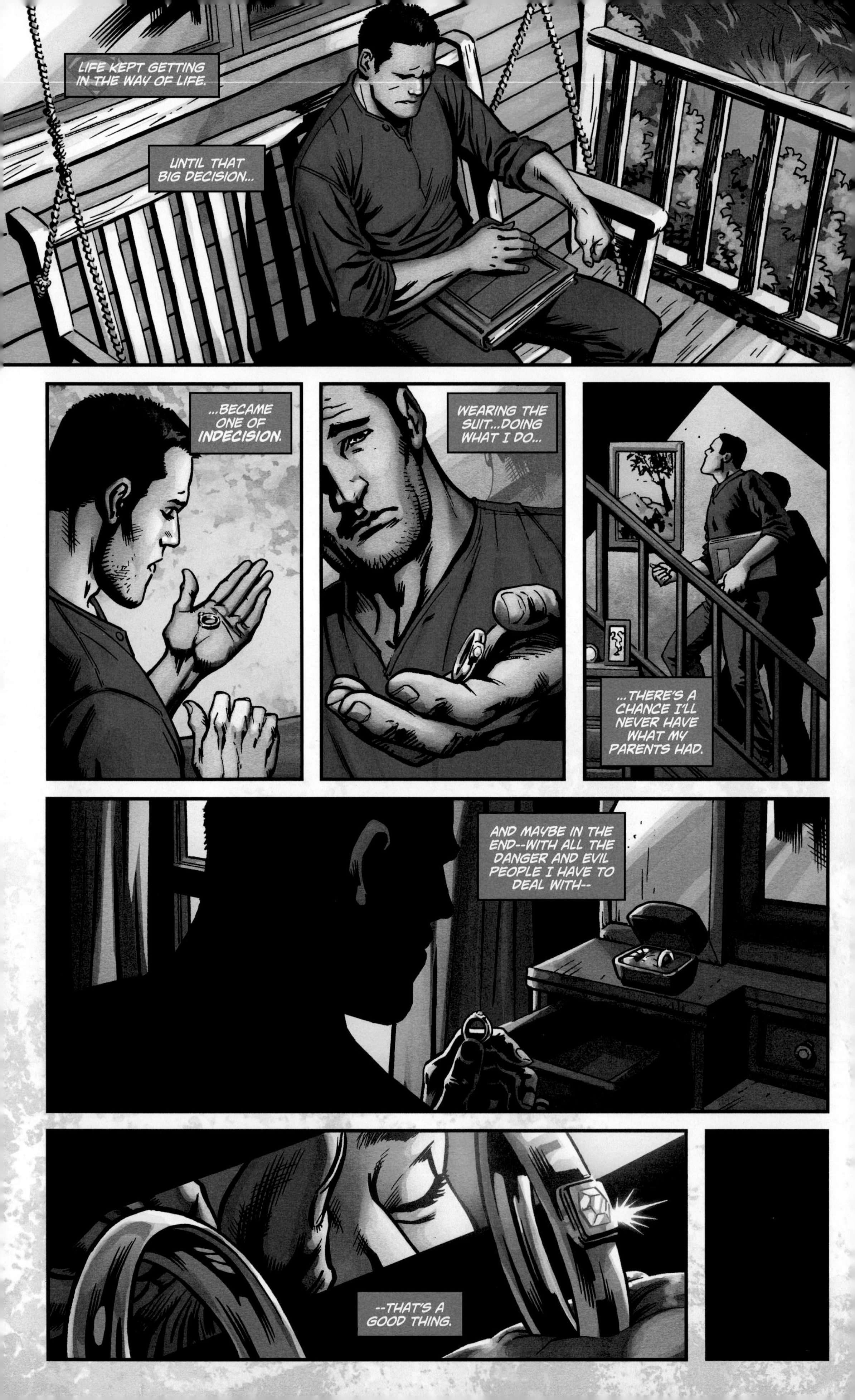
LIFE KEPT GETTING IN THE WAY OF LIFE.
UNTIL THAT BIG DECISION...
...BECAME ONE OF INDECISION.
WEARING THE SUIT...DOING WHAT I DO...
...THERE'S A CHANCE I'LL NEVER HAVE WHAT MY PARENTS HAD.
AND MAYBE IN THE END--WITH ALL THE DANGER AND EVIL PEOPLE I HAVE TO DEAL WITH--
--THAT'S A GOOD THING.

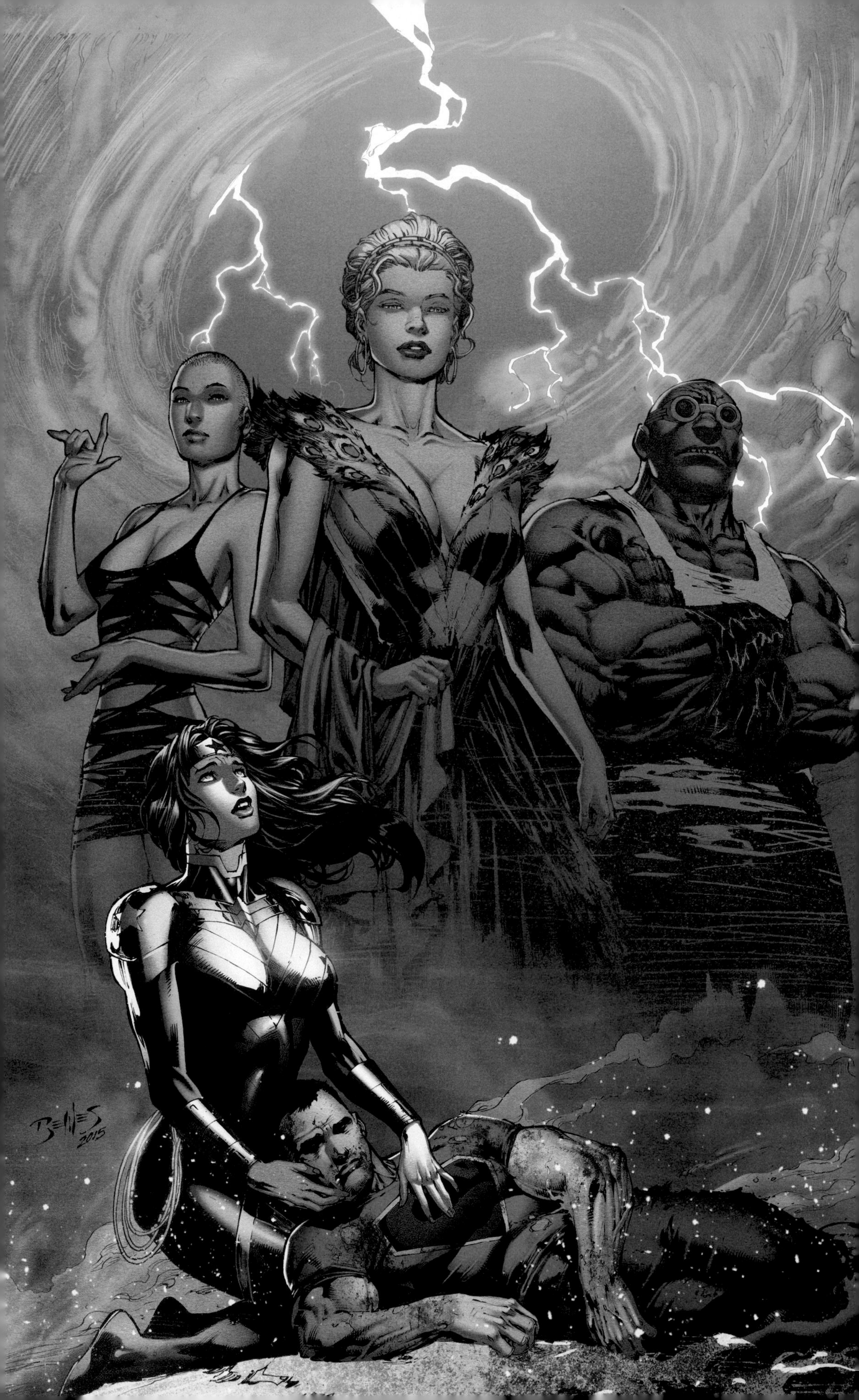
BENES
2015

A GOD SOMEWHERE

PETER J. TOMASI writer **DOUG MAHNKE** penciller **JAIME MENDOZA, JONATHAN GLAPION, SCOTT HANNA** inkers **WIL QUINTANA** colorist
ROB LEIGH letterer cover by **ED BENES & WIL QUINTANA**

Previously,
in SUPERMAN ANNUAL #3 and ACTION COMICS #48...

How ironic that a Kryptonian scientist, upon successfully deflecting a comet that threatened his planet, would inadvertently give rise to the Last Son of Krypton's greatest adversary. With his powers gone and his identity revealed to the world, Superman discovers that the culprit behind his months of misery is Vandal Savage, whose aeons-old obsession with reclaiming the comet that first granted him immortality now endangers every living human being on Earth.

Using the Man of Steel's stolen powers to defeat the Justice League and siphon their combined might, Savage successfully merges the League Watchtower and Stormwatch Carrier. Uncertain what the tyrant hopes to accomplish, Superman temporarily rejuvenates his cells inside Metallo's original Kryptonite-powered armor, then joins members of the Justice League United to liberate their fallen friends. Though they succeed in freeing Wonder Woman, the rest of their mission ends in disaster. As Savage's forces capture the remaining Leaguers and power up his spacecraft for the next phase of his grand design, Superman lays motionless...

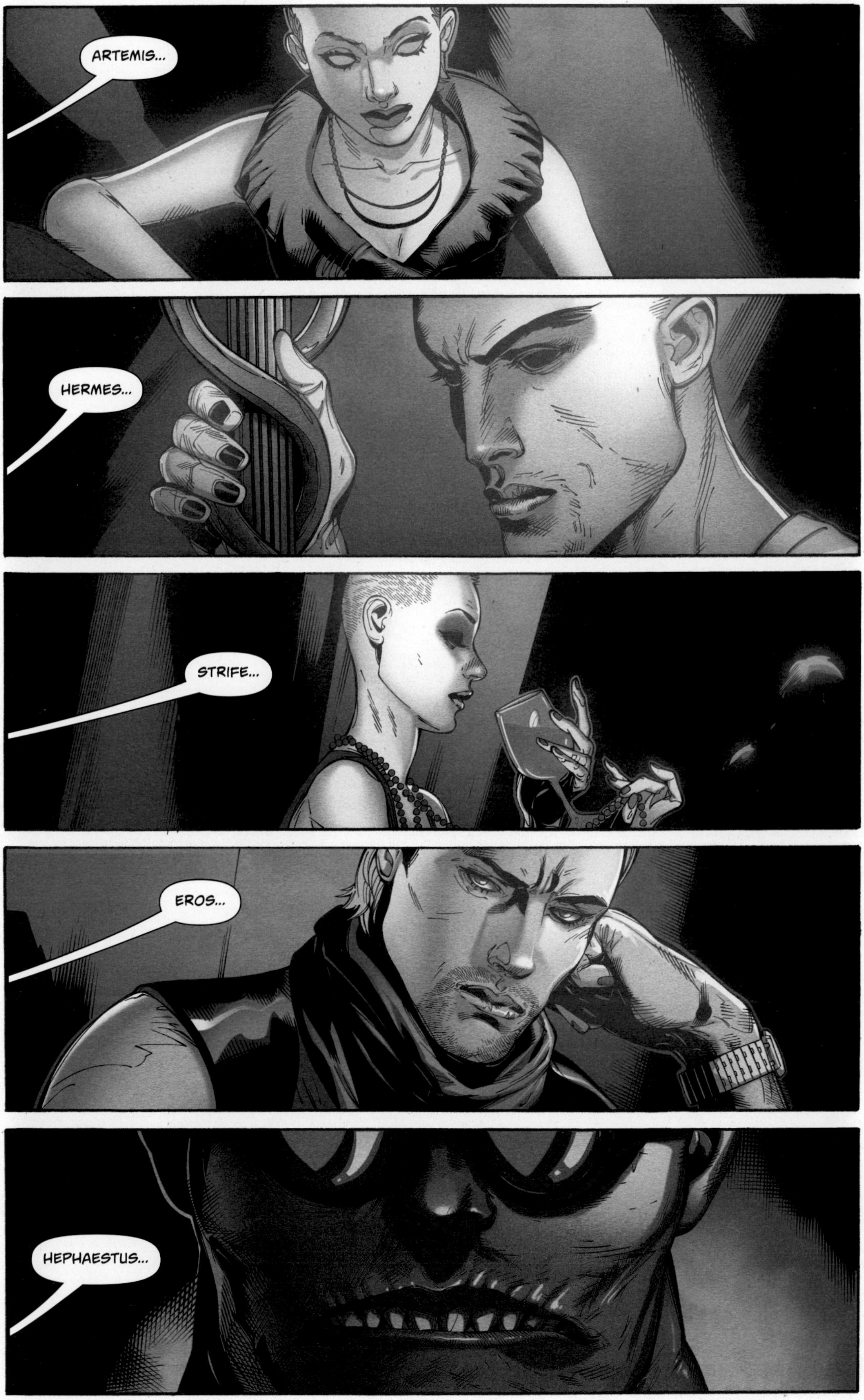
ARTEMIS...
HERMES...
STRIFE...
EROS...
HEPHAESTUS...

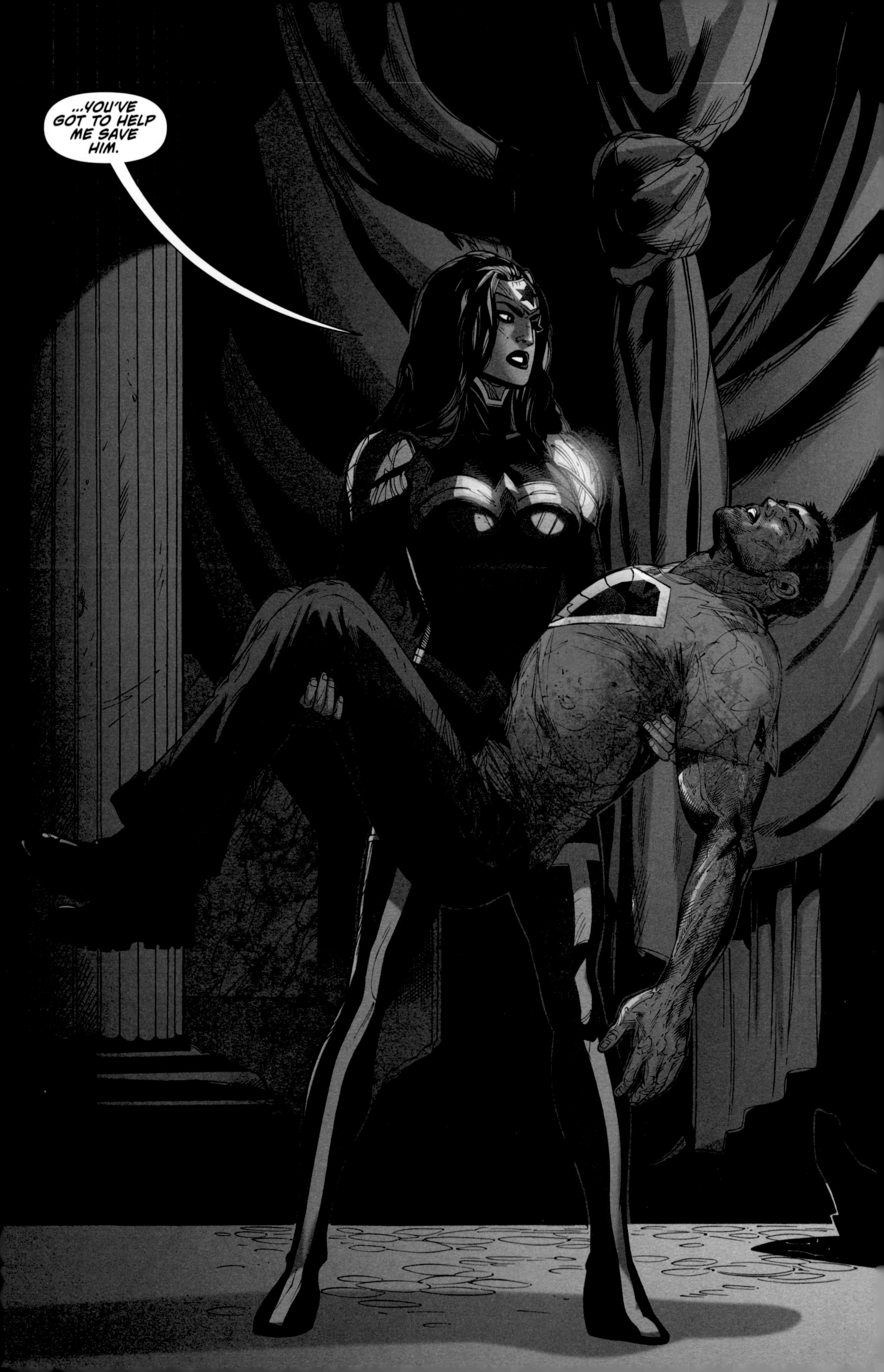
...YOU'VE GOT TO HELP ME SAVE HIM.

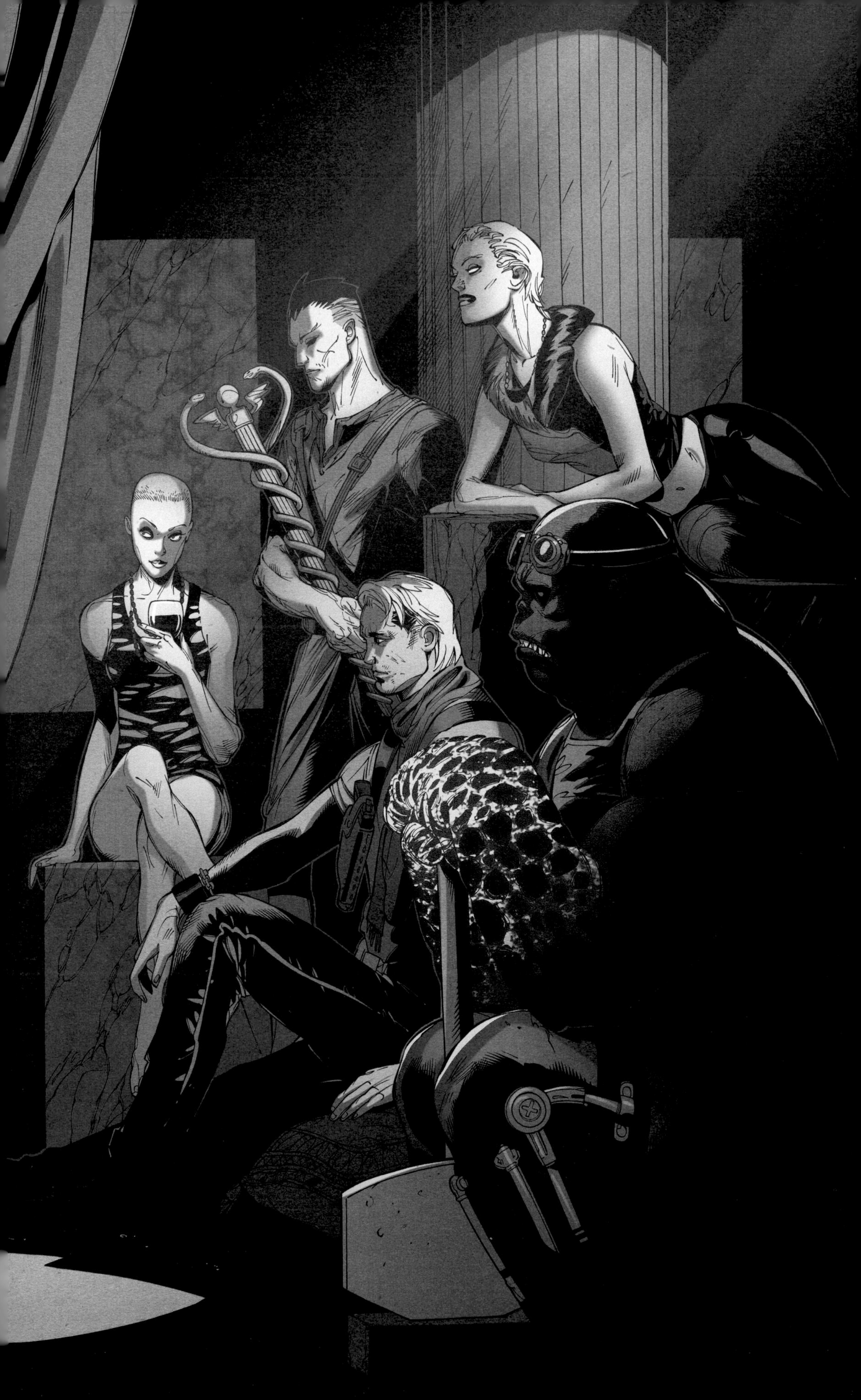

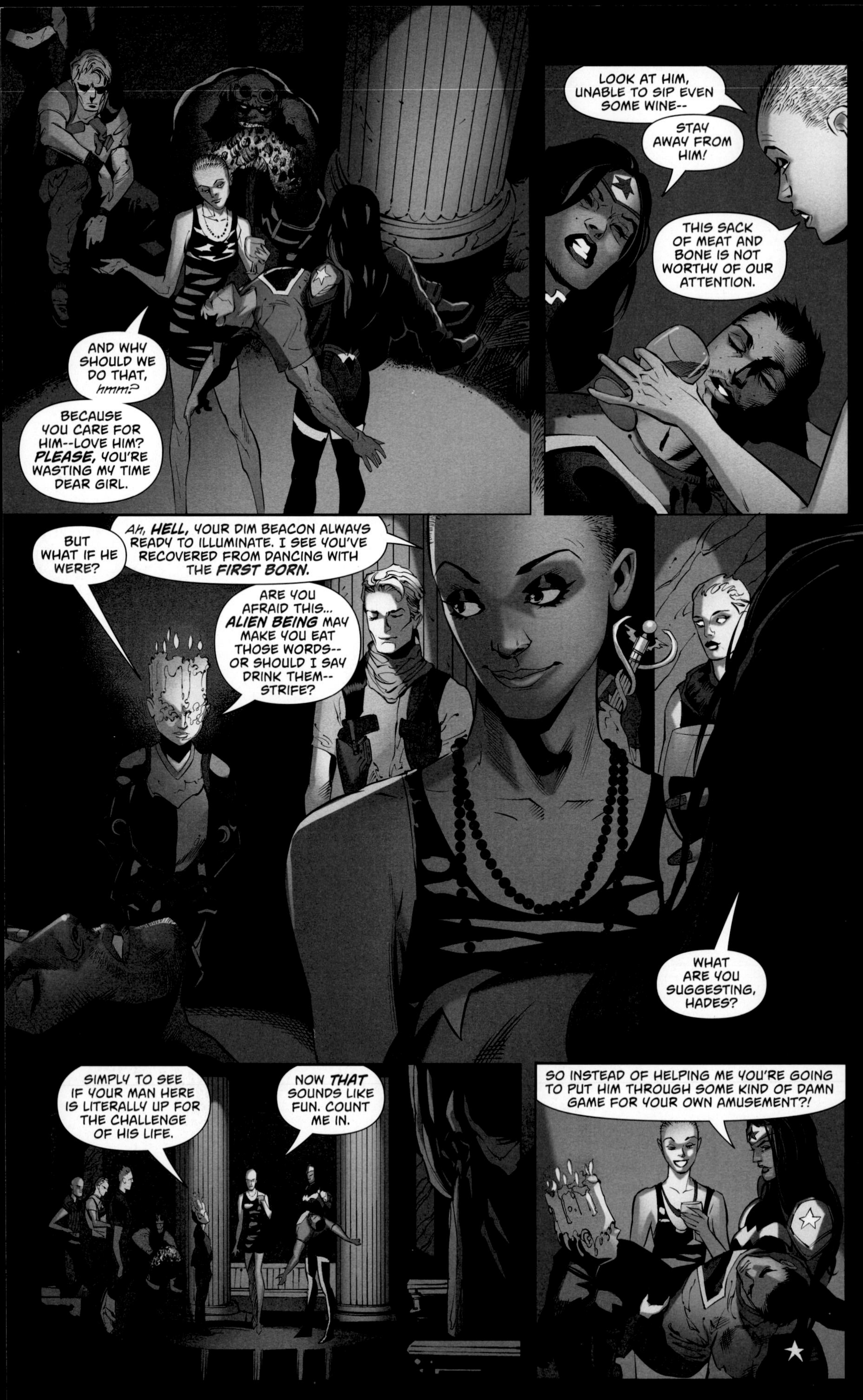
AND WHY SHOULD WE DO THAT, *hmm?*
BECAUSE YOU CARE FOR HIM--LOVE HIM? **PLEASE,** YOU'RE WASTING MY TIME DEAR GIRL.
LOOK AT HIM, UNABLE TO SIP EVEN SOME WINE--
STAY AWAY FROM HIM!
THIS SACK OF MEAT AND BONE IS NOT WORTHY OF OUR ATTENTION.
BUT WHAT IF HE WERE?
Ah, **HELL,** YOUR DIM BEACON ALWAYS READY TO ILLUMINATE. I SEE YOU'VE RECOVERED FROM DANCING WITH THE **FIRST BORN.**
ARE YOU AFRAID THIS... **ALIEN BEING** MAY MAKE YOU EAT THOSE WORDS-- OR SHOULD I SAY DRINK THEM-- STRIFE?
WHAT ARE YOU SUGGESTING, HADES?
SIMPLY TO SEE IF YOUR MAN HERE IS LITERALLY UP FOR THE CHALLENGE OF HIS LIFE.
NOW **THAT** SOUNDS LIKE FUN. COUNT ME IN.
SO INSTEAD OF HELPING ME YOU'RE GOING TO PUT HIM THROUGH SOME KIND OF DAMN GAME FOR YOUR OWN AMUSEMENT?!

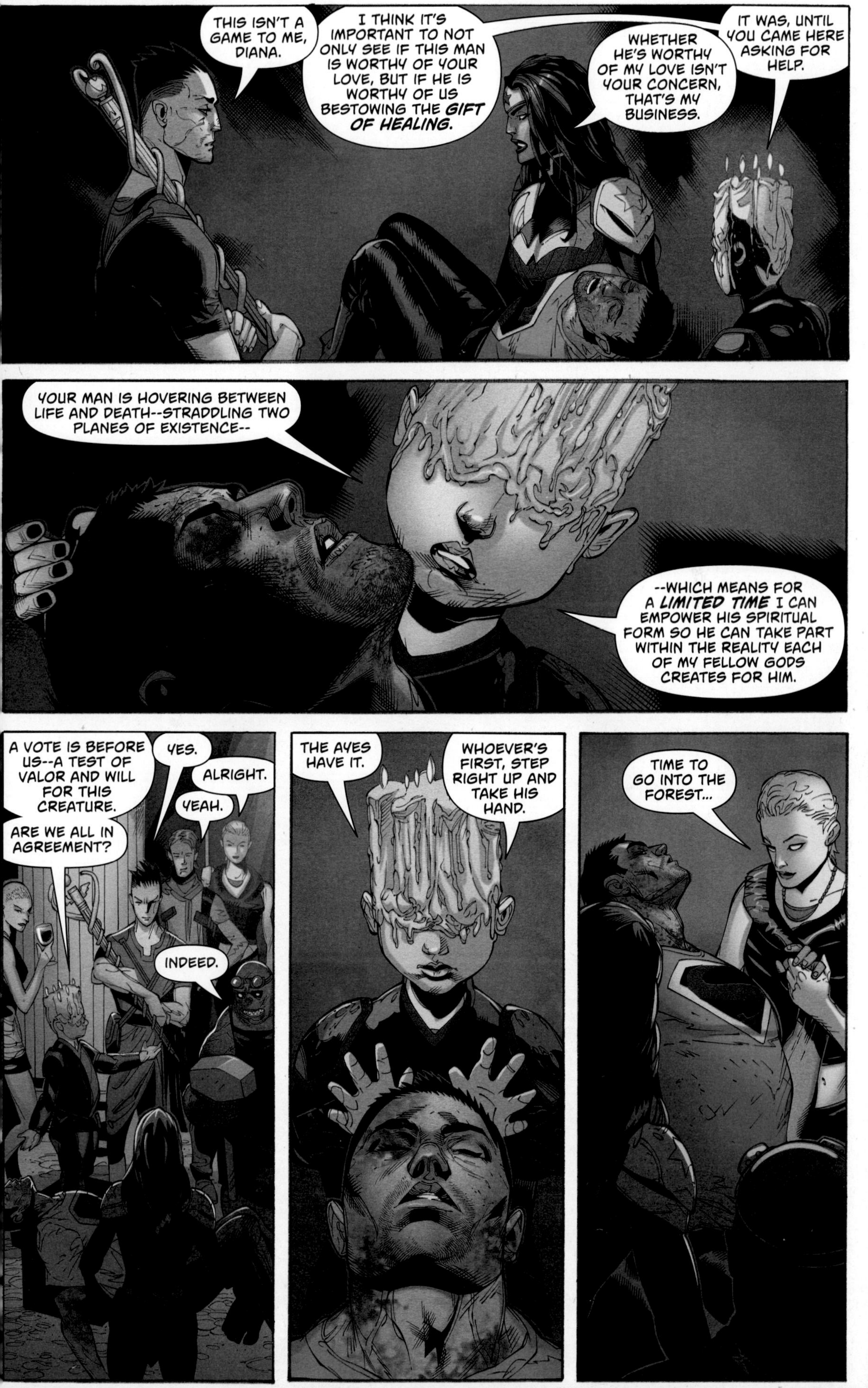
THIS ISN'T A GAME TO ME, DIANA.
I THINK IT'S IMPORTANT TO NOT ONLY SEE IF THIS MAN IS WORTHY OF YOUR LOVE, BUT IF HE IS WORTHY OF US BESTOWING THE GIFT OF HEALING.
WHETHER HE'S WORTHY OF MY LOVE ISN'T YOUR CONCERN, THAT'S MY BUSINESS.
IT WAS, UNTIL YOU CAME HERE ASKING FOR HELP.
YOUR MAN IS HOVERING BETWEEN LIFE AND DEATH--STRADDLING TWO PLANES OF EXISTENCE--
--WHICH MEANS FOR A LIMITED TIME I CAN EMPOWER HIS SPIRITUAL FORM SO HE CAN TAKE PART WITHIN THE REALITY EACH OF MY FELLOW GODS CREATES FOR HIM.
A VOTE IS BEFORE US--A TEST OF VALOR AND WILL FOR THIS CREATURE.
ARE WE ALL IN AGREEMENT?
YES.
ALRIGHT.
YEAH.
INDEED.
THE AYES HAVE IT.
WHOEVER'S FIRST, STEP RIGHT UP AND TAKE HIS HAND.
TIME TO GO INTO THE FOREST...

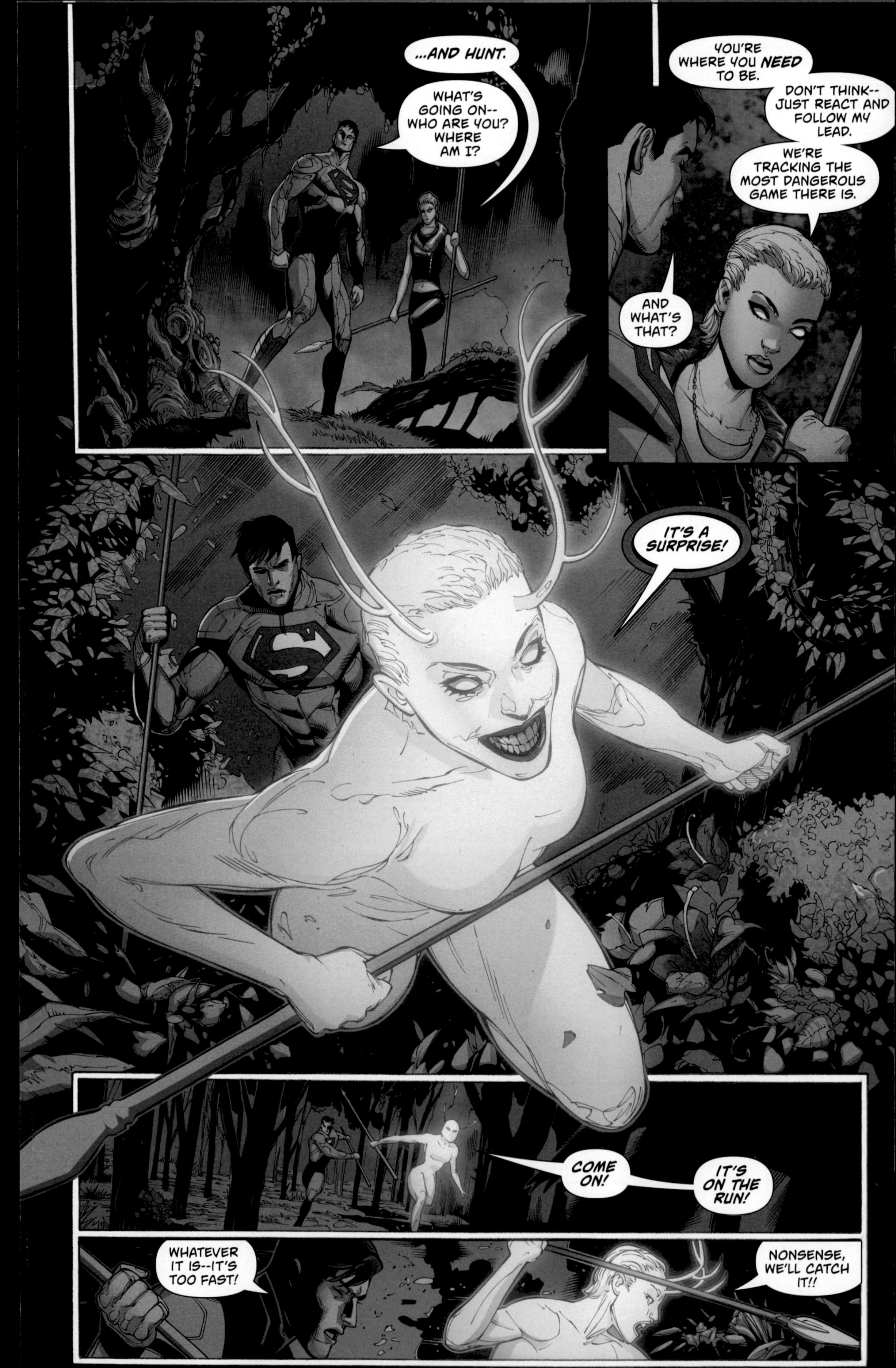
...AND HUNT.
WHAT'S GOING ON--WHO ARE YOU? WHERE AM I?
YOU'RE WHERE YOU NEED TO BE.
DON'T THINK--JUST REACT AND FOLLOW MY LEAD.
WE'RE TRACKING THE MOST DANGEROUS GAME THERE IS.
AND WHAT'S THAT?
IT'S A SURPRISE!
COME ON!
IT'S ON THE RUN!
WHATEVER IT IS--IT'S TOO FAST!
NONSENSE, WE'LL CATCH IT!!

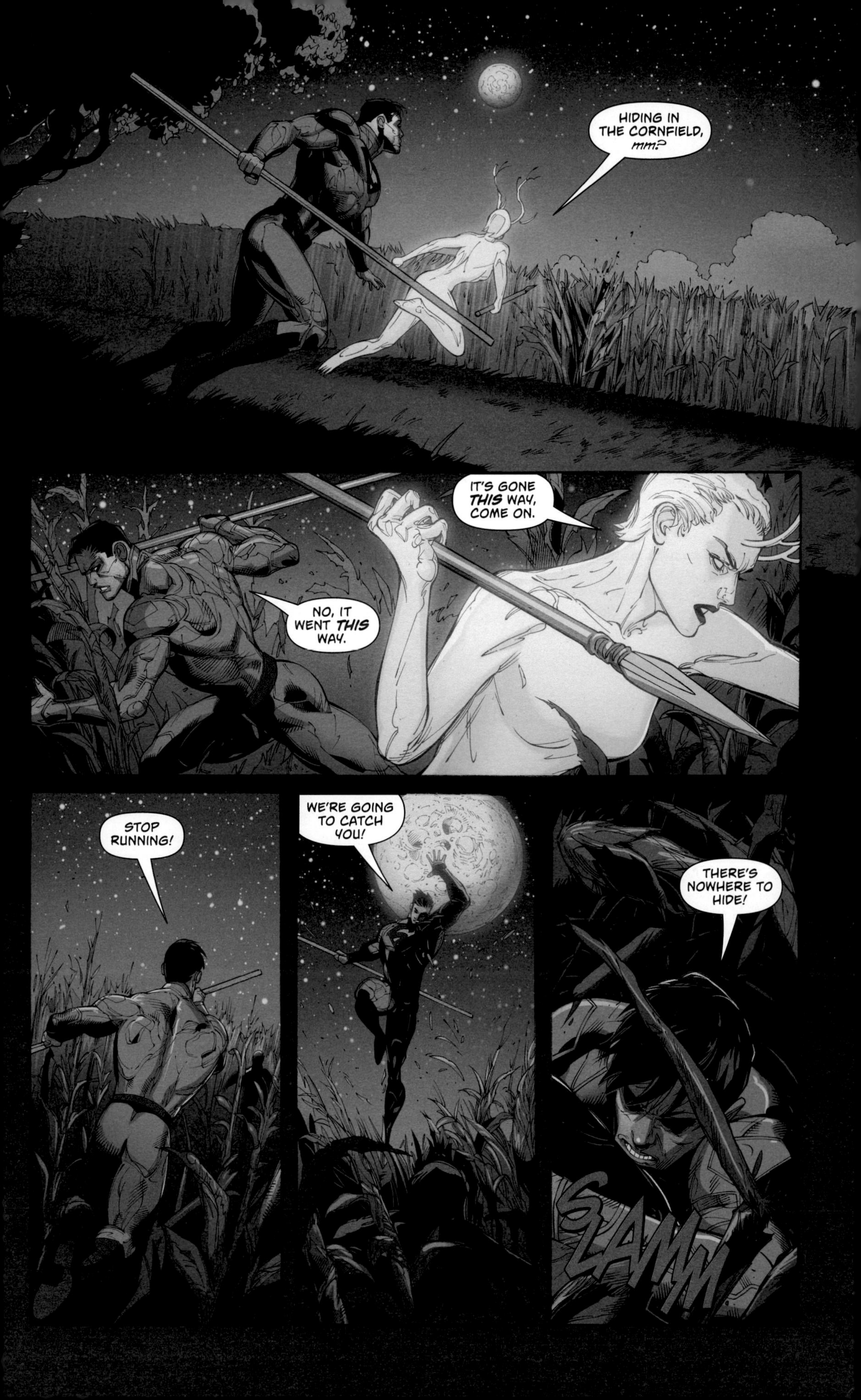
HIDING IN THE CORNFIELD, mm?
IT'S GONE THIS WAY, COME ON.
NO, IT WENT THIS WAY.
STOP RUNNING!
WE'RE GOING TO CATCH YOU!
THERE'S NOWHERE TO HIDE!
SLAMM

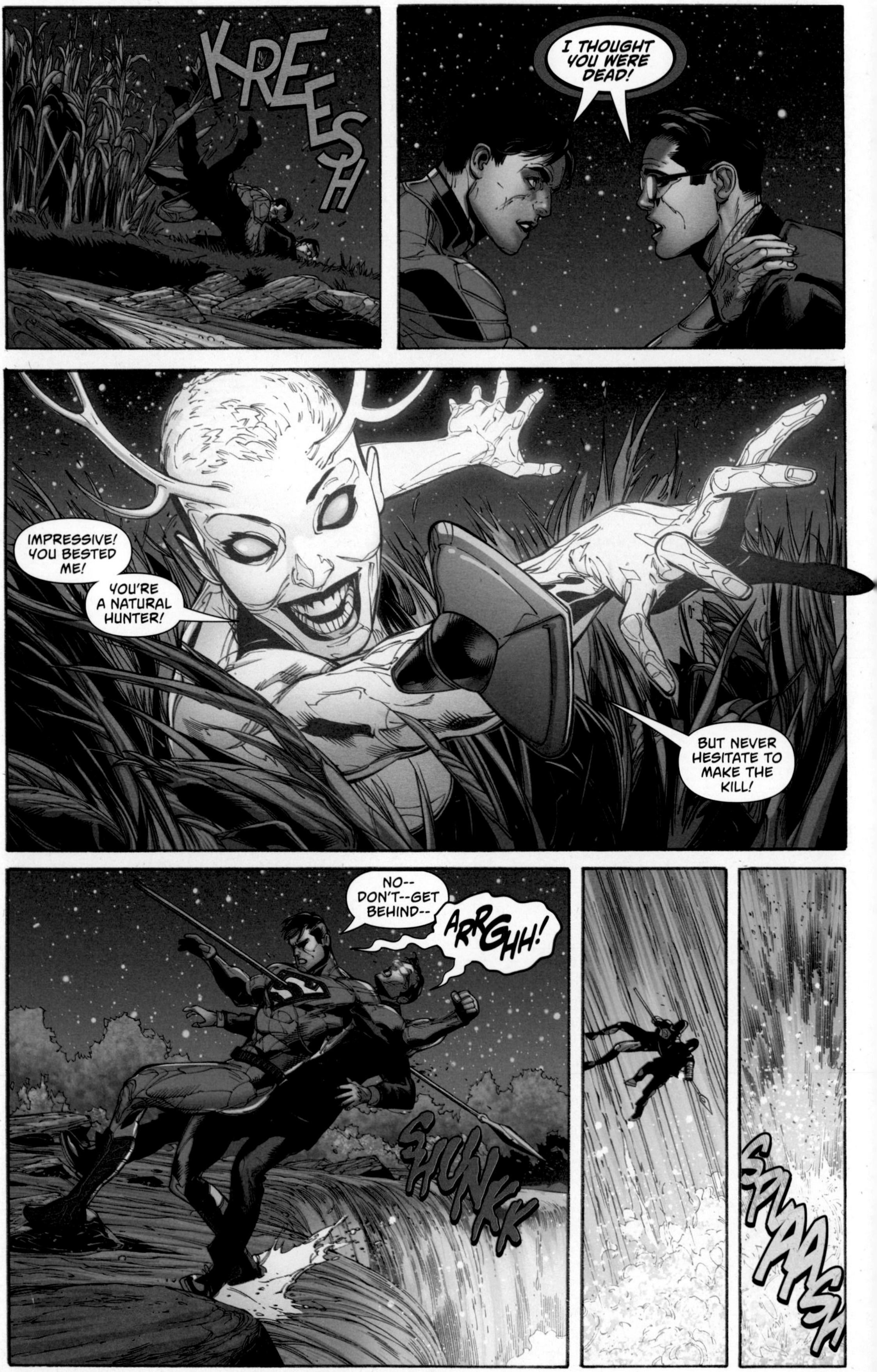
KREESH
I THOUGHT YOU WERE DEAD!
IMPRESSIVE! YOU BESTED ME!
YOU'RE A NATURAL HUNTER!
BUT NEVER HESITATE TO MAKE THE KILL!
NO-- DON'T--GET BEHIND--
ARRGHH!
SHUNKK
SPLAASH

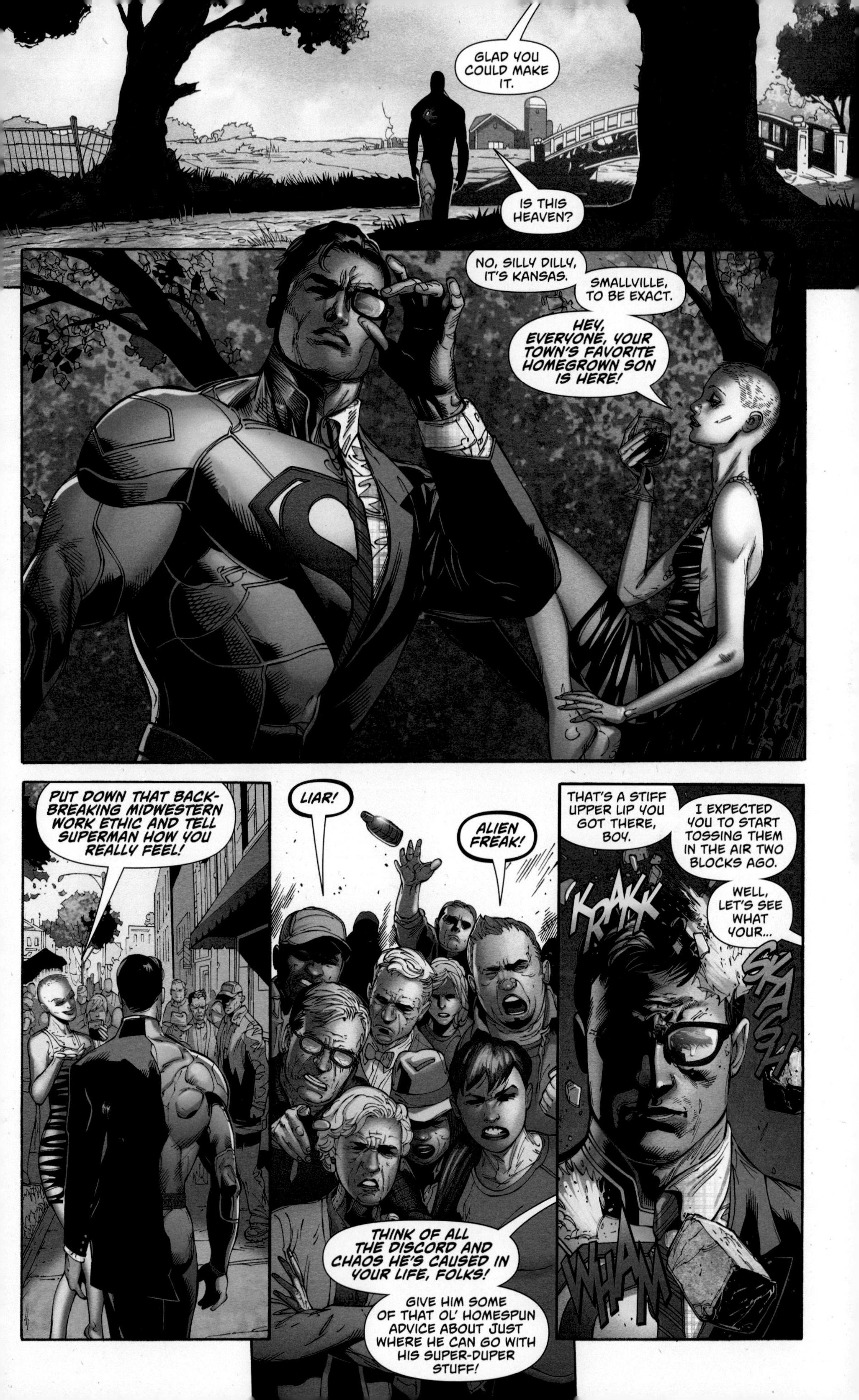
GLAD YOU COULD MAKE IT.
IS THIS HEAVEN?
NO, SILLY DILLY, IT'S KANSAS.
SMALLVILLE, TO BE EXACT.
HEY, EVERYONE, YOUR TOWN'S FAVORITE HOMEGROWN SON IS HERE!
PUT DOWN THAT BACK-BREAKING MIDWESTERN WORK ETHIC AND TELL SUPERMAN HOW YOU REALLY FEEL!
LIAR!
ALIEN FREAK!
THINK OF ALL THE DISCORD AND CHAOS HE'S CAUSED IN YOUR LIFE, FOLKS!
GIVE HIM SOME OF THAT OL' HOMESPUN ADVICE ABOUT JUST WHERE HE CAN GO WITH HIS SUPER-DUPER STUFF!
THAT'S A STIFF UPPER LIP YOU GOT THERE, BOY.
I EXPECTED YOU TO START TOSSING THEM IN THE AIR TWO BLOCKS AGO.
WELL, LET'S SEE WHAT YOUR...
KRAKK
SHASH
WHAM

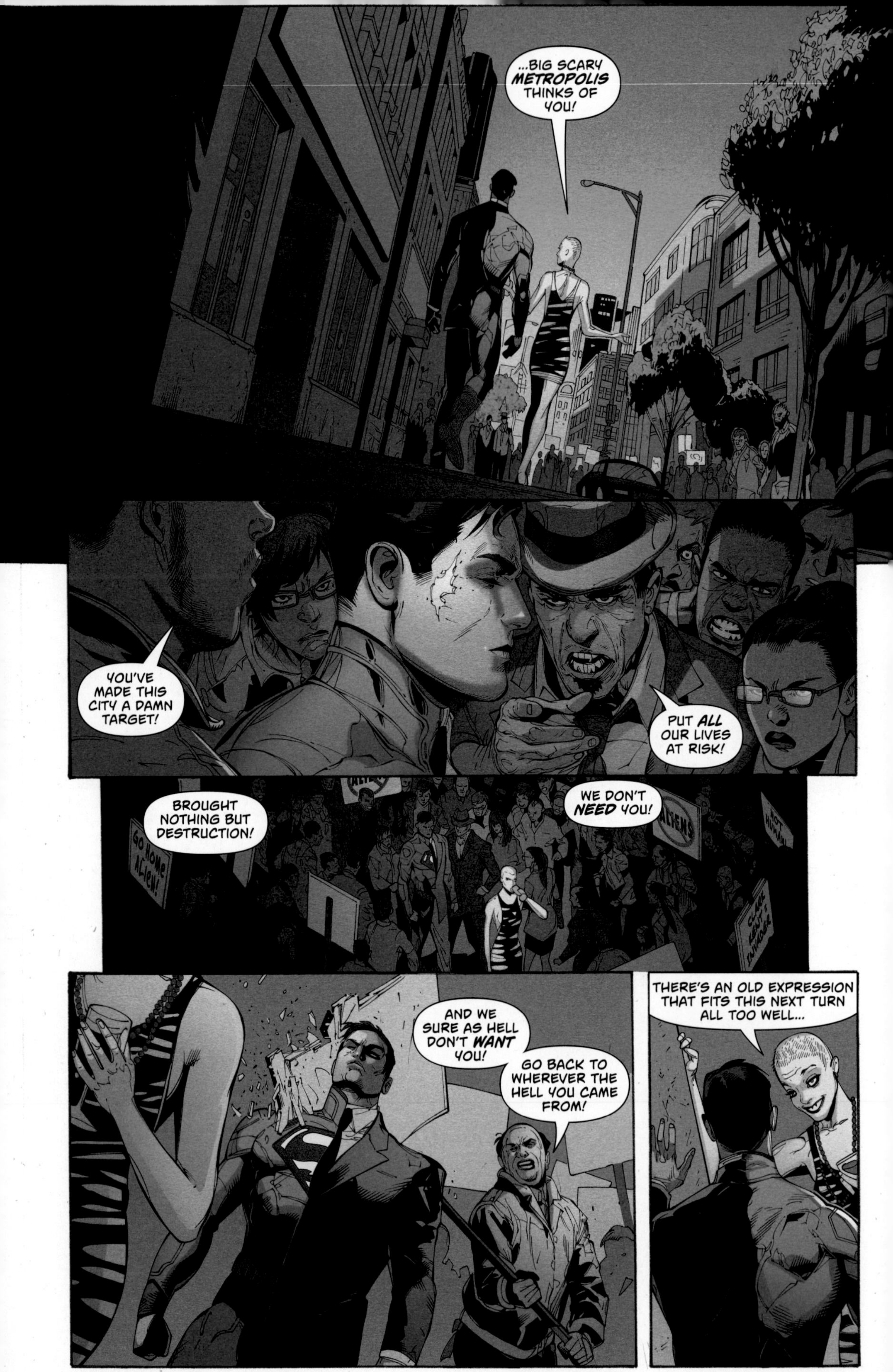
...BIG SCARY METROPOLIS THINKS OF YOU!
YOU'VE MADE THIS CITY A DAMN TARGET!
PUT ALL OUR LIVES AT RISK!
BROUGHT NOTHING BUT DESTRUCTION!
WE DON'T NEED YOU!
AND WE SURE AS HELL DON'T WANT YOU!
GO BACK TO WHEREVER THE HELL YOU CAME FROM!
THERE'S AN OLD EXPRESSION THAT FITS THIS NEXT TURN ALL TOO WELL...

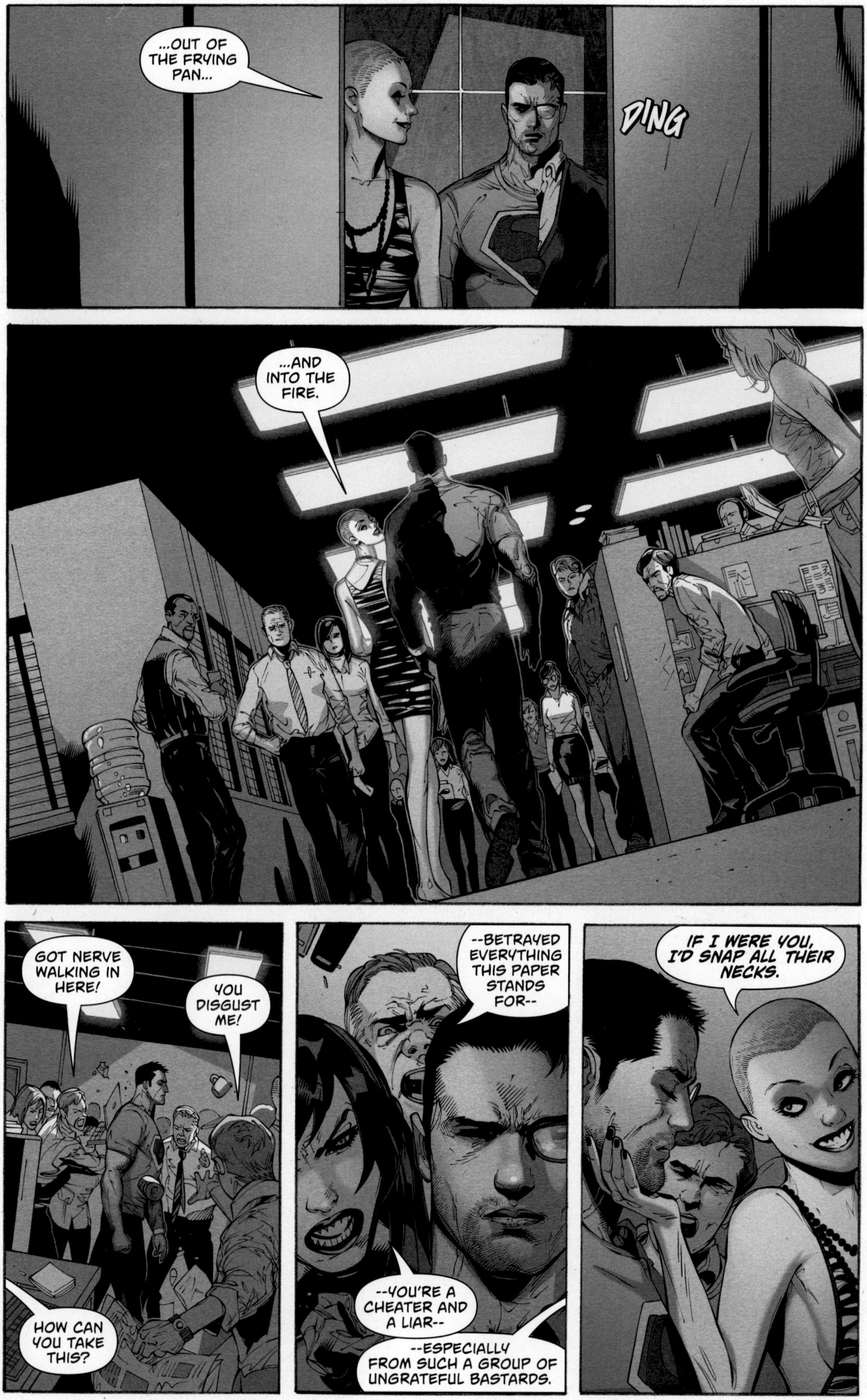

...OUT OF THE FRYING PAN...
DING
...AND INTO THE FIRE.
GOT NERVE WALKING IN HERE!
YOU DISGUST ME!
HOW CAN YOU TAKE THIS?
--BETRAYED EVERYTHING THIS PAPER STANDS FOR--
--YOU'RE A CHEATER AND A LIAR--
--ESPECIALLY FROM SUCH A GROUP OF UNGRATEFUL BASTARDS.
IF I WERE YOU, I'D SNAP ALL THEIR NECKS.

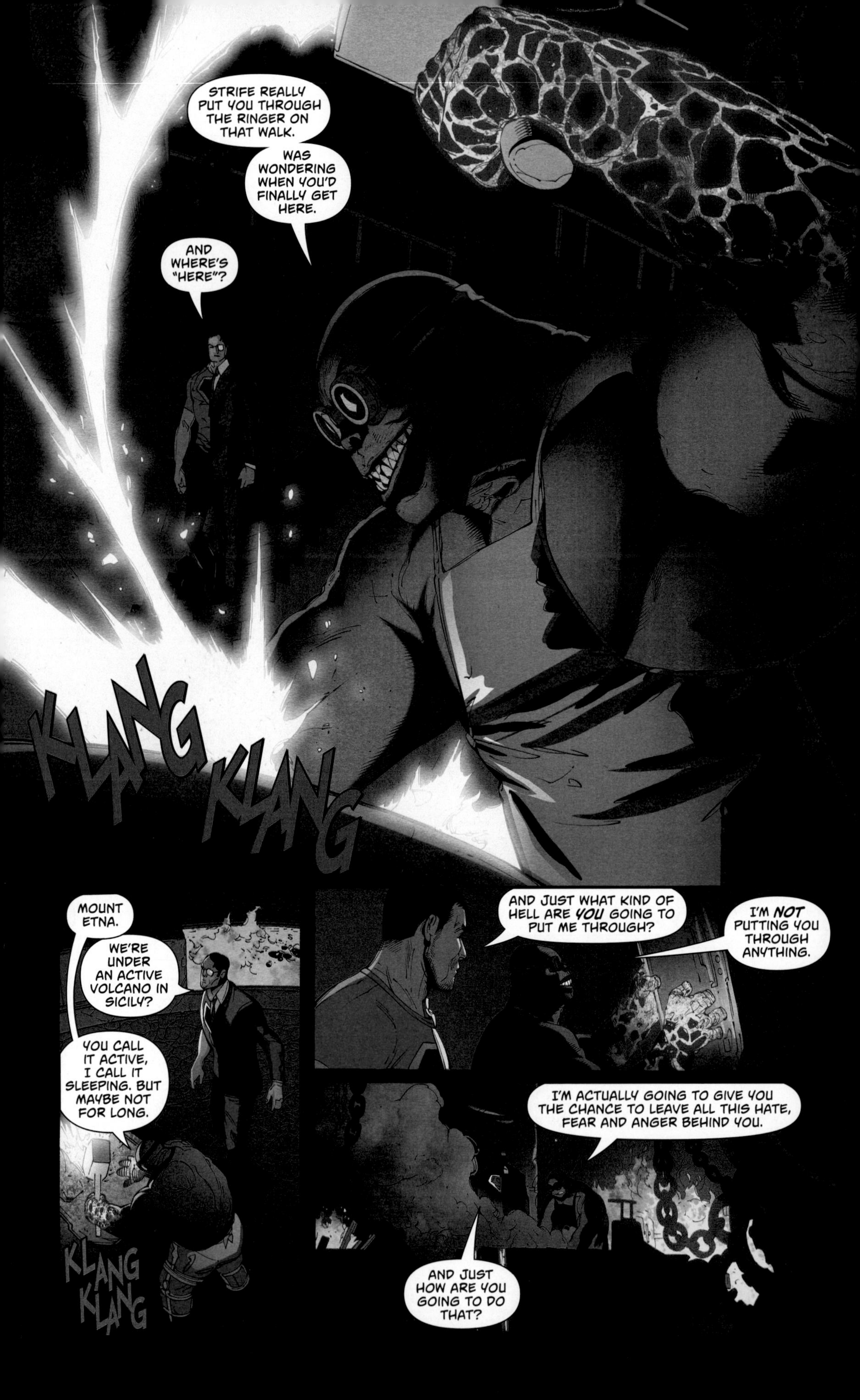
STRIFE REALLY PUT YOU THROUGH THE RINGER ON THAT WALK.
WAS WONDERING WHEN YOU'D FINALLY GET HERE.
AND WHERE'S "HERE"?
KLANG KLANG
MOUNT ETNA.
WE'RE UNDER AN ACTIVE VOLCANO IN SICILY?
YOU CALL IT ACTIVE, I CALL IT SLEEPING. BUT MAYBE NOT FOR LONG.
KLANG KLANG
AND JUST WHAT KIND OF HELL ARE *YOU* GOING TO PUT ME THROUGH?
I'M ***NOT*** PUTTING YOU THROUGH ANYTHING.
I'M ACTUALLY GOING TO GIVE YOU THE CHANCE TO LEAVE ALL THIS HATE, FEAR AND ANGER BEHIND YOU.
AND JUST HOW ARE YOU GOING TO DO THAT?

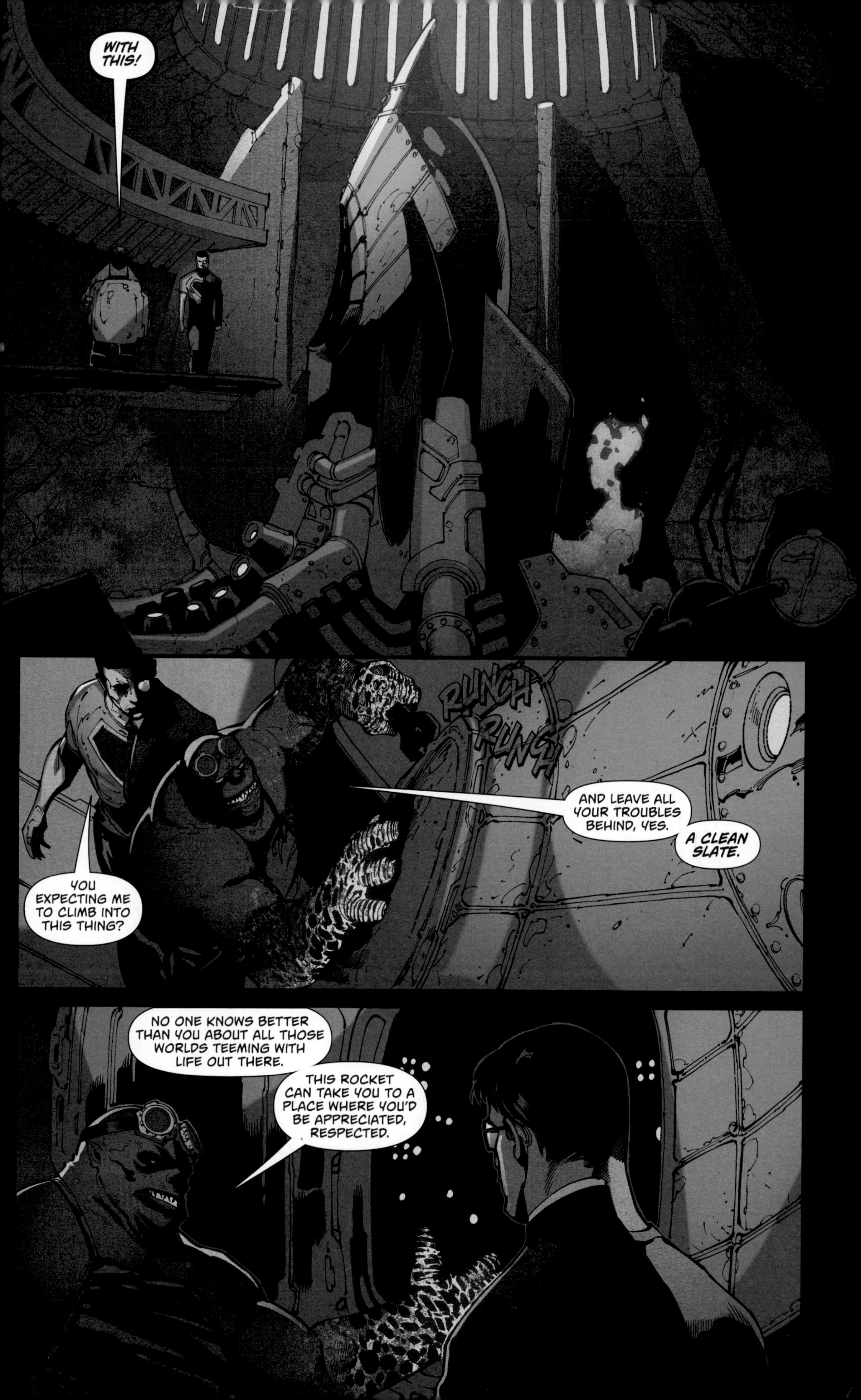
WITH THIS!
RUNCH
RUNCH
YOU EXPECTING ME TO CLIMB INTO THIS THING?
AND LEAVE ALL YOUR TROUBLES BEHIND, YES.
A CLEAN SLATE.
NO ONE KNOWS BETTER THAN YOU ABOUT ALL THOSE WORLDS TEEMING WITH LIFE OUT THERE.
THIS ROCKET CAN TAKE YOU TO A PLACE WHERE YOU'D BE APPRECIATED, RESPECTED.

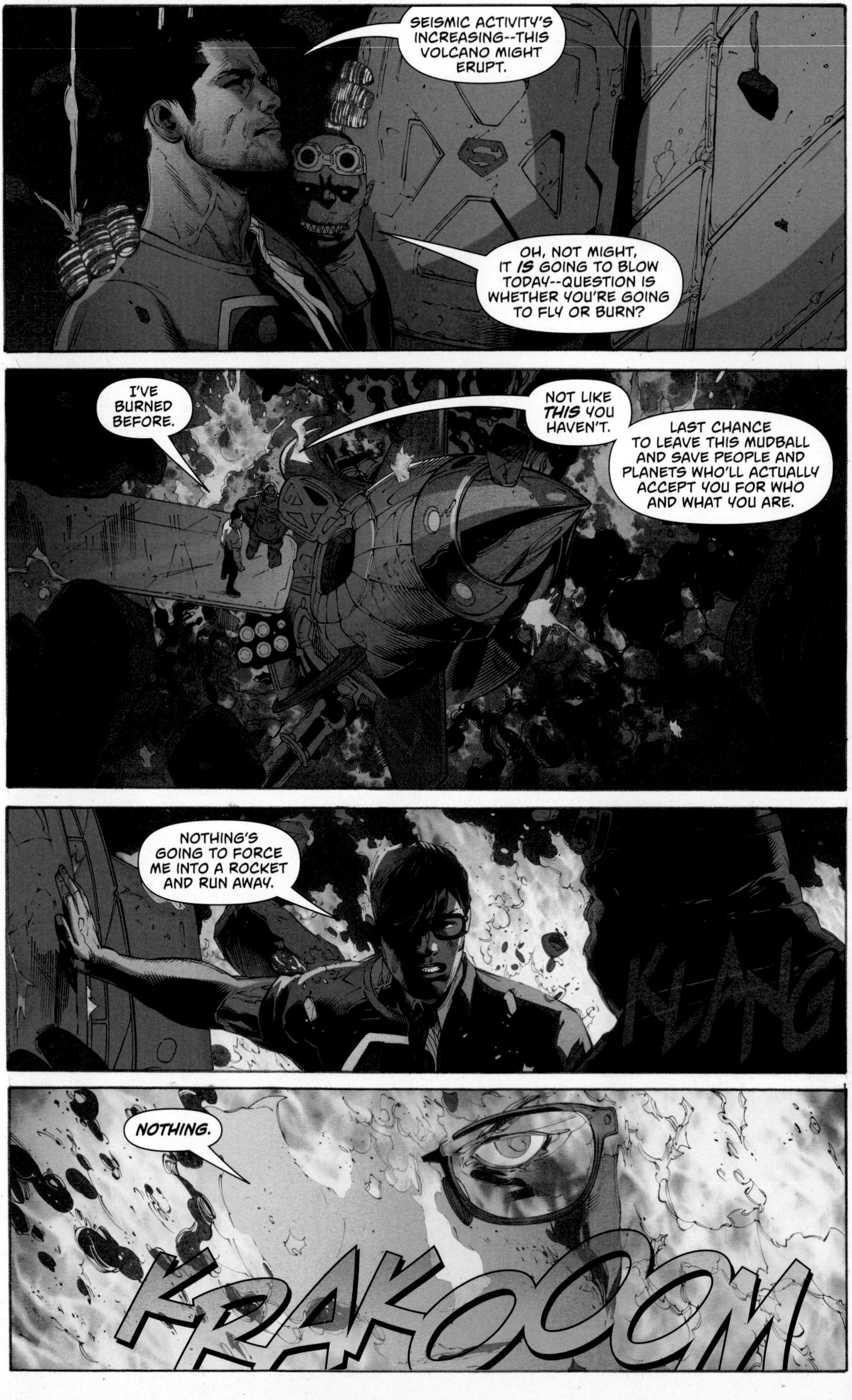
SEISMIC ACTIVITY'S INCREASING--THIS VOLCANO MIGHT ERUPT.
OH, NOT MIGHT, IT *IS* GOING TO BLOW TODAY--QUESTION IS WHETHER YOU'RE GOING TO FLY OR BURN?
I'VE BURNED BEFORE.
NOT LIKE *THIS* YOU HAVEN'T.
LAST CHANCE TO LEAVE THIS MUDBALL AND SAVE PEOPLE AND PLANETS WHO'LL ACTUALLY ACCEPT YOU FOR WHO AND WHAT YOU ARE.
NOTHING'S GOING TO FORCE ME INTO A ROCKET AND RUN AWAY.
KLANG
NOTHING.
KRAKOOOM

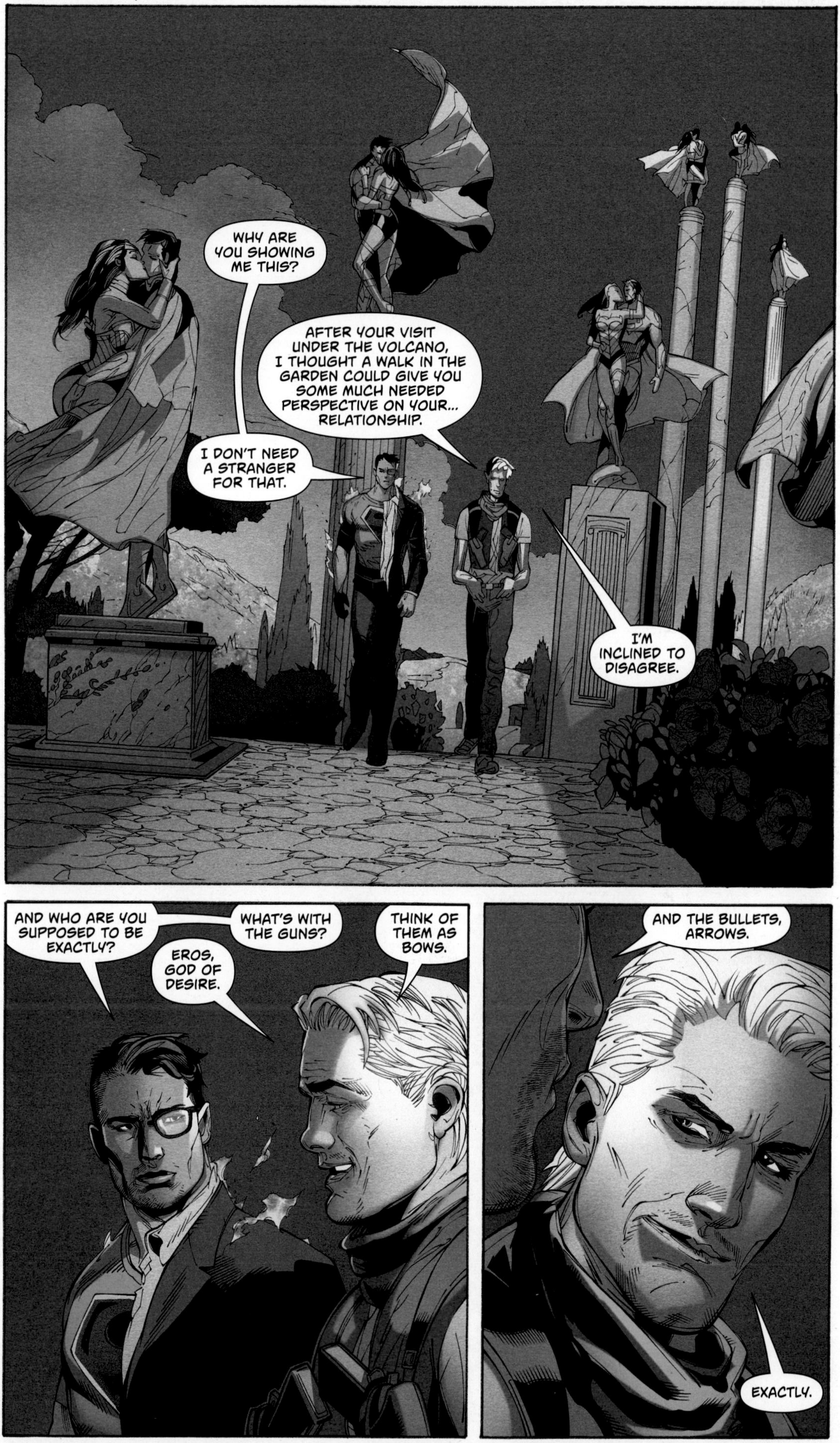
WHY ARE YOU SHOWING ME THIS?
AFTER YOUR VISIT UNDER THE VOLCANO, I THOUGHT A WALK IN THE GARDEN COULD GIVE YOU SOME MUCH NEEDED PERSPECTIVE ON YOUR... RELATIONSHIP.
I DON'T NEED A STRANGER FOR THAT.
I'M INCLINED TO DISAGREE.
AND WHO ARE YOU SUPPOSED TO BE EXACTLY?
EROS, GOD OF DESIRE.
WHAT'S WITH THE GUNS?
THINK OF THEM AS BOWS.
AND THE BULLETS, ARROWS.
EXACTLY.

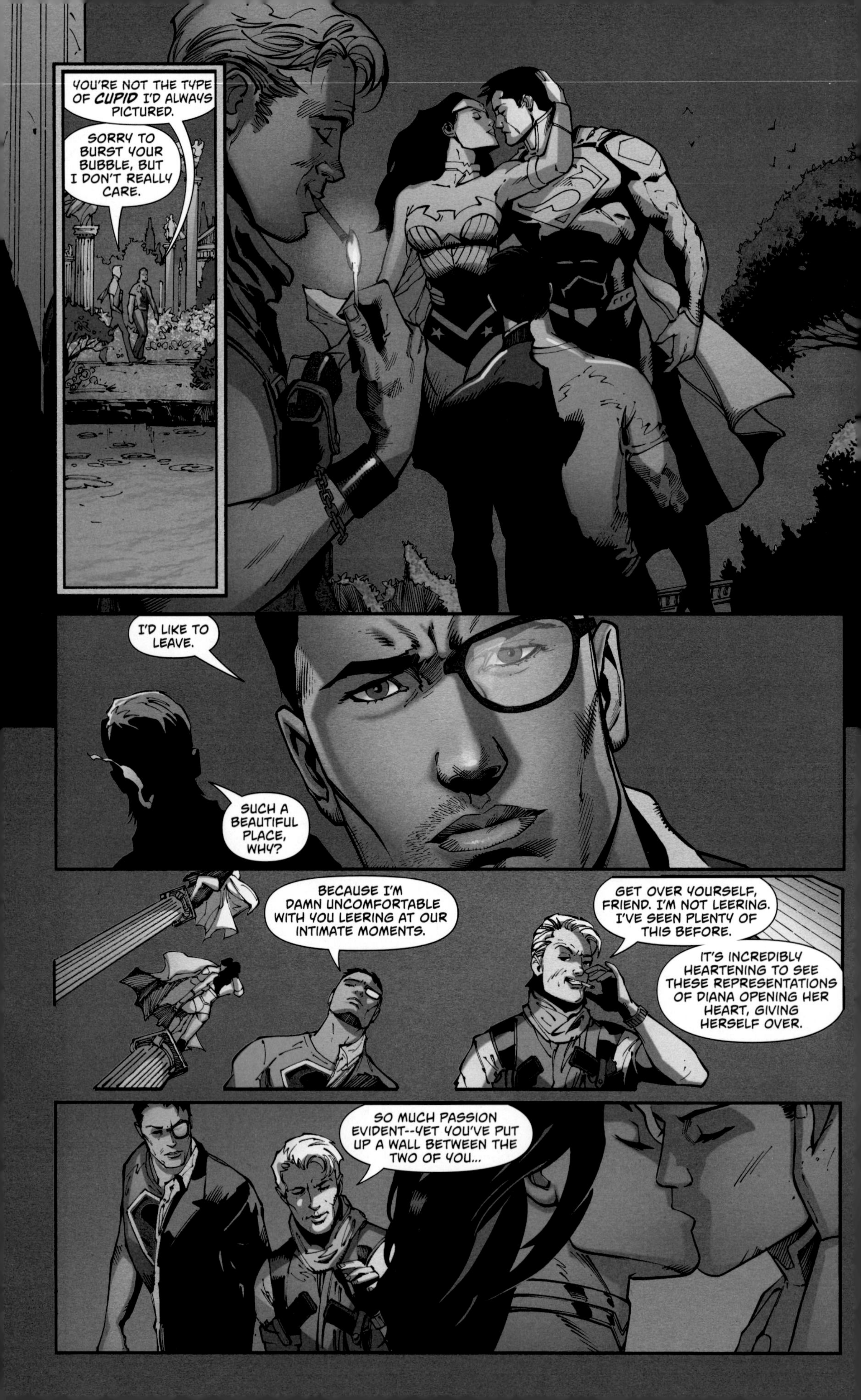
YOU'RE NOT THE TYPE OF CUPID I'D ALWAYS PICTURED.
SORRY TO BURST YOUR BUBBLE, BUT I DON'T REALLY CARE.
I'D LIKE TO LEAVE.
SUCH A BEAUTIFUL PLACE, WHY?
BECAUSE I'M DAMN UNCOMFORTABLE WITH YOU LEERING AT OUR INTIMATE MOMENTS.
GET OVER YOURSELF, FRIEND. I'M NOT LEERING. I'VE SEEN PLENTY OF THIS BEFORE.
IT'S INCREDIBLY HEARTENING TO SEE THESE REPRESENTATIONS OF DIANA OPENING HER HEART, GIVING HERSELF OVER.
SO MUCH PASSION EVIDENT--YET YOU'VE PUT UP A WALL BETWEEN THE TWO OF YOU...

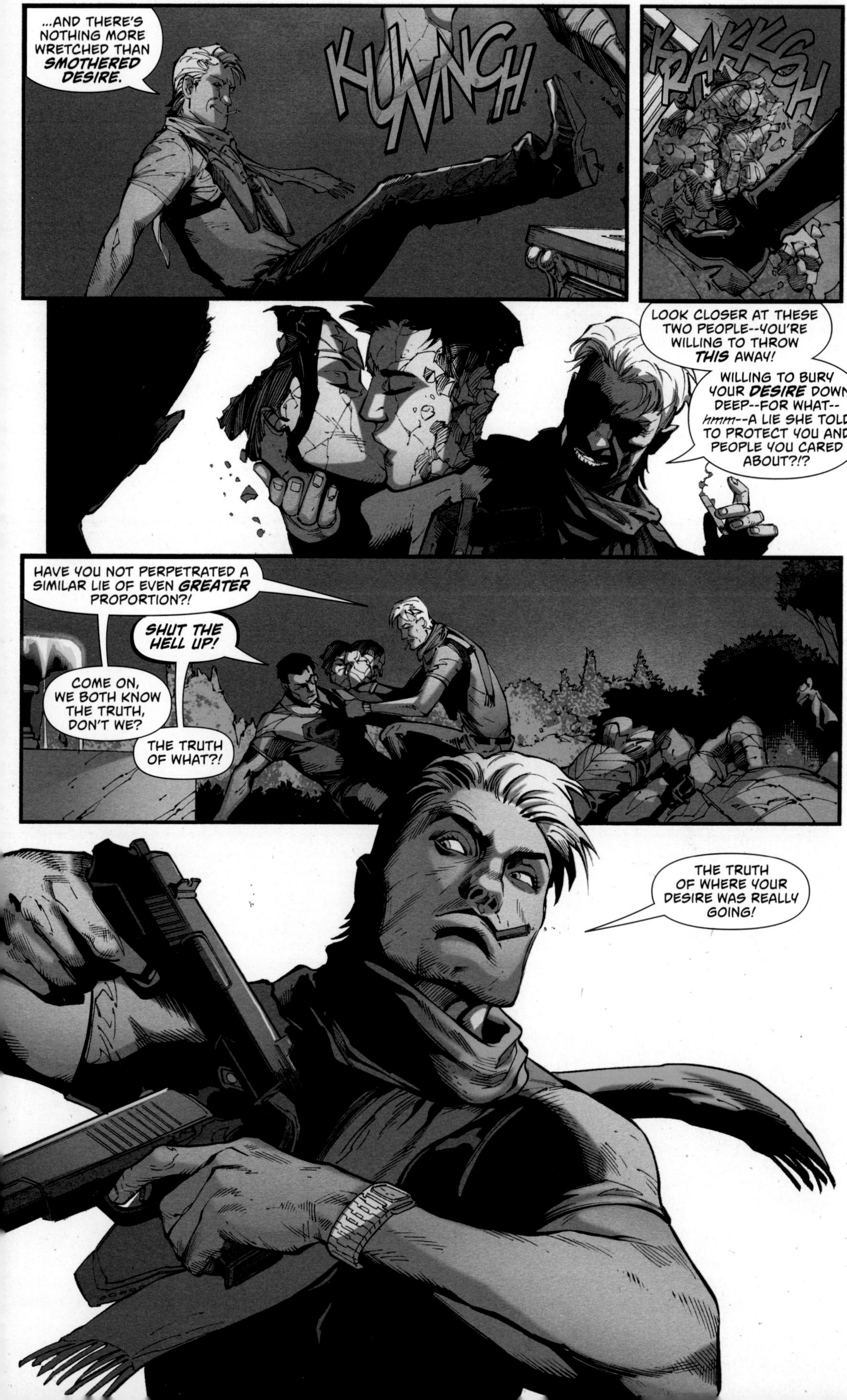

...AND THERE'S NOTHING MORE WRETCHED THAN SMOTHERED DESIRE.
KUNNCH
KRAKKSH
LOOK CLOSER AT THESE TWO PEOPLE--YOU'RE WILLING TO THROW THIS AWAY!
WILLING TO BURY YOUR DESIRE DOWN DEEP--FOR WHAT--hmm--A LIE SHE TOLD TO PROTECT YOU AND PEOPLE YOU CARED ABOUT?!?
HAVE YOU NOT PERPETRATED A SIMILAR LIE OF EVEN GREATER PROPORTION?!
SHUT THE HELL UP!
COME ON, WE BOTH KNOW THE TRUTH, DON'T WE?
THE TRUTH OF WHAT?!
THE TRUTH OF WHERE YOUR DESIRE WAS REALLY GOING!

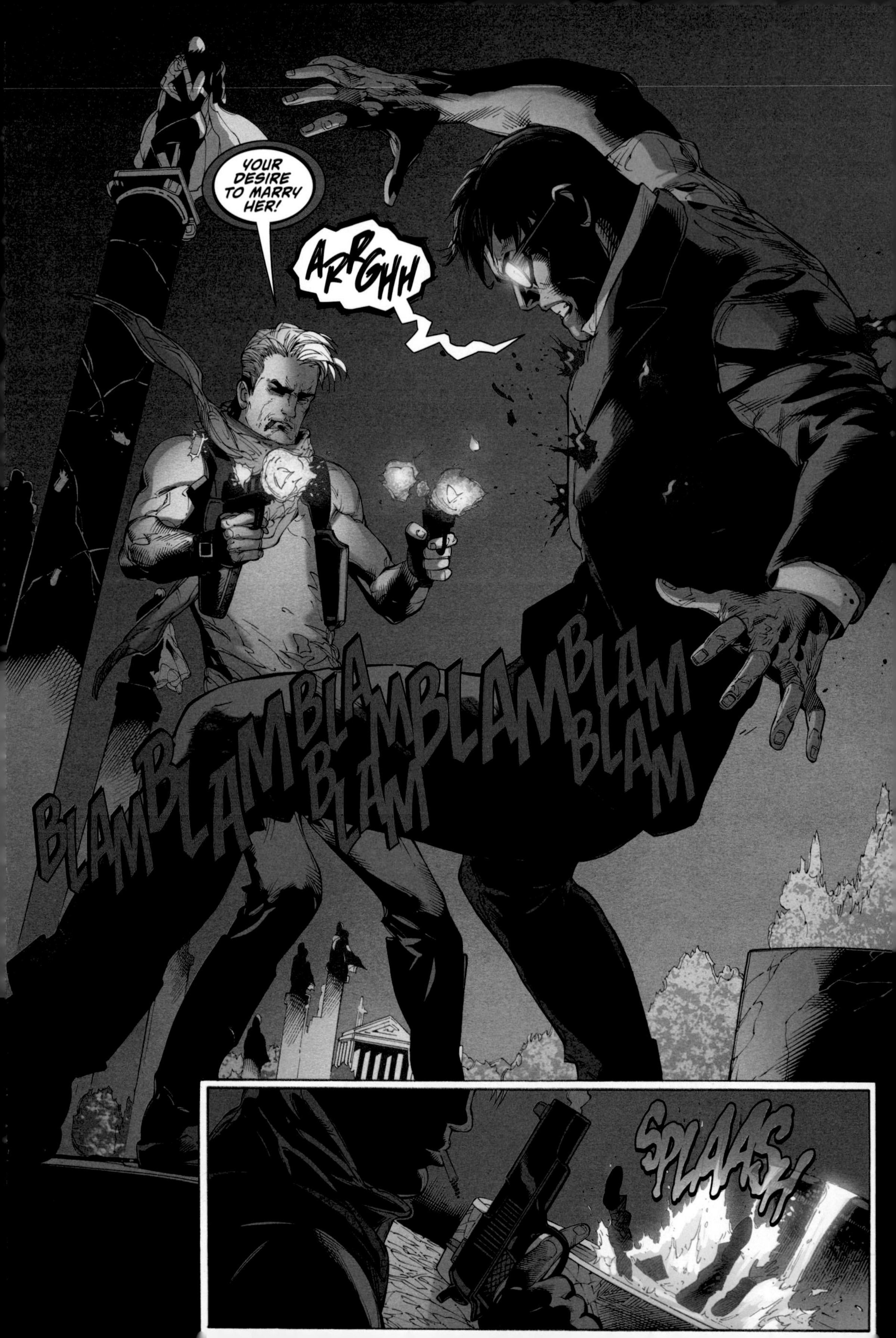
YOUR DESIRE TO MARRY HER!
ARRGHH
BLAMBLAMBLAMBLAMBLAMBLAM BLAM BLAM
SPLAASH

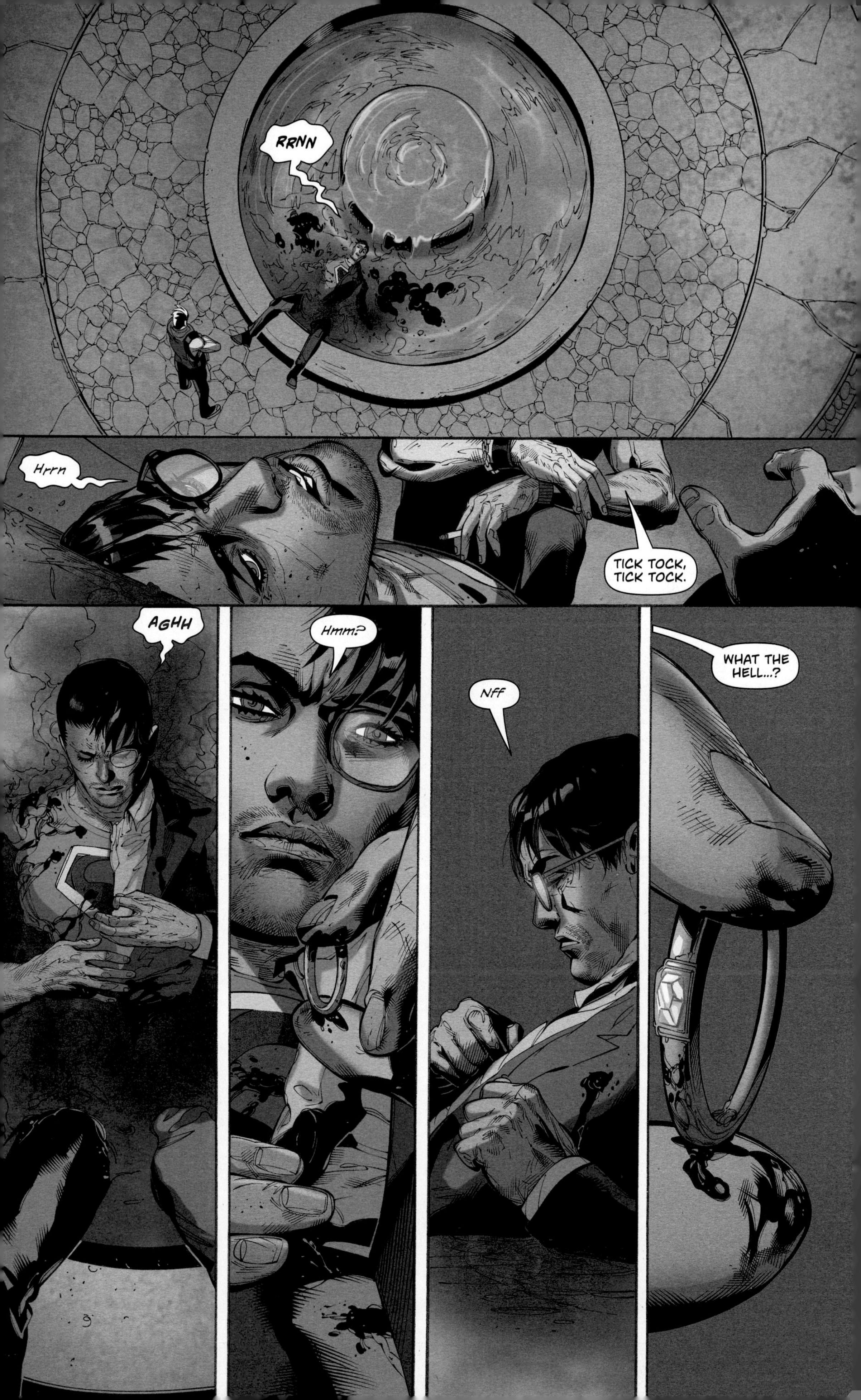
RRNN
Hrrn
TICK TOCK,
TICK TOCK.
AGHH
Hmm?
Nff
WHAT THE
HELL...?

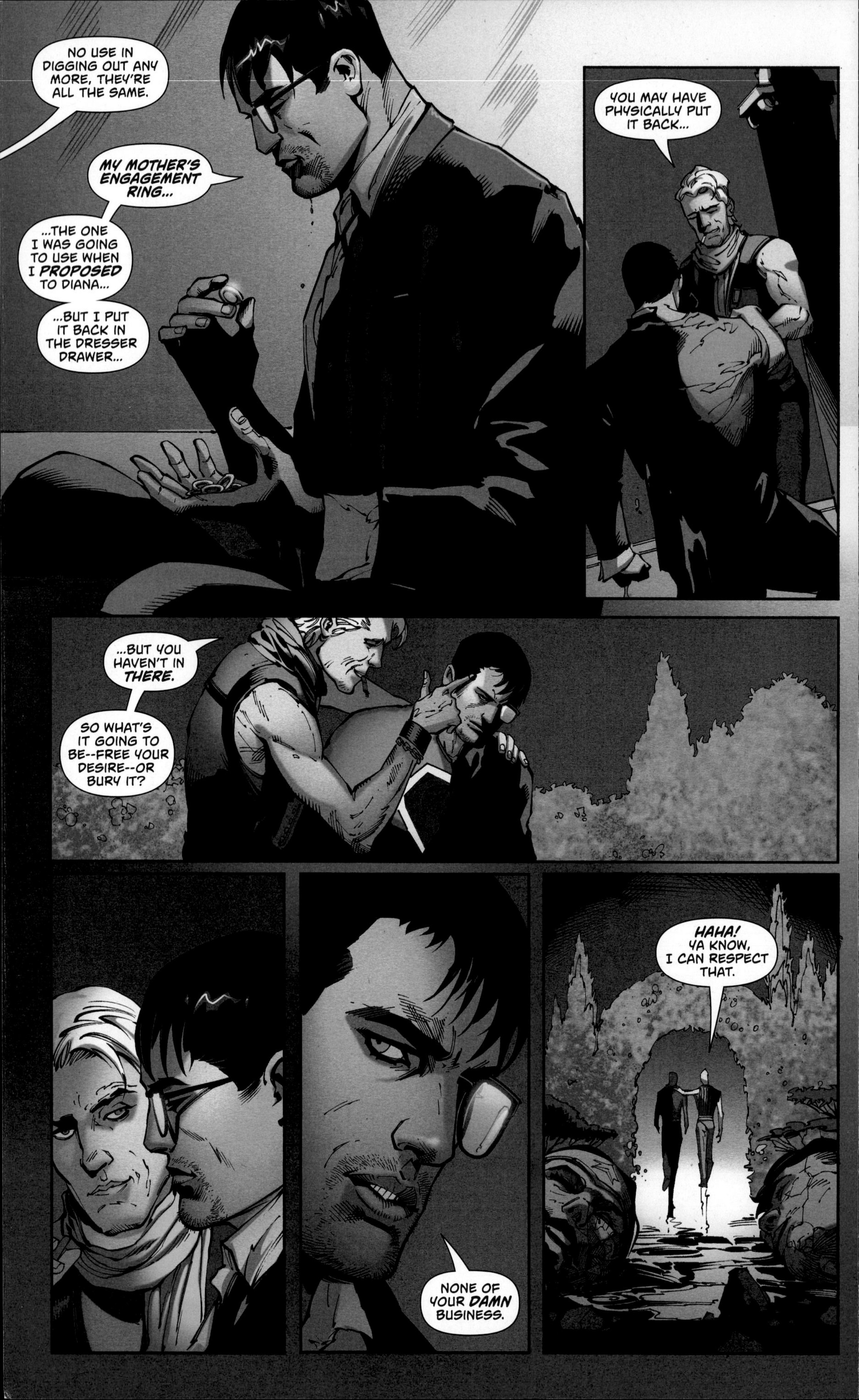
NO USE IN DIGGING OUT ANY MORE, THEY'RE ALL THE SAME.
MY MOTHER'S ENGAGEMENT RING...
...THE ONE I WAS GOING TO USE WHEN I PROPOSED TO DIANA...
...BUT I PUT IT BACK IN THE DRESSER DRAWER...
YOU MAY HAVE PHYSICALLY PUT IT BACK...
...BUT YOU HAVEN'T IN THERE.
SO WHAT'S IT GOING TO BE--FREE YOUR DESIRE--OR BURY IT?
NONE OF YOUR DAMN BUSINESS.
HAHA! YA KNOW, I CAN RESPECT THAT.

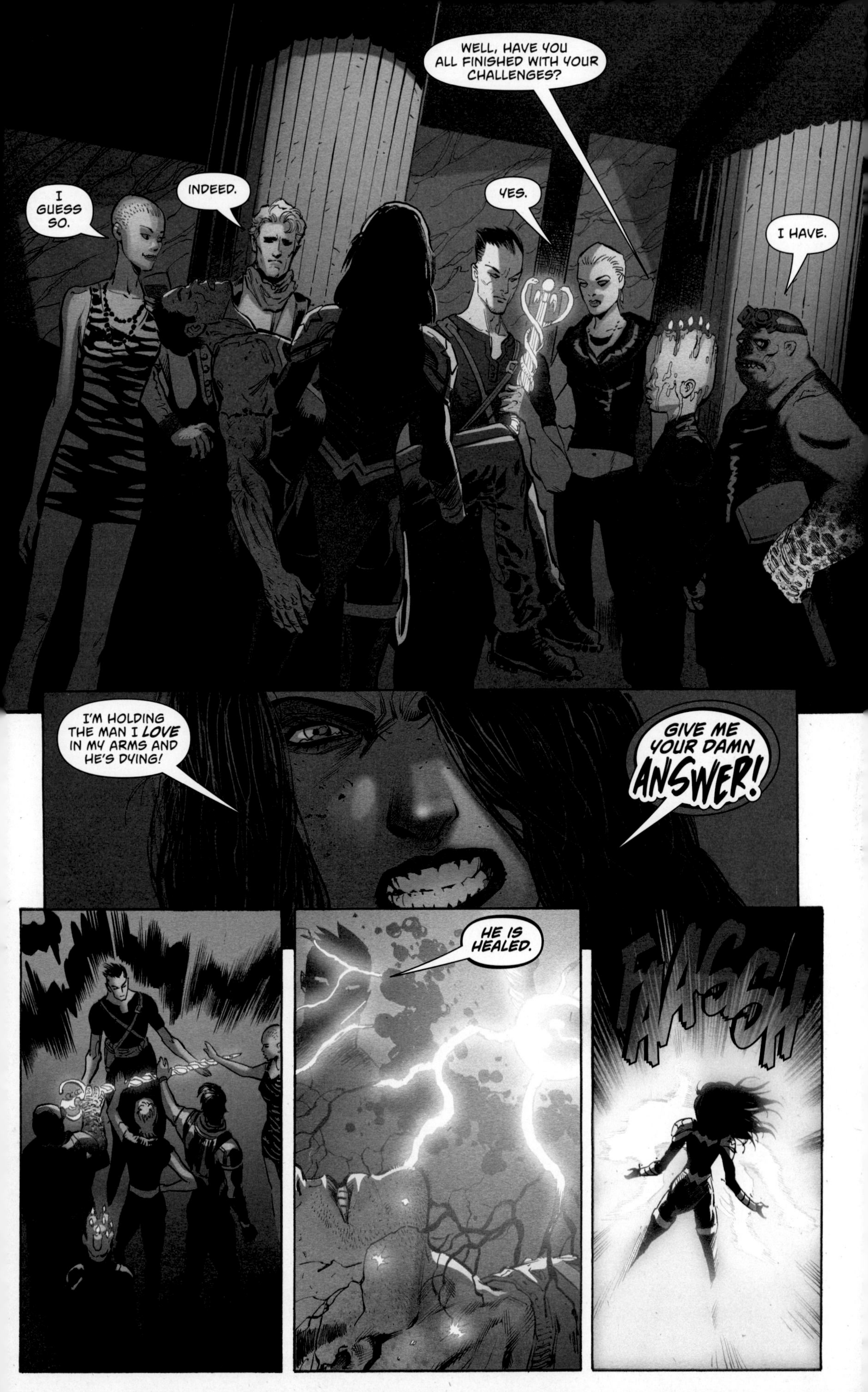
WELL, HAVE YOU ALL FINISHED WITH YOUR CHALLENGES?
I GUESS SO.
INDEED.
YES.
I HAVE.
I'M HOLDING THE MAN I LOVE IN MY ARMS AND HE'S DYING!
GIVE ME YOUR DAMN ANSWER!
HE IS HEALED.
FTAASCH

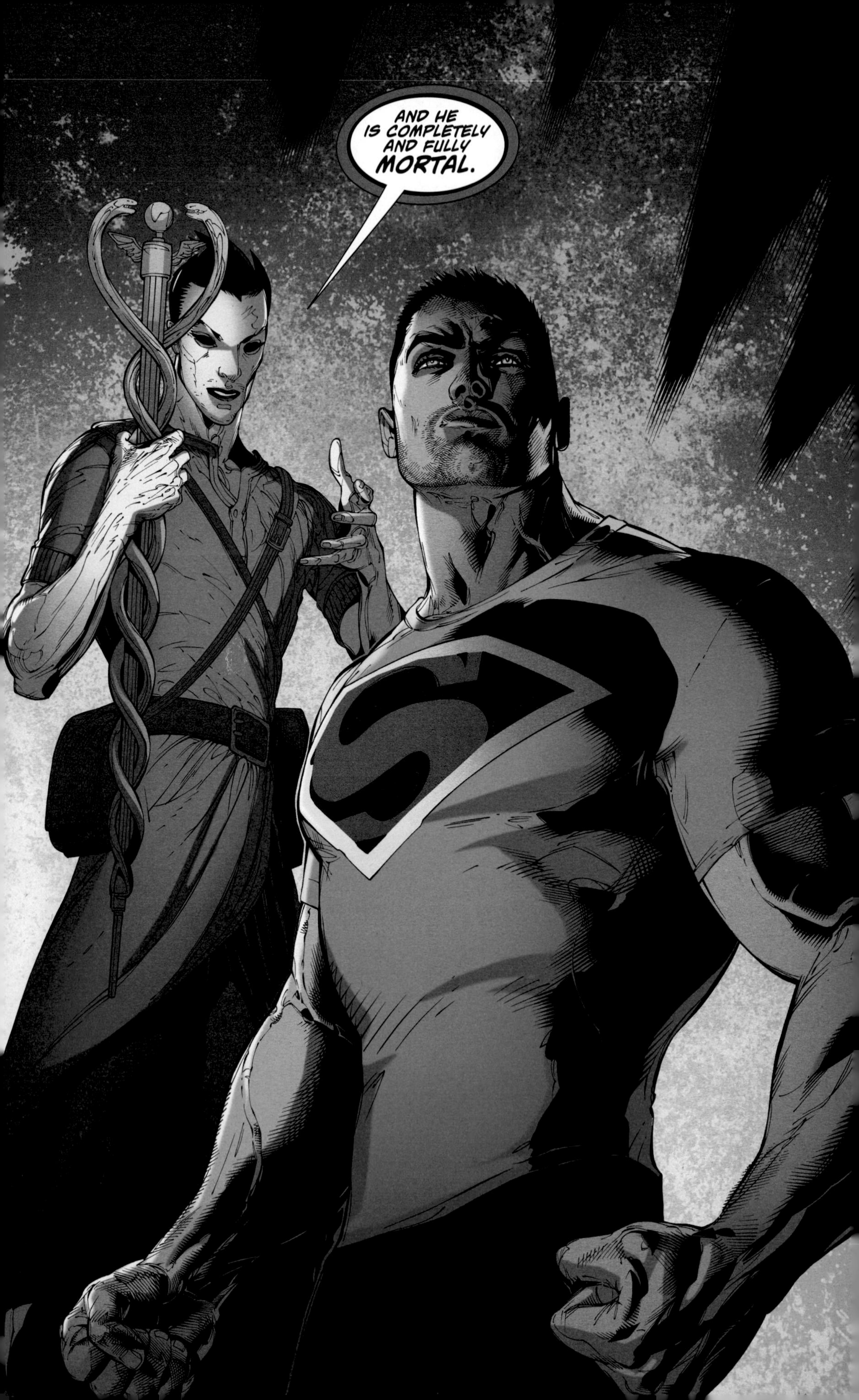
AND HE IS COMPLETELY AND FULLY MORTAL.

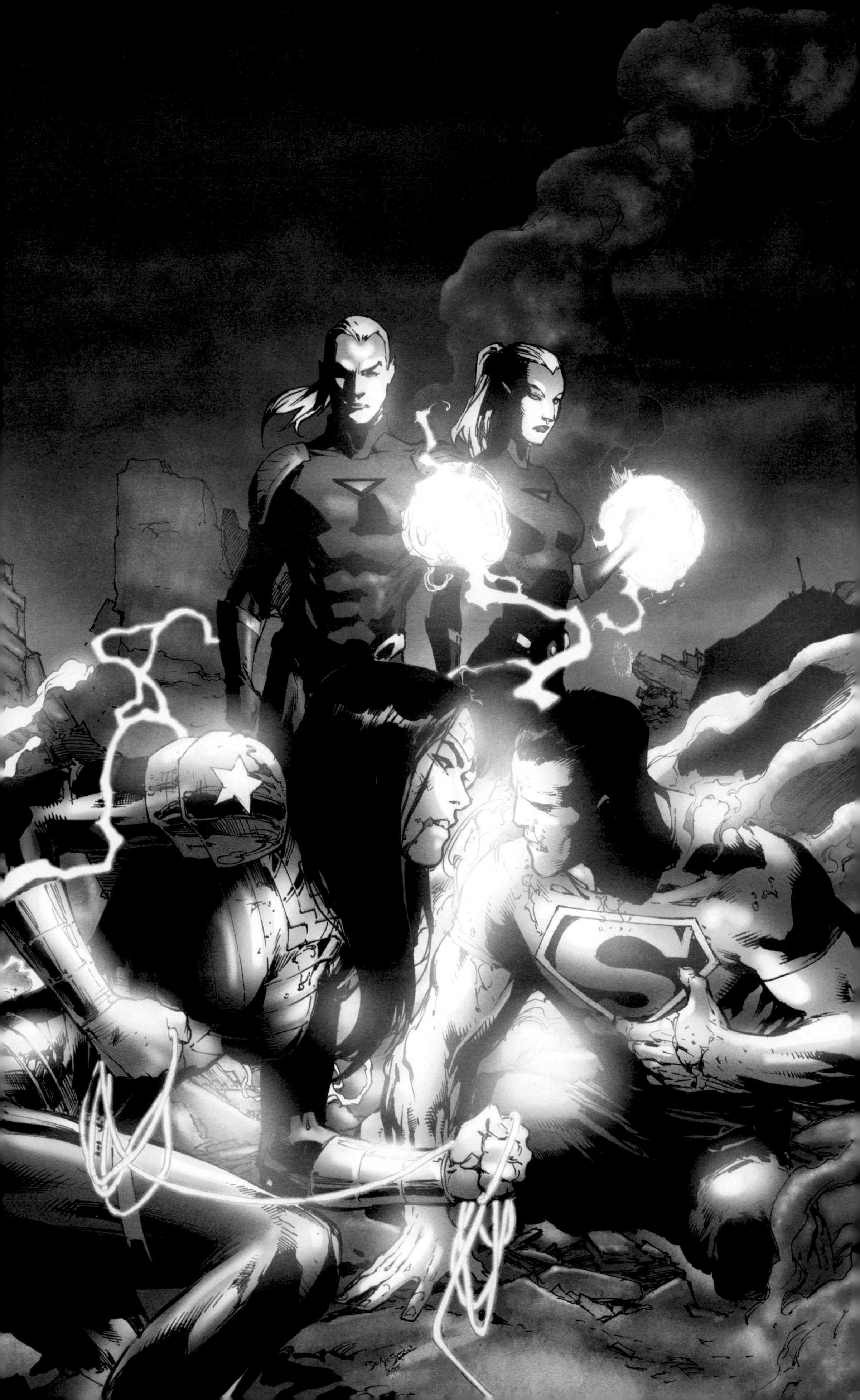

SKYFALL
PETER J. TOMASI writer DOUG MAHNKE penciller JAIME MENDOZA, DOUG MAHNKE inkers WIL QUINTANA colorist ROB LEIGH letterer cover by ED BENES & PETE PANTAZIS

Previously,
in SUPERMAN #48 and ACTION COMICS #49...

Rendered "completely and fully mortal" by the Olympian gods, Superman approaches Steve Trevor—top field agent of A.R.G.U.S. (Advanced Research Group Uniting Super-Humans), and the previous ex-boyfriend of Kal-El's ex-girlfriend, Wonder Woman—with an odd request: to grant him access to A.R.G.U.S.'s massive deposit of Kryptonite. With a layer of his cells mutating to the point where he can no longer absorb solar energy, Superman theorizes that Kryptonite may burn away the poisoned cells and enable him to power up...provided it doesn't kill him first.

The Man of Steel soon proves his theory right—sort of. Hurling himself into A.R.G.U.S.'s Kryptonite chamber, he powers up in unpredictable ways long enough to defeat the Puzzler, a mechanical menace Vandal Savage has ordered to destroy the compound and Superman. Though the Kryptonite is also killing off his healthy cells, Superman uses his renewed strength to unite with Wonder Woman in an orchestrated attack against Savage. Unfortunately, the first of the immortal's Black Mist-saturated "offspring," a boy turned brute called Salvaxe, offsets the duo's offensive, allowing Savage to realign Jupiter's moons and merge the Man of Steel's Fortress of Solitude with the already-fused Justice League Watchtower and Stormwatch Carrier...

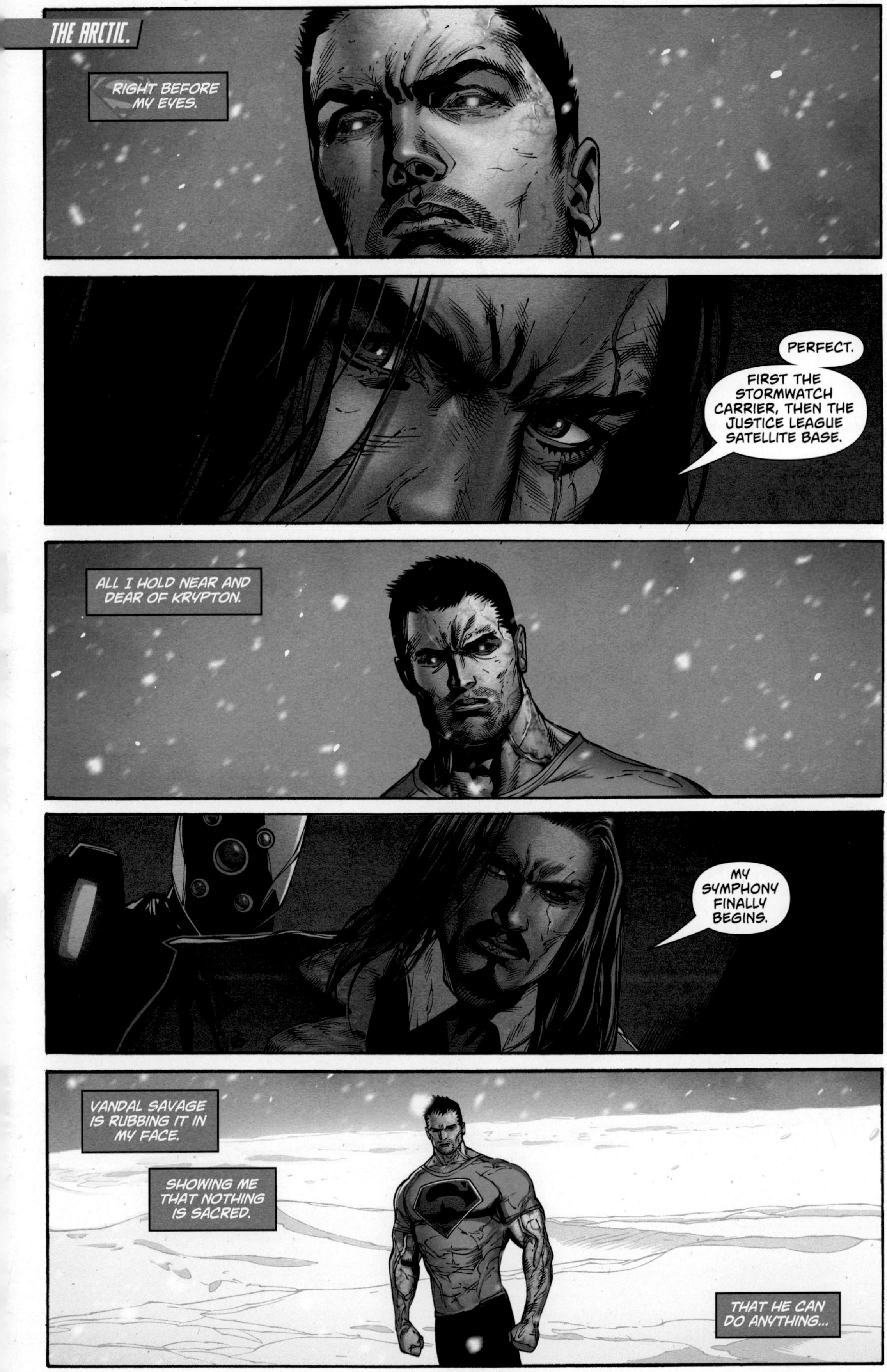
THE ARCTIC.
RIGHT BEFORE MY EYES.
PERFECT.
FIRST THE STORMWATCH CARRIER, THEN THE JUSTICE LEAGUE SATELLITE BASE.
ALL I HOLD NEAR AND DEAR OF KRYPTON.
MY SYMPHONY FINALLY BEGINS.
VANDAL SAVAGE IS RUBBING IT IN MY FACE.
SHOWING ME THAT NOTHING IS SACRED.
THAT HE CAN DO ANYTHING...

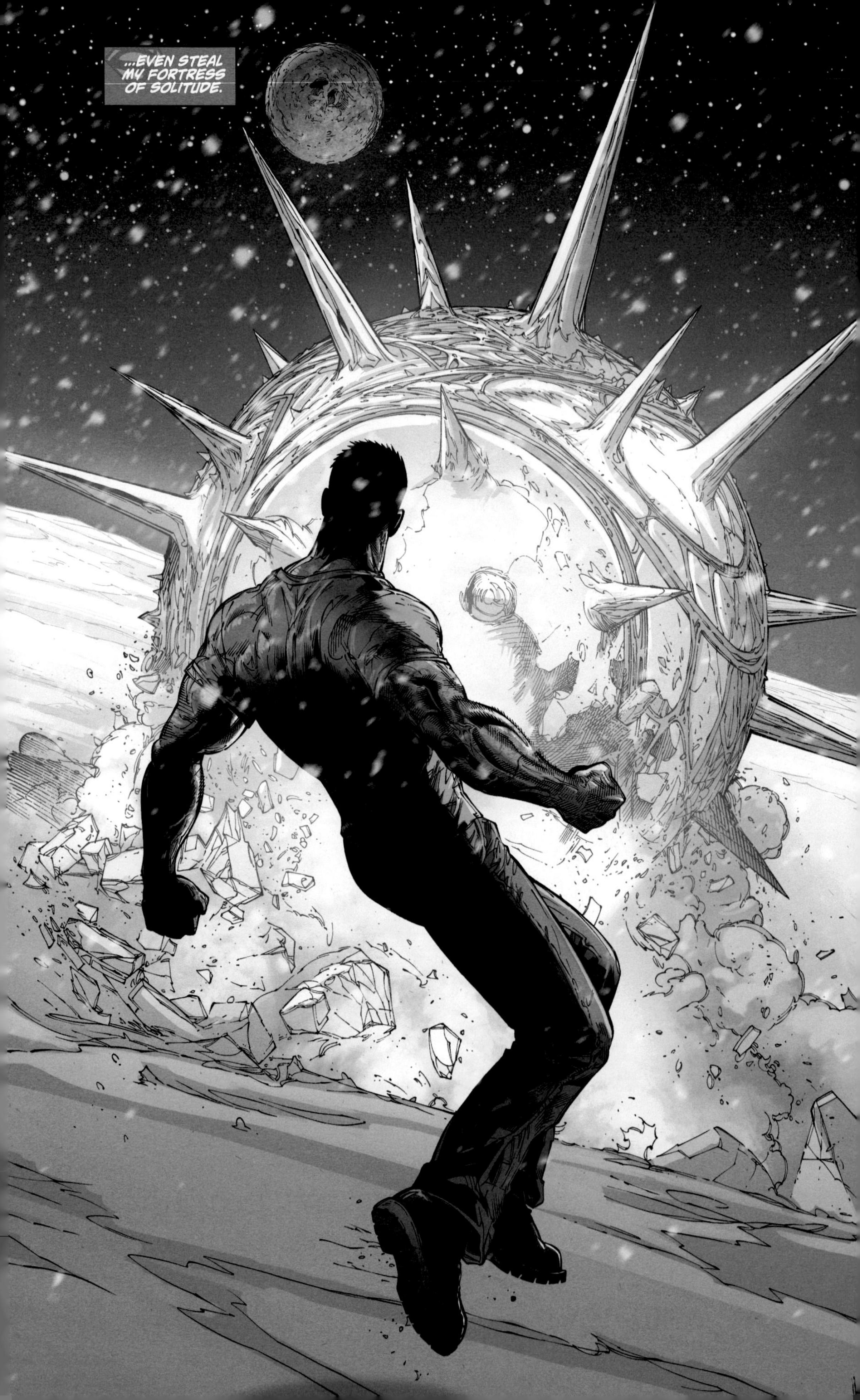
...EVEN STEAL MY FORTRESS OF SOLITUDE.

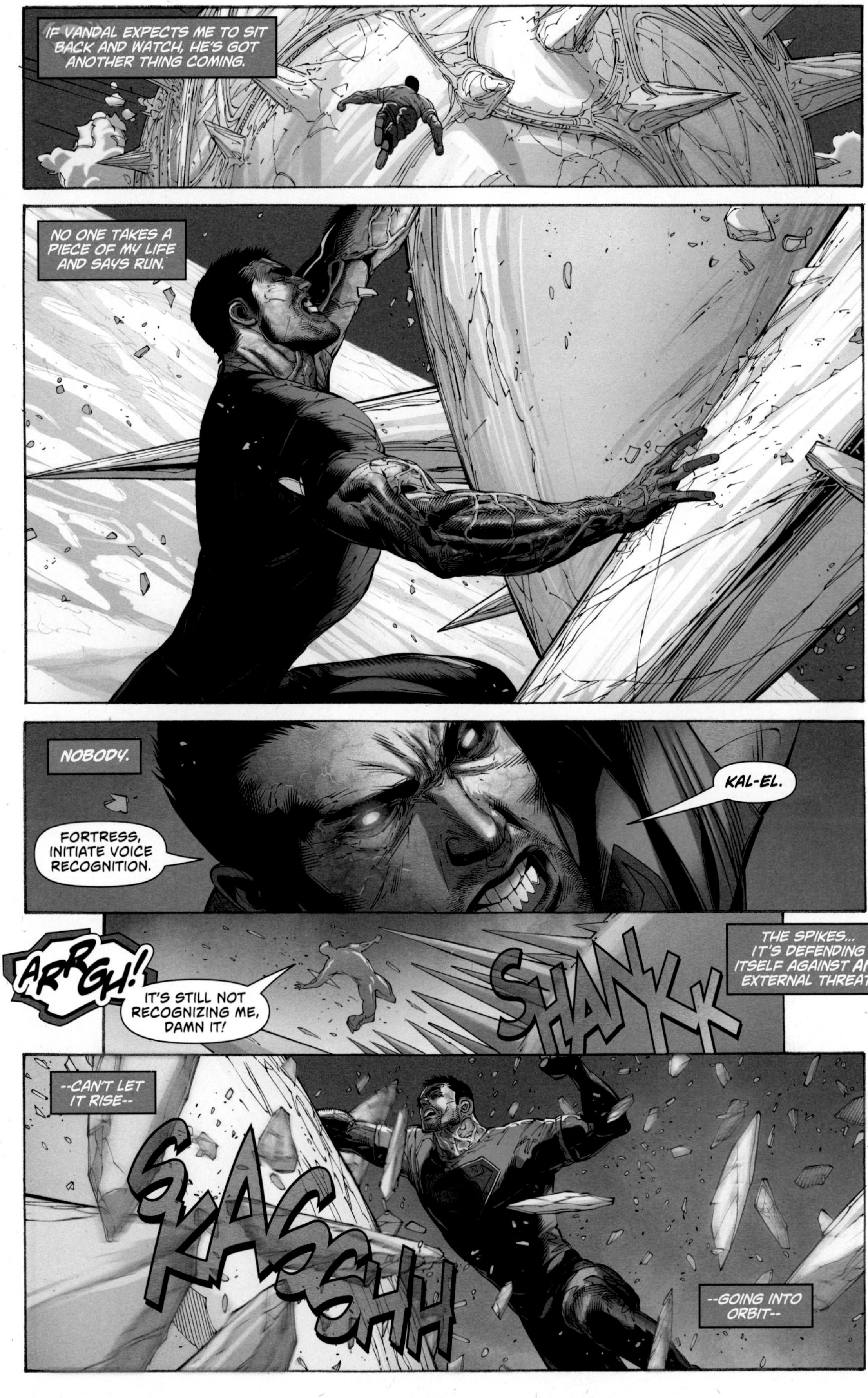

IF VANDAL EXPECTS ME TO SIT BACK AND WATCH, HE'S GOT ANOTHER THING COMING.
NO ONE TAKES A PIECE OF MY LIFE AND SAYS RUN.
NOBODY.
FORTRESS, INITIATE VOICE RECOGNITION.
KAL-EL.
ARRRGH!
IT'S STILL NOT RECOGNIZING ME, DAMN IT!
SHANKK
THE SPIKES... IT'S DEFENDING ITSELF AGAINST ANY EXTERNAL THREAT.
--CAN'T LET IT RISE--
SKASSHH
--GOING INTO ORBIT--

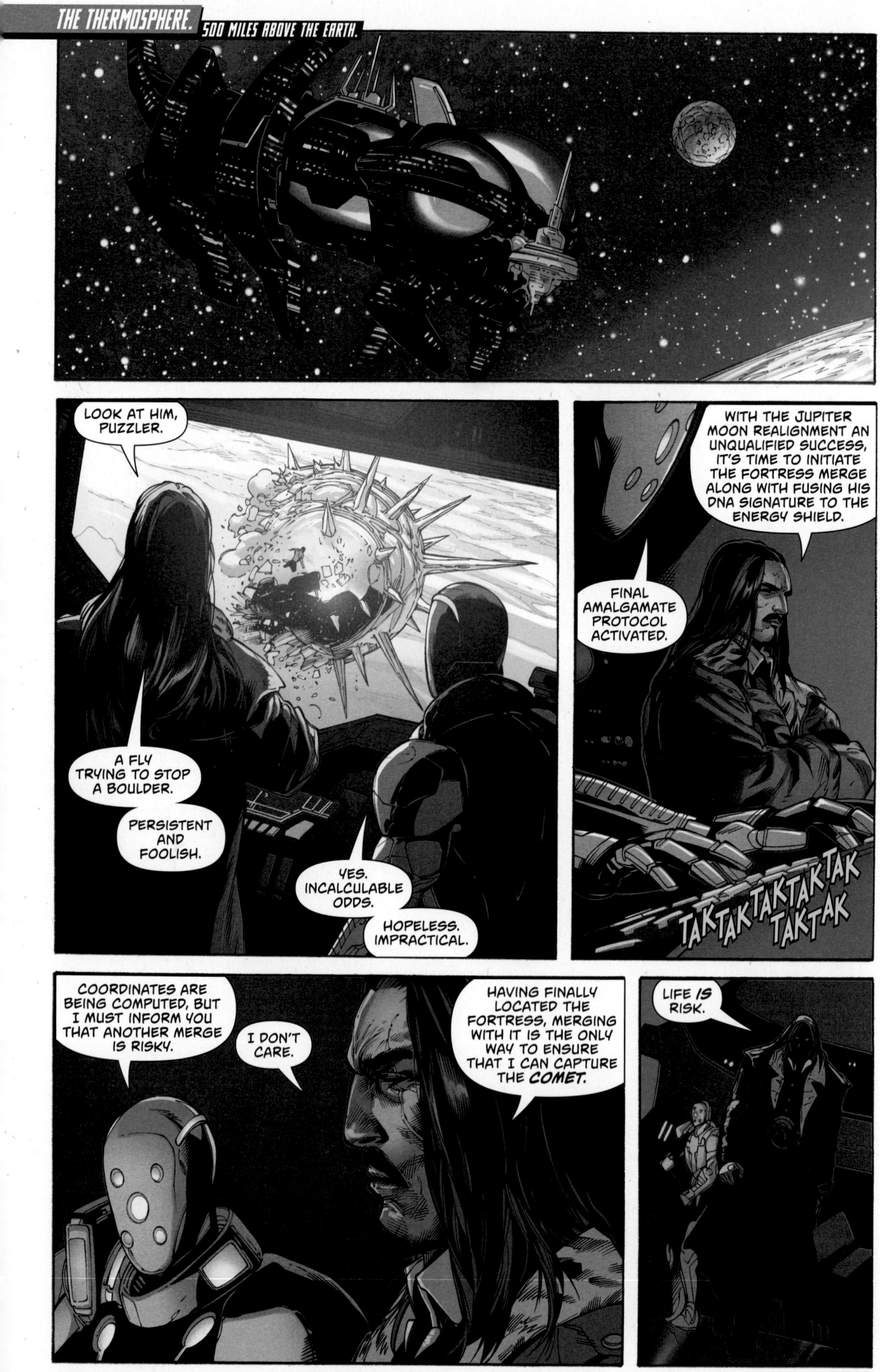
THE THERMOSPHERE.
500 MILES ABOVE THE EARTH.
LOOK AT HIM, PUZZLER.
A FLY TRYING TO STOP A BOULDER.
PERSISTENT AND FOOLISH.
YES. INCALCULABLE ODDS.
HOPELESS. IMPRACTICAL.
WITH THE JUPITER MOON REALIGNMENT AN UNQUALIFIED SUCCESS, IT'S TIME TO INITIATE THE FORTRESS MERGE ALONG WITH FUSING HIS DNA SIGNATURE TO THE ENERGY SHIELD.
FINAL AMALGAMATE PROTOCOL ACTIVATED.
TAKTAKTAKTAKTAK TAKTAK
COORDINATES ARE BEING COMPUTED, BUT I MUST INFORM YOU THAT ANOTHER MERGE IS RISKY.
I DON'T CARE.
HAVING FINALLY LOCATED THE FORTRESS, MERGING WITH IT IS THE ONLY WAY TO ENSURE THAT I CAN CAPTURE THE COMET.
LIFE IS RISK.

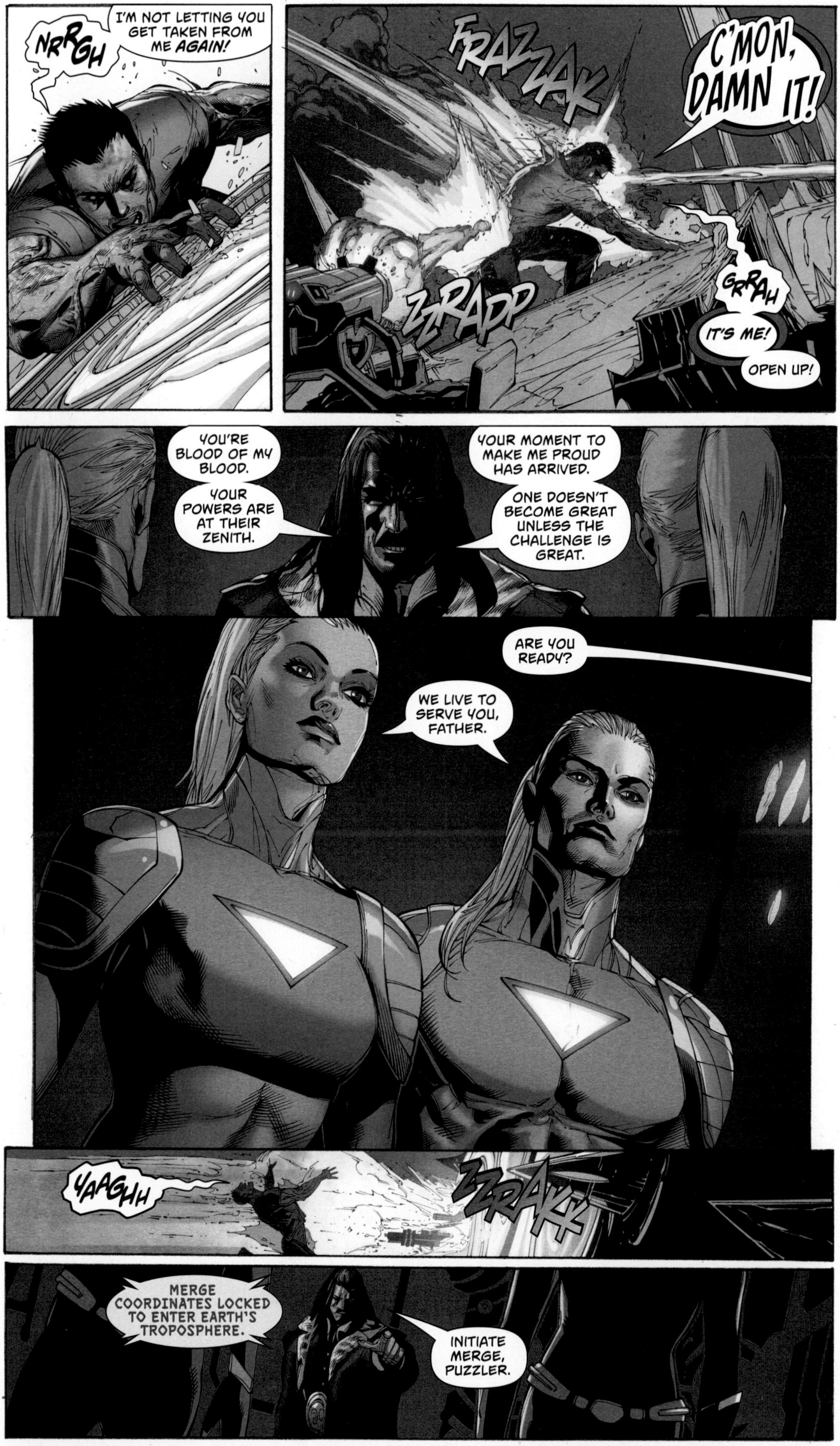
NRRGH
I'M NOT LETTING YOU GET TAKEN FROM ME AGAIN!
FRAZZAK
C'MON, DAMN IT!
ZZRADP
GRRAH
IT'S ME!
OPEN UP!
YOU'RE BLOOD OF MY BLOOD.
YOUR POWERS ARE AT THEIR ZENITH.
YOUR MOMENT TO MAKE ME PROUD HAS ARRIVED.
ONE DOESN'T BECOME GREAT UNLESS THE CHALLENGE IS GREAT.
ARE YOU READY?
WE LIVE TO SERVE YOU, FATHER.
YAAGHH
ZZRAKK
MERGE COORDINATES LOCKED TO ENTER EARTH'S TROPOSPHERE.
INITIATE MERGE, PUZZLER.

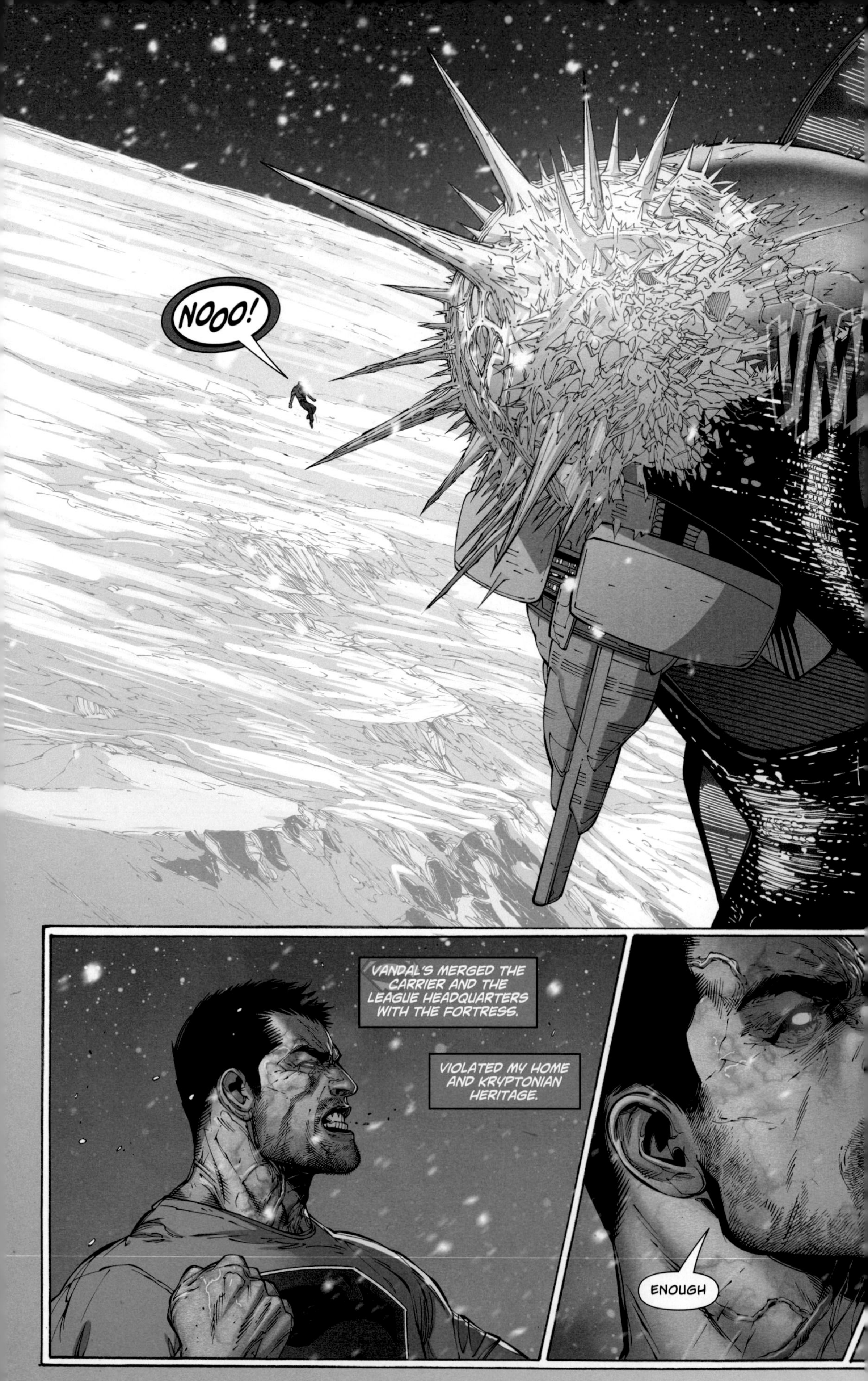
NOOO!
VANDAL'S MERGED THE CARRIER AND THE LEAGUE HEADQUARTERS WITH THE FORTRESS.
VIOLATED MY HOME AND KRYPTONIAN HERITAGE.
ENOUGH

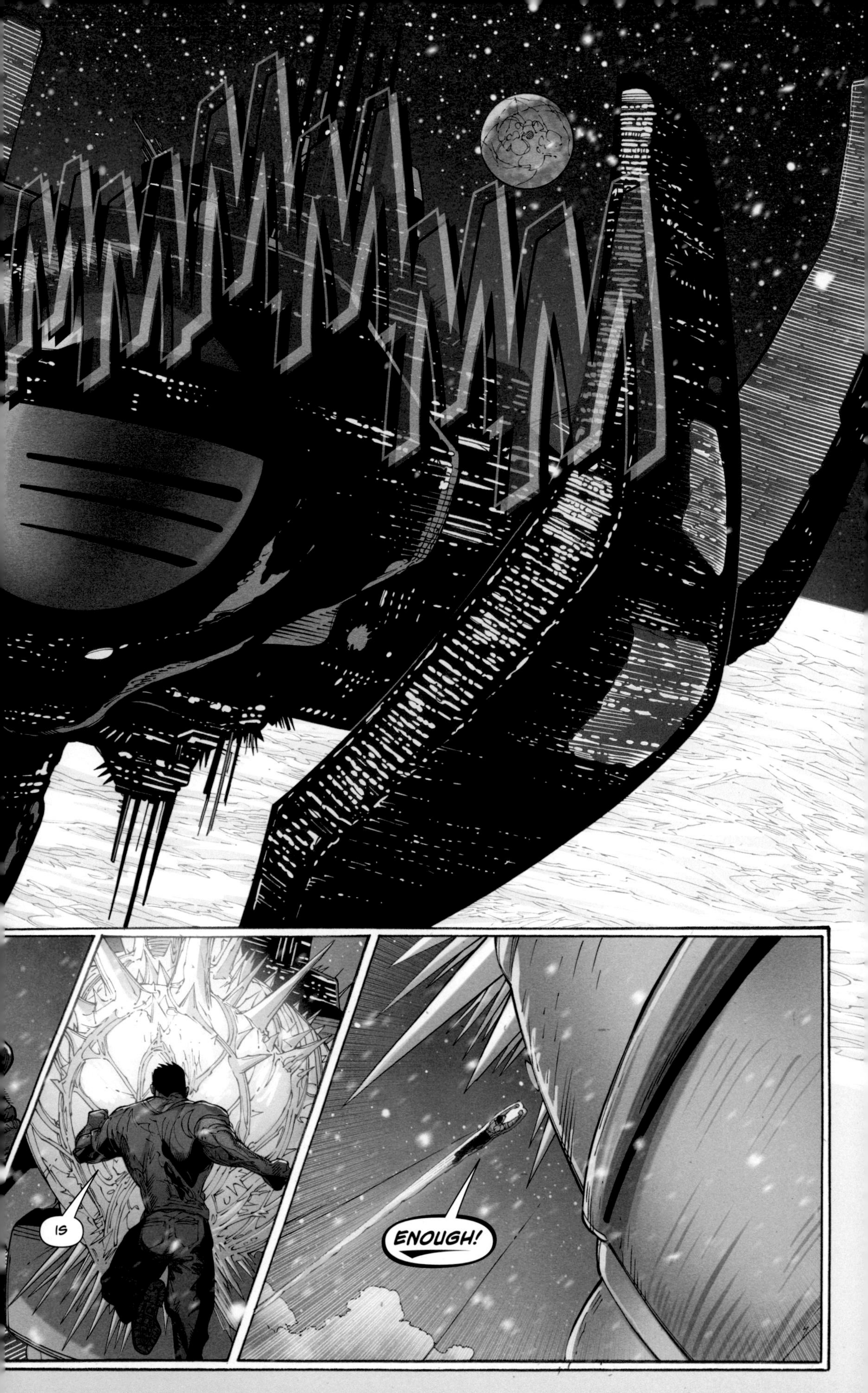
IS
ENOUGH!

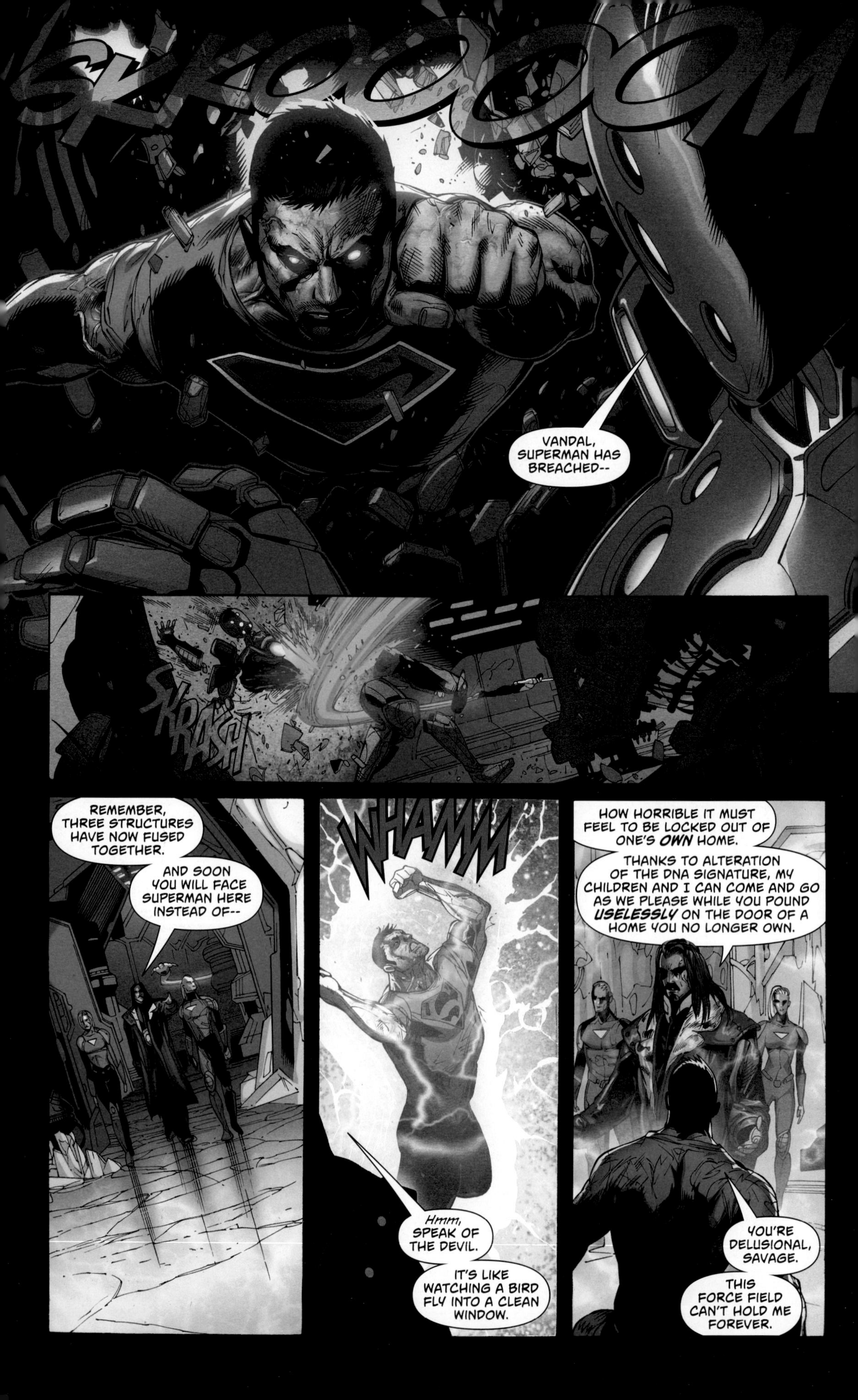
SKRAKOOOOOM
VANDAL, SUPERMAN HAS BREACHED--
SKRASH
REMEMBER, THREE STRUCTURES HAVE NOW FUSED TOGETHER.
AND SOON YOU WILL FACE SUPERMAN HERE INSTEAD OF--
WHAMM
Hmm, SPEAK OF THE DEVIL.
IT'S LIKE WATCHING A BIRD FLY INTO A CLEAN WINDOW.
HOW HORRIBLE IT MUST FEEL TO BE LOCKED OUT OF ONE'S OWN HOME.
THANKS TO ALTERATION OF THE DNA SIGNATURE, MY CHILDREN AND I CAN COME AND GO AS WE PLEASE WHILE YOU POUND USELESSLY ON THE DOOR OF A HOME YOU NO LONGER OWN.
YOU'RE DELUSIONAL, SAVAGE.
THIS FORCE FIELD CAN'T HOLD ME FOREVER.

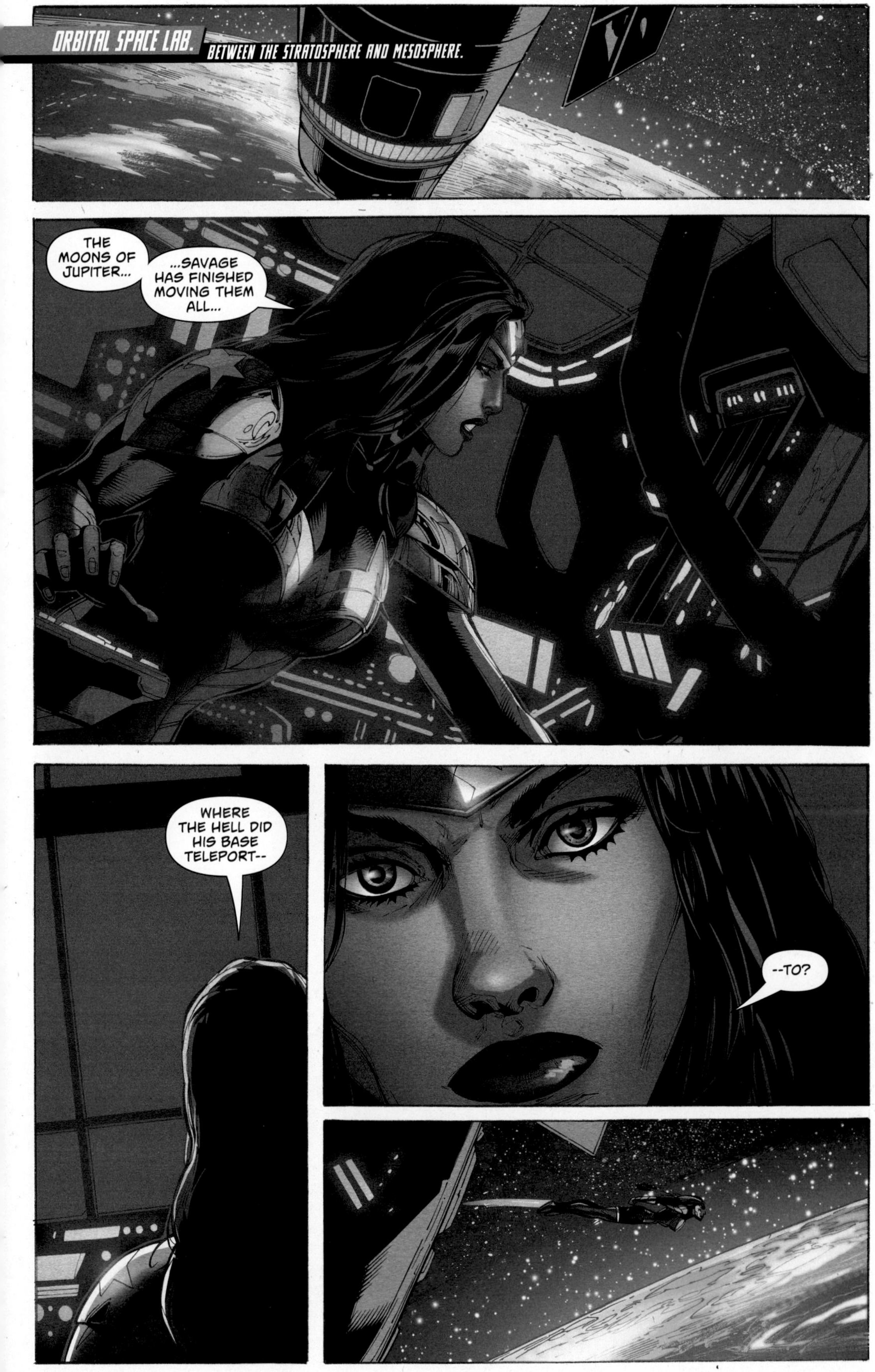
ORBITAL SPACE LAB.
BETWEEN THE STRATOSPHERE AND MESOSPHERE.
THE MOONS OF JUPITER...
...SAVAGE HAS FINISHED MOVING THEM ALL...
WHERE THE HELL DID HIS BASE TELEPORT--
--TO?

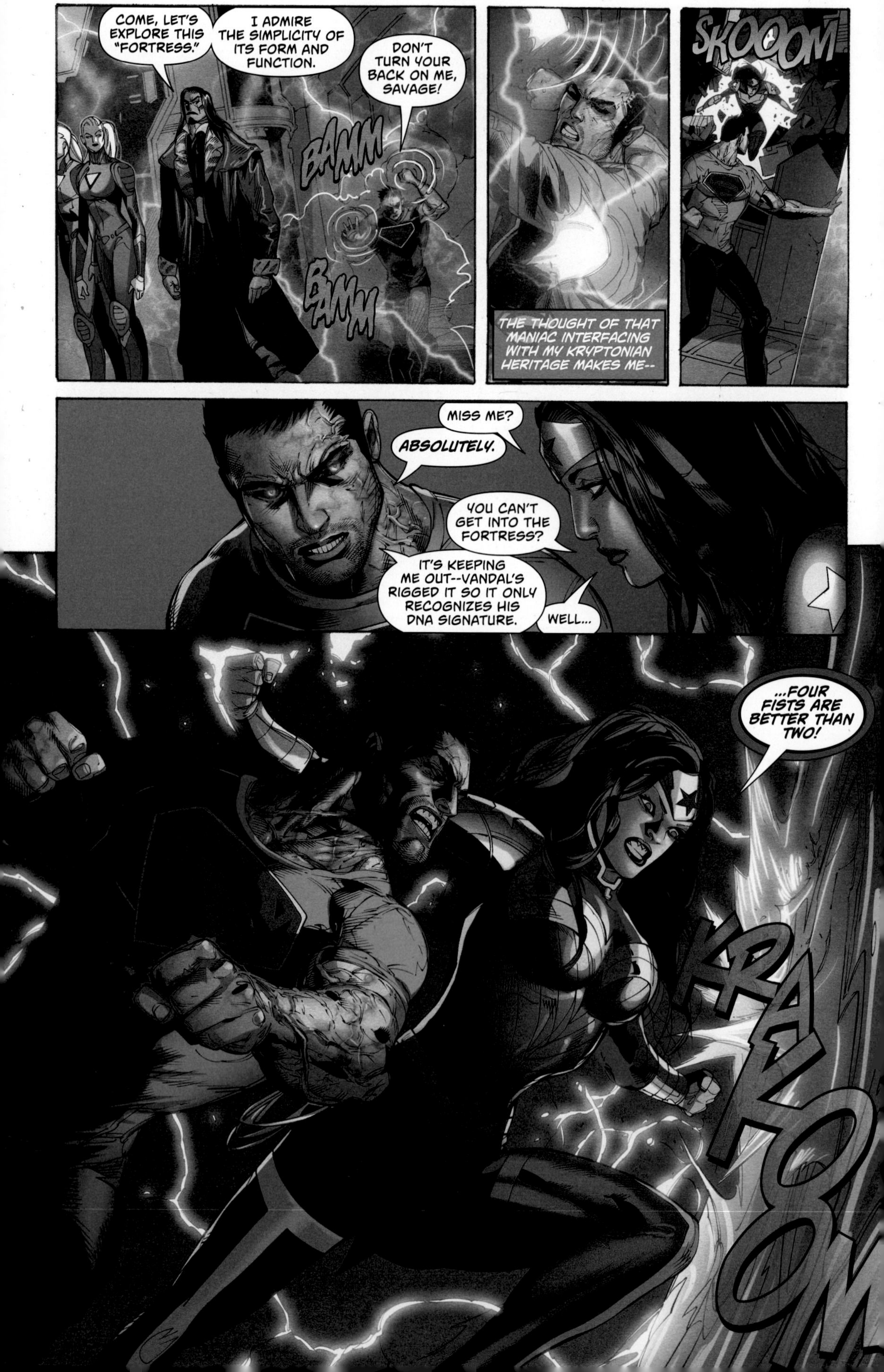
COME, LET'S EXPLORE THIS "FORTRESS."
I ADMIRE THE SIMPLICITY OF ITS FORM AND FUNCTION.
DON'T TURN YOUR BACK ON ME, SAVAGE!
BAMM
BAMM
THE THOUGHT OF THAT MANIAC INTERFACING WITH MY KRYPTONIAN HERITAGE MAKES ME--
SKOOOM
MISS ME?
ABSOLUTELY.
YOU CAN'T GET INTO THE FORTRESS?
IT'S KEEPING ME OUT--VANDAL'S RIGGED IT SO IT ONLY RECOGNIZES HIS DNA SIGNATURE.
WELL...
...FOUR FISTS ARE BETTER THAN TWO!
KRAKOOM

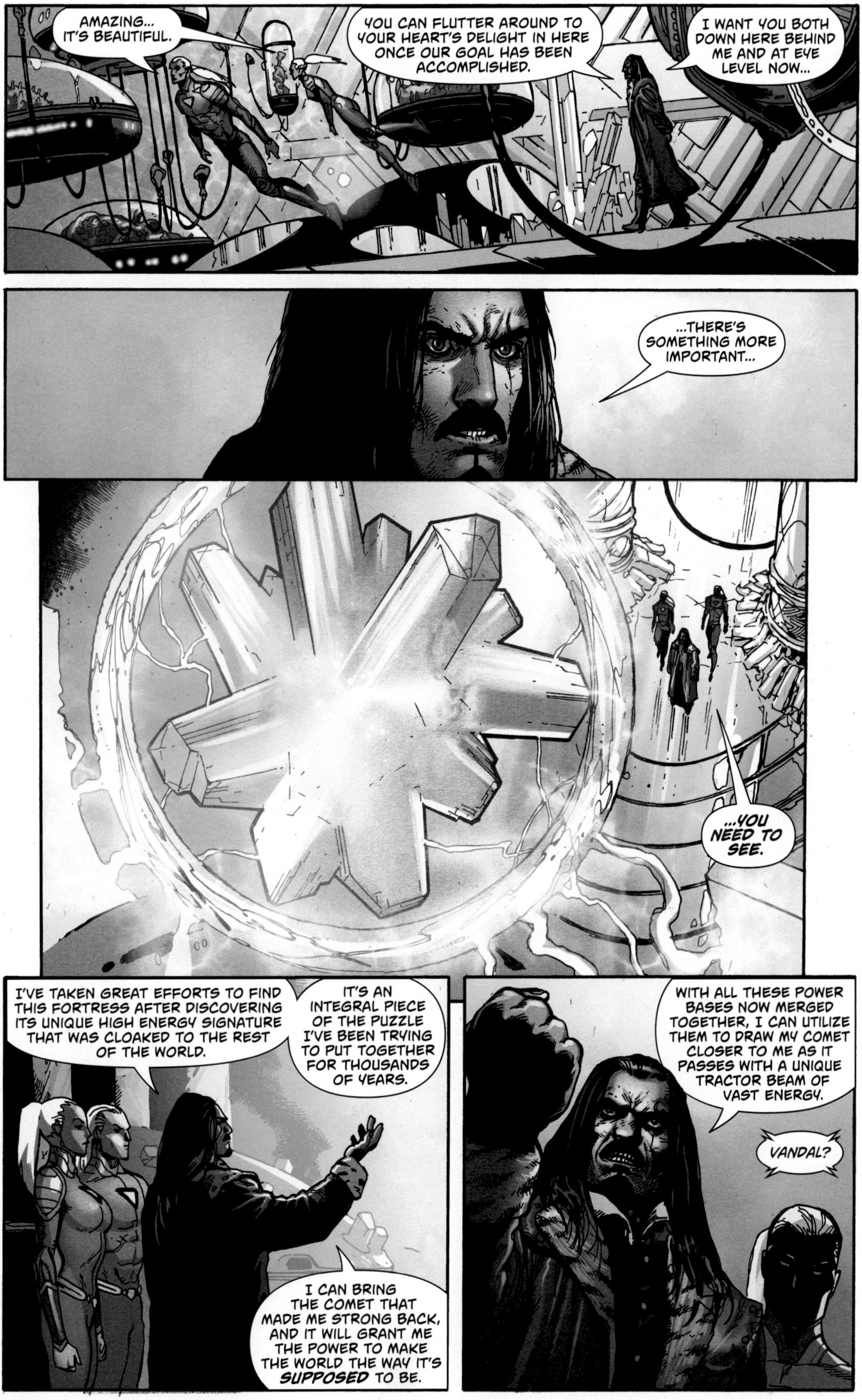
AMAZING... IT'S BEAUTIFUL.
YOU CAN FLUTTER AROUND TO YOUR HEART'S DELIGHT IN HERE ONCE OUR GOAL HAS BEEN ACCOMPLISHED.
I WANT YOU BOTH DOWN HERE BEHIND ME AND AT EYE LEVEL NOW...
...THERE'S SOMETHING MORE IMPORTANT...
...YOU NEED TO SEE.
I'VE TAKEN GREAT EFFORTS TO FIND THIS FORTRESS AFTER DISCOVERING ITS UNIQUE HIGH ENERGY SIGNATURE THAT WAS CLOAKED TO THE REST OF THE WORLD.
IT'S AN INTEGRAL PIECE OF THE PUZZLE I'VE BEEN TRYING TO PUT TOGETHER FOR THOUSANDS OF YEARS.
I CAN BRING THE COMET THAT MADE ME STRONG BACK, AND IT WILL GRANT ME THE POWER TO MAKE THE WORLD THE WAY IT'S *SUPPOSED* TO BE.
WITH ALL THESE POWER BASES NOW MERGED TOGETHER, I CAN UTILIZE THEM TO DRAW MY COMET CLOSER TO ME AS IT PASSES WITH A UNIQUE TRACTOR BEAM OF VAST ENERGY.
VANDAL?

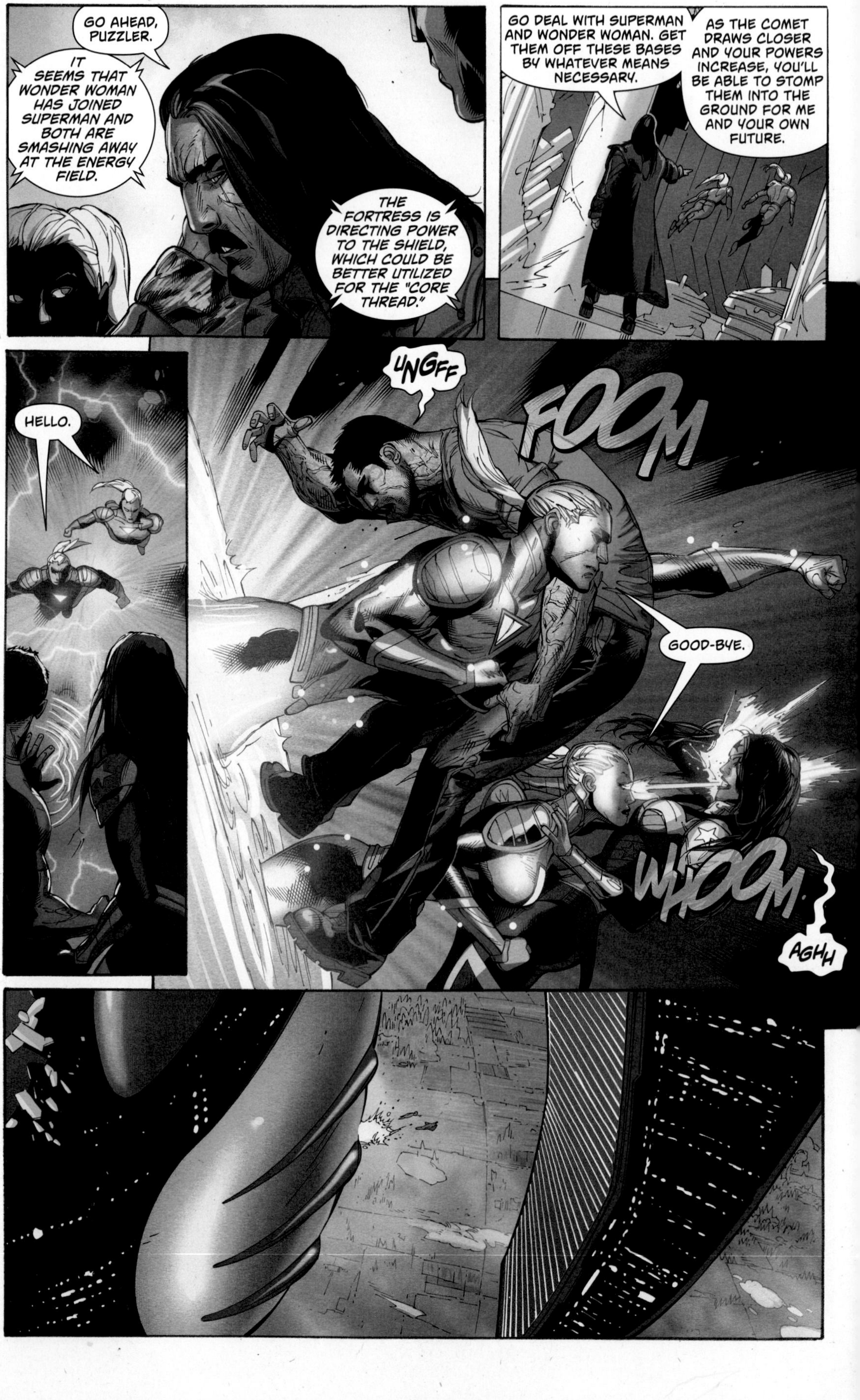
GO AHEAD, PUZZLER.
IT SEEMS THAT WONDER WOMAN HAS JOINED SUPERMAN AND BOTH ARE SMASHING AWAY AT THE ENERGY FIELD.
THE FORTRESS IS DIRECTING POWER TO THE SHIELD, WHICH COULD BE BETTER UTILIZED FOR THE "CORE THREAD."
GO DEAL WITH SUPERMAN AND WONDER WOMAN. GET THEM OFF THESE BASES BY WHATEVER MEANS NECESSARY.
AS THE COMET DRAWS CLOSER AND YOUR POWERS INCREASE, YOU'LL BE ABLE TO STOMP THEM INTO THE GROUND FOR ME AND YOUR OWN FUTURE.
HELLO.
UNGFF
FOOM
GOOD-BYE.
WHOOM
AGHH

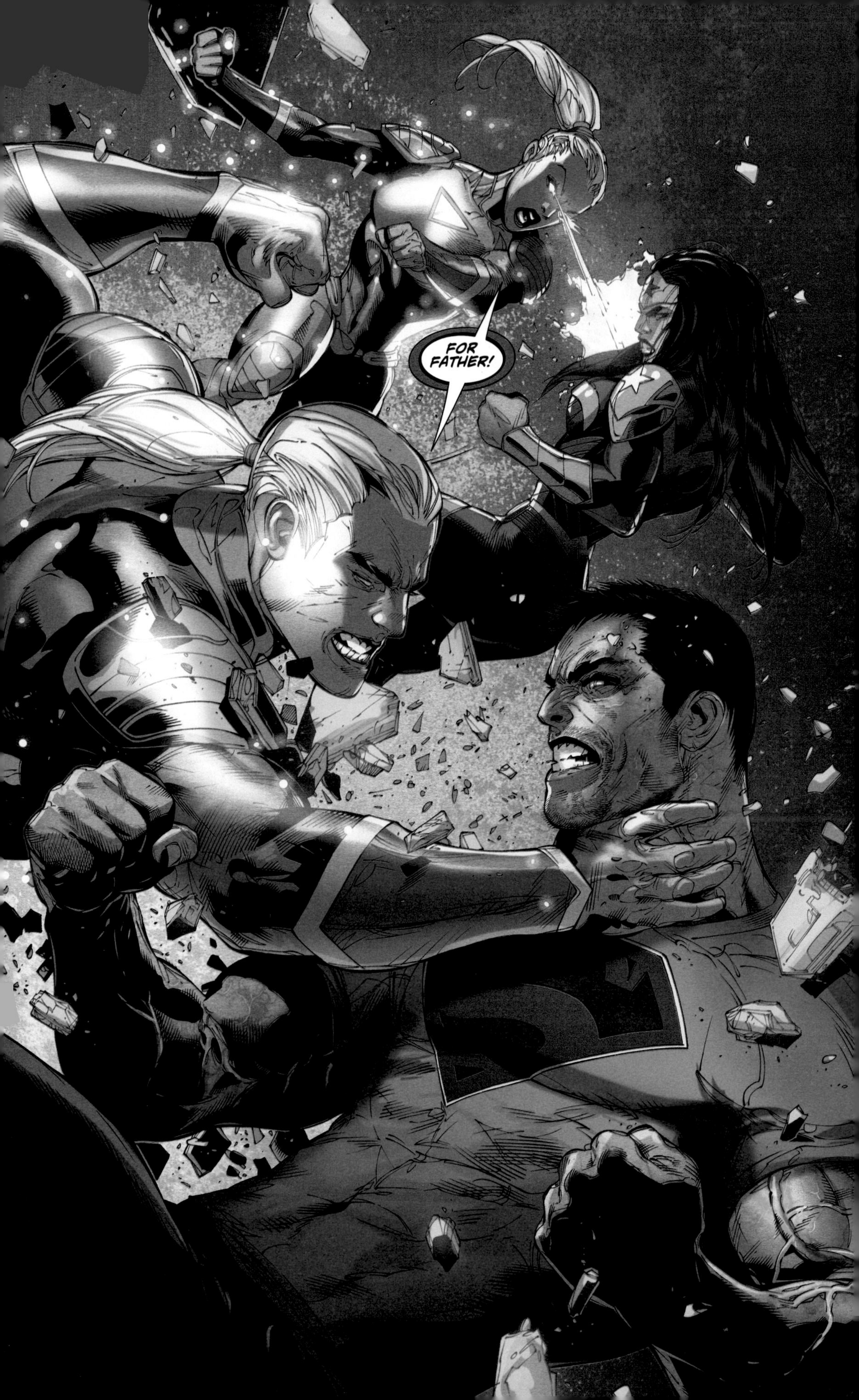
FOR FATHER!

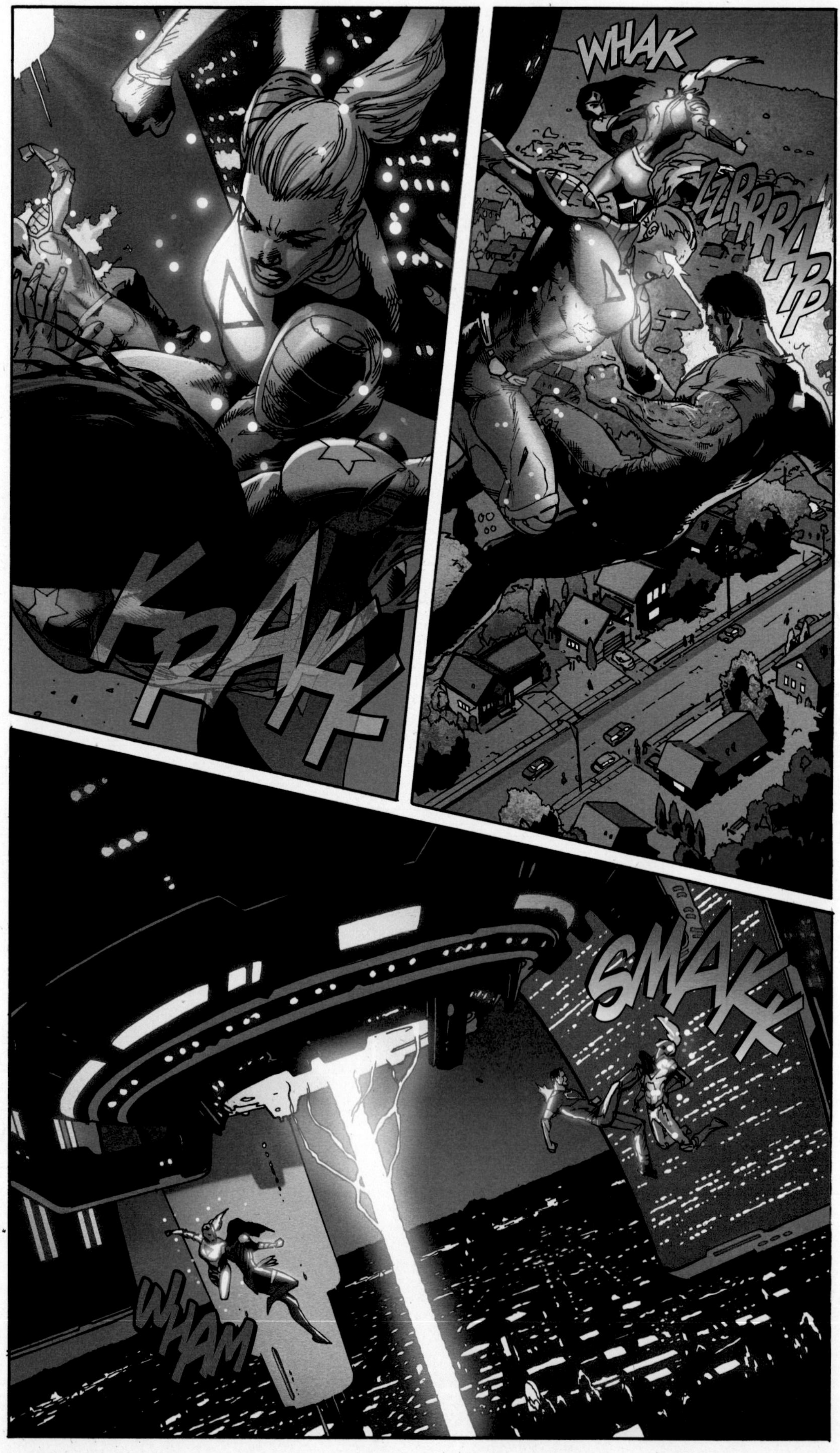
KRAKK
WHAK
ZZRRRAP
SMAKK
WHAM

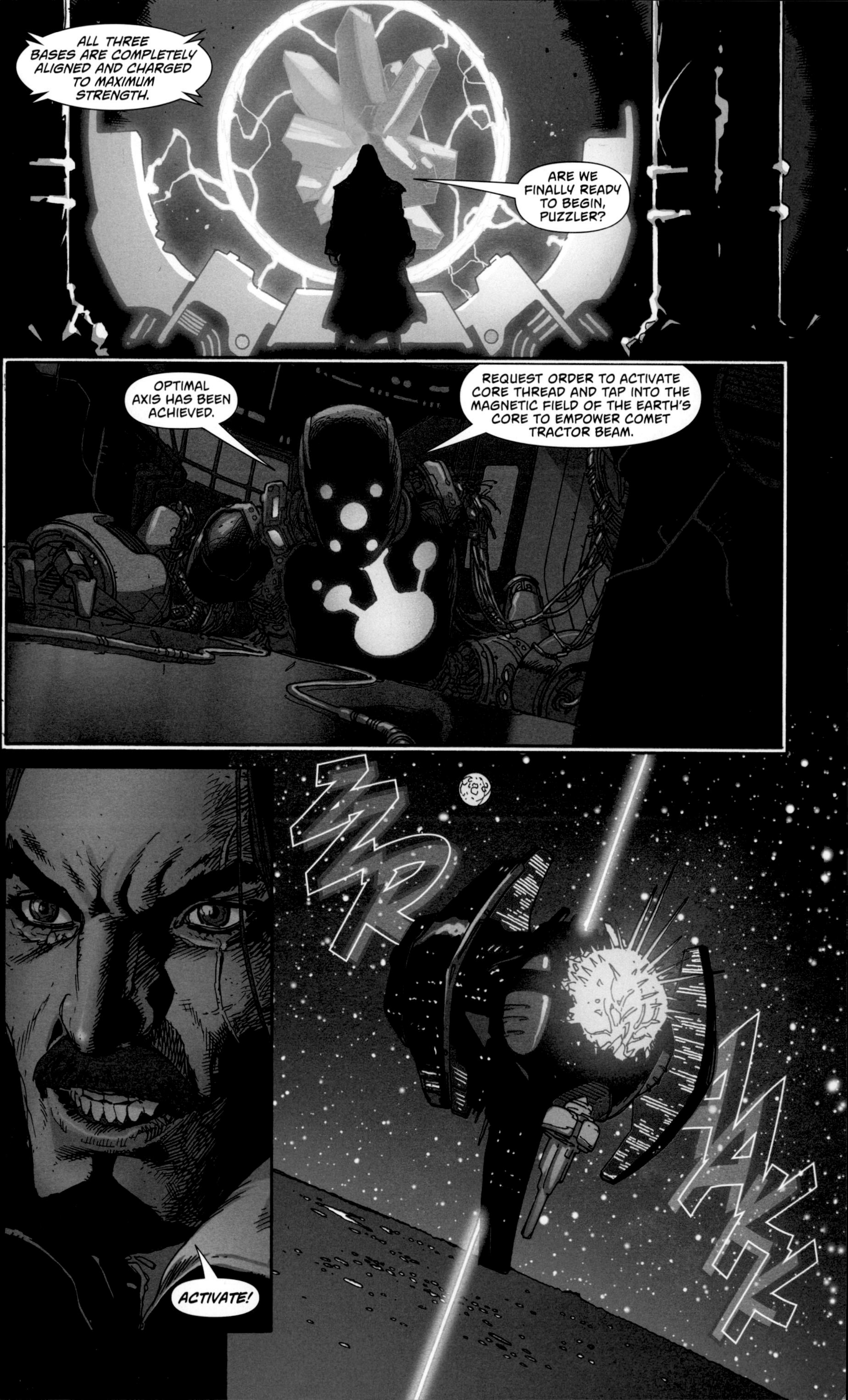
ALL THREE BASES ARE COMPLETELY ALIGNED AND CHARGED TO MAXIMUM STRENGTH.
ARE WE FINALLY READY TO BEGIN, PUZZLER?
OPTIMAL AXIS HAS BEEN ACHIEVED.
REQUEST ORDER TO ACTIVATE CORE THREAD AND TAP INTO THE MAGNETIC FIELD OF THE EARTH'S CORE TO EMPOWER COMET TRACTOR BEAM.
ACTIVATE!

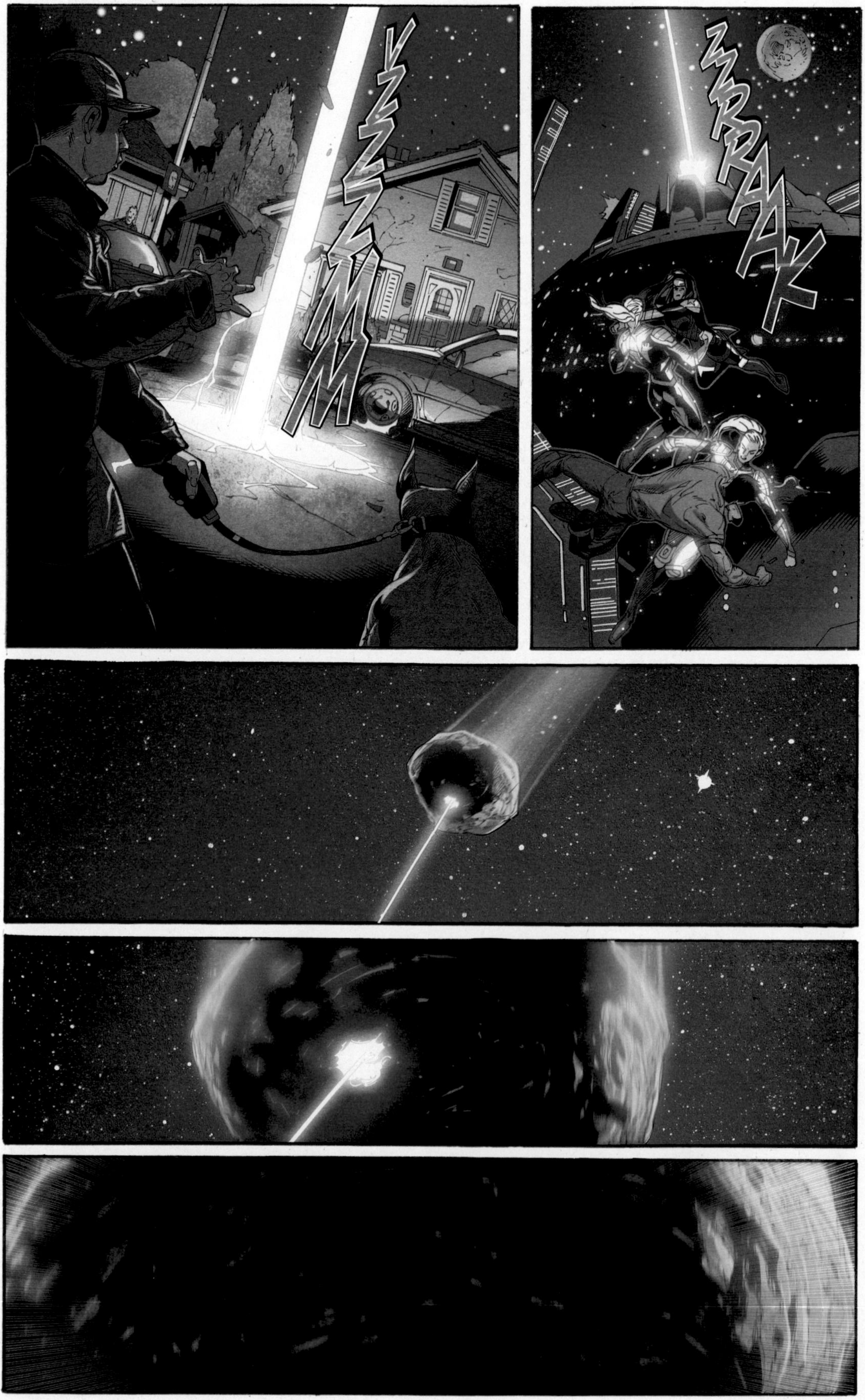
VZZZMMM
ZZRRAAK

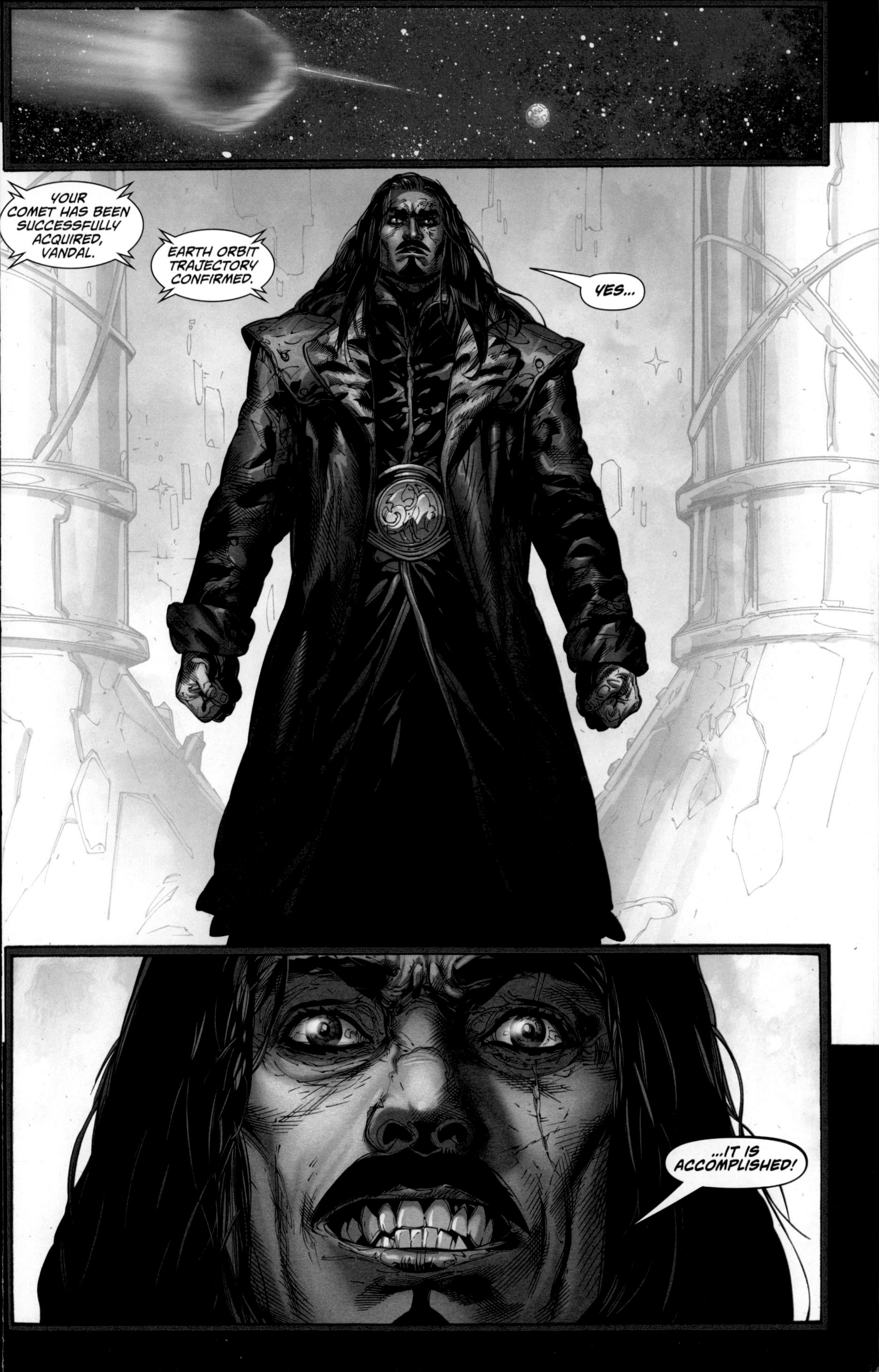
YOUR COMET HAS BEEN SUCCESSFULLY ACQUIRED, VANDAL.
EARTH ORBIT TRAJECTORY CONFIRMED.
YES...
...IT IS ACCOMPLISHED!

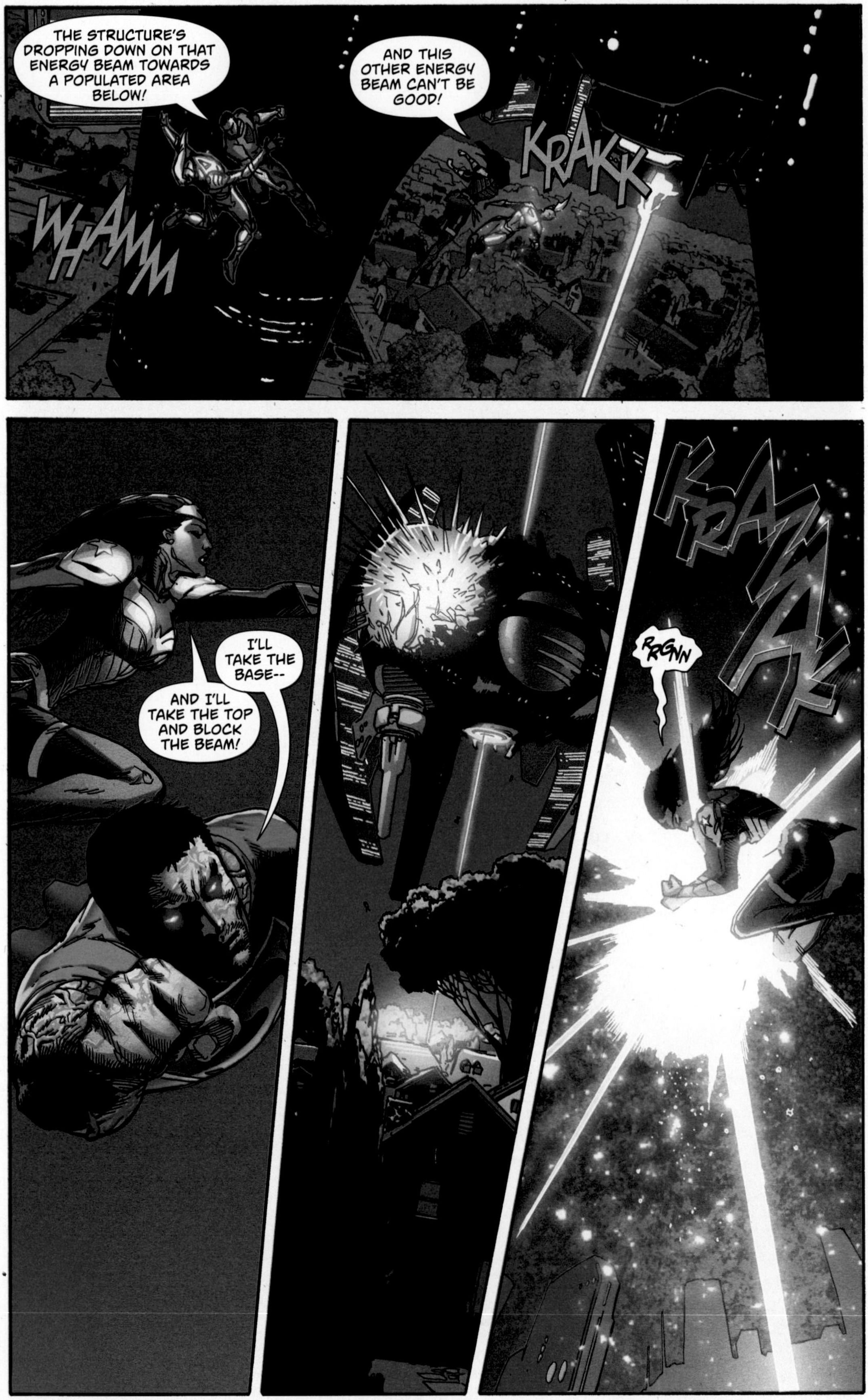
THE STRUCTURE'S DROPPING DOWN ON THAT ENERGY BEAM TOWARDS A POPULATED AREA BELOW!
AND THIS OTHER ENERGY BEAM CAN'T BE GOOD!
WHAMM
KRAKK
I'LL TAKE THE BASE--
AND I'LL TAKE THE TOP AND BLOCK THE BEAM!
KRAZAK
RRGNN

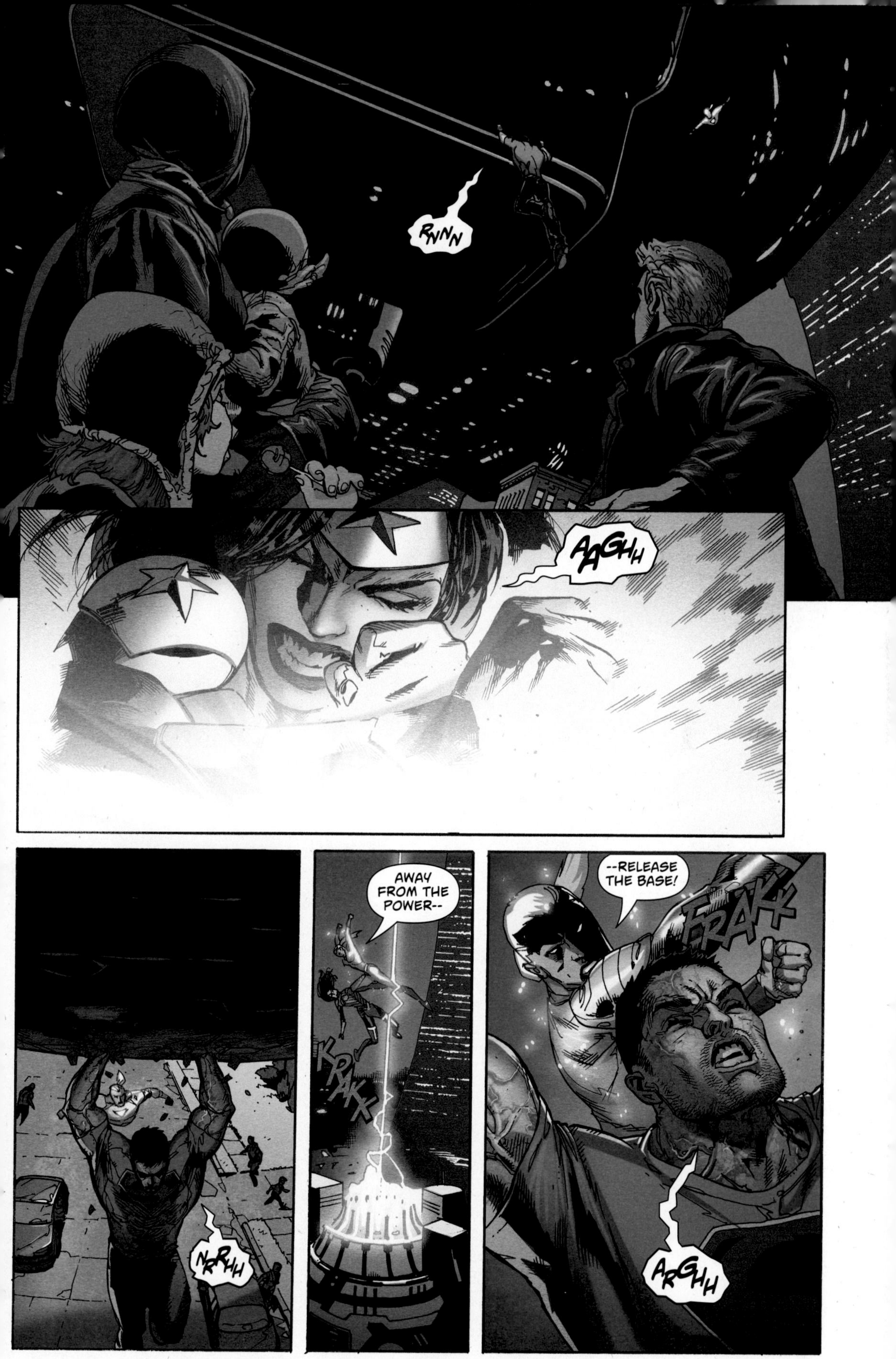
RNNN
AAGHH
NRRHH
AWAY FROM THE POWER--
KRAKK
--RELEASE THE BASE!
FRAKK
ARGHH

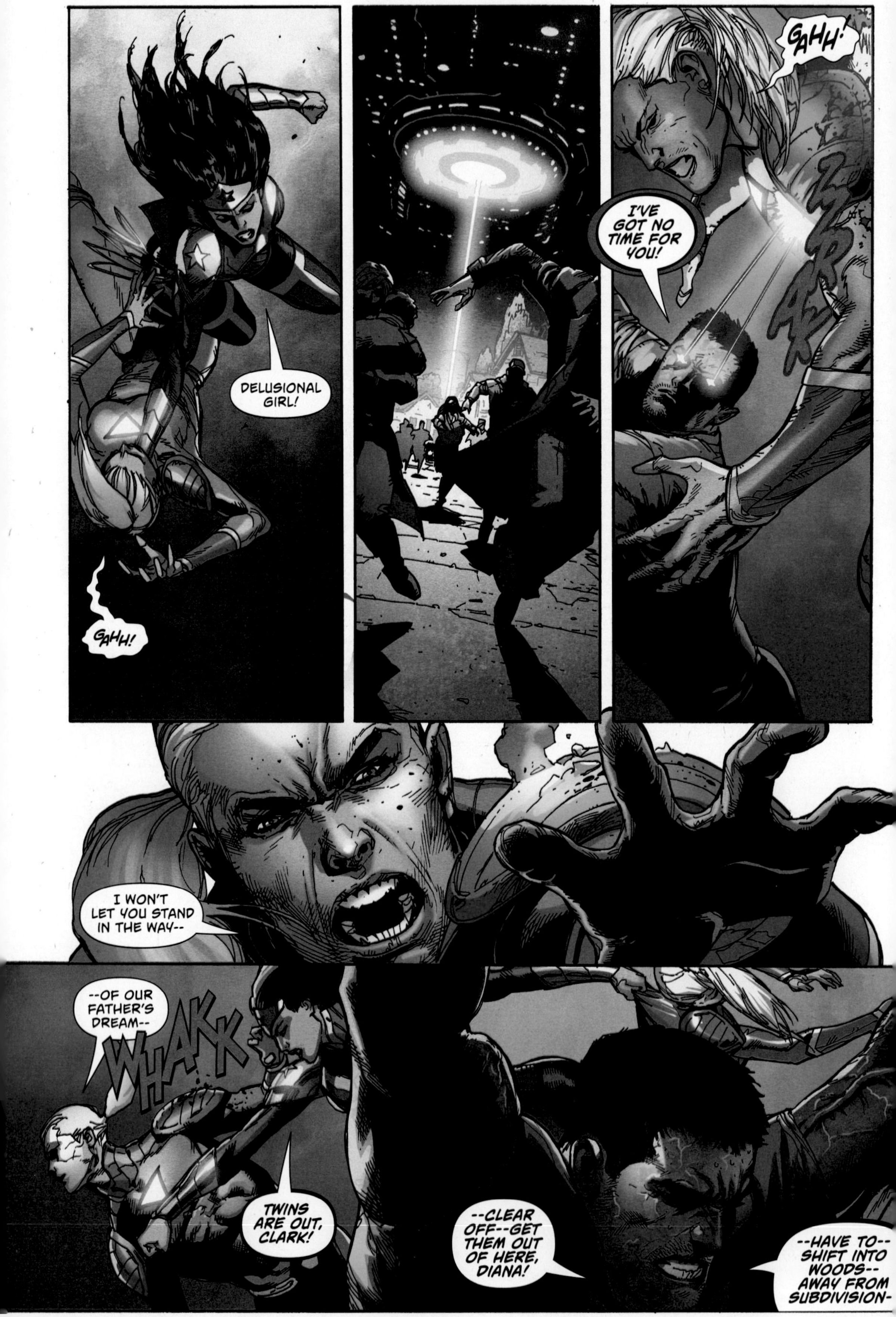
DELUSIONAL GIRL!
GAHH!
I'VE GOT NO TIME FOR YOU!
GAHH!
I WON'T LET YOU STAND IN THE WAY--
--OF OUR FATHER'S DREAM--
WHAKK
TWINS ARE OUT, CLARK!
--CLEAR OFF--GET THEM OUT OF HERE, DIANA!
--HAVE TO--SHIFT INTO WOODS--AWAY FROM SUBDIVISION-

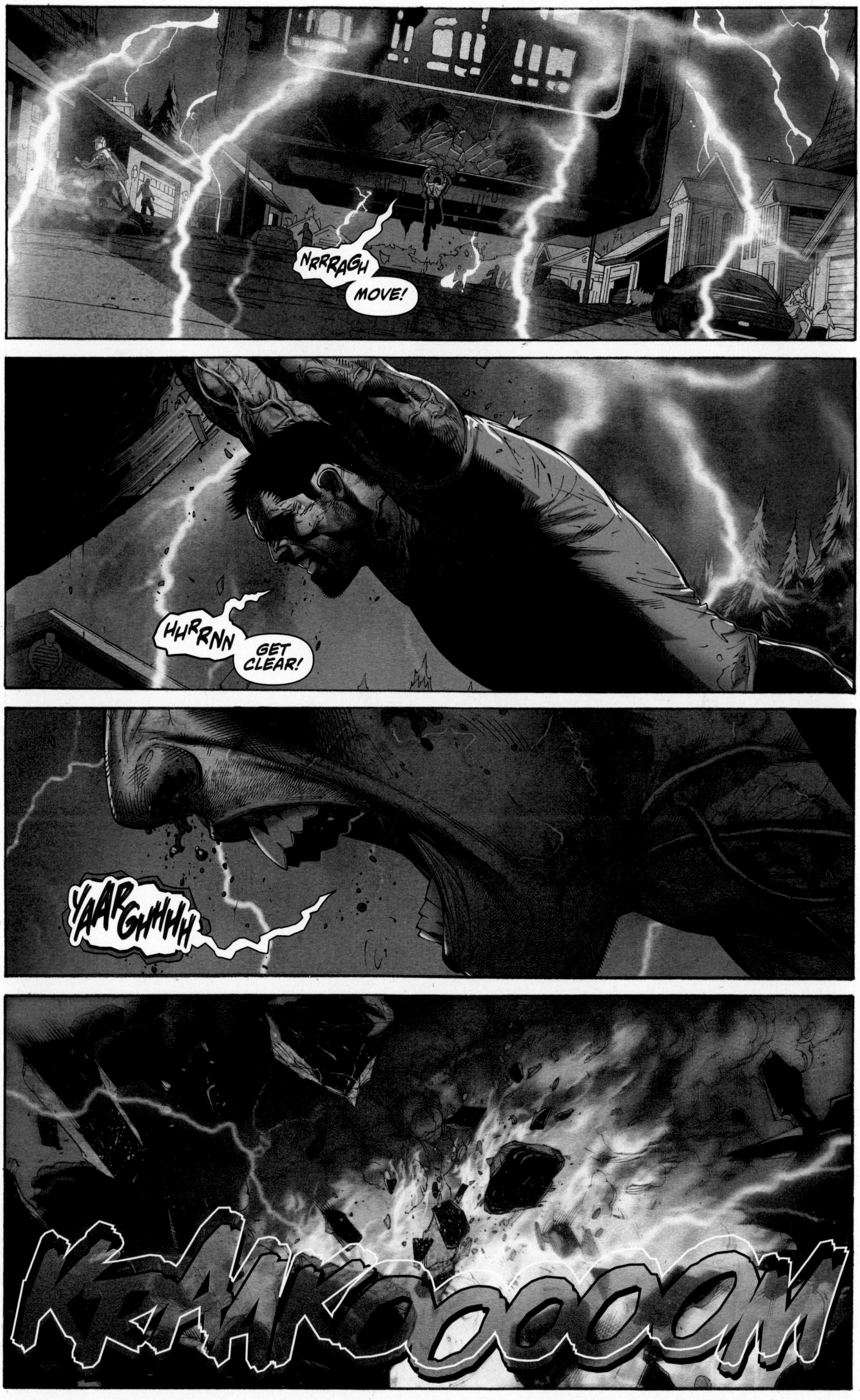
NRRRAGH
MOVE!
HHRNN
GET CLEAR!
YAARGHHHH
KRAKOOOOOM

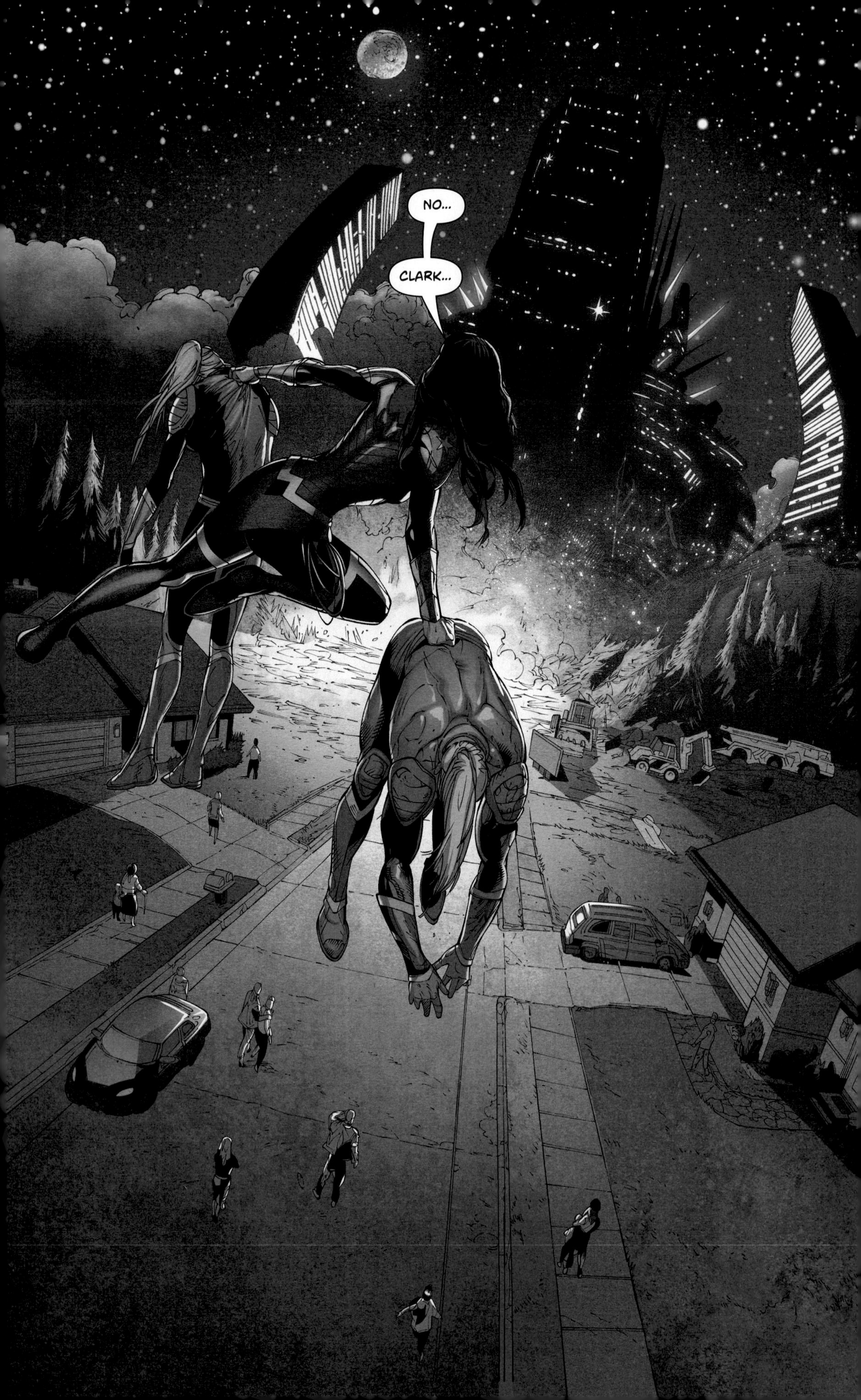
NO...
CLARK...

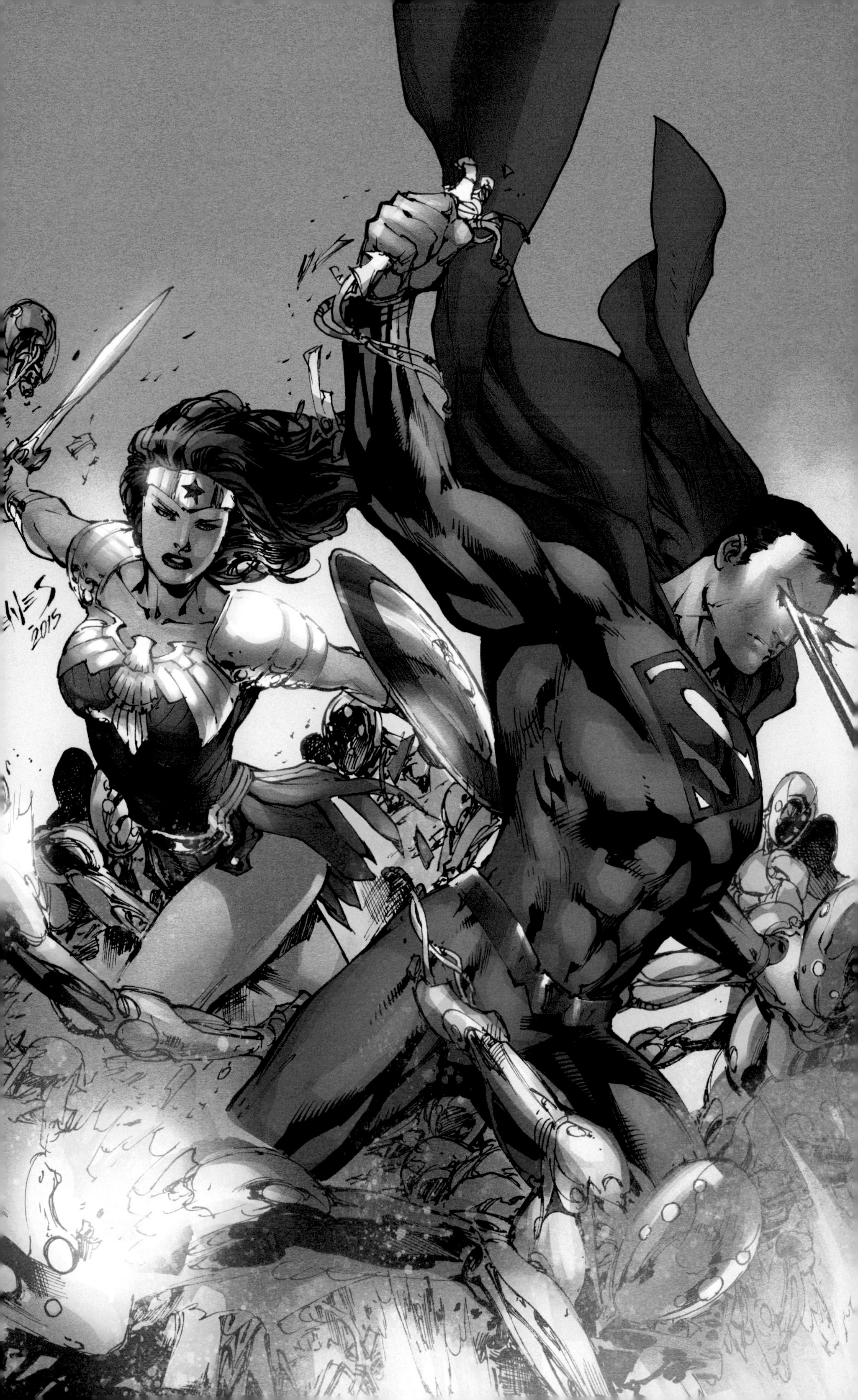

SLAM BANG
PETER J. TOMASI writer CLIFF RICHARDS artist WIL QUINTANA colorist ROB LEIGH letterer cover by ED BENES & ALEX SINCLAIR

Previously,
in SUPERMAN #49 and ACTION COMICS #50...

After seeing the man she loves buried under the fused Fortress of Solitude, Justice League Watchtower and Stormwatch Carrier, Wonder Woman punches her way through the rubble long enough to help Superman ultimately free himself. Together, they and Lois Lane's personal bodyguard, Metallo, try to fight their way into the base to stop Vandal Savage. However, as the comet draws closer to Earth, more of Savage's power-maddened progeny rise to thwart the trio.

Diana and Earth's only remaining heroes make their stand against the immortal's offspring army, while a mortally wounded Metallo makes the ultimate sacrifice and literally offers Superman his Kryptonite heart, hoping it will give the Man of Steel the power necessary to take Savage down. He succeeds in rescuing the imprisoned Justice League members, but as Superman attempts to stop Savage from shuttling his children toward the comet, the tyrant shoots him with cell-decaying toxins and sends him plummeting from the sky, seemingly to his death.

What Savage didn't expect, however, was that the Fortress below would recognize Kal-El's recharged DNA and restore the Man of Steel to full power. Superman is back, but is he in time...?

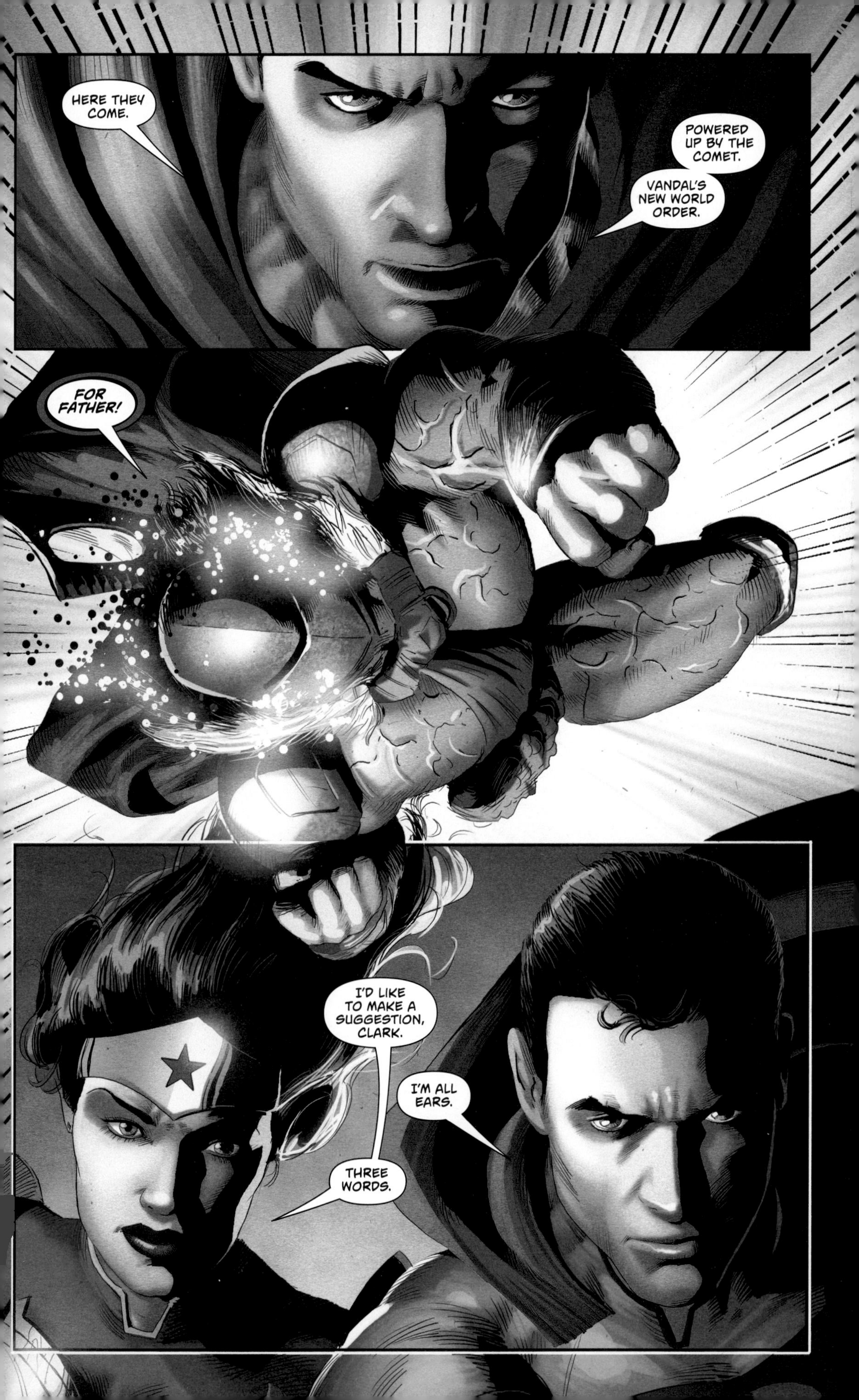
HERE THEY COME.
POWERED UP BY THE COMET.
VANDAL'S NEW WORLD ORDER.
FOR FATHER!
I'D LIKE TO MAKE A SUGGESTION, CLARK.
I'M ALL EARS.
THREE WORDS.

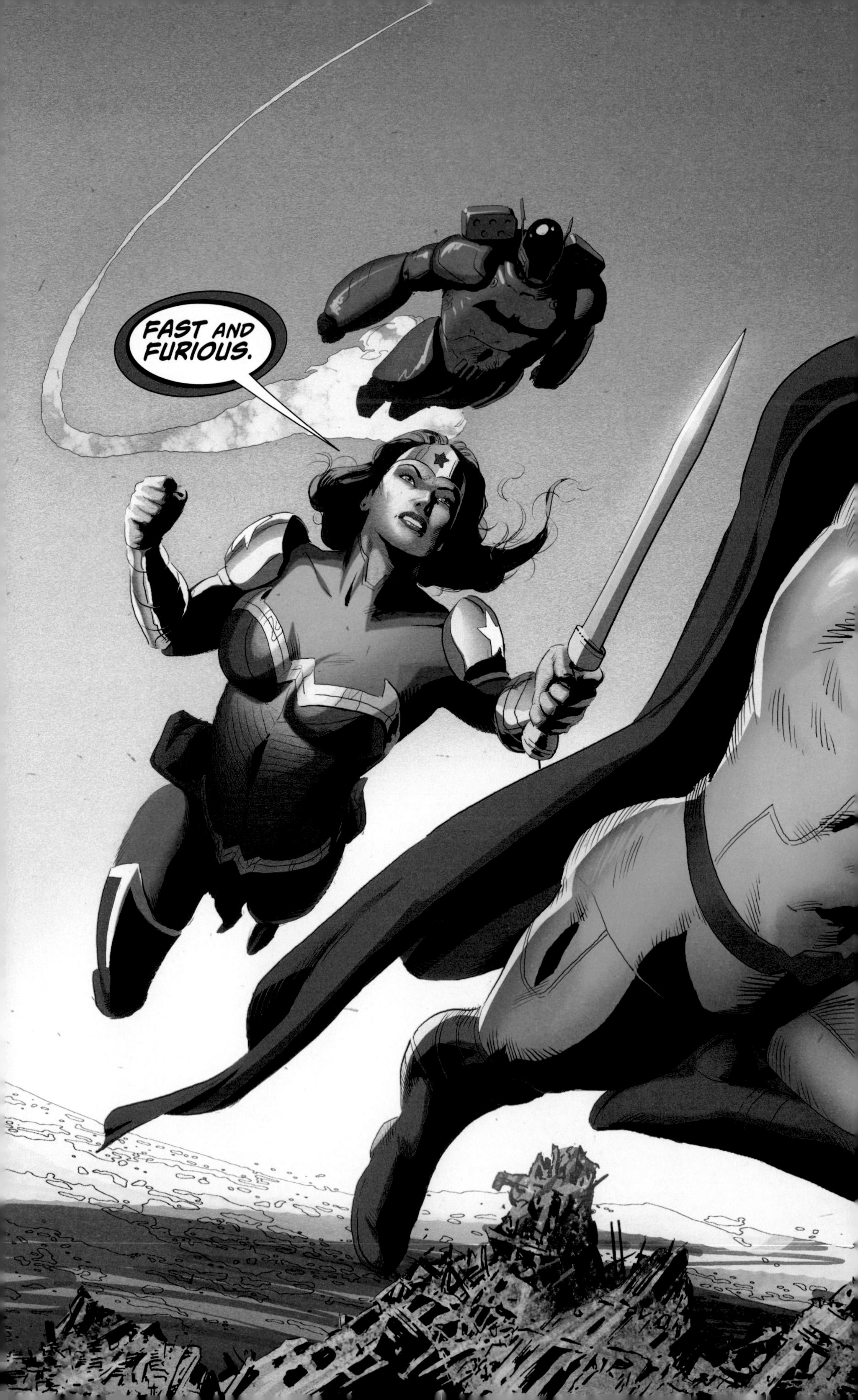
FAST AND FURIOUS.

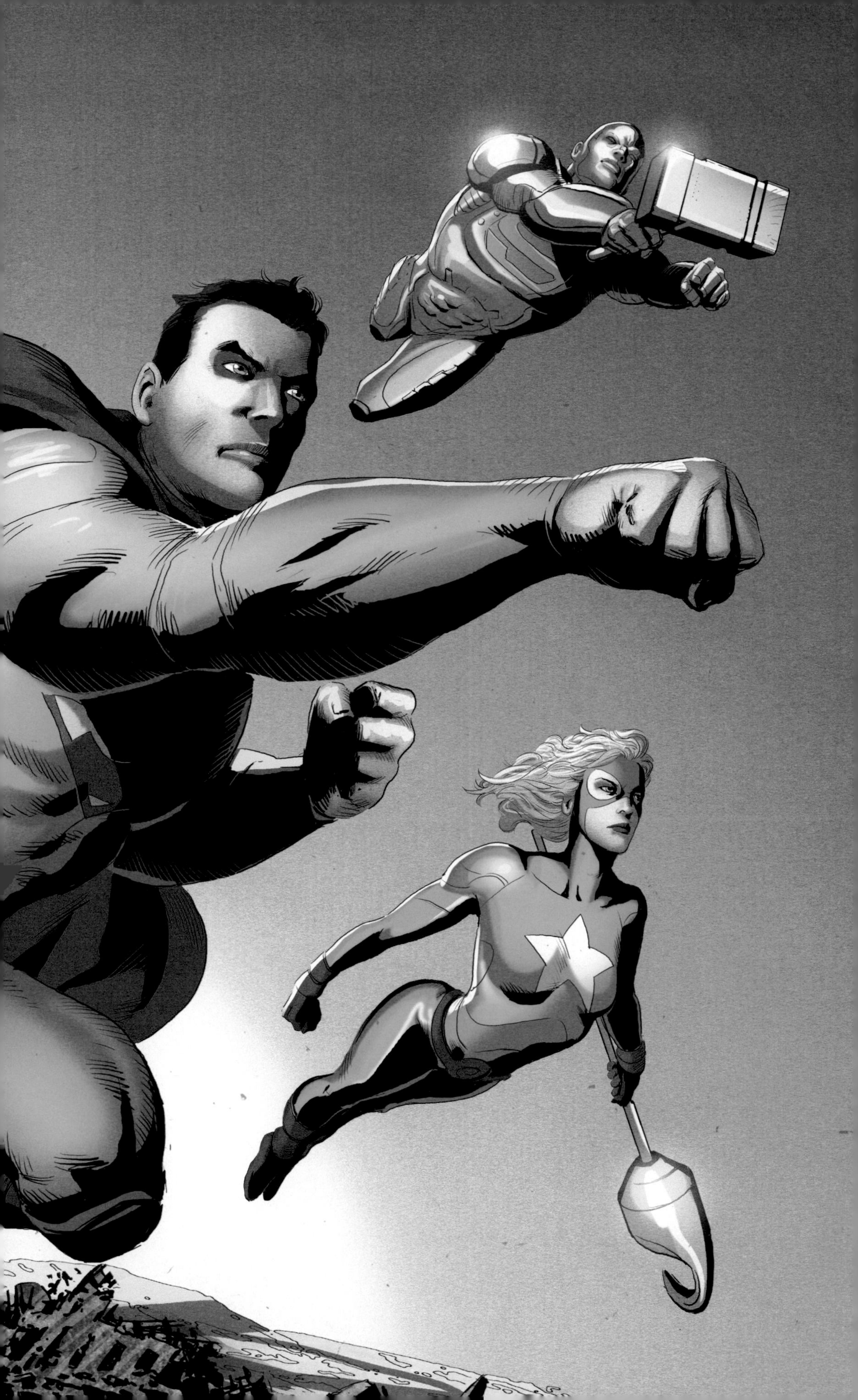

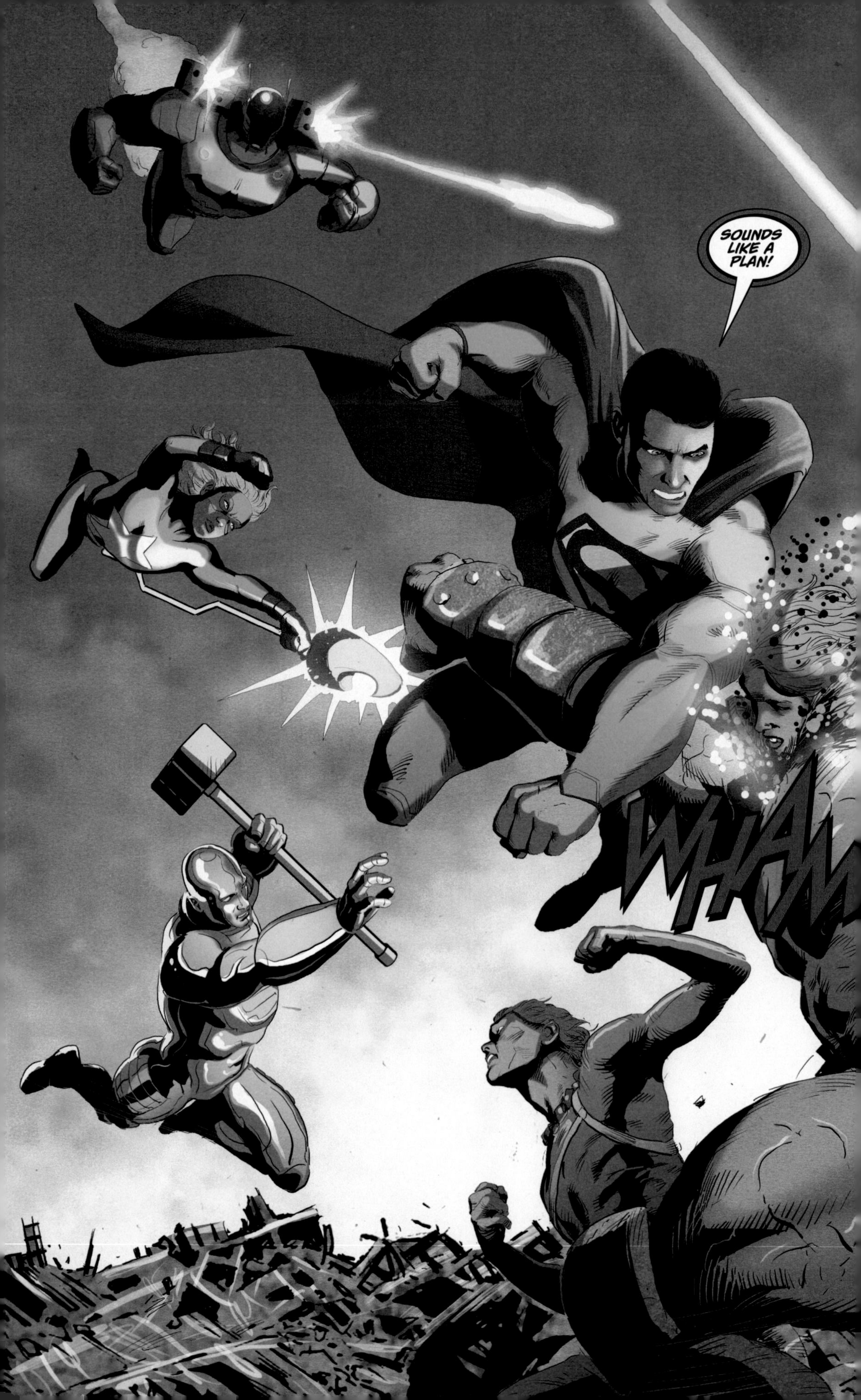
SOUNDS LIKE A PLAN!
WHAM

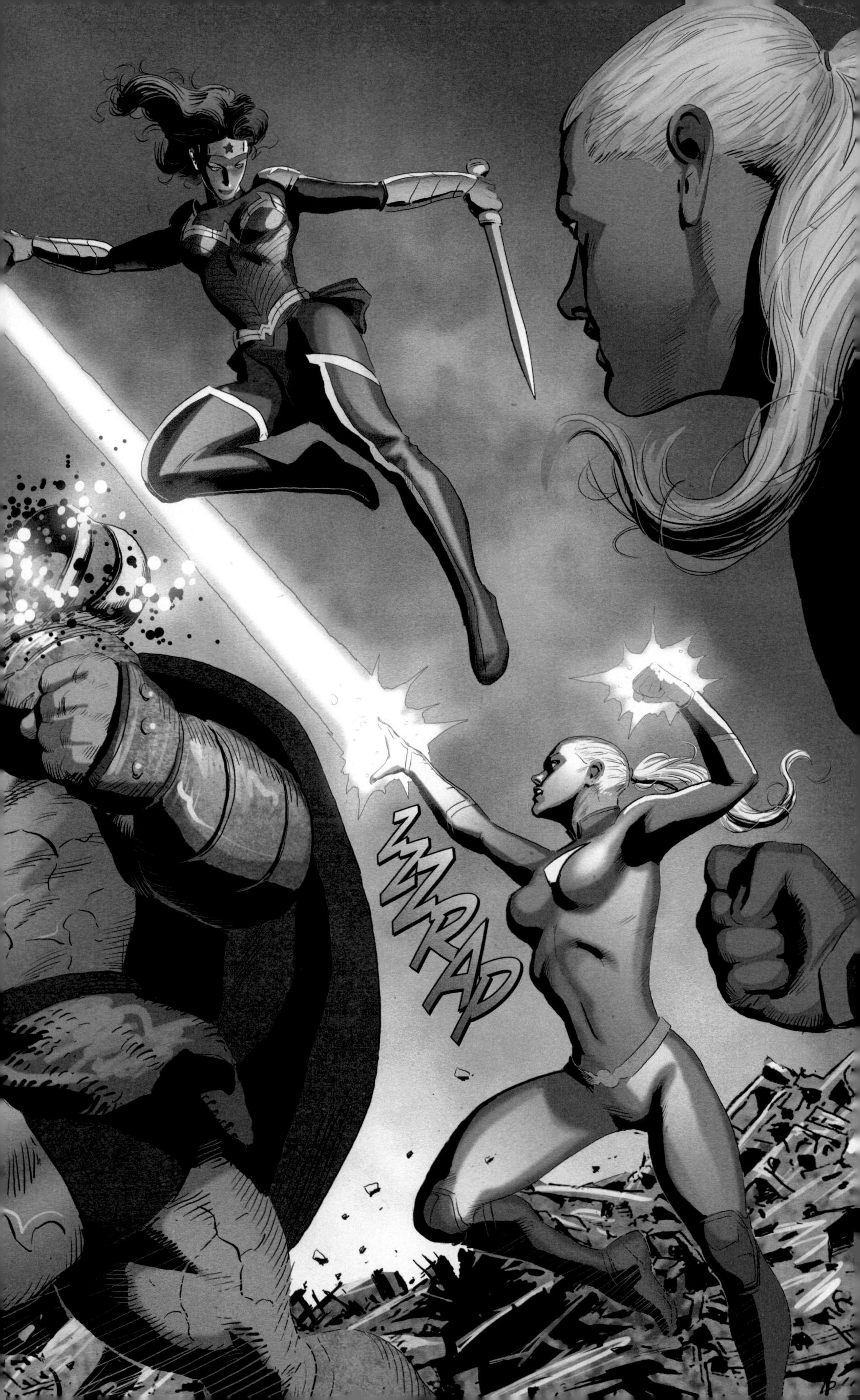
ZZZRAD

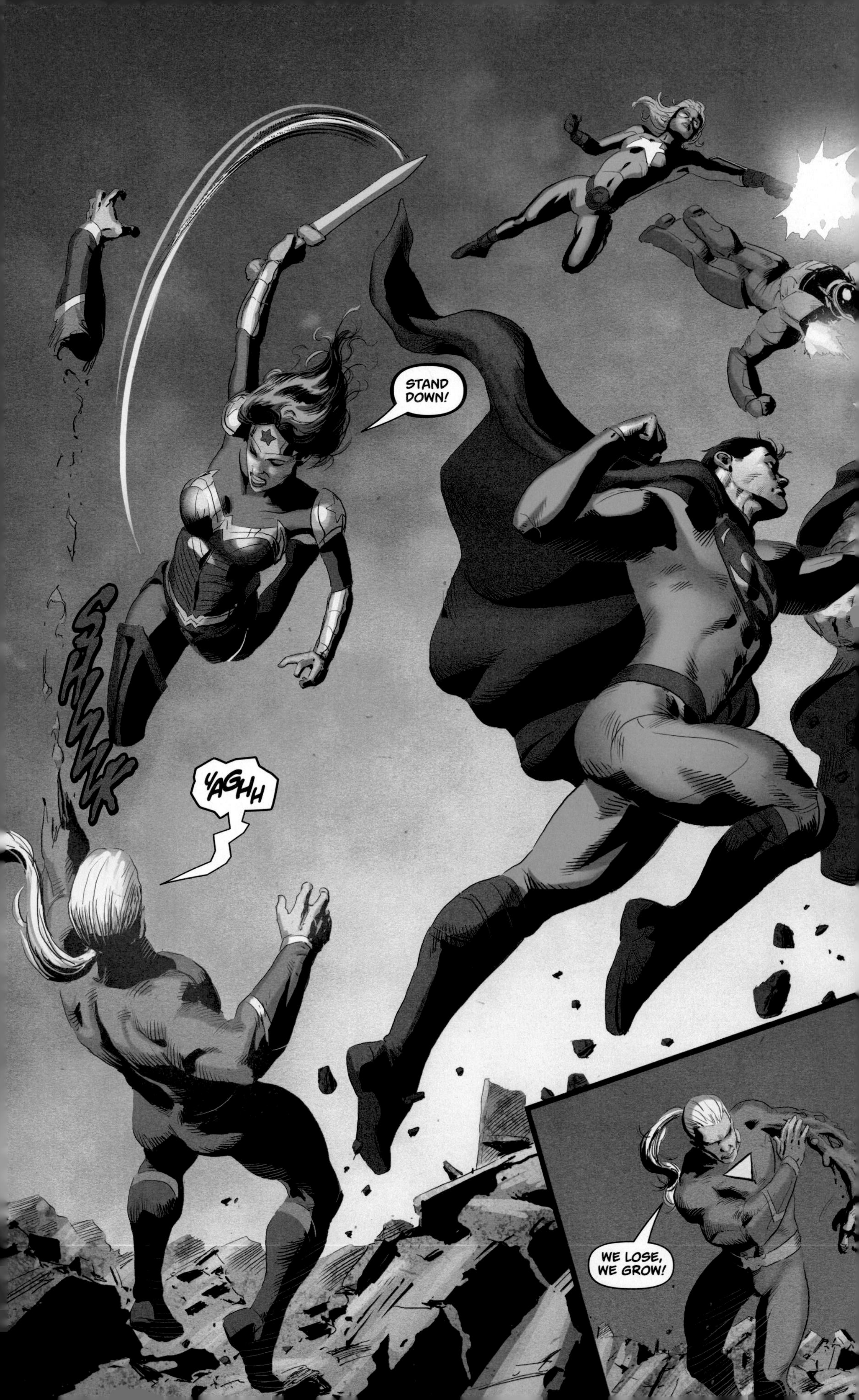
STAND DOWN!
SHUNK
YAGHH
WE LOSE, WE GROW!

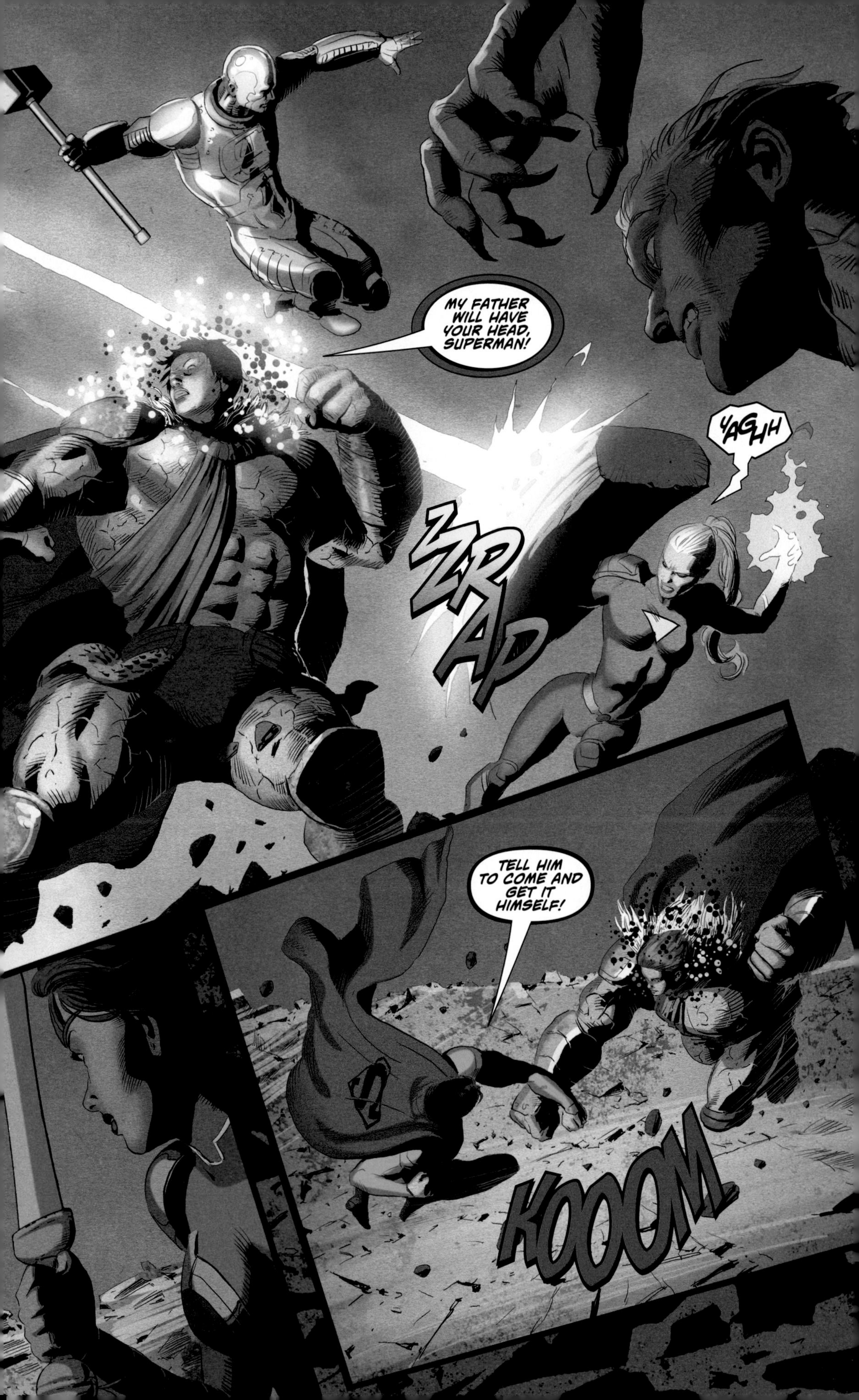
MY FATHER WILL HAVE YOUR HEAD, SUPERMAN!
YAGHH
ZZRAP
TELL HIM TO COME AND GET IT HIMSELF!
KOOOM

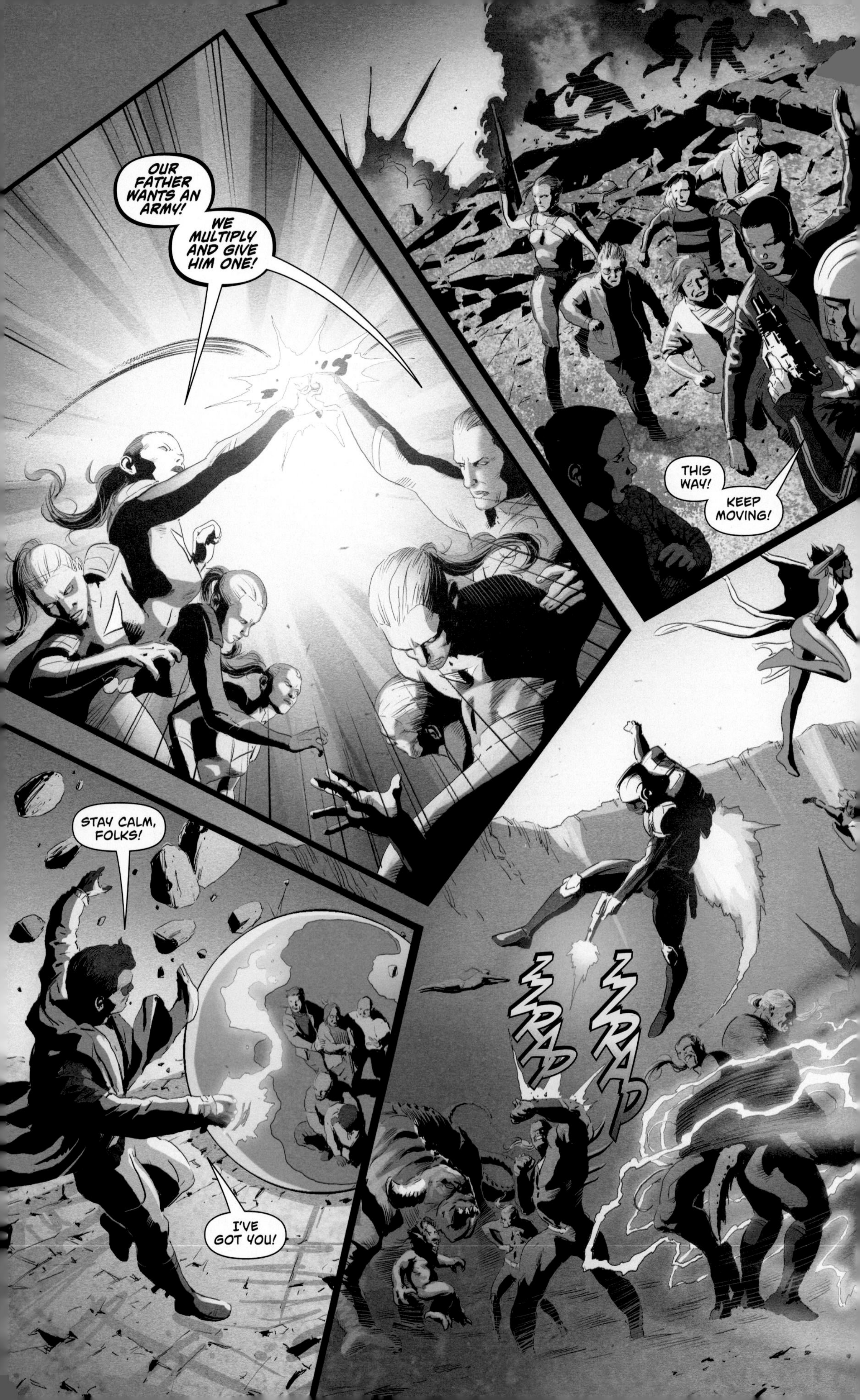
OUR FATHER WANTS AN ARMY!
WE MULTIPLY AND GIVE HIM ONE!
THIS WAY!
KEEP MOVING!
STAY CALM, FOLKS!
I'VE GOT YOU!
ZZRAP
ZZRAP

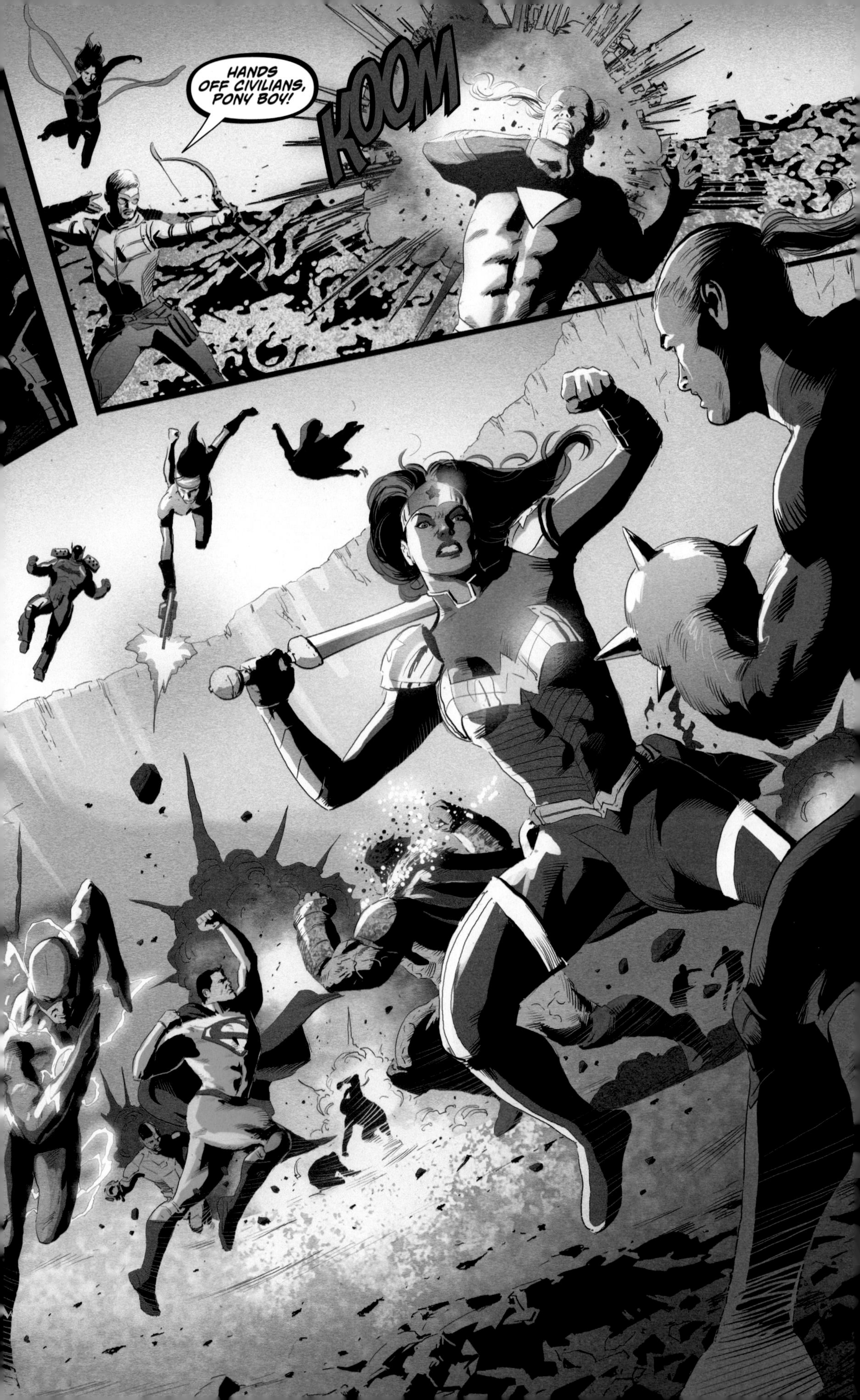
HANDS OFF CIVILIANS, PONY BOY!
KOOM

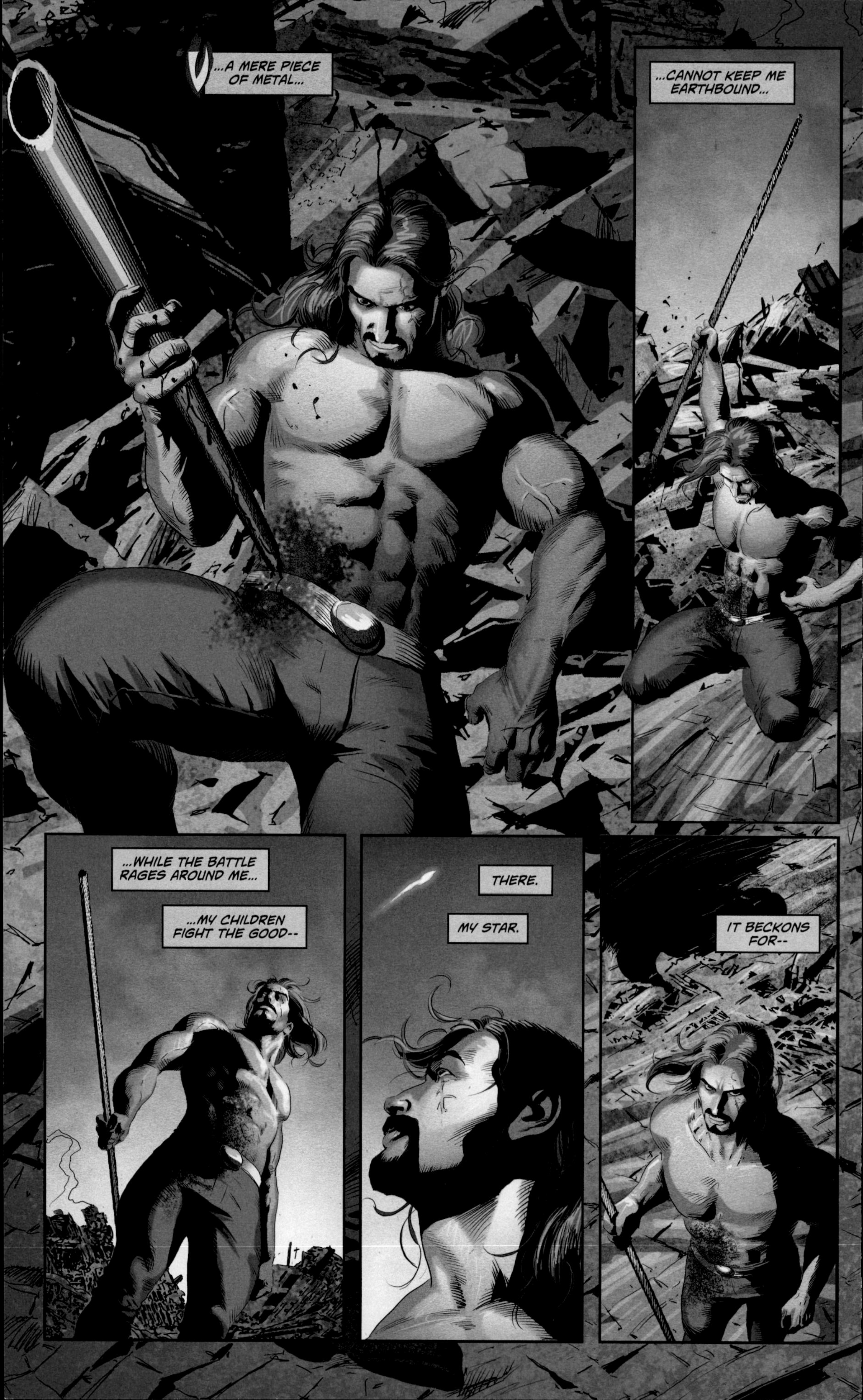
...A MERE PIECE OF METAL...
...CANNOT KEEP ME EARTHBOUND...
...WHILE THE BATTLE RAGES AROUND ME...
...MY CHILDREN FIGHT THE GOOD--
THERE.
MY STAR.
IT BECKONS FOR--

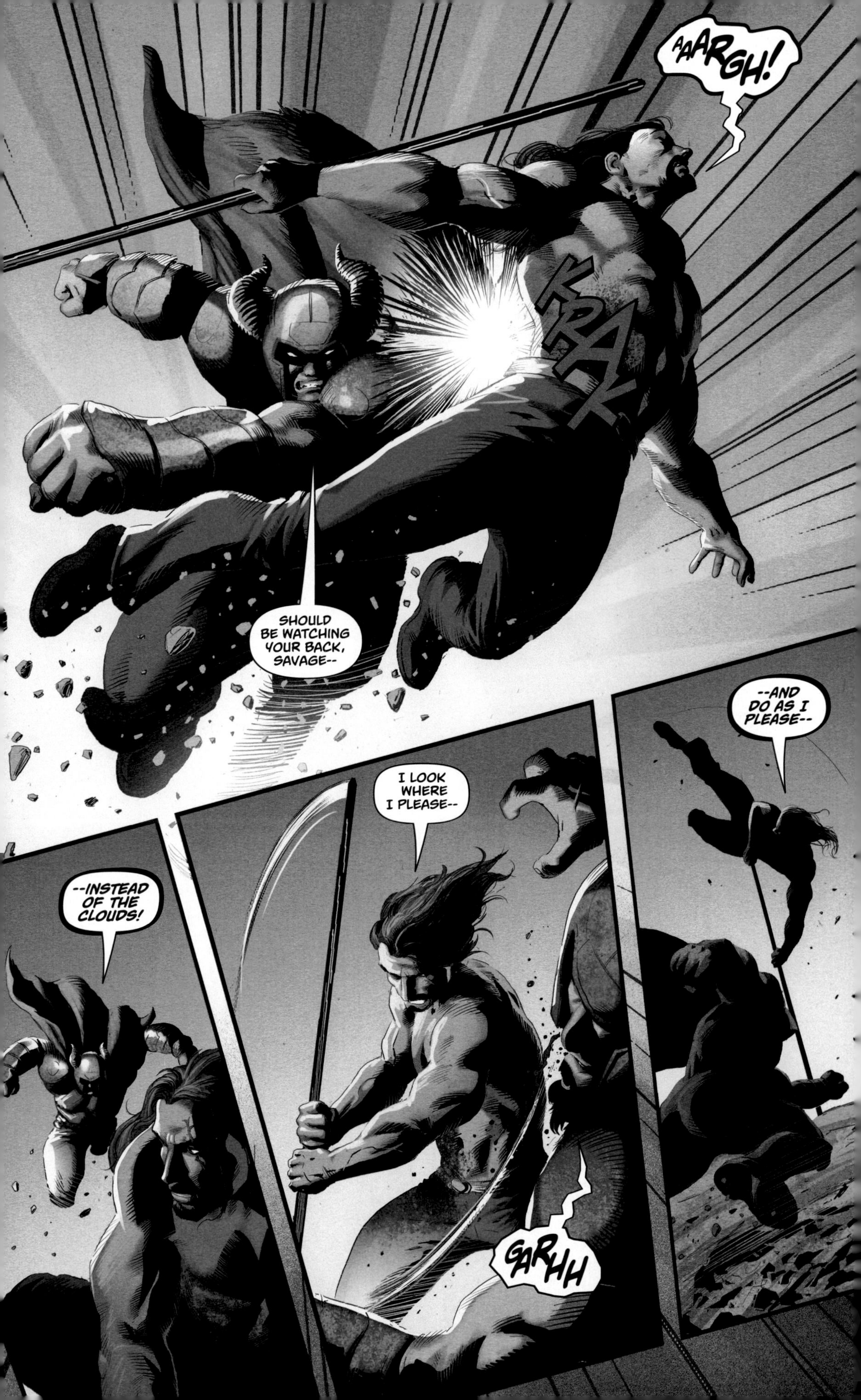
AAARGH!
KRAK
SHOULD BE WATCHING YOUR BACK, SAVAGE--
--INSTEAD OF THE CLOUDS!
I LOOK WHERE I PLEASE--
--AND DO AS I PLEASE--
GARHH

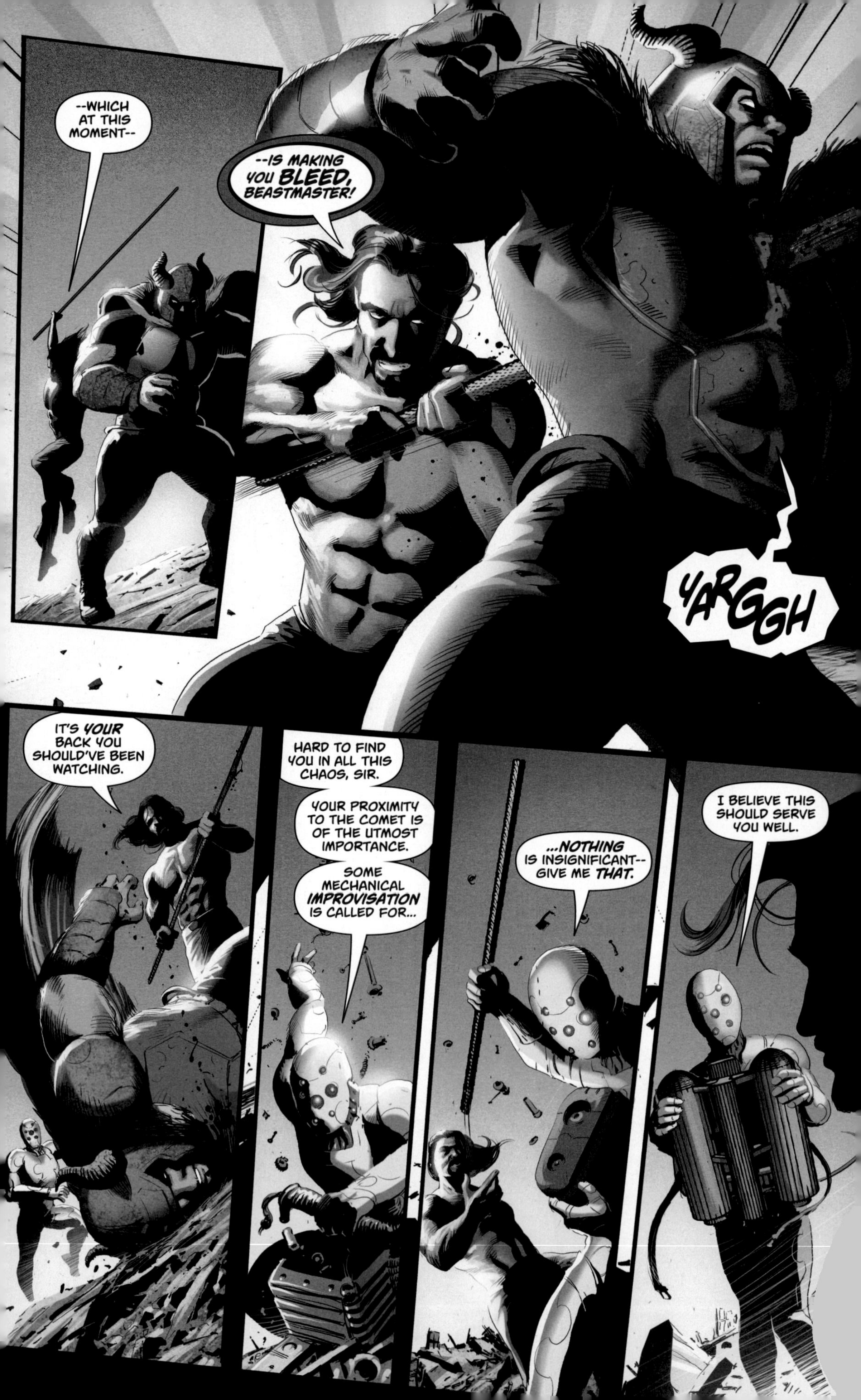
--WHICH AT THIS MOMENT--
--IS MAKING YOU BLEED, BEASTMASTER!
YARGGH
IT'S YOUR BACK YOU SHOULD'VE BEEN WATCHING.
HARD TO FIND YOU IN ALL THIS CHAOS, SIR.
YOUR PROXIMITY TO THE COMET IS OF THE UTMOST IMPORTANCE.
SOME MECHANICAL IMPROVISATION IS CALLED FOR...
...NOTHING IS INSIGNIFICANT--GIVE ME THAT.
I BELIEVE THIS SHOULD SERVE YOU WELL.

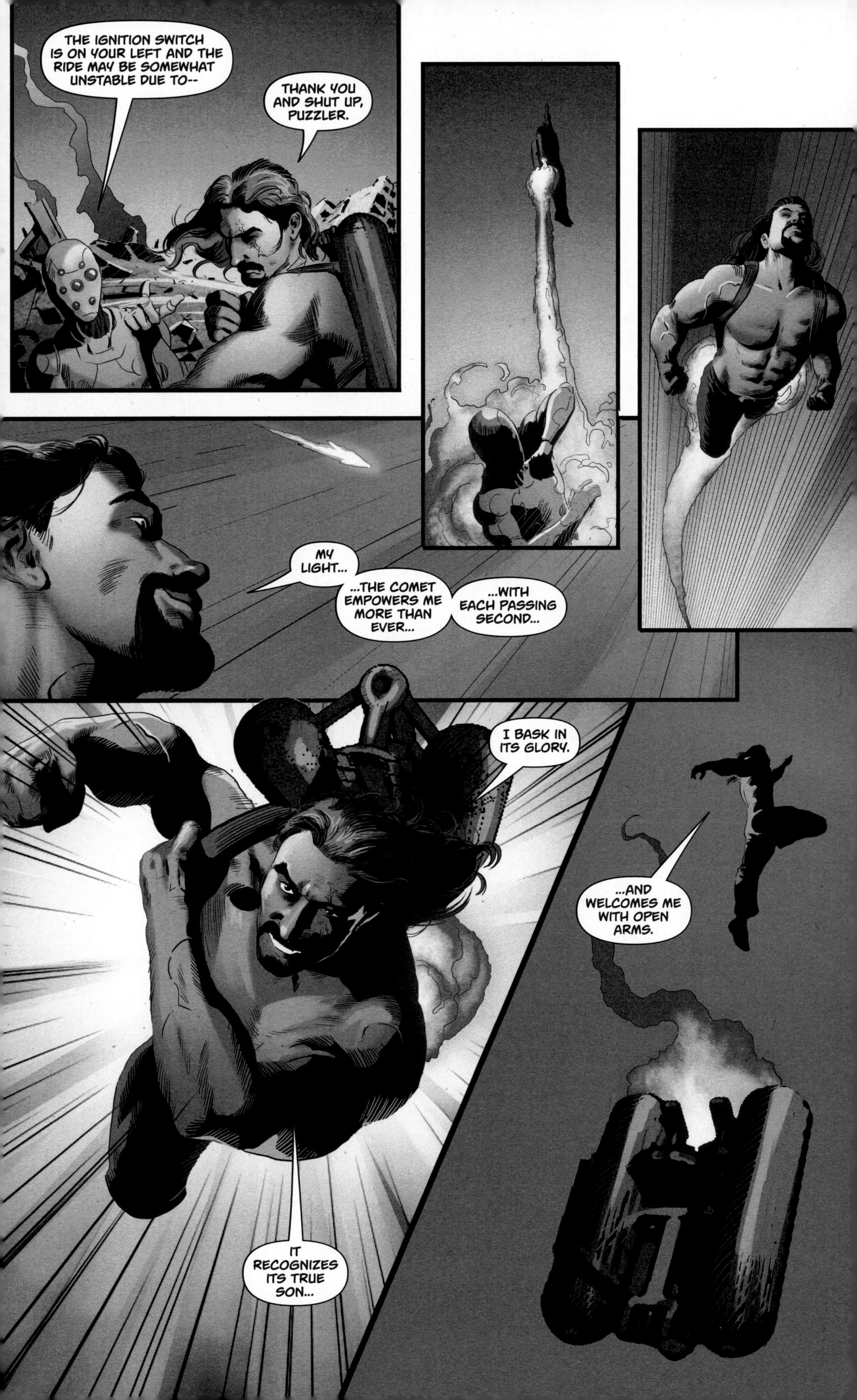
THE IGNITION SWITCH IS ON YOUR LEFT AND THE RIDE MAY BE SOMEWHAT UNSTABLE DUE TO--
THANK YOU AND SHUT UP, PUZZLER.
MY LIGHT...
...THE COMET EMPOWERS ME MORE THAN EVER...
...WITH EACH PASSING SECOND...
I BASK IN ITS GLORY.
IT RECOGNIZES ITS TRUE SON...
...AND WELCOMES ME WITH OPEN ARMS.

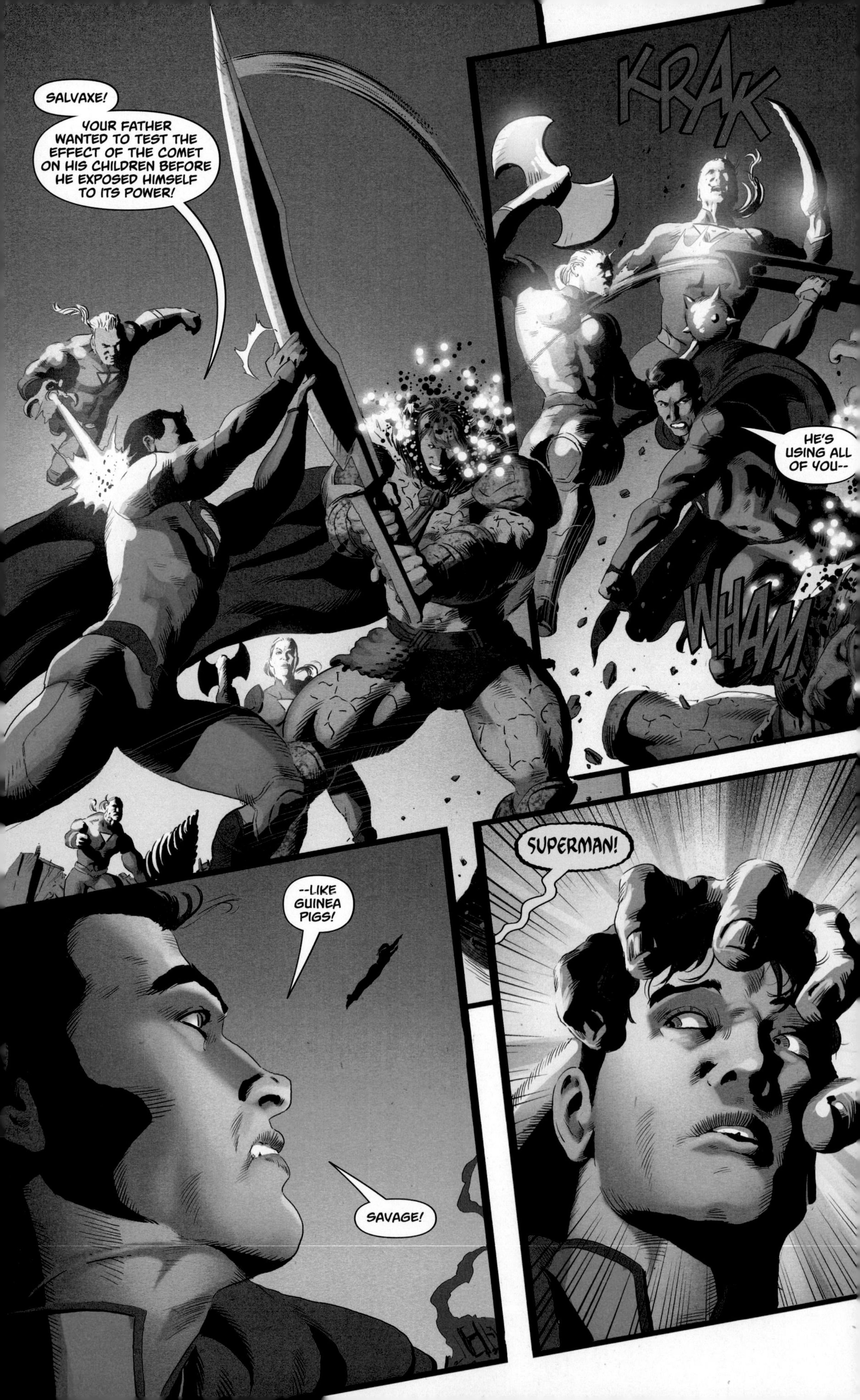
SALVAXE!
YOUR FATHER WANTED TO TEST THE EFFECT OF THE COMET ON HIS CHILDREN BEFORE HE EXPOSED HIMSELF TO ITS POWER!
KRAK
HE'S USING ALL OF YOU--
WHAM
--LIKE GUINEA PIGS!
SAVAGE!
SUPERMAN!

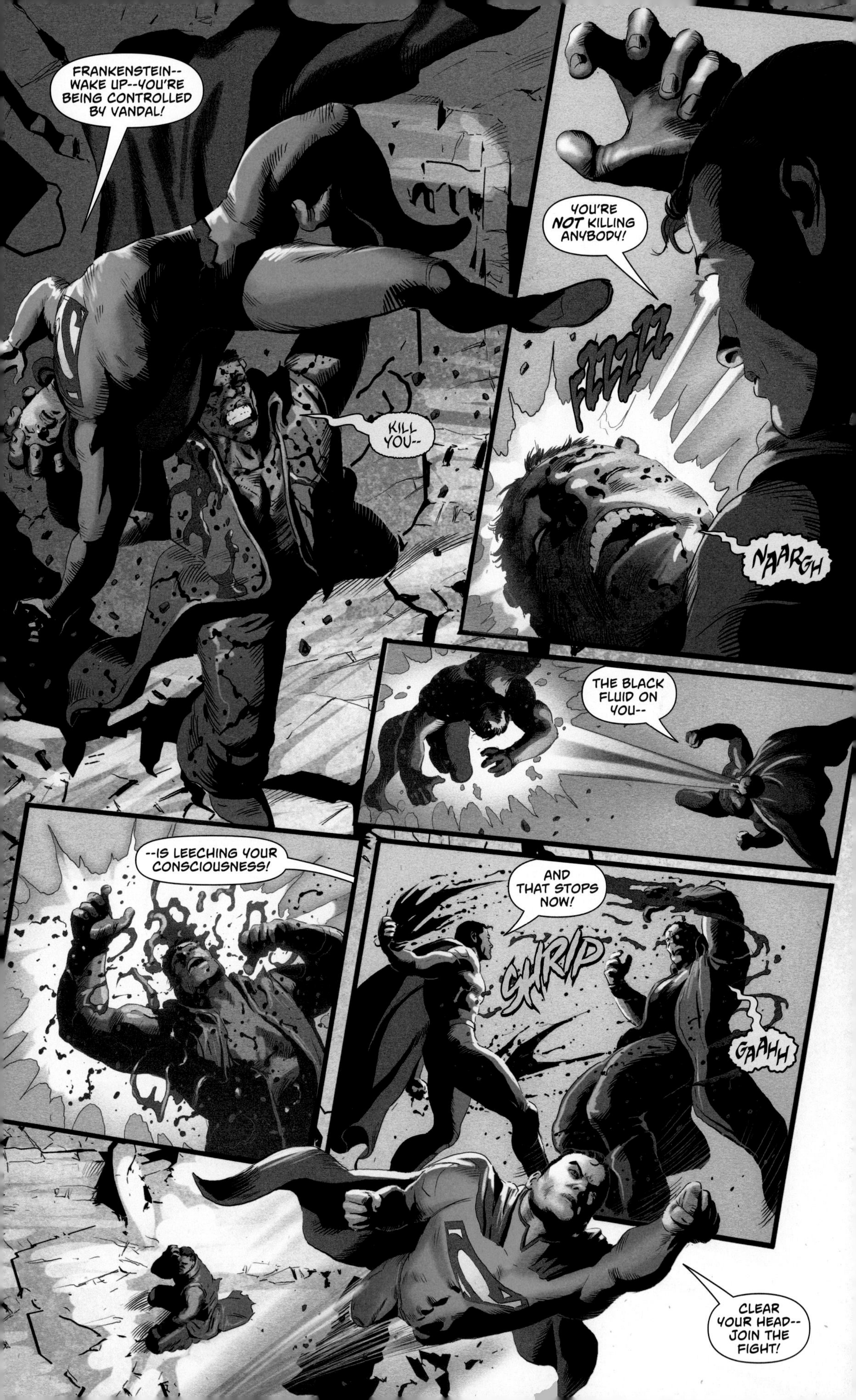
FRANKENSTEIN--
WAKE UP--YOU'RE
BEING CONTROLLED
BY VANDAL!
KILL
YOU--
YOU'RE
NOT KILLING
ANYBODY!
FZZZZ
NAARGH
THE BLACK
FLUID ON
YOU--
--IS LEECHING YOUR
CONSCIOUSNESS!
AND
THAT STOPS
NOW!
SHRIP
GAAHH
CLEAR
YOUR HEAD--
JOIN THE
FIGHT!

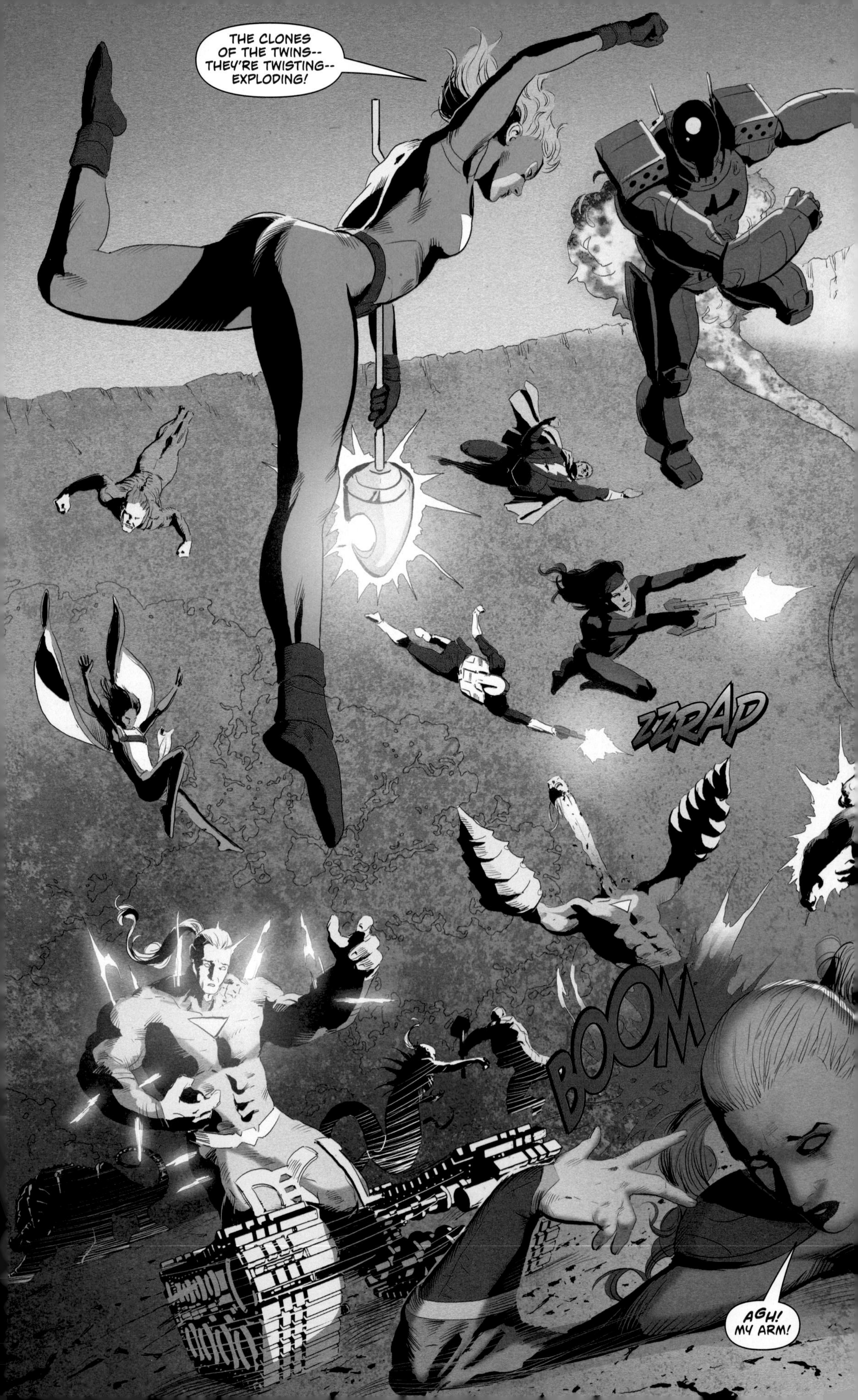
THE CLONES OF THE TWINS-- THEY'RE TWISTING-- EXPLODING!
ZZRAP
BOOM
AGH! MY ARM!

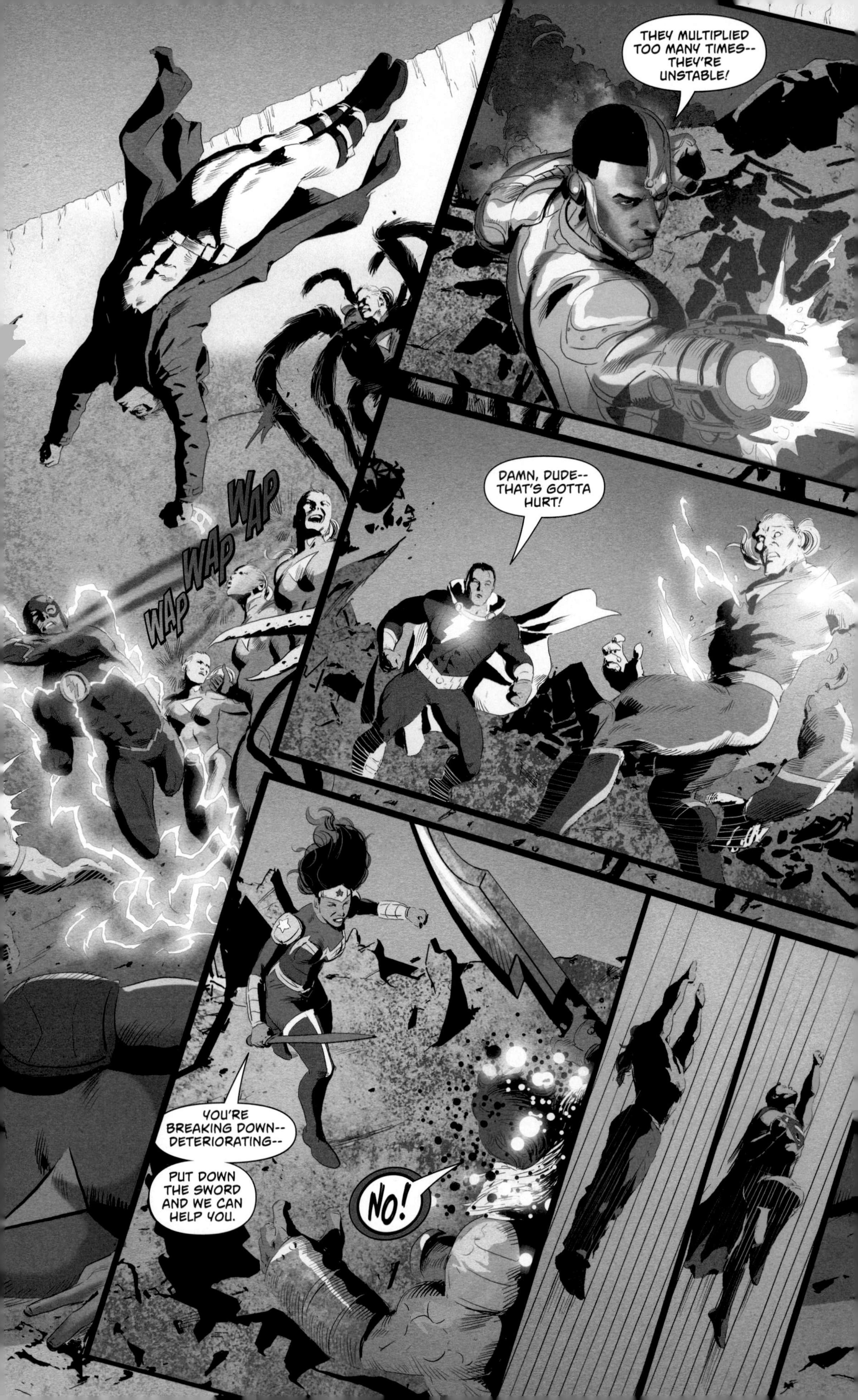

WAP
WAP
WAP
THEY MULTIPLIED TOO MANY TIMES-- THEY'RE UNSTABLE!
DAMN, DUDE-- THAT'S GOTTA HURT!
YOU'RE BREAKING DOWN-- DETERIORATING--
PUT DOWN THE SWORD AND WE CAN HELP YOU.
NO!

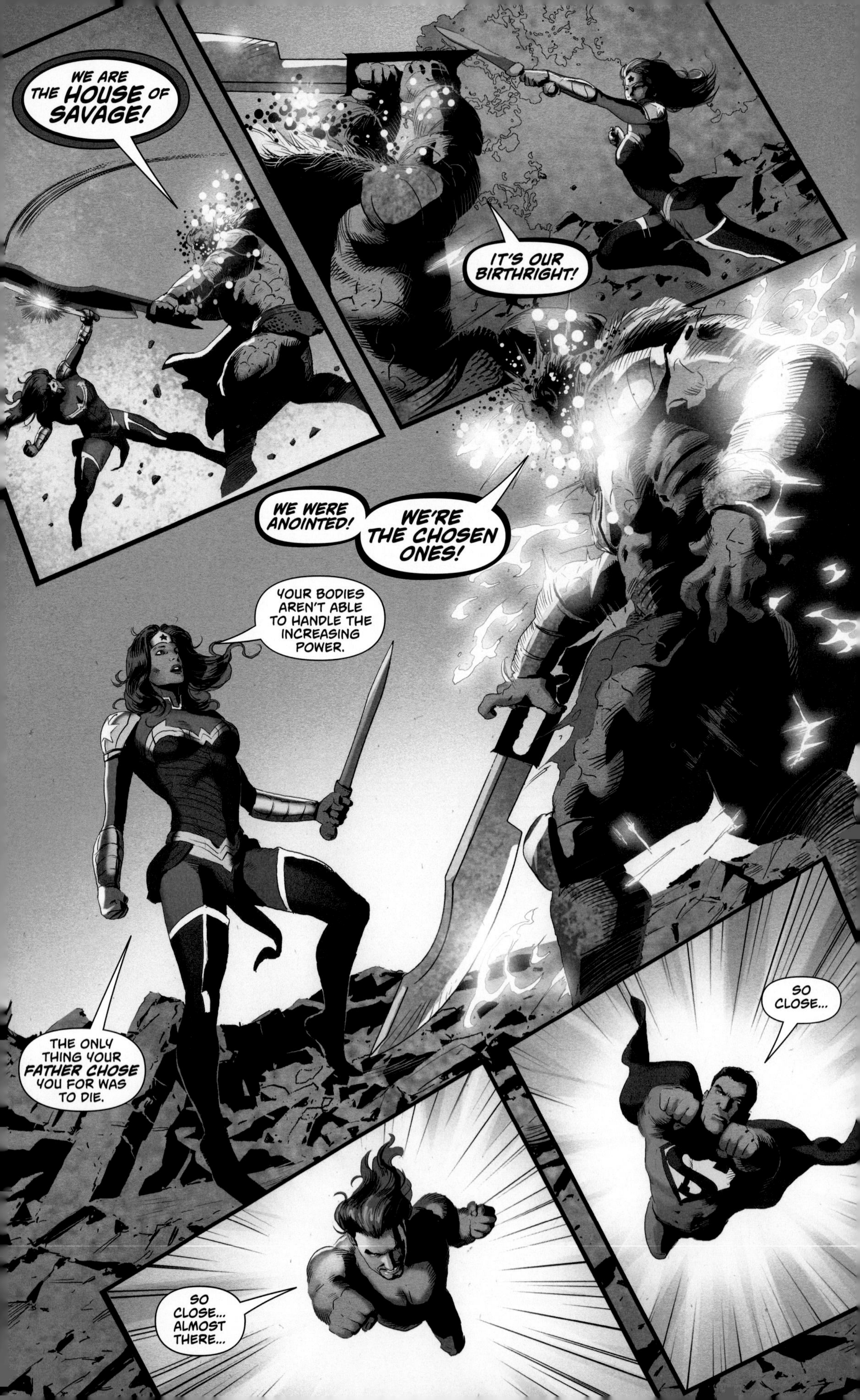
WE ARE THE HOUSE OF SAVAGE!
IT'S OUR BIRTHRIGHT!
WE WERE ANOINTED!
WE'RE THE CHOSEN ONES!
YOUR BODIES AREN'T ABLE TO HANDLE THE INCREASING POWER.
THE ONLY THING YOUR FATHER CHOSE YOU FOR WAS TO DIE.
SO CLOSE...
SO CLOSE... ALMOST THERE...

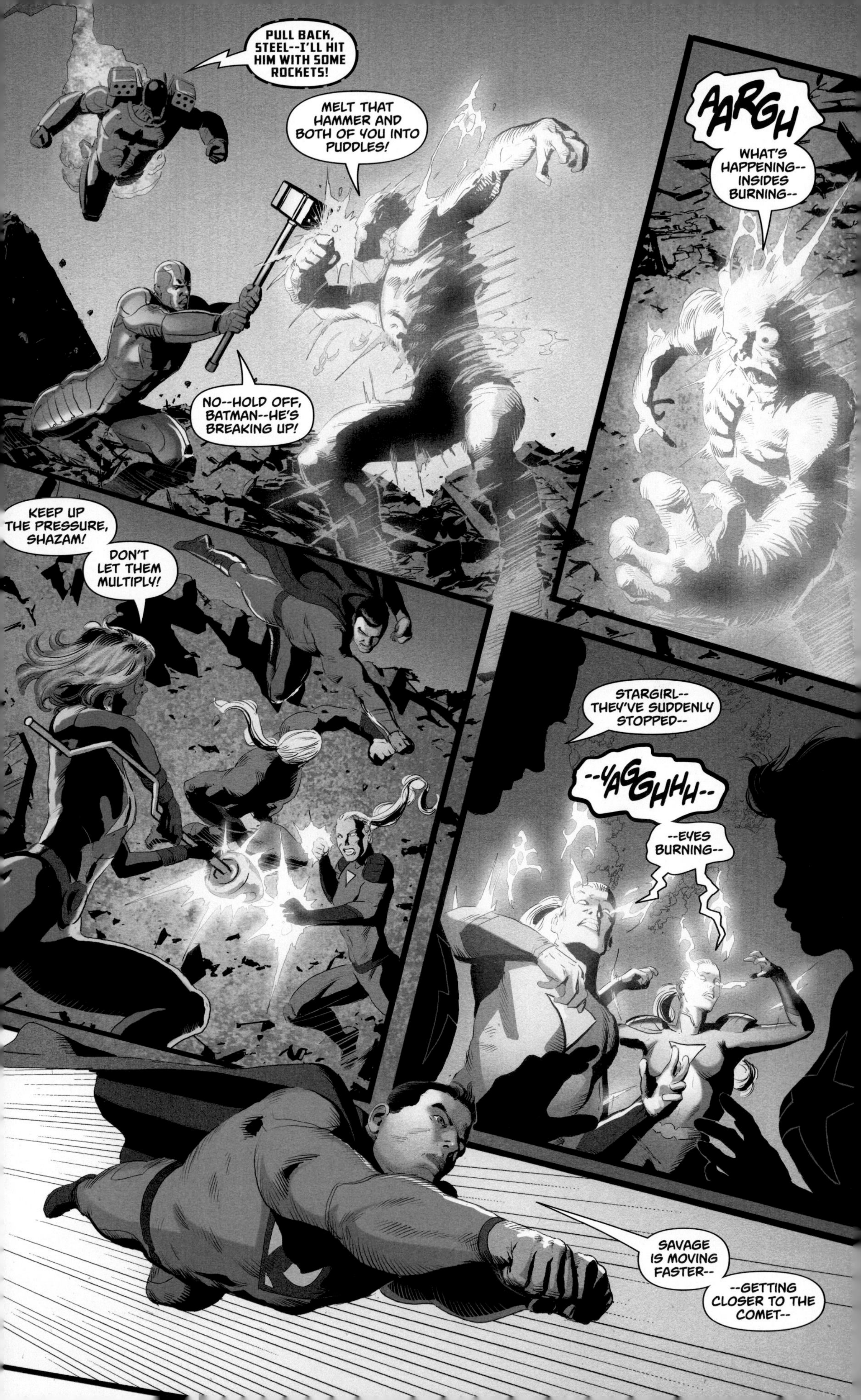
PULL BACK, STEEL--I'LL HIT HIM WITH SOME ROCKETS!
MELT THAT HAMMER AND BOTH OF YOU INTO PUDDLES!
NO--HOLD OFF, BATMAN--HE'S BREAKING UP!
AARGH
WHAT'S HAPPENING-- INSIDES BURNING--
KEEP UP THE PRESSURE, SHAZAM!
DON'T LET THEM MULTIPLY!
STARGIRL-- THEY'VE SUDDENLY STOPPED--
--YAGGHHH--
--EYES BURNING--
SAVAGE IS MOVING FASTER--
--GETTING CLOSER TO THE COMET--

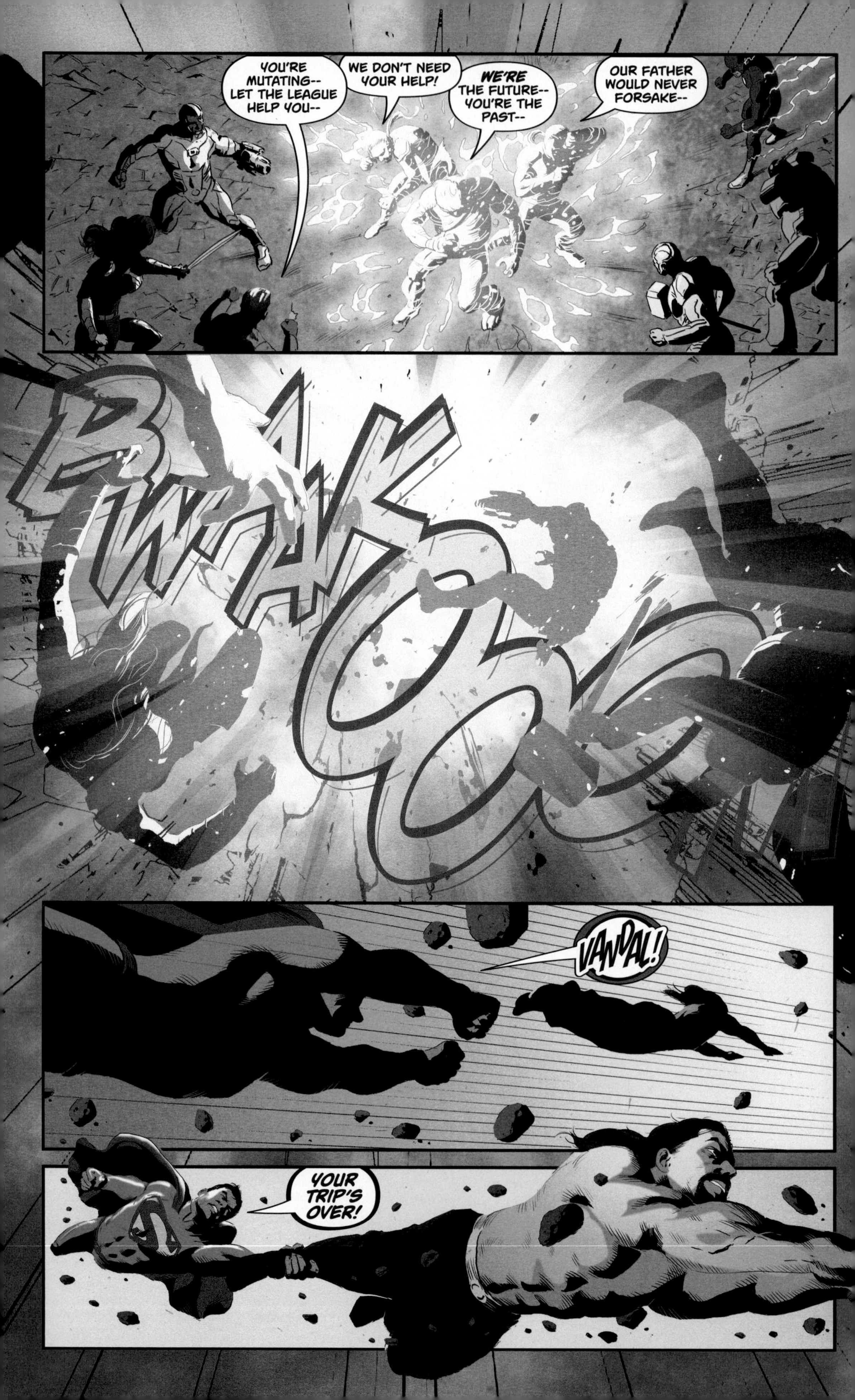
YOU'RE MUTATING-- LET THE LEAGUE HELP YOU--
WE DON'T NEED YOUR HELP!
WE'RE THE FUTURE-- YOU'RE THE PAST--
OUR FATHER WOULD NEVER FORSAKE--
BWAKOOM
VANDAL!
YOUR TRIP'S OVER!

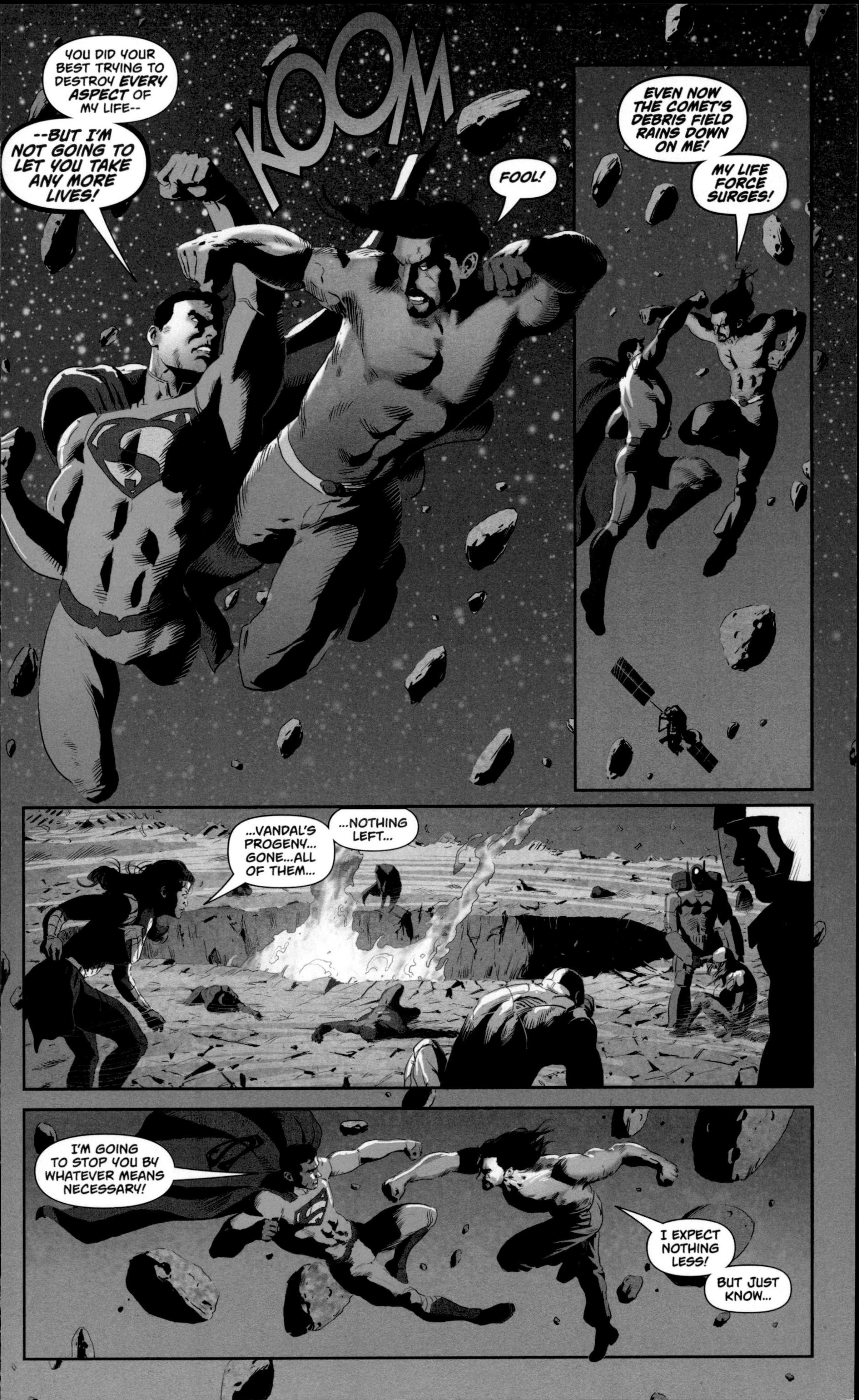

YOU DID YOUR BEST TRYING TO DESTROY EVERY ASPECT OF MY LIFE--
--BUT I'M NOT GOING TO LET YOU TAKE ANY MORE LIVES!
KOOM
FOOL!
EVEN NOW THE COMET'S DEBRIS FIELD RAINS DOWN ON ME!
MY LIFE FORCE SURGES!
...VANDAL'S PROGENY... GONE...ALL OF THEM...
...NOTHING LEFT...
I'M GOING TO STOP YOU BY WHATEVER MEANS NECESSARY!
I EXPECT NOTHING LESS!
BUT JUST KNOW...

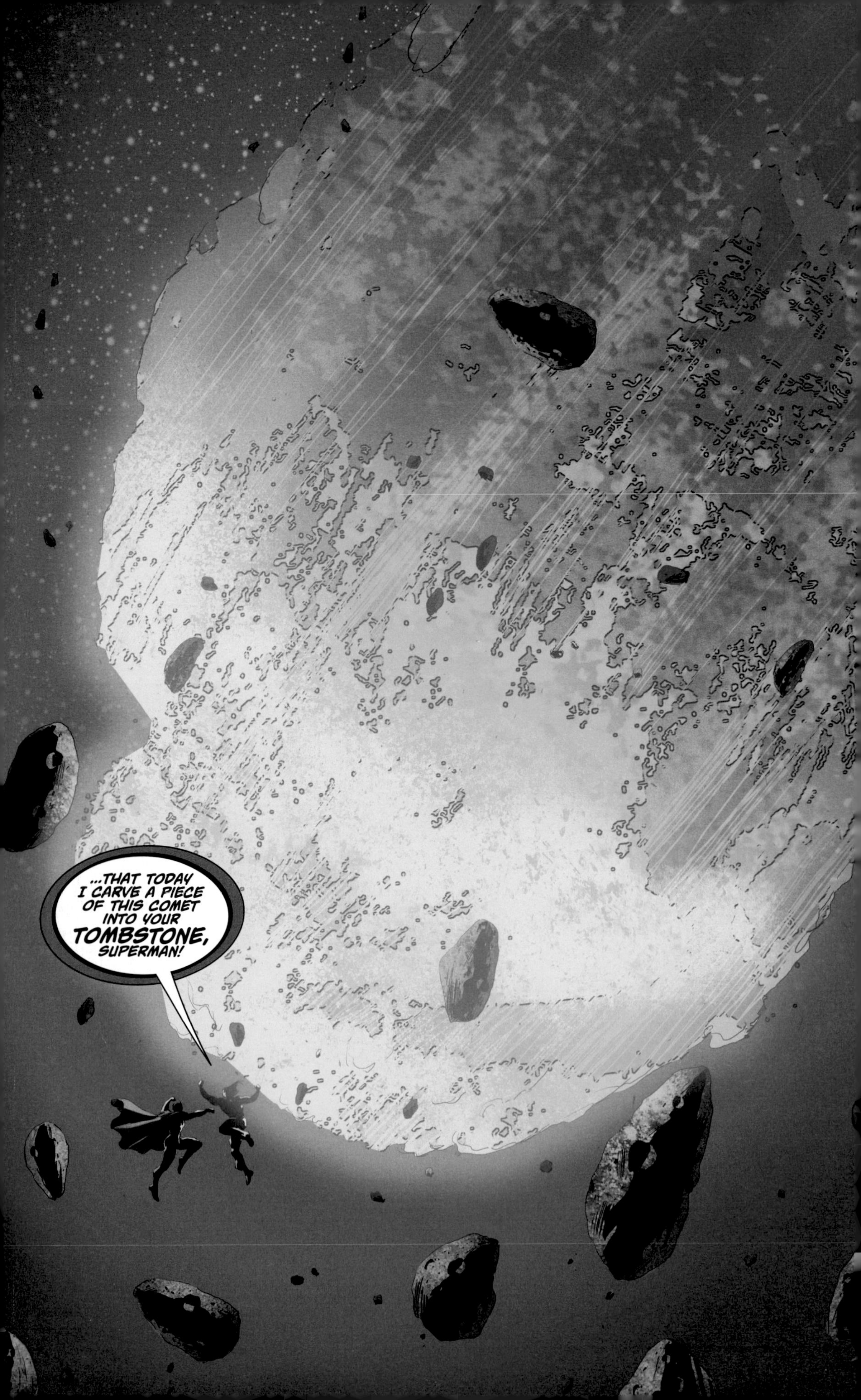
...THAT TODAY I CARVE A PIECE OF THIS COMET INTO YOUR TOMBSTONE, SUPERMAN!

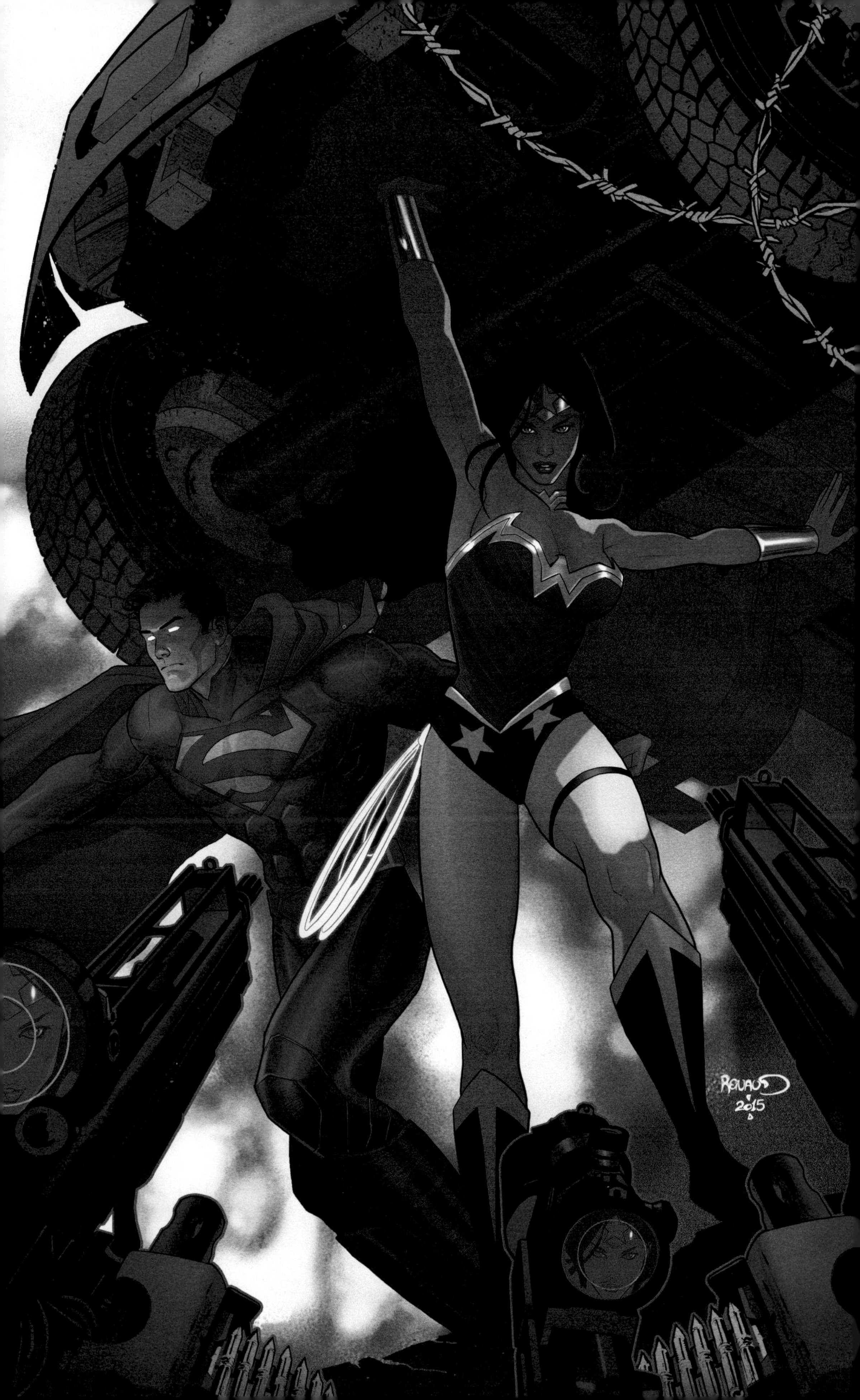
RENAUD
2015

THE FINAL DAYS OF SUPERMAN PART 4: LAST KISS
PETER J. TOMASI writer ED BENES artist ALEX SINCLAIR colorist ROB LEIGH letterer cover by PAUL RENAUD

Previously,
in SUPERMAN #50-51, BATMAN/SUPERMAN #31
and ACTION COMICS #51...

Resisting visions and an offer to "benefit" Earth by serving under Vandal
Savage, Superman destroys the immortal's comet, the source of his eternal
power, and sends his adversary hurtling out into space. Unfortunately, the Man
of Steel's greatest victory has come at the highest price. Numerous medical
scans inside his Fortress of Solitude reveal that his exposure to A.R.G.U.S.'s
Kryptonite chamber, plus recent battles inside Apokolips' fire pits and against
the Kryptonian deity Rao, have taken their toll. Krypton's last son is dying.

While Kal-El begins sharing his prognosis with loved ones, in Minnesota
escaped convict Denny Swan is unexpectedly transformed by the Man of
Steel's residual solar energy flares into a "Solar-Superman." Believing himself
to be Superman, the unstable Swan initially behaves in a heroic—if uneasy—
manner. However, a disastrous attempt to take over the duties of "Clark Kent"
at the Daily Planet results in casualties, until Lois Lane manages to catch Swan
off guard and subdue him.

Traveling to Gotham City, the real Man of Steel requests Batman's help in
locating his missing cousin Kara, a.k.a. Supergirl. After fending off an attack
by brutish embodiments of the Chinese Zodiac, one of which manages to draw
Superman's blood, the world's finest duo track Supergirl down to National
City and a ghost site for the D.E.O., where she's been undergoing tests to
recoup the missing powers that Savage had stolen from her.

Superman brings Kara to the Arctic Circle, where he tells her the Fortress is
now her sanctuary as the last surviving member of the House of El. He asks
her to take care of Earth when he's gone and, with a heavy heart, Supergirl
agrees. But as the two start to exit the Fortress, they encounter a visibly upset
Wonder Woman...

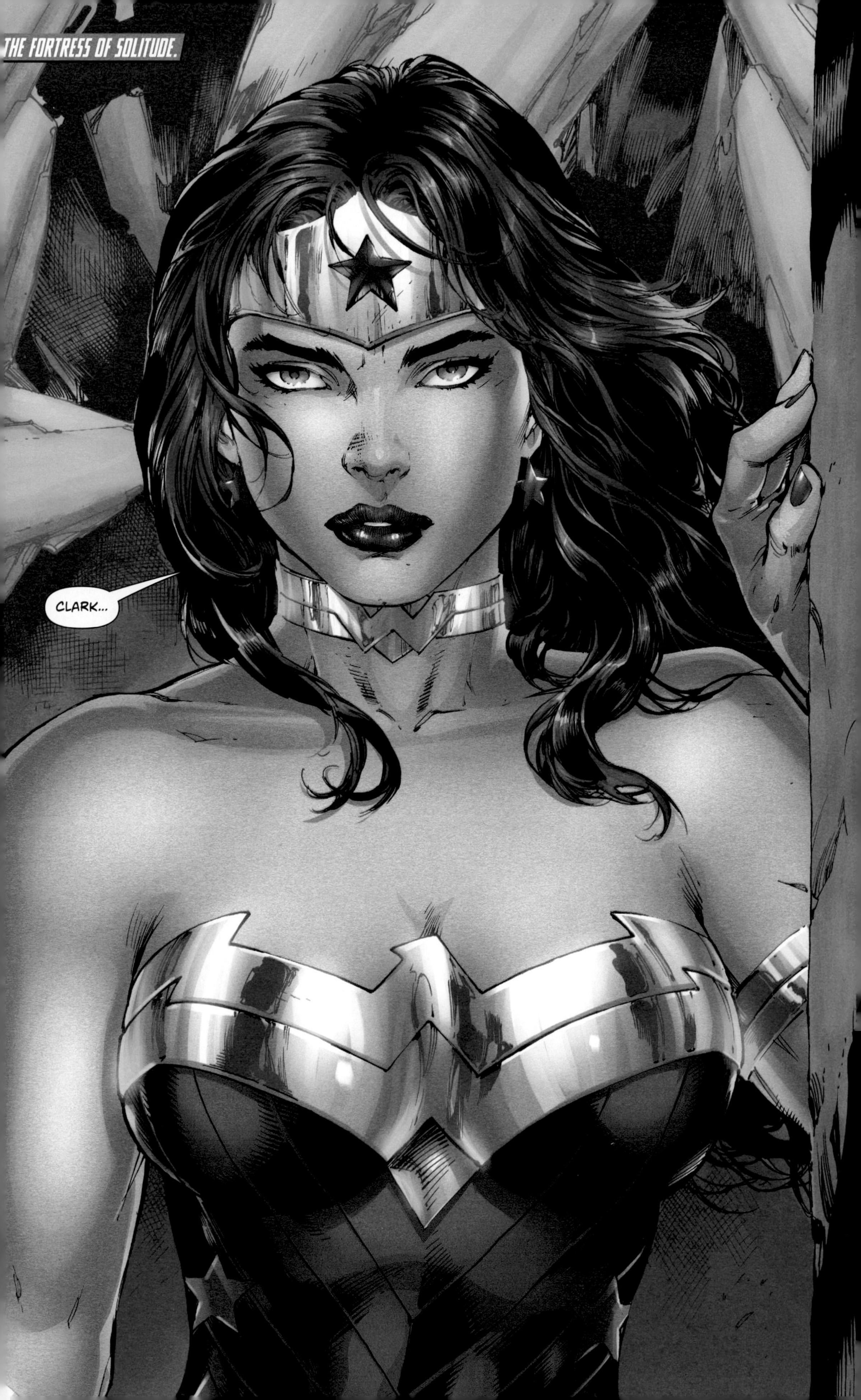
THE FORTRESS OF SOLITUDE.
CLARK...

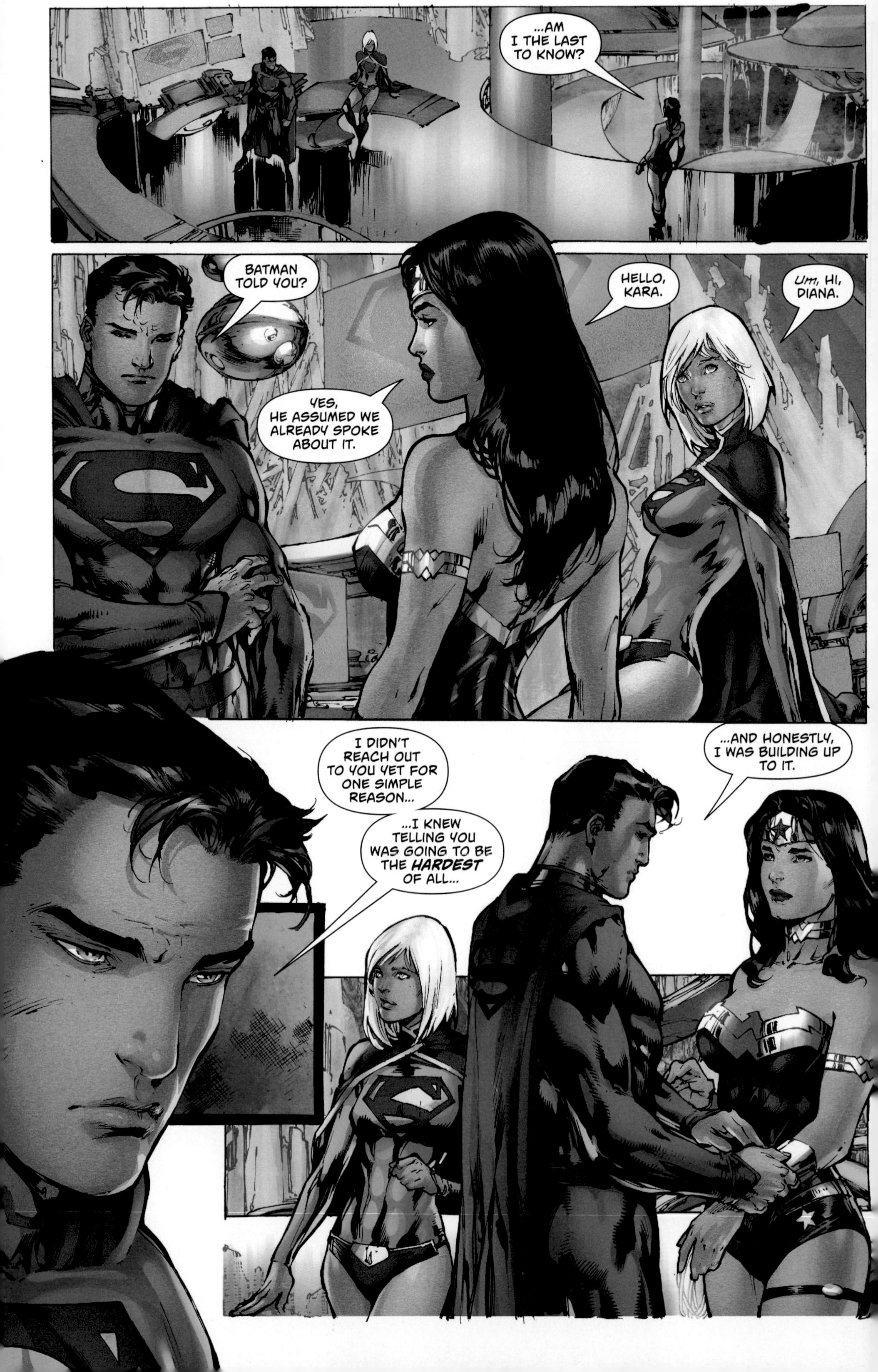
...AM I THE LAST TO KNOW?
BATMAN TOLD YOU?
YES, HE ASSUMED WE ALREADY SPOKE ABOUT IT.
HELLO, KARA.
Um, HI, DIANA.
I DIDN'T REACH OUT TO YOU YET FOR ONE SIMPLE REASON...
...I KNEW TELLING YOU WAS GOING TO BE THE HARDEST OF ALL...
...AND HONESTLY, I WAS BUILDING UP TO IT.

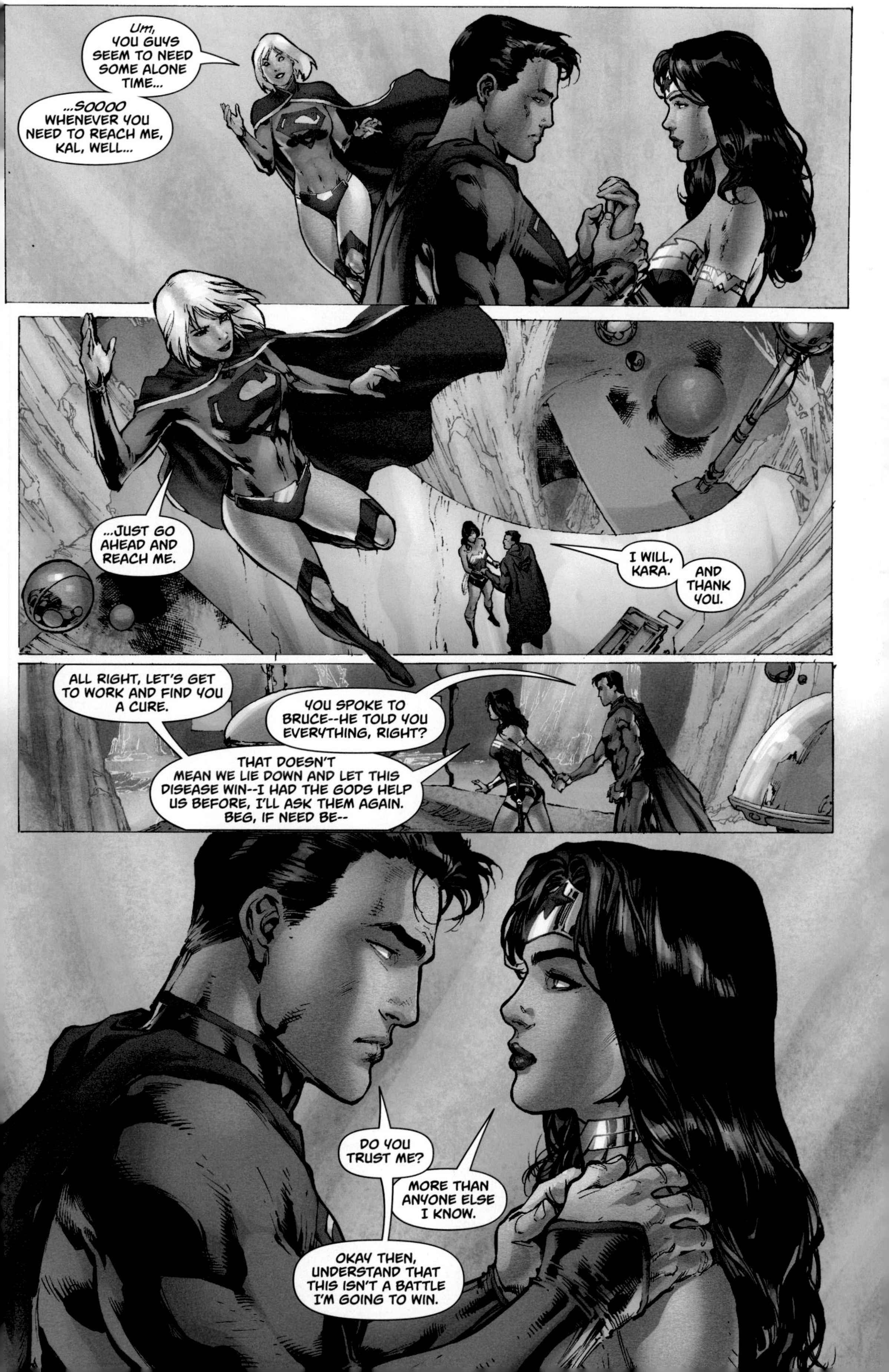
Um, YOU GUYS SEEM TO NEED SOME ALONE TIME...
...SOOOO WHENEVER YOU NEED TO REACH ME, KAL, WELL...
...JUST GO AHEAD AND REACH ME.
I WILL, KARA.
AND THANK YOU.
ALL RIGHT, LET'S GET TO WORK AND FIND YOU A CURE.
YOU SPOKE TO BRUCE--HE TOLD YOU EVERYTHING, RIGHT?
THAT DOESN'T MEAN WE LIE DOWN AND LET THIS DISEASE WIN--I HAD THE GODS HELP US BEFORE, I'LL ASK THEM AGAIN. BEG, IF NEED BE--
DO YOU TRUST ME?
MORE THAN ANYONE ELSE I KNOW.
OKAY THEN, UNDERSTAND THAT THIS ISN'T A BATTLE I'M GOING TO WIN.

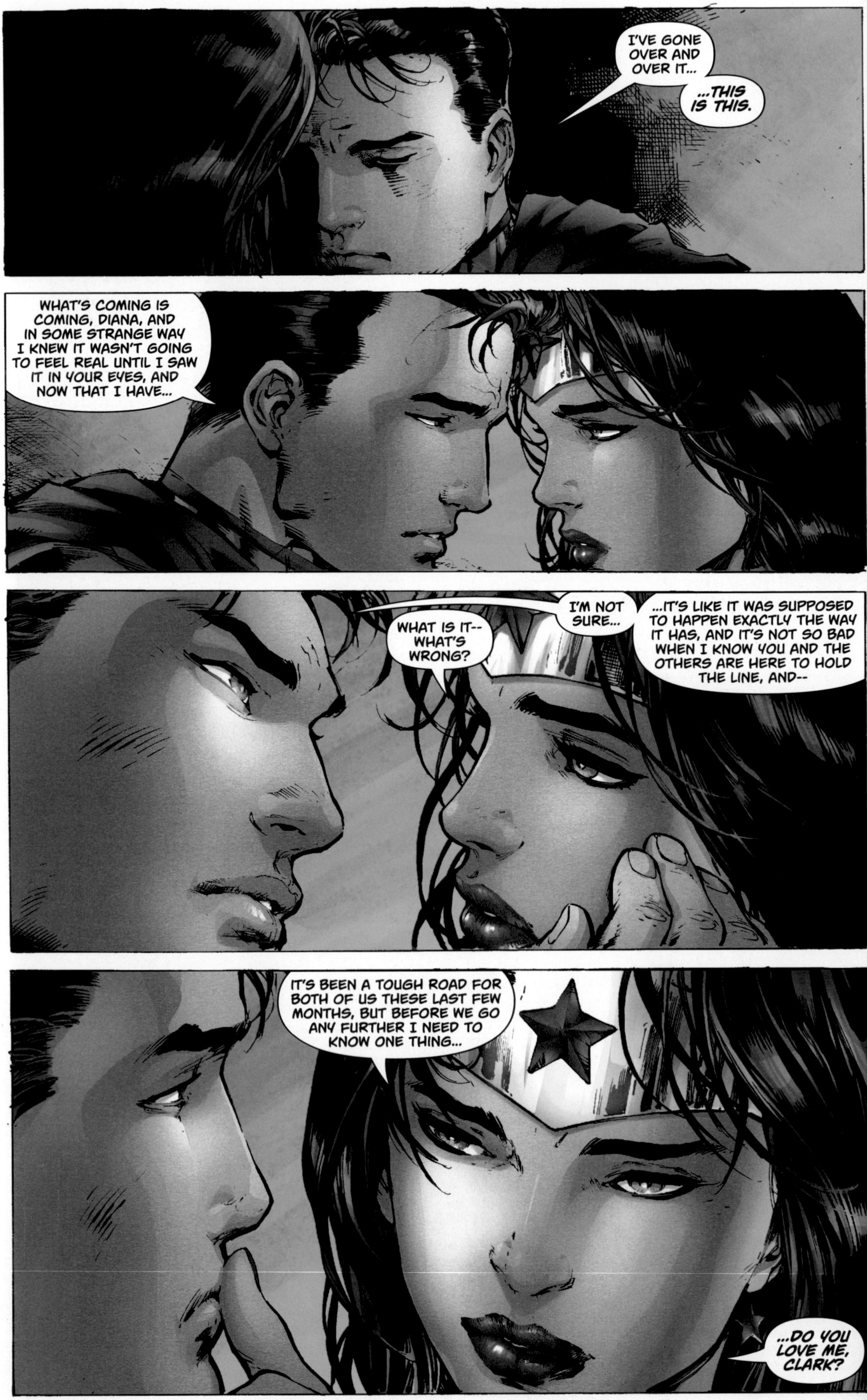
I'VE GONE OVER AND OVER IT...
...THIS IS THIS.
WHAT'S COMING IS COMING, DIANA, AND IN SOME STRANGE WAY I KNEW IT WASN'T GOING TO FEEL REAL UNTIL I SAW IT IN YOUR EYES, AND NOW THAT I HAVE...
WHAT IS IT-- WHAT'S WRONG?
I'M NOT SURE...
...IT'S LIKE IT WAS SUPPOSED TO HAPPEN EXACTLY THE WAY IT HAS, AND IT'S NOT SO BAD WHEN I KNOW YOU AND THE OTHERS ARE HERE TO HOLD THE LINE, AND--
IT'S BEEN A TOUGH ROAD FOR BOTH OF US THESE LAST FEW MONTHS, BUT BEFORE WE GO ANY FURTHER I NEED TO KNOW ONE THING...
...DO YOU LOVE ME, CLARK?

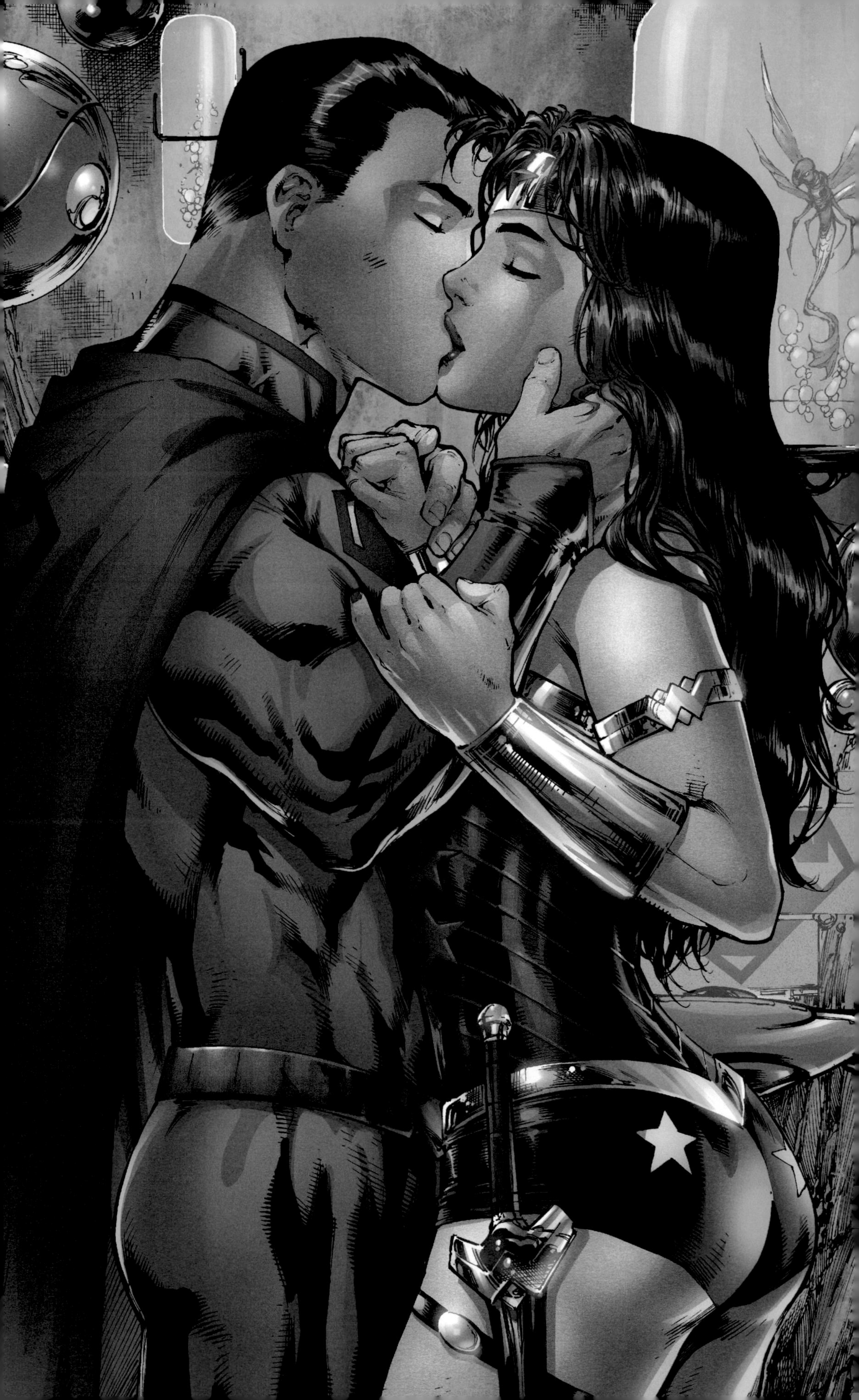

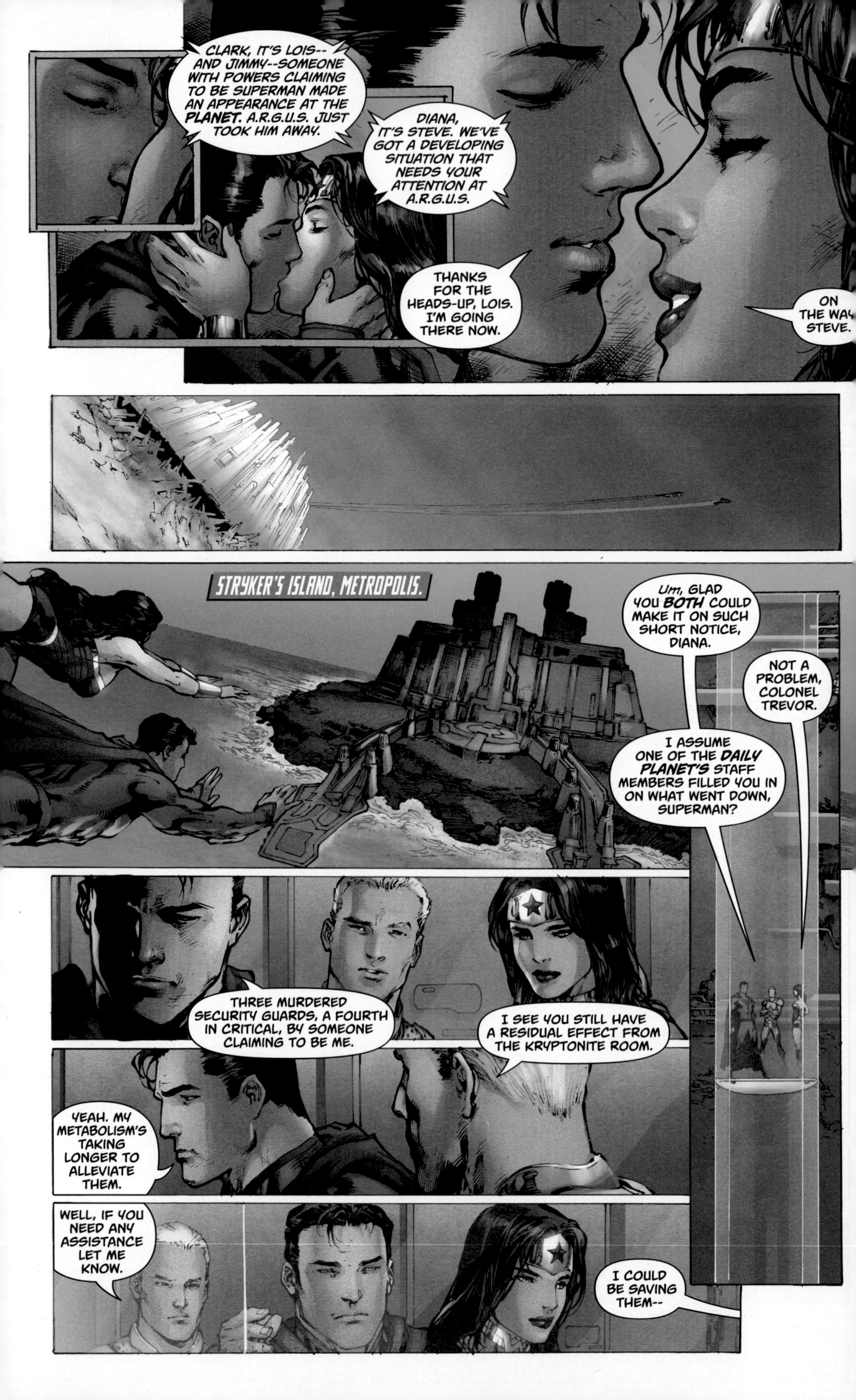
CLARK, IT'S LOIS--AND JIMMY--SOMEONE WITH POWERS CLAIMING TO BE SUPERMAN MADE AN APPEARANCE AT THE PLANET. A.R.G.U.S. JUST TOOK HIM AWAY.
DIANA, IT'S STEVE. WE'VE GOT A DEVELOPING SITUATION THAT NEEDS YOUR ATTENTION AT A.R.G.U.S.
THANKS FOR THE HEADS-UP, LOIS. I'M GOING THERE NOW.
ON THE WAY STEVE.
STRYKER'S ISLAND, METROPOLIS.
Um, GLAD YOU BOTH COULD MAKE IT ON SUCH SHORT NOTICE, DIANA.
NOT A PROBLEM, COLONEL TREVOR.
I ASSUME ONE OF THE DAILY PLANET'S STAFF MEMBERS FILLED YOU IN ON WHAT WENT DOWN, SUPERMAN?
THREE MURDERED SECURITY GUARDS, A FOURTH IN CRITICAL, BY SOMEONE CLAIMING TO BE ME.
I SEE YOU STILL HAVE A RESIDUAL EFFECT FROM THE KRYPTONITE ROOM.
YEAH. MY METABOLISM'S TAKING LONGER TO ALLEVIATE THEM.
WELL, IF YOU NEED ANY ASSISTANCE LET ME KNOW.
I COULD BE SAVING THEM--

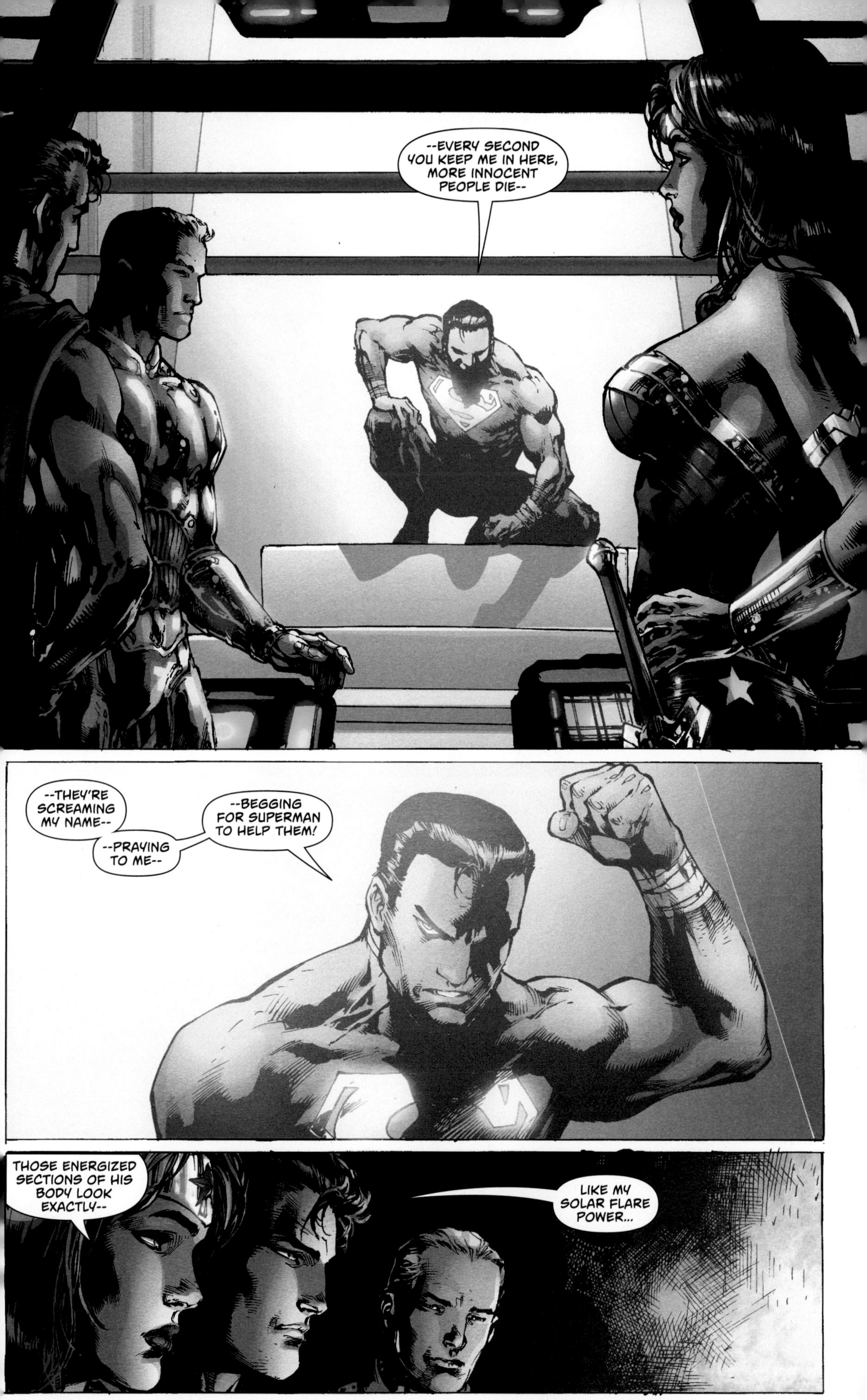
--EVERY SECOND YOU KEEP ME IN HERE, MORE INNOCENT PEOPLE DIE--
--THEY'RE SCREAMING MY NAME--
--PRAYING TO ME--
--BEGGING FOR SUPERMAN TO HELP THEM!
THOSE ENERGIZED SECTIONS OF HIS BODY LOOK EXACTLY--
LIKE MY SOLAR FLARE POWER...

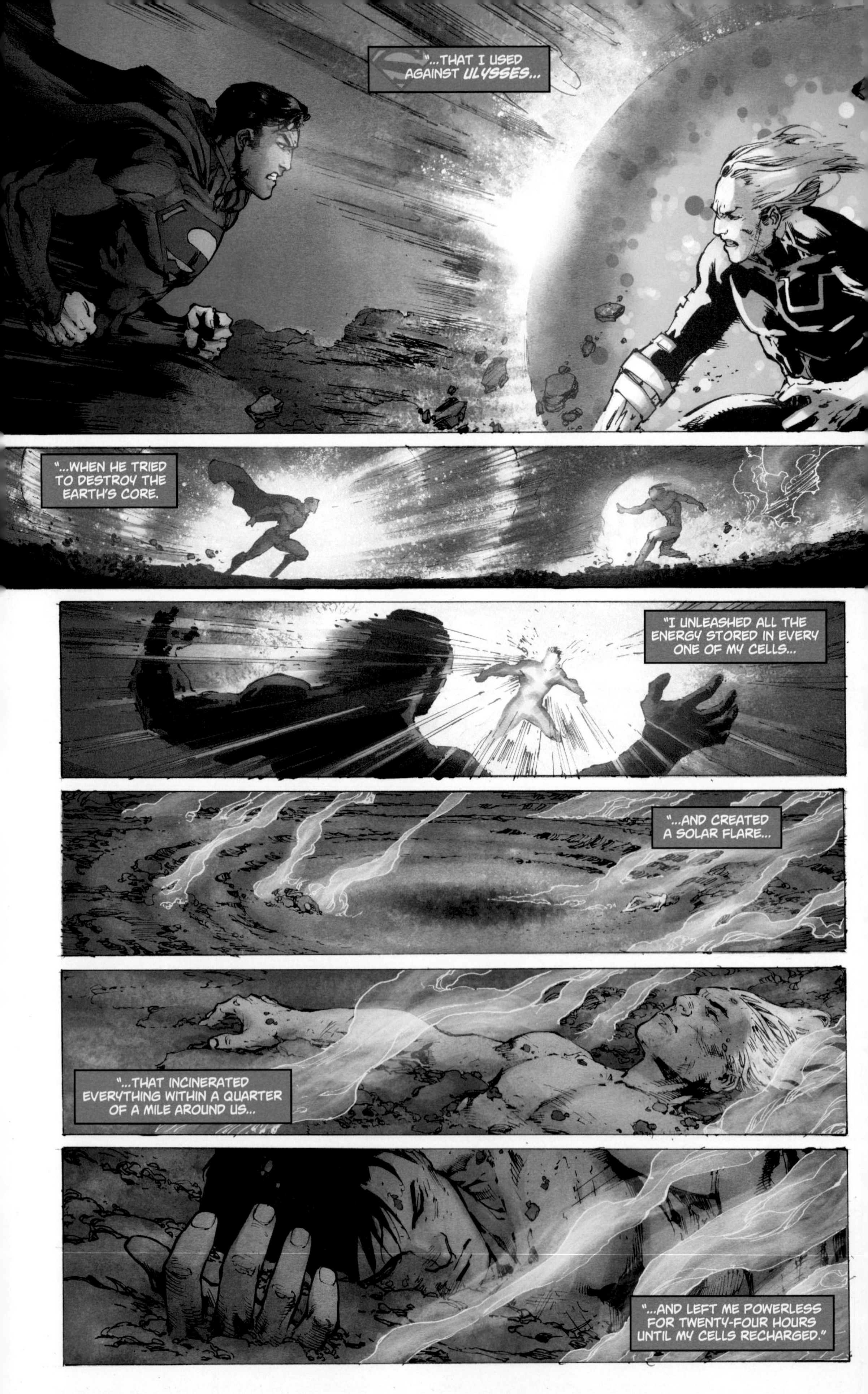
"...THAT I USED AGAINST ULYSSES...
"...WHEN HE TRIED TO DESTROY THE EARTH'S CORE.
"I UNLEASHED ALL THE ENERGY STORED IN EVERY ONE OF MY CELLS...
"...AND CREATED A SOLAR FLARE...
"...THAT INCINERATED EVERYTHING WITHIN A QUARTER OF A MILE AROUND US...
"...AND LEFT ME POWERLESS FOR TWENTY-FOUR HOURS UNTIL MY CELLS RECHARGED."

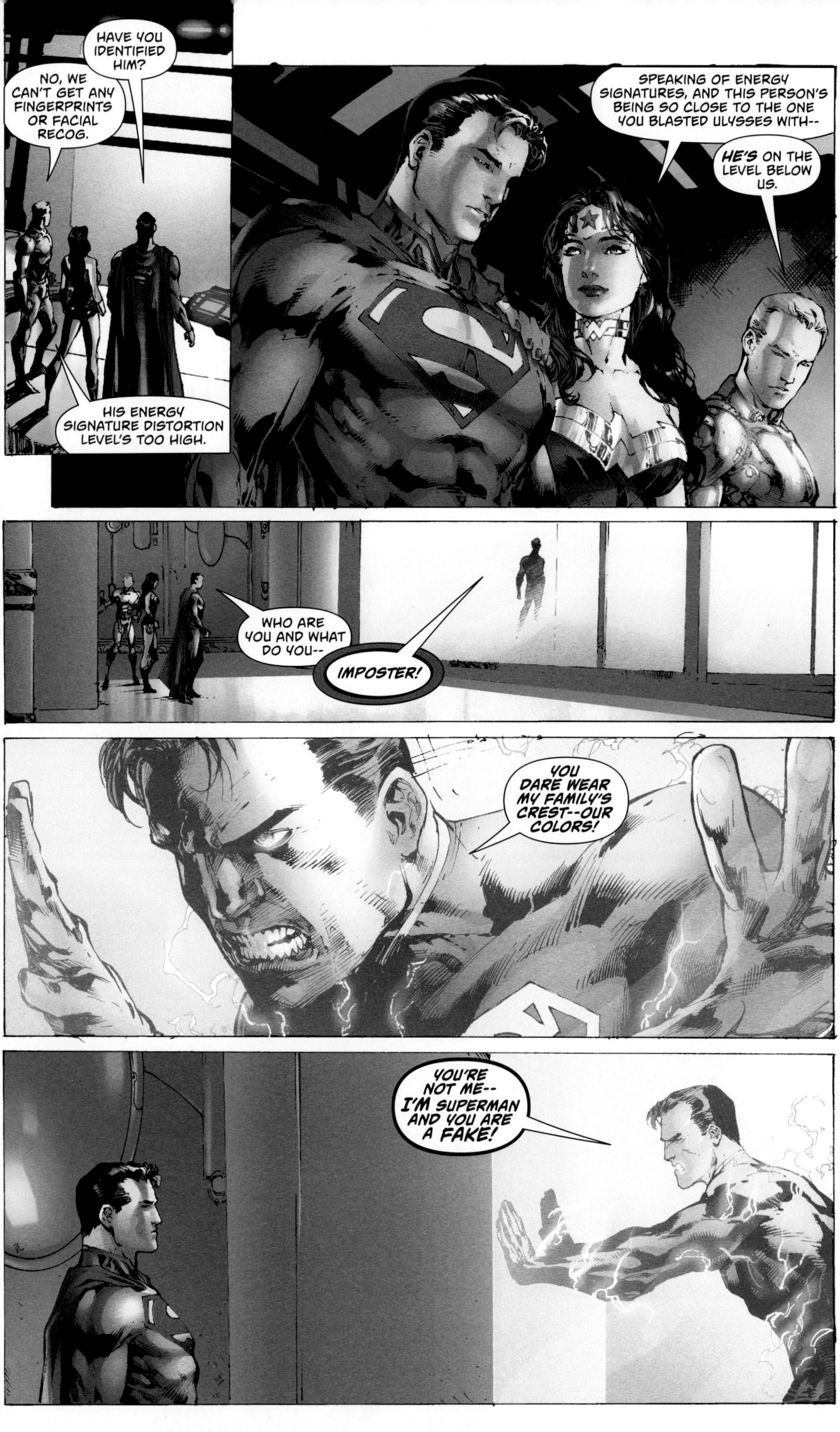
HAVE YOU IDENTIFIED HIM?
NO, WE CAN'T GET ANY FINGERPRINTS OR FACIAL RECOG.
HIS ENERGY SIGNATURE DISTORTION LEVEL'S TOO HIGH.
SPEAKING OF ENERGY SIGNATURES, AND THIS PERSON'S BEING SO CLOSE TO THE ONE YOU BLASTED ULYSSES WITH--
HE'S ON THE LEVEL BELOW US.
WHO ARE YOU AND WHAT DO YOU--
IMPOSTER!
YOU DARE WEAR MY FAMILY'S CREST--OUR COLORS!
YOU'RE NOT ME-- I'M SUPERMAN AND YOU ARE A FAKE!

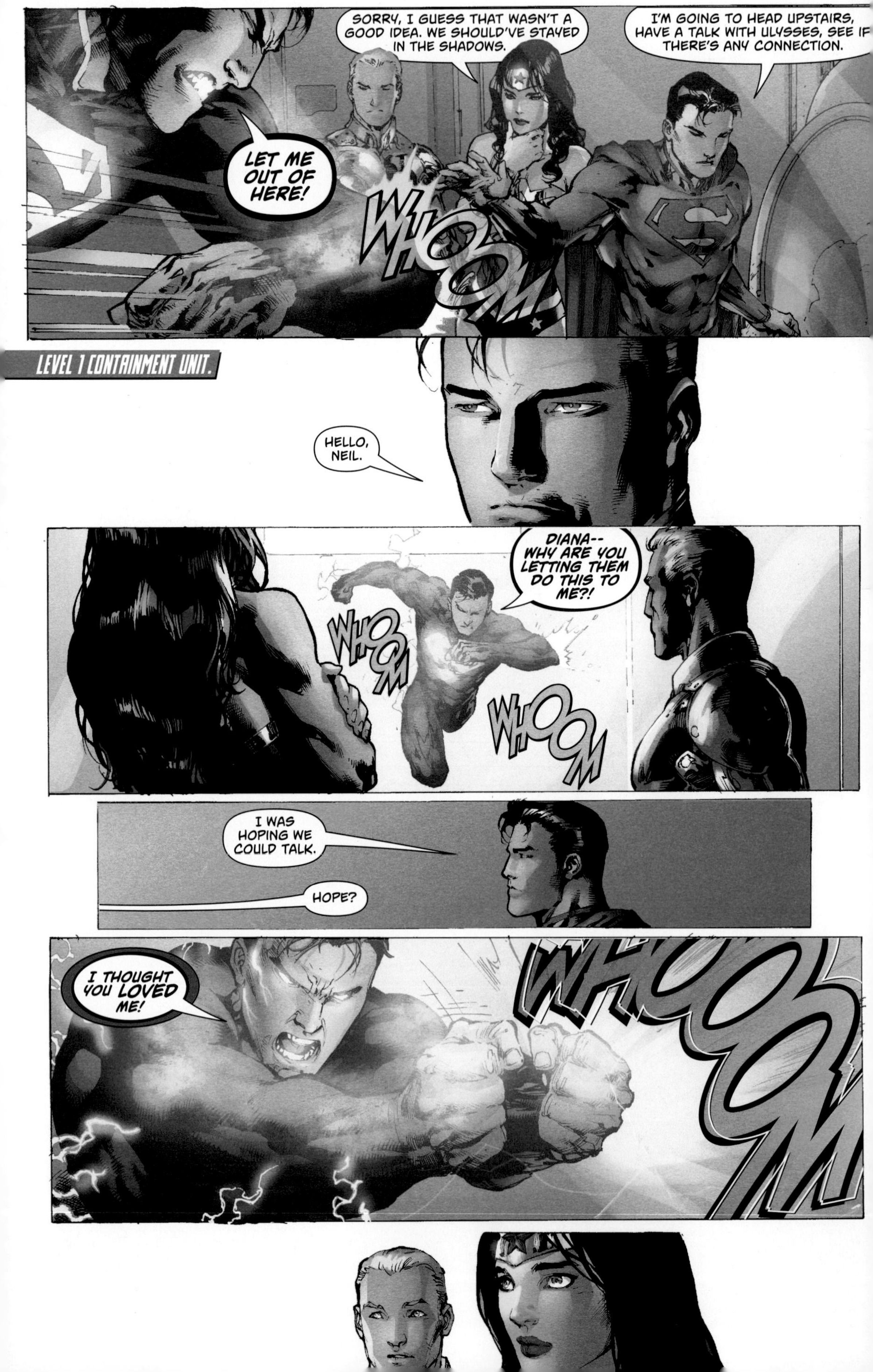
SORRY, I GUESS THAT WASN'T A GOOD IDEA. WE SHOULD'VE STAYED IN THE SHADOWS.
I'M GOING TO HEAD UPSTAIRS, HAVE A TALK WITH ULYSSES, SEE IF THERE'S ANY CONNECTION.
LET ME OUT OF HERE!
WHOOOM
LEVEL 1 CONTAINMENT UNIT.
HELLO, NEIL.
DIANA-- WHY ARE YOU LETTING THEM DO THIS TO ME?!
WHOOM
WHOOM
I WAS HOPING WE COULD TALK.
HOPE?
I THOUGHT YOU LOVED ME!

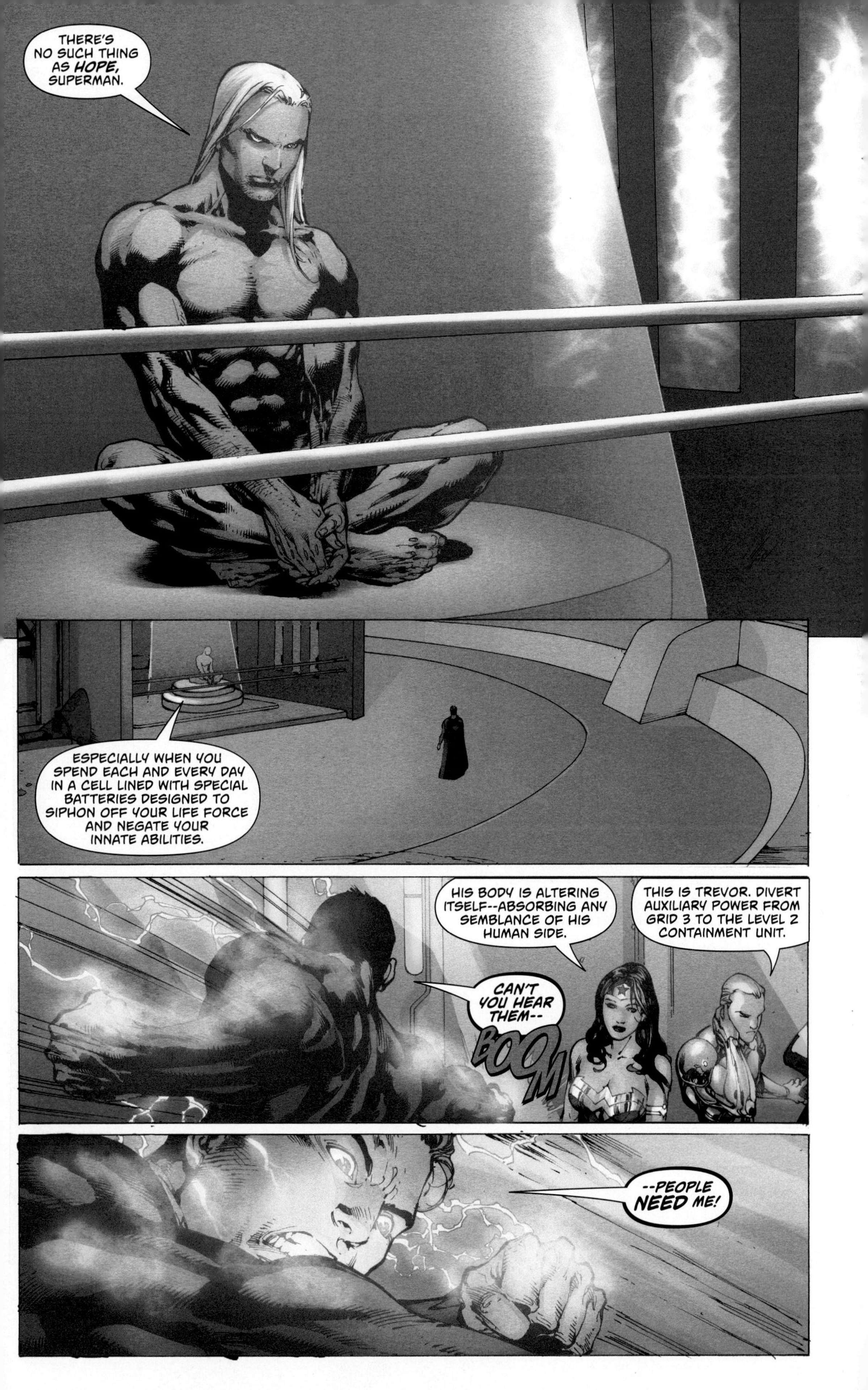
THERE'S NO SUCH THING AS HOPE, SUPERMAN.
ESPECIALLY WHEN YOU SPEND EACH AND EVERY DAY IN A CELL LINED WITH SPECIAL BATTERIES DESIGNED TO SIPHON OFF YOUR LIFE FORCE AND NEGATE YOUR INNATE ABILITIES.
HIS BODY IS ALTERING ITSELF--ABSORBING ANY SEMBLANCE OF HIS HUMAN SIDE.
THIS IS TREVOR. DIVERT AUXILIARY POWER FROM GRID 3 TO THE LEVEL 2 CONTAINMENT UNIT.
CAN'T YOU HEAR THEM--
BOOOM
--PEOPLE NEED ME!

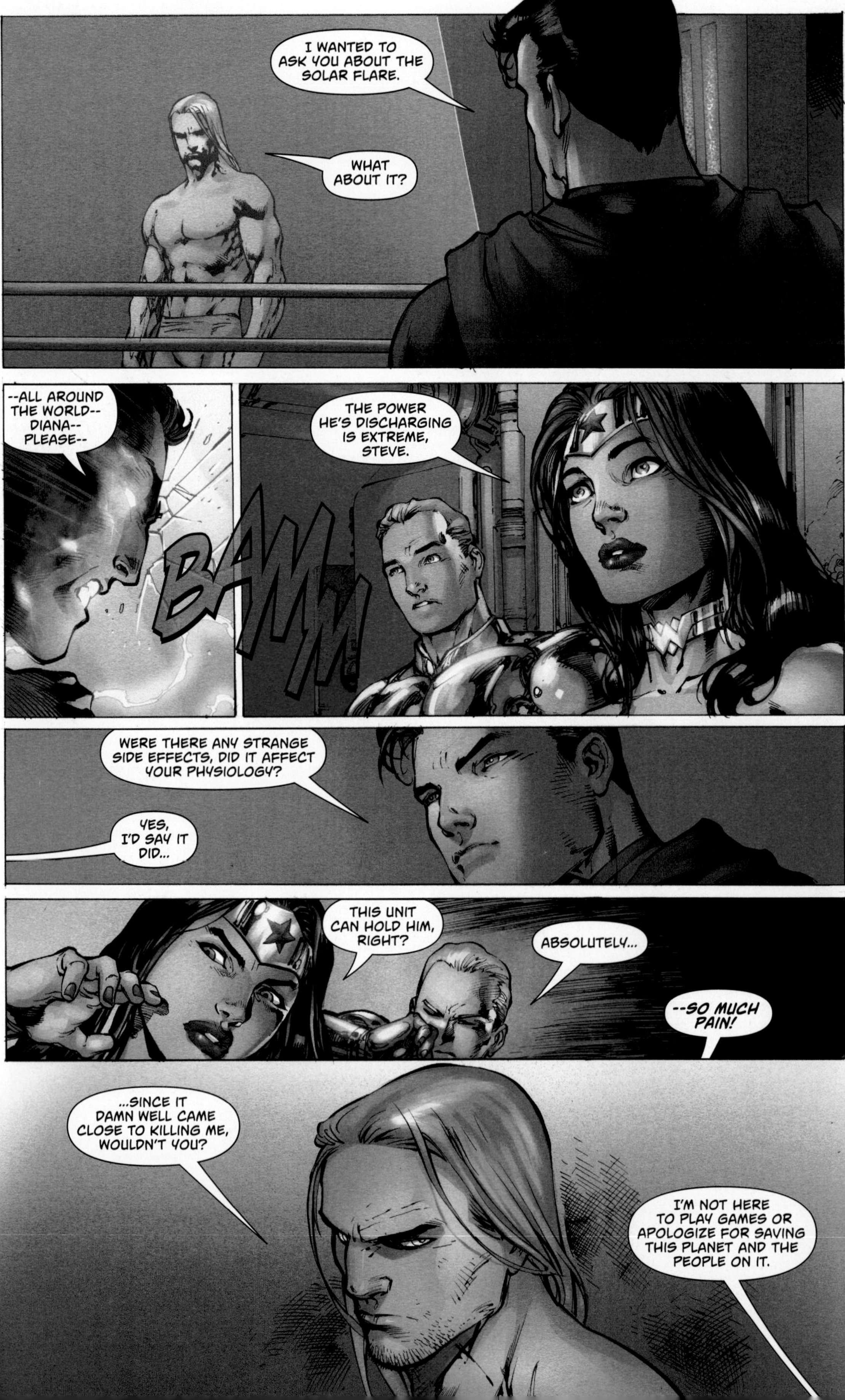
I WANTED TO ASK YOU ABOUT THE SOLAR FLARE.
WHAT ABOUT IT?
--ALL AROUND THE WORLD-- DIANA-- PLEASE--
BAMM
THE POWER HE'S DISCHARGING IS EXTREME, STEVE.
WERE THERE ANY STRANGE SIDE EFFECTS, DID IT AFFECT YOUR PHYSIOLOGY?
YES, I'D SAY IT DID...
THIS UNIT CAN HOLD HIM, RIGHT?
ABSOLUTELY...
--SO MUCH PAIN!
...SINCE IT DAMN WELL CAME CLOSE TO KILLING ME, WOULDN'T YOU?
I'M NOT HERE TO PLAY GAMES OR APOLOGIZE FOR SAVING THIS PLANET AND THE PEOPLE ON IT.

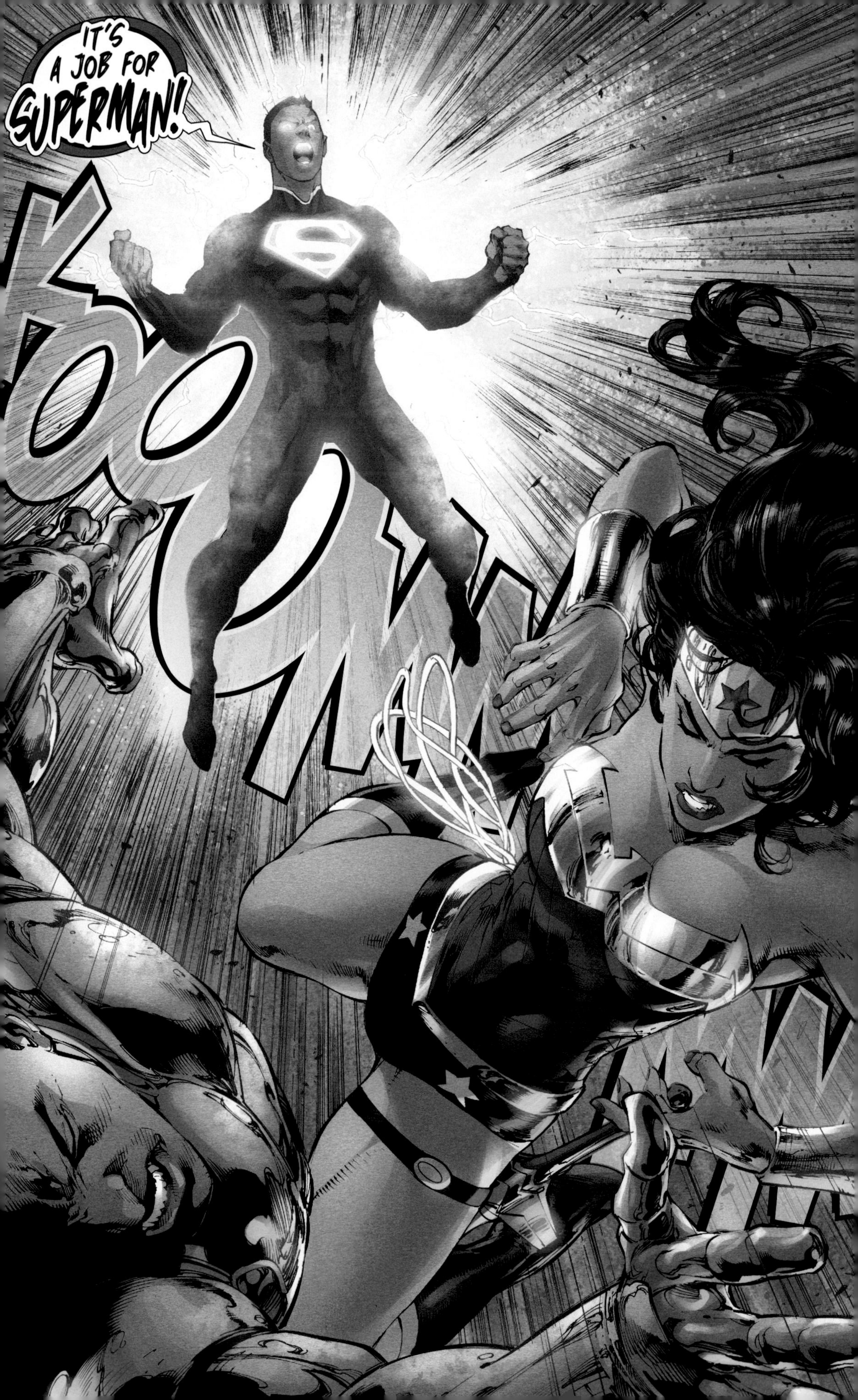
IT'S A JOB FOR SUPERMAN!

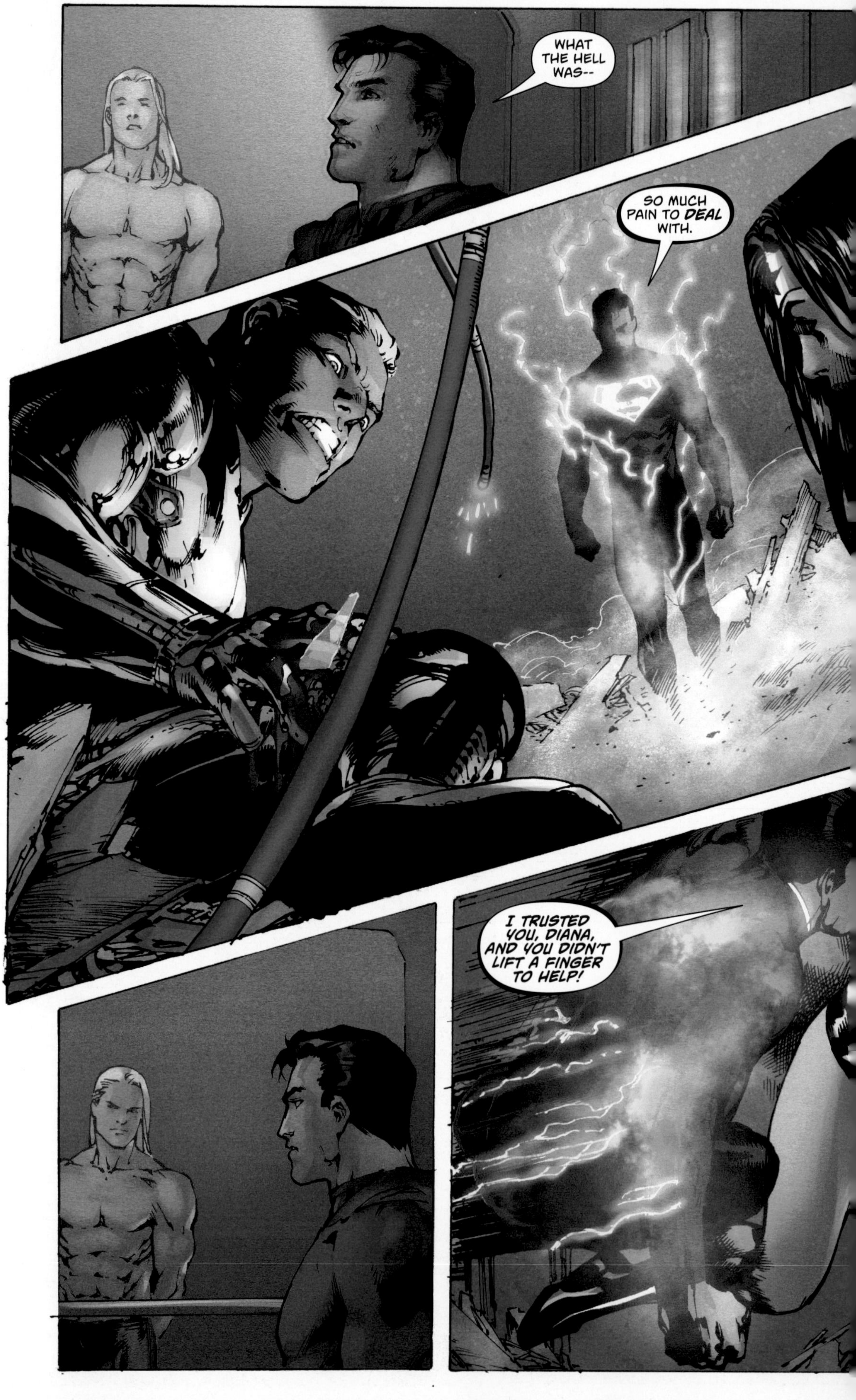
WHAT THE HELL WAS--
SO MUCH PAIN TO DEAL WITH.
I TRUSTED YOU, DIANA, AND YOU DIDN'T LIFT A FINGER TO HELP!

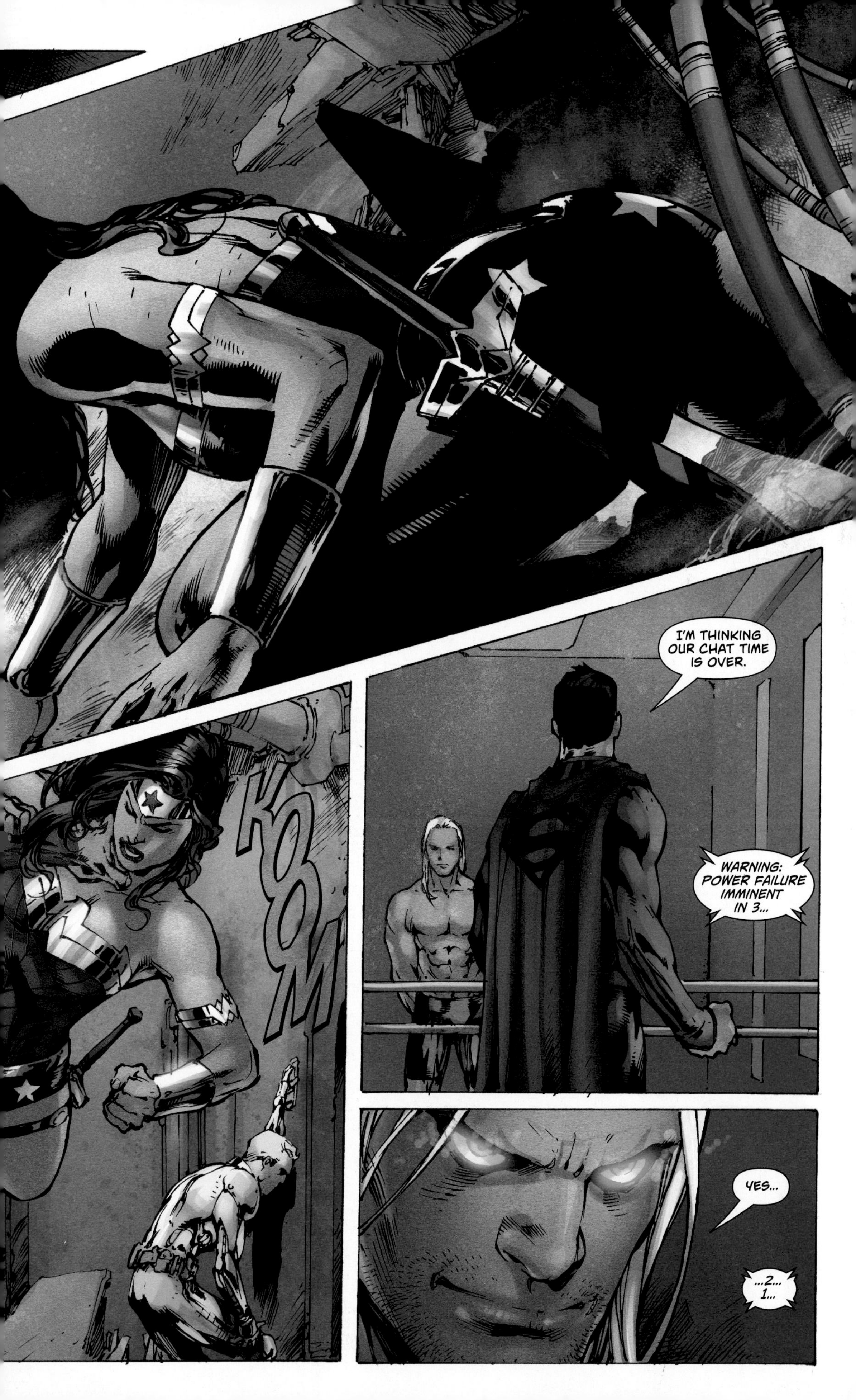
KOOM
I'M THINKING OUR CHAT TIME IS OVER.
WARNING: POWER FAILURE IMMINENT IN 3...
YES...
...2... 1...

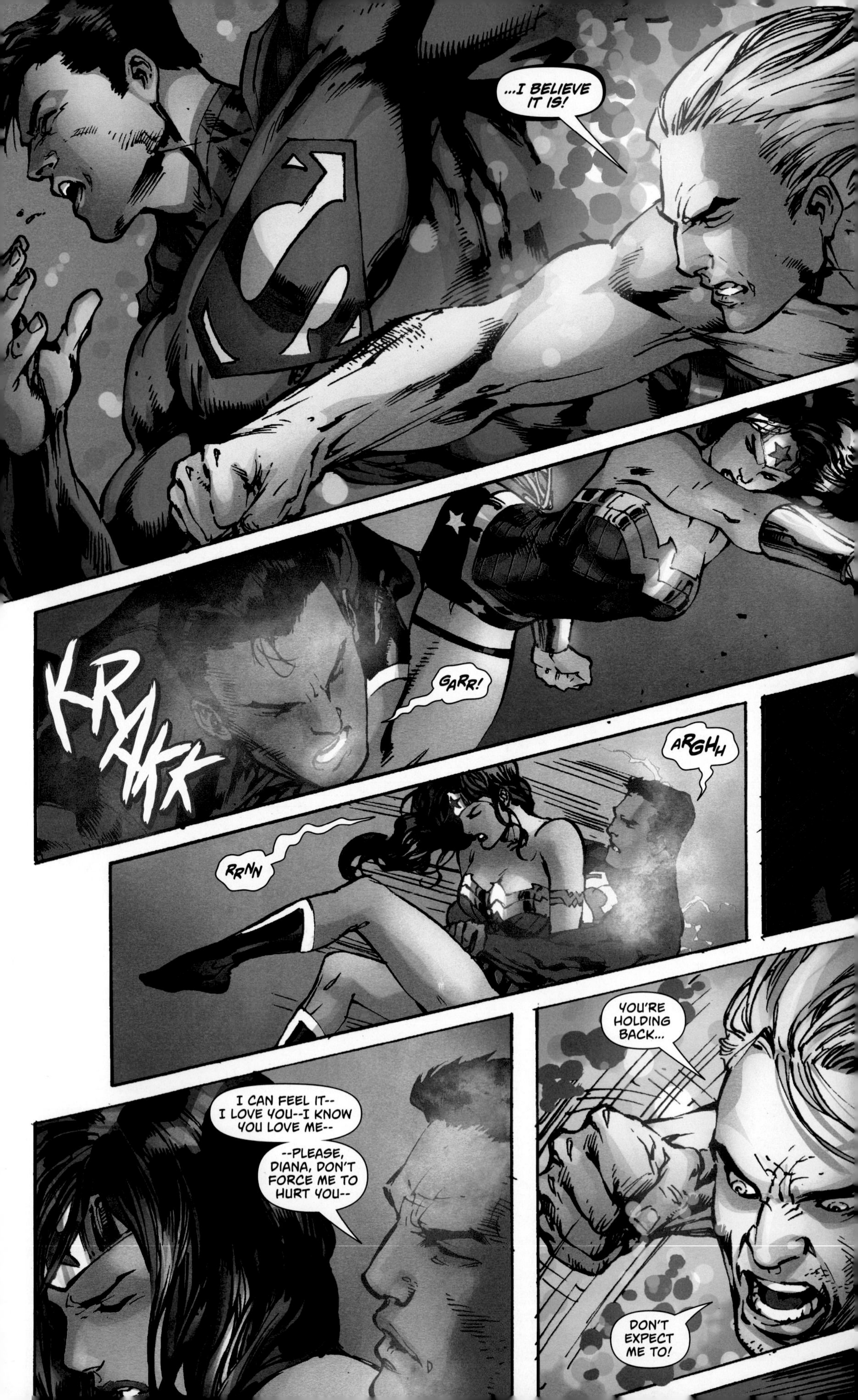
...I BELIEVE IT IS!
KRAKK
GARR!
ARGHH
RRNN
YOU'RE HOLDING BACK...
I CAN FEEL IT-- I LOVE YOU--I KNOW YOU LOVE ME--
--PLEASE, DIANA, DON'T FORCE ME TO HURT YOU--
DON'T EXPECT ME TO!

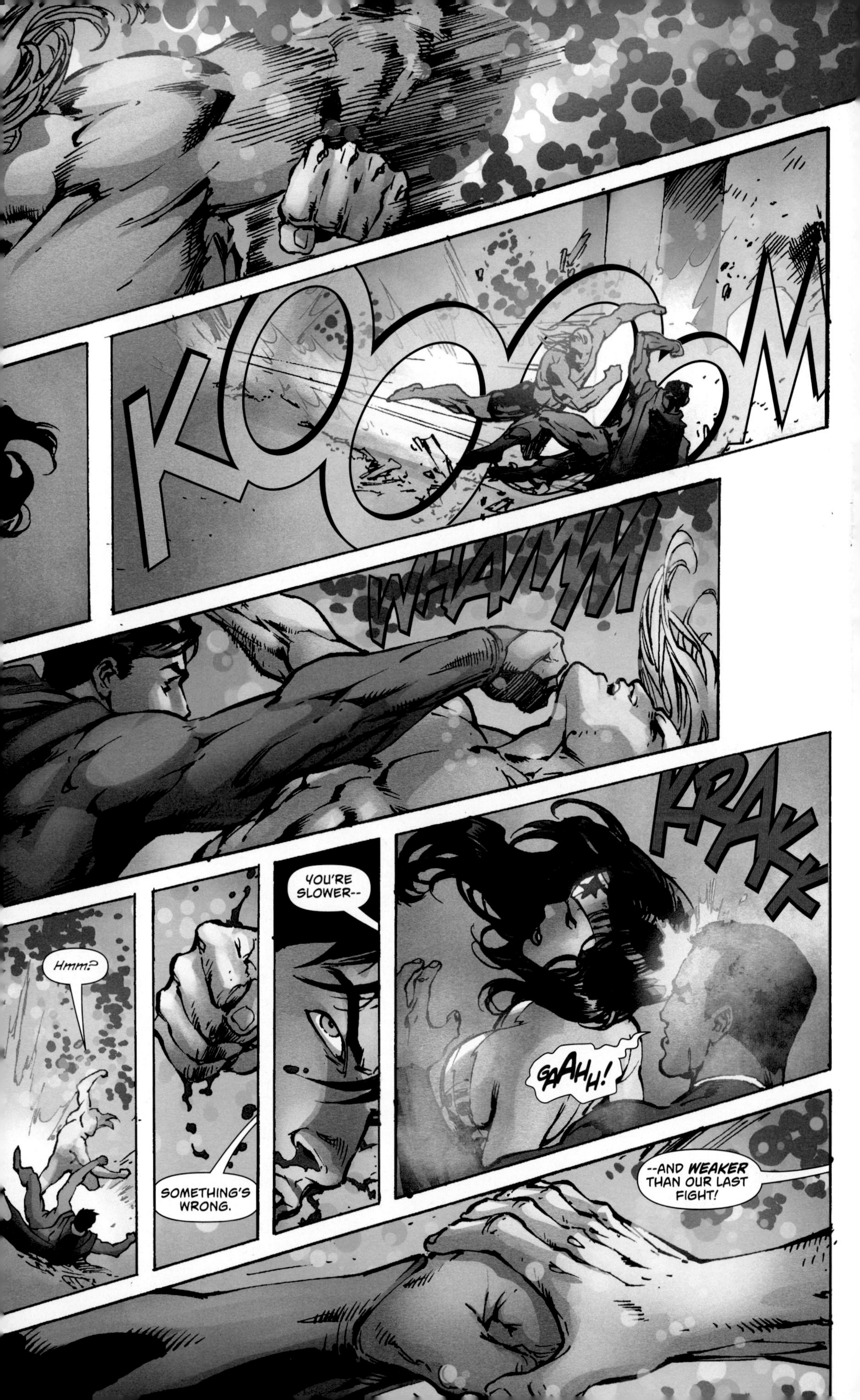
KOOOOM
WHAMM
KRAKK
Hmm?
SOMETHING'S WRONG.
YOU'RE SLOWER--
GAAHH!
--AND WEAKER THAN OUR LAST FIGHT!

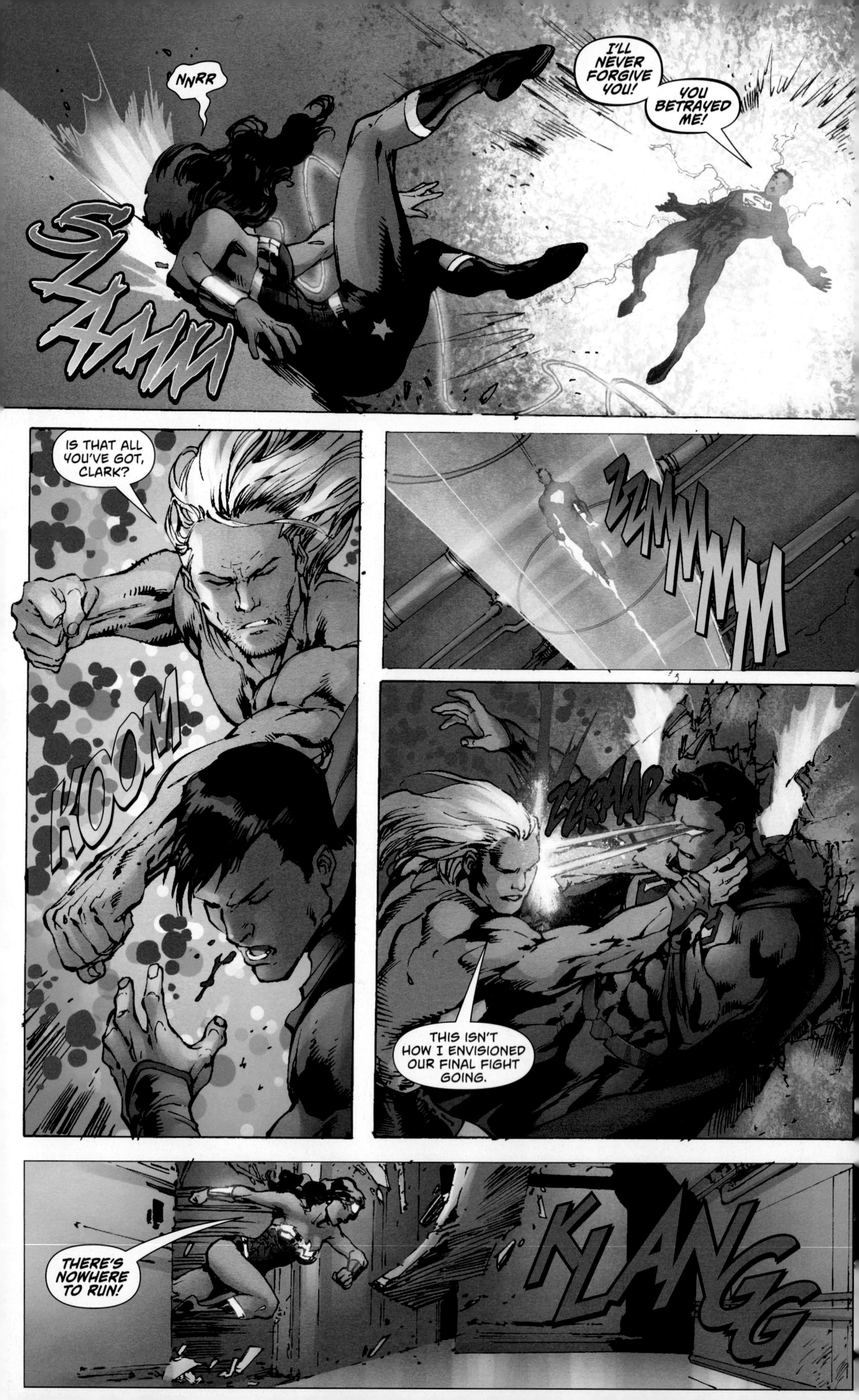
NNRR
SLAMM
I'LL NEVER FORGIVE YOU!
YOU BETRAYED ME!
IS THAT ALL YOU'VE GOT, CLARK?
KOOM
ZZMMMMM
ZZRAAAP
THIS ISN'T HOW I ENVISIONED OUR FINAL FIGHT GOING.
THERE'S NOWHERE TO RUN!
KLANGG

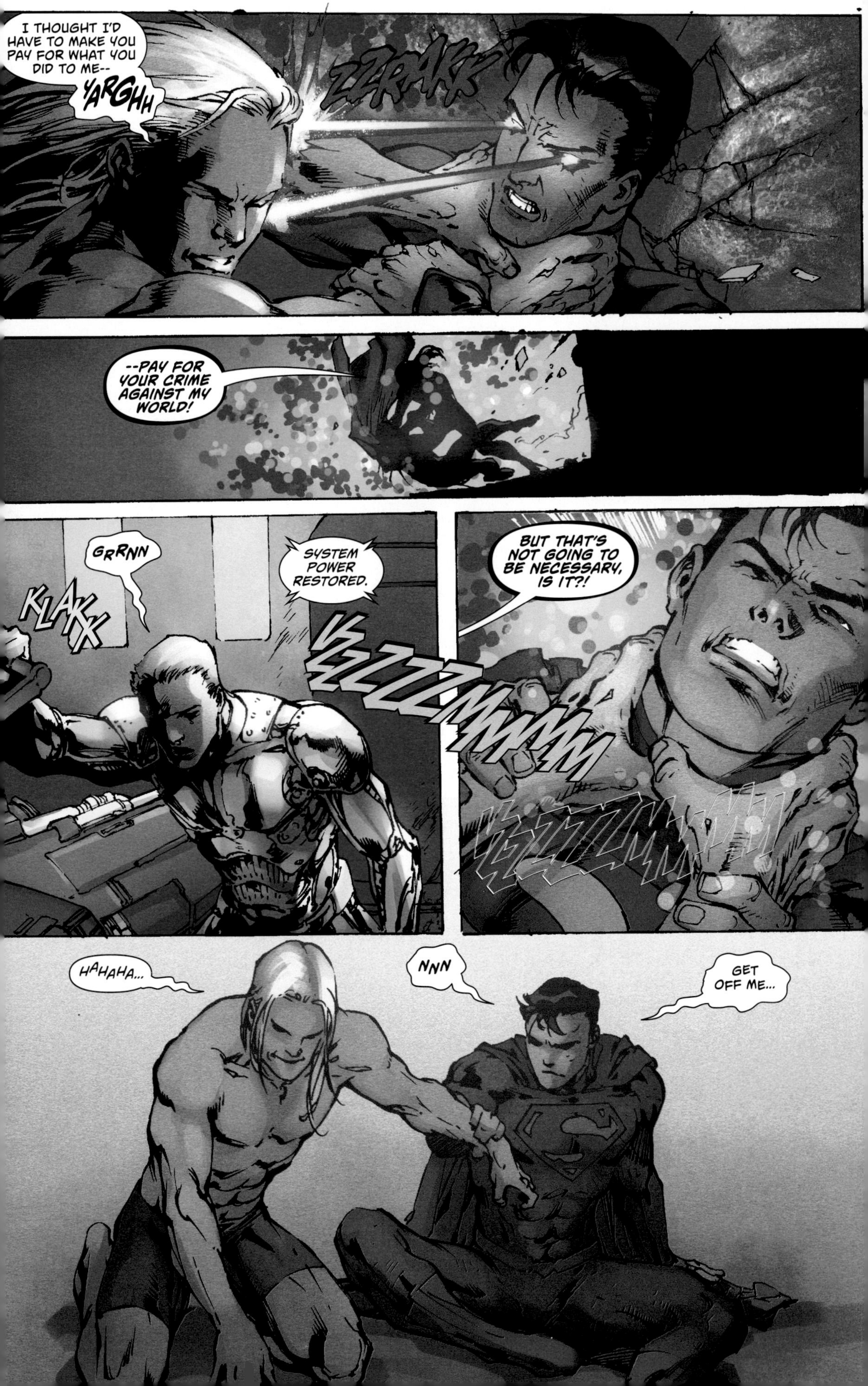
I THOUGHT I'D HAVE TO MAKE YOU PAY FOR WHAT YOU DID TO ME--
YARGHH
ZZRAKK
--PAY FOR YOUR CRIME AGAINST MY WORLD!
GRRNN
KLAKK
SYSTEM POWER RESTORED.
VSZZZZMMMM
BUT THAT'S NOT GOING TO BE NECESSARY, IS IT?!
HAHAHA...
NNN
GET OFF ME...

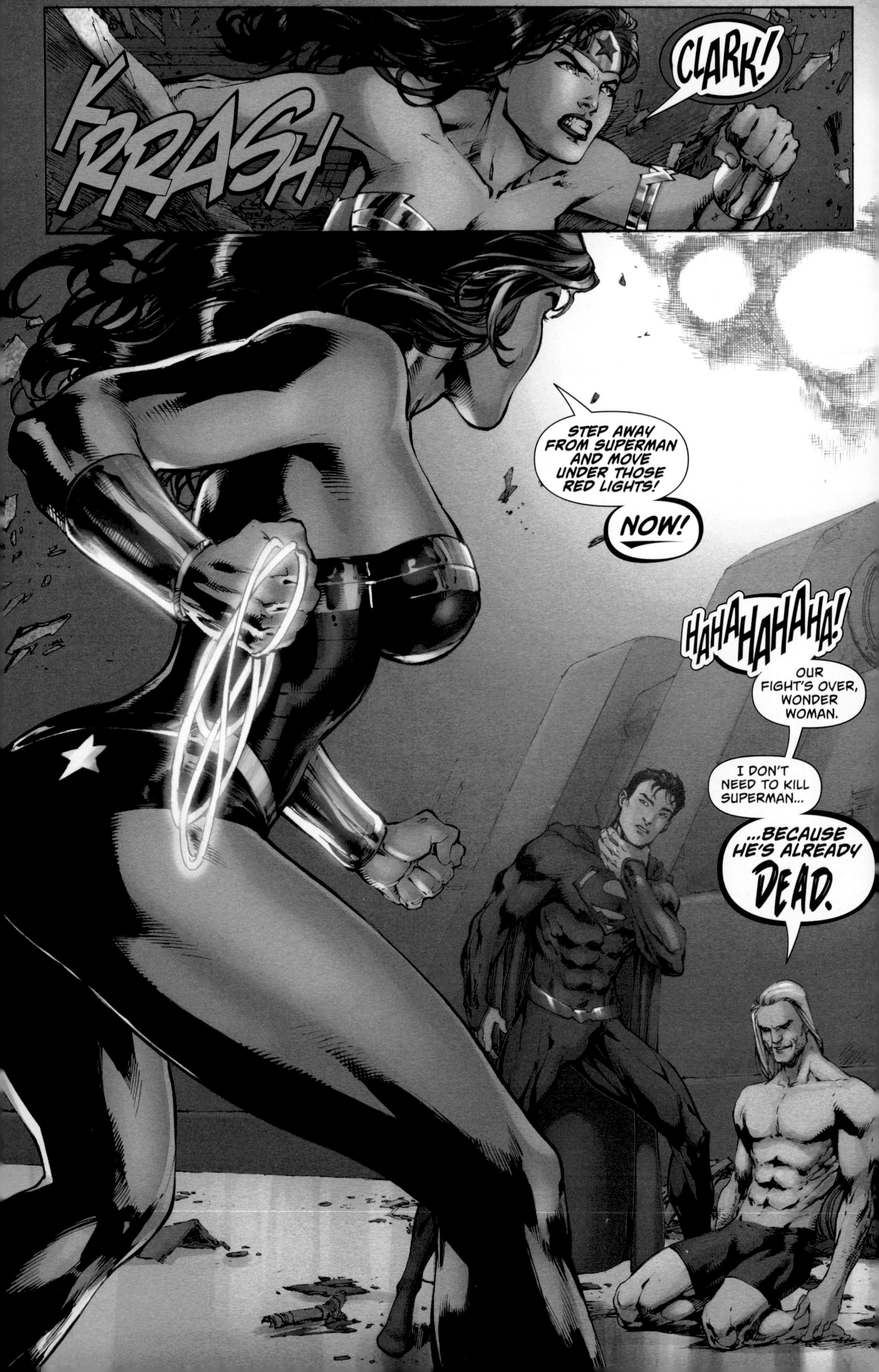
KRRASH
CLARK!
STEP AWAY FROM SUPERMAN AND MOVE UNDER THOSE RED LIGHTS!
NOW!
HAHAHAHAHA!
OUR FIGHT'S OVER, WONDER WOMAN.
I DON'T NEED TO KILL SUPERMAN...
...BECAUSE HE'S ALREADY DEAD.

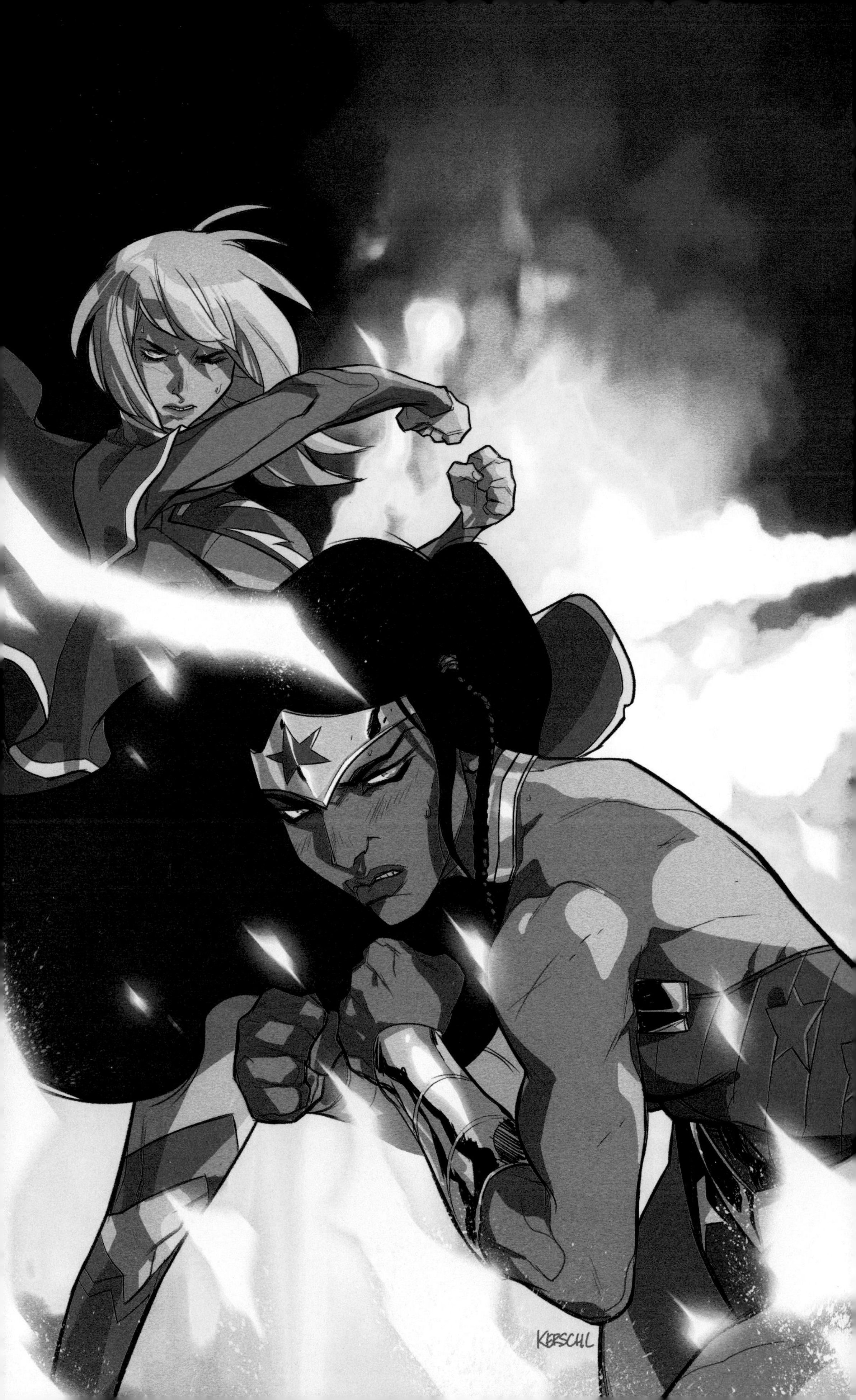
KERSCHL

THE FINAL DAYS OF SUPERMAN PART 7: FIRE LINE

PETER J. TOMASI writer JORGE JIMÉNEZ artist ALEJANDRO SÁNCHEZ colorist ROB LEIGH letterer cover by KARL KERSCHL

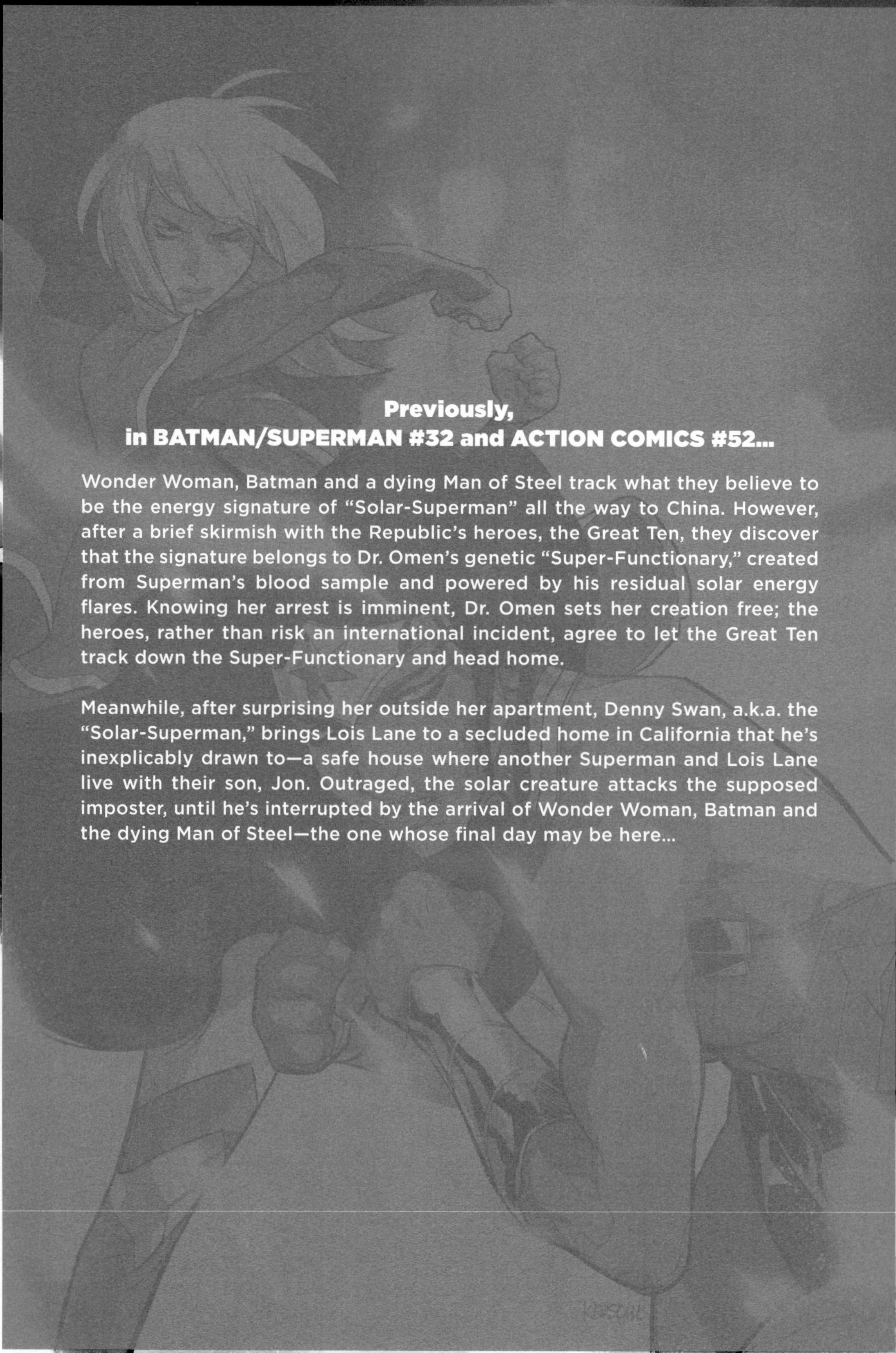

Previously, in BATMAN/SUPERMAN #32 and ACTION COMICS #52...

Wonder Woman, Batman and a dying Man of Steel track what they believe to be the energy signature of "Solar-Superman" all the way to China. However, after a brief skirmish with the Republic's heroes, the Great Ten, they discover that the signature belongs to Dr. Omen's genetic "Super-Functionary," created from Superman's blood sample and powered by his residual solar energy flares. Knowing her arrest is imminent, Dr. Omen sets her creation free; the heroes, rather than risk an international incident, agree to let the Great Ten track down the Super-Functionary and head home.

Meanwhile, after surprising her outside her apartment, Denny Swan, a.k.a. the "Solar-Superman," brings Lois Lane to a secluded home in California that he's inexplicably drawn to—a safe house where another Superman and Lois Lane live with their son, Jon. Outraged, the solar creature attacks the supposed imposter, until he's interrupted by the arrival of Wonder Woman, Batman and the dying Man of Steel—the one whose final day may be here...

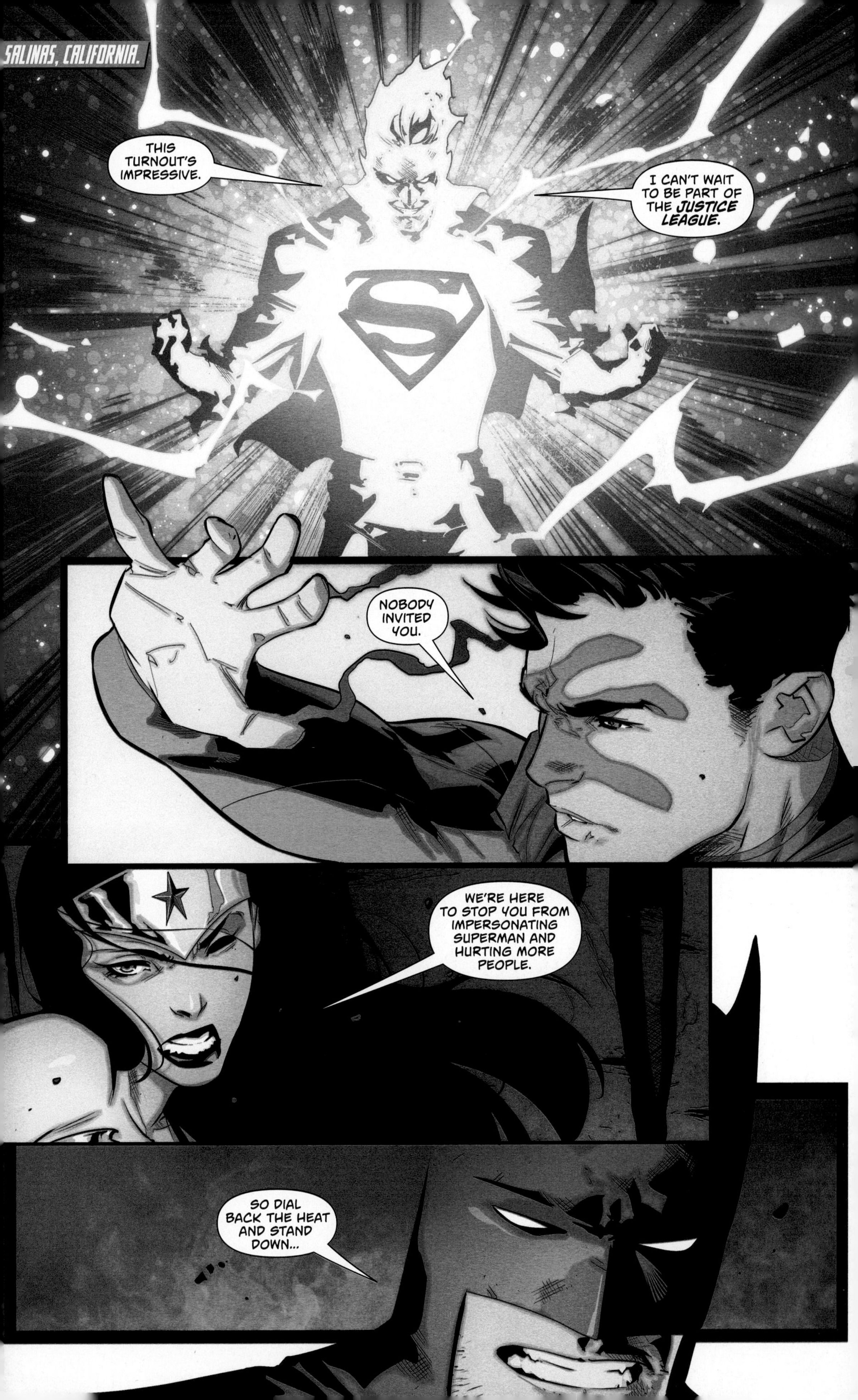
SALINAS, CALIFORNIA.
THIS TURNOUT'S IMPRESSIVE.
I CAN'T WAIT TO BE PART OF THE JUSTICE LEAGUE.
NOBODY INVITED YOU.
WE'RE HERE TO STOP YOU FROM IMPERSONATING SUPERMAN AND HURTING MORE PEOPLE.
SO DIAL BACK THE HEAT AND STAND DOWN...

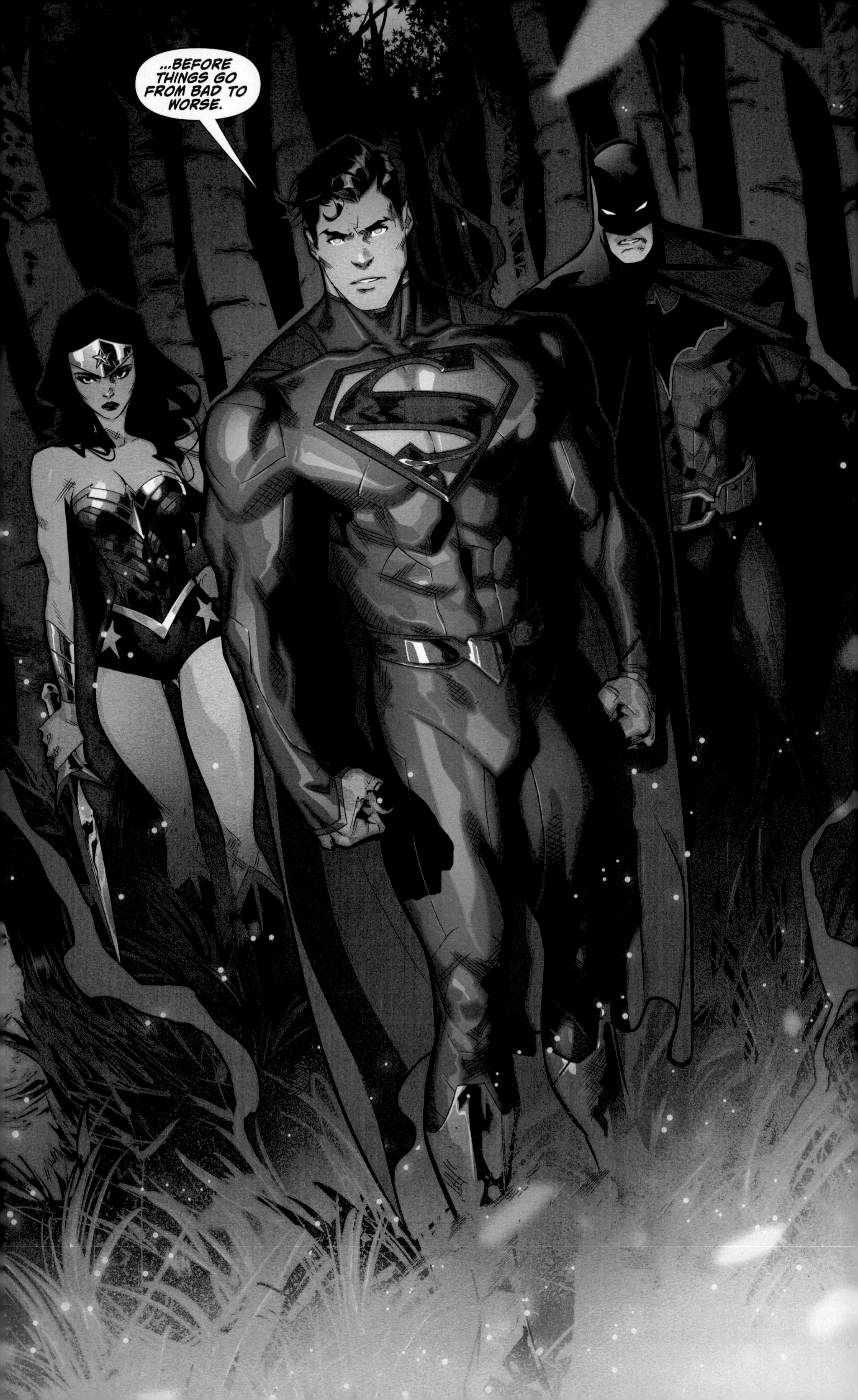
...BEFORE THINGS GO FROM BAD TO WORSE.

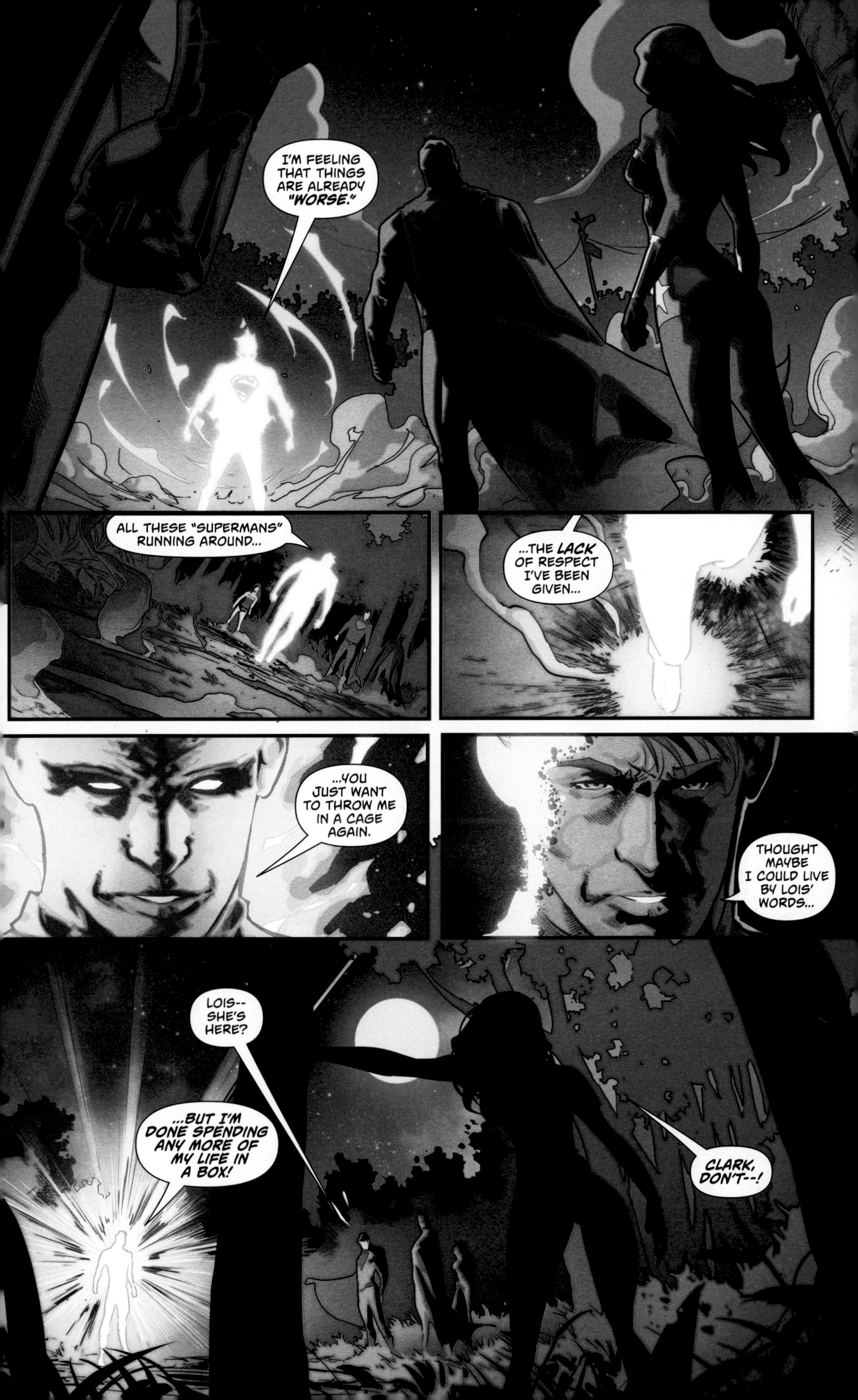

I'M FEELING THAT THINGS ARE ALREADY "WORSE."
ALL THESE "SUPERMANS" RUNNING AROUND...
...THE LACK OF RESPECT I'VE BEEN GIVEN...
...YOU JUST WANT TO THROW ME IN A CAGE AGAIN.
THOUGHT MAYBE I COULD LIVE BY LOIS' WORDS...
LOIS-- SHE'S HERE?
...BUT I'M DONE SPENDING ANY MORE OF MY LIFE IN A BOX!
CLARK, DON'T--!

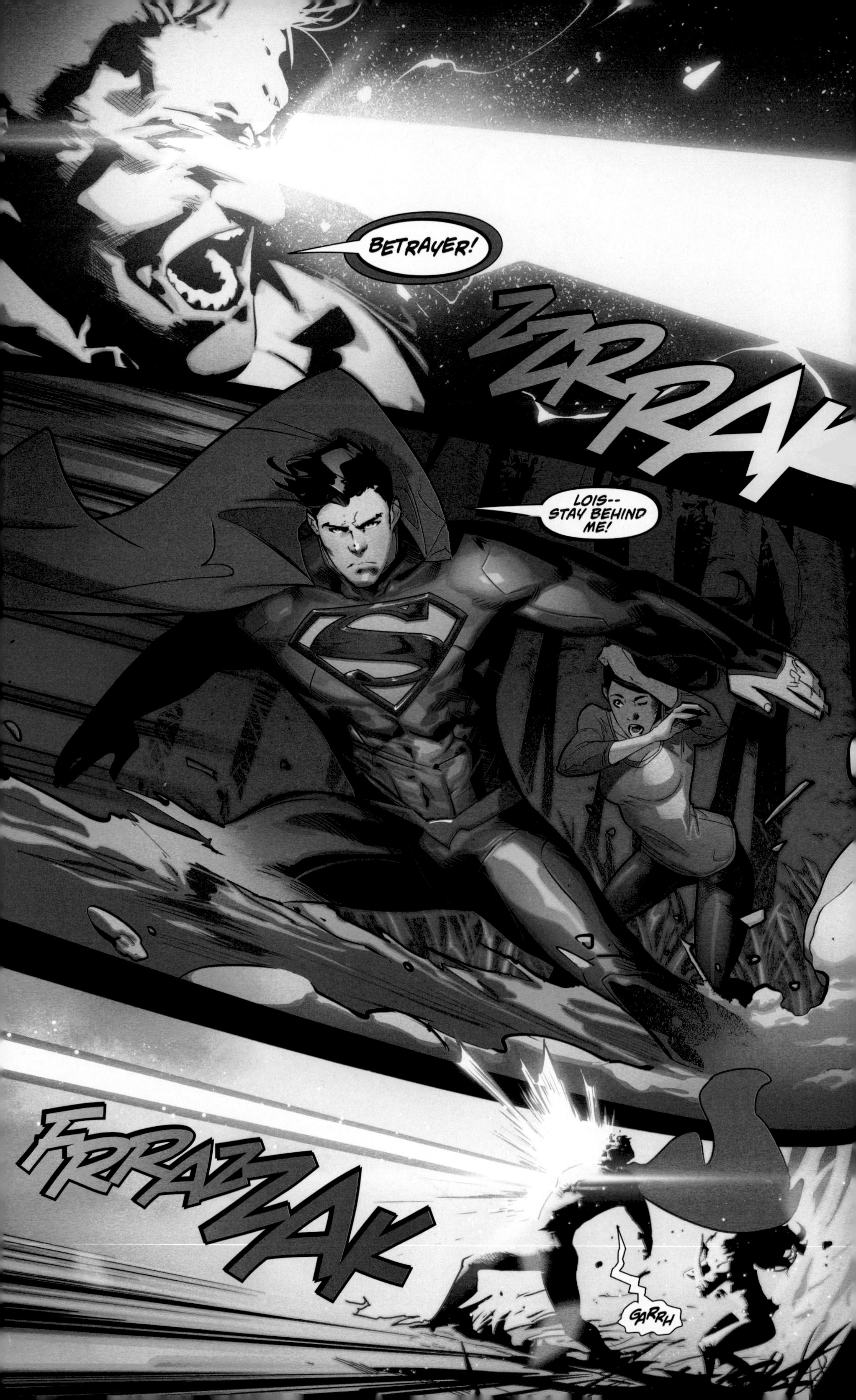
BETRAYER!
ZZRRAK
LOIS-- STAY BEHIND ME!
FRRAZZAK
GARRH

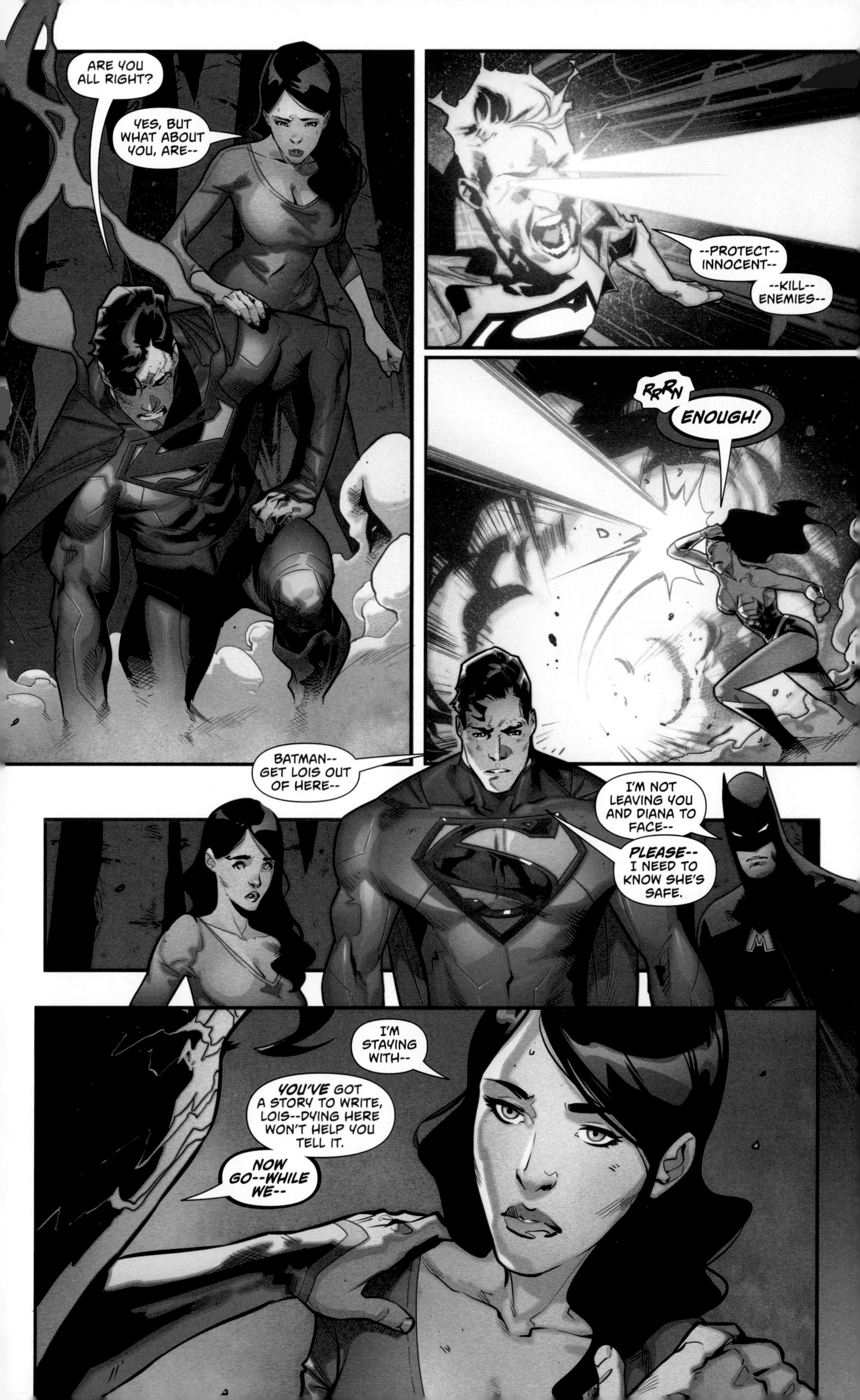
ARE YOU ALL RIGHT?
YES, BUT WHAT ABOUT YOU, ARE--
--PROTECT-- INNOCENT--
--KILL-- ENEMIES--
RRRN
ENOUGH!
BATMAN-- GET LOIS OUT OF HERE--
I'M NOT LEAVING YOU AND DIANA TO FACE--
PLEASE-- I NEED TO KNOW SHE'S SAFE.
I'M STAYING WITH--
YOU'VE GOT A STORY TO WRITE, LOIS--DYING HERE WON'T HELP YOU TELL IT.
NOW GO--WHILE WE--

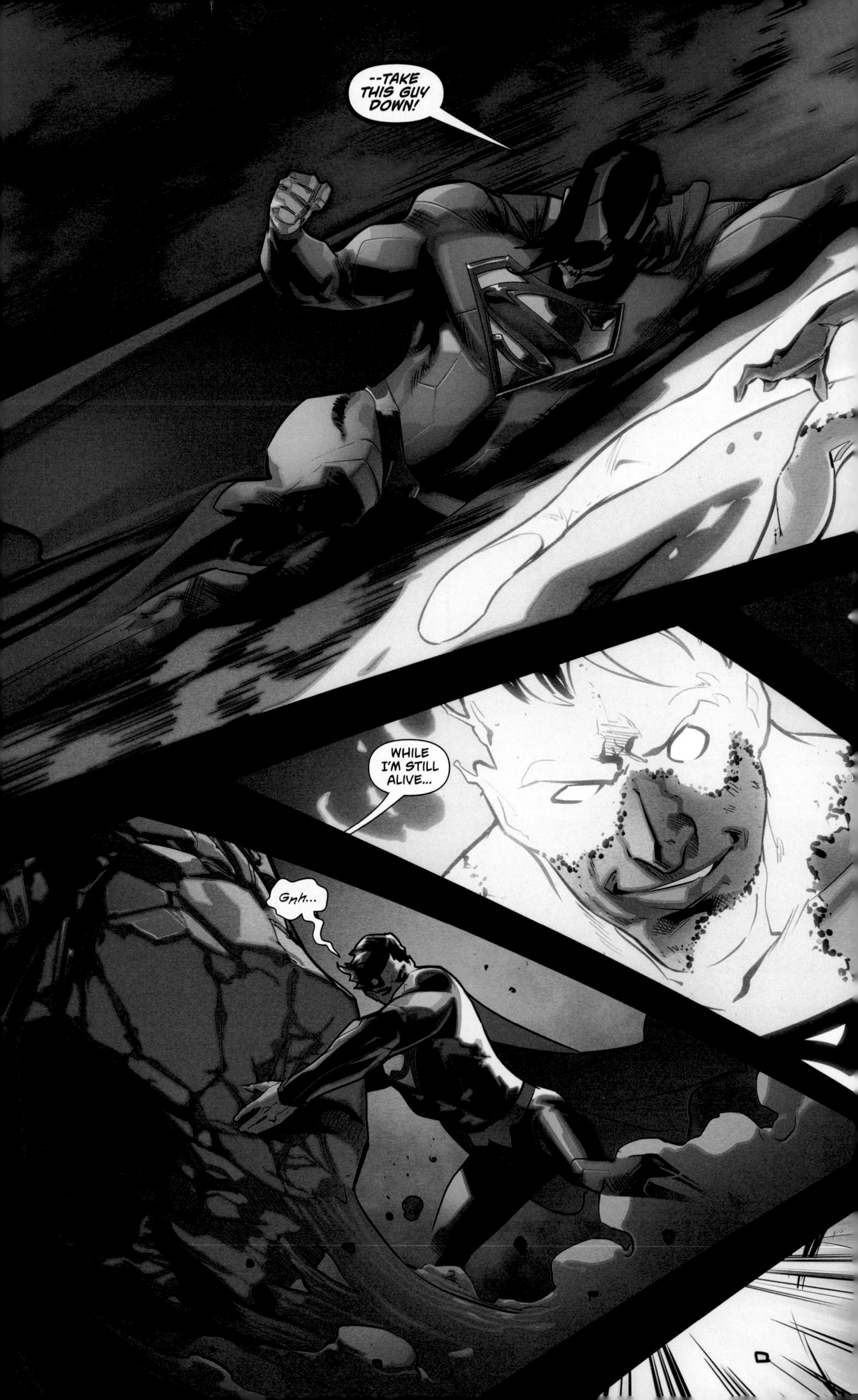
--TAKE THIS GUY DOWN!
WHILE I'M STILL ALIVE...
Gnh...

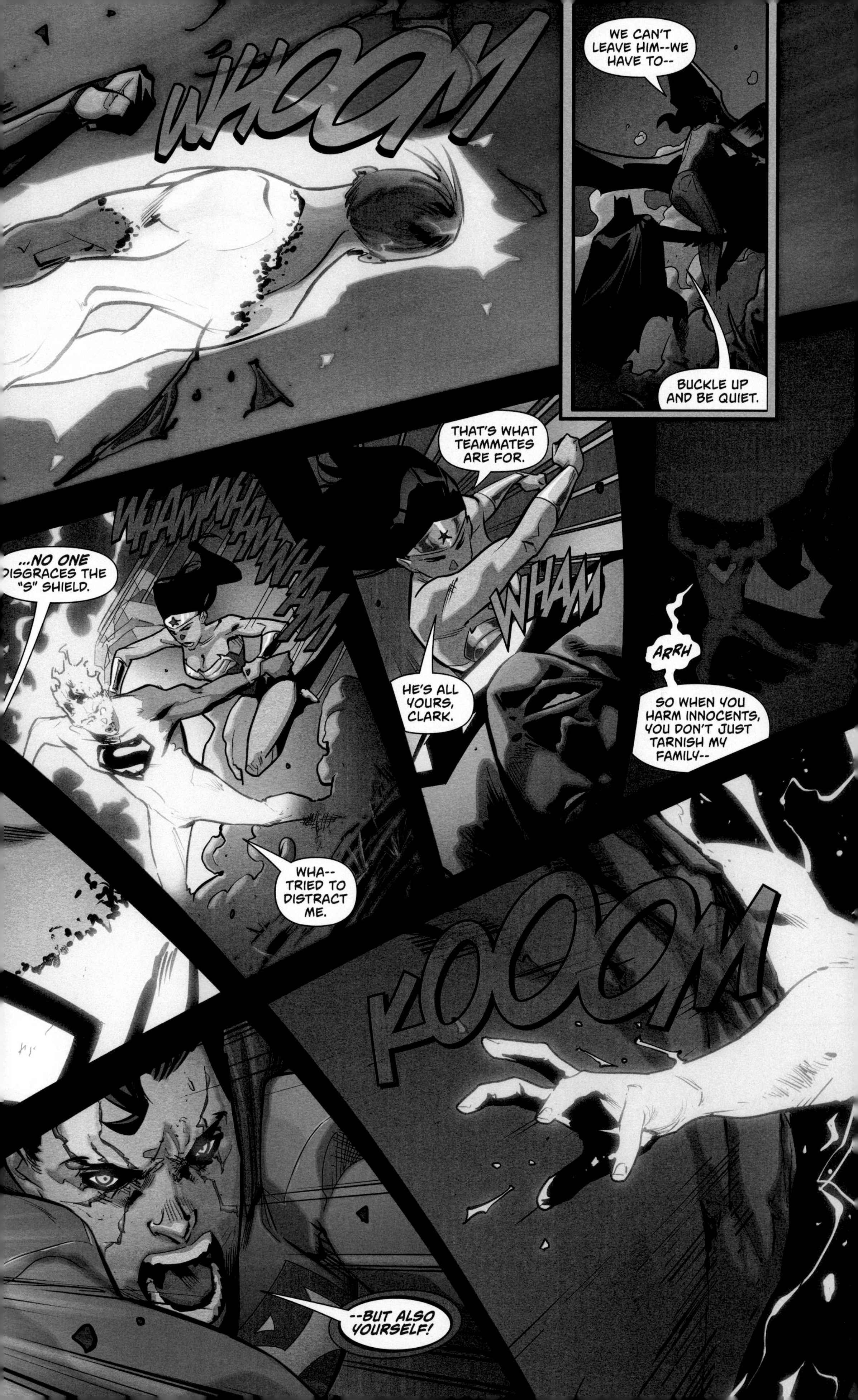
WHOOM
WE CAN'T LEAVE HIM--WE HAVE TO--
BUCKLE UP AND BE QUIET.
THAT'S WHAT TEAMMATES ARE FOR.
WHAMWHAMWHAMWHAM
...NO ONE DISGRACES THE "S" SHIELD.
WHAM
HE'S ALL YOURS, CLARK.
ARRH
SO WHEN YOU HARM INNOCENTS, YOU DON'T JUST TARNISH MY FAMILY--
WHA-- TRIED TO DISTRACT ME.
KOOOM
--BUT ALSO YOURSELF!

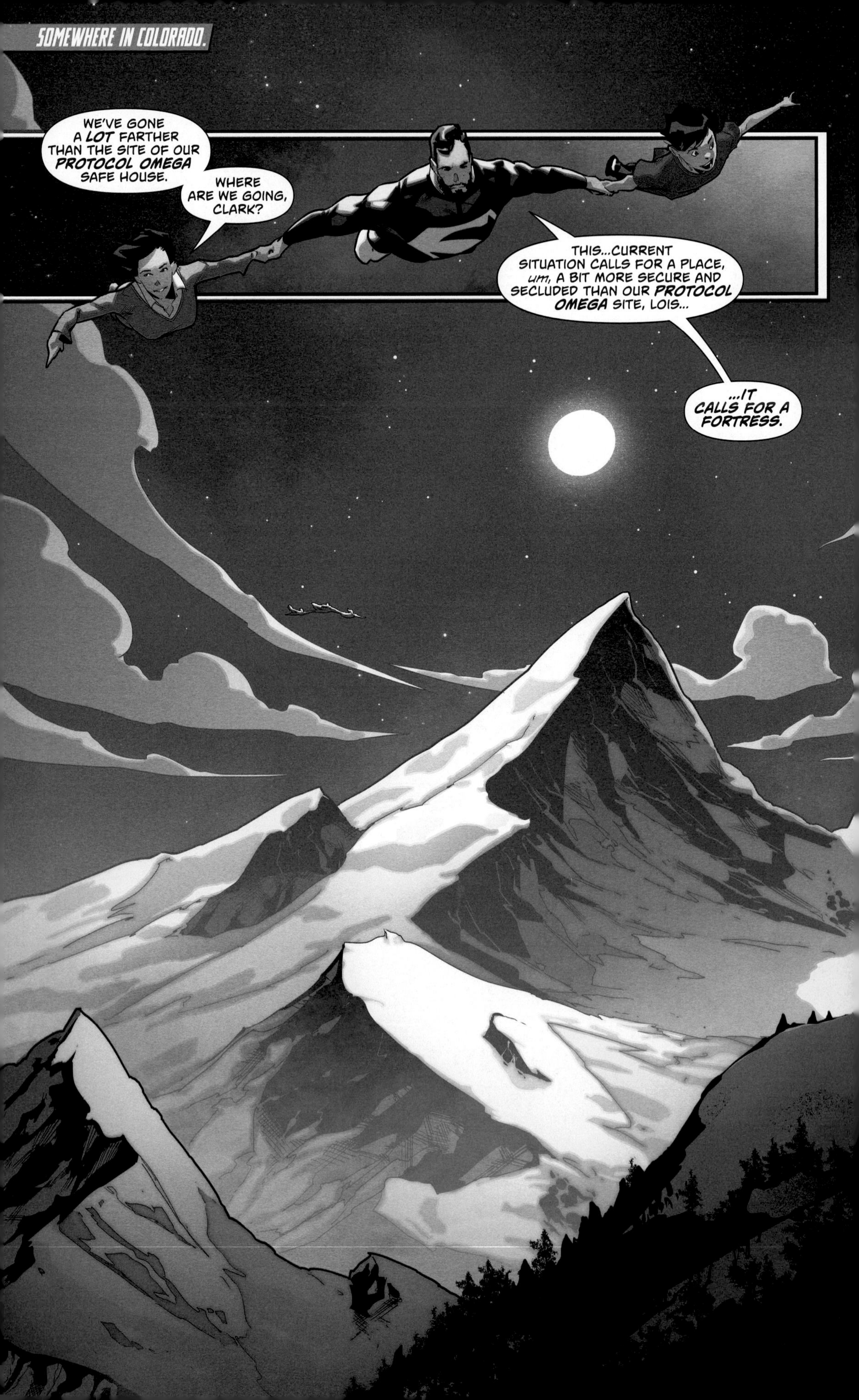
SOMEWHERE IN COLORADO.
WE'VE GONE A LOT FARTHER THAN THE SITE OF OUR PROTOCOL OMEGA SAFE HOUSE.
WHERE ARE WE GOING, CLARK?
THIS...CURRENT SITUATION CALLS FOR A PLACE, um, A BIT MORE SECURE AND SECLUDED THAN OUR PROTOCOL OMEGA SITE, LOIS...
...IT CALLS FOR A FORTRESS.

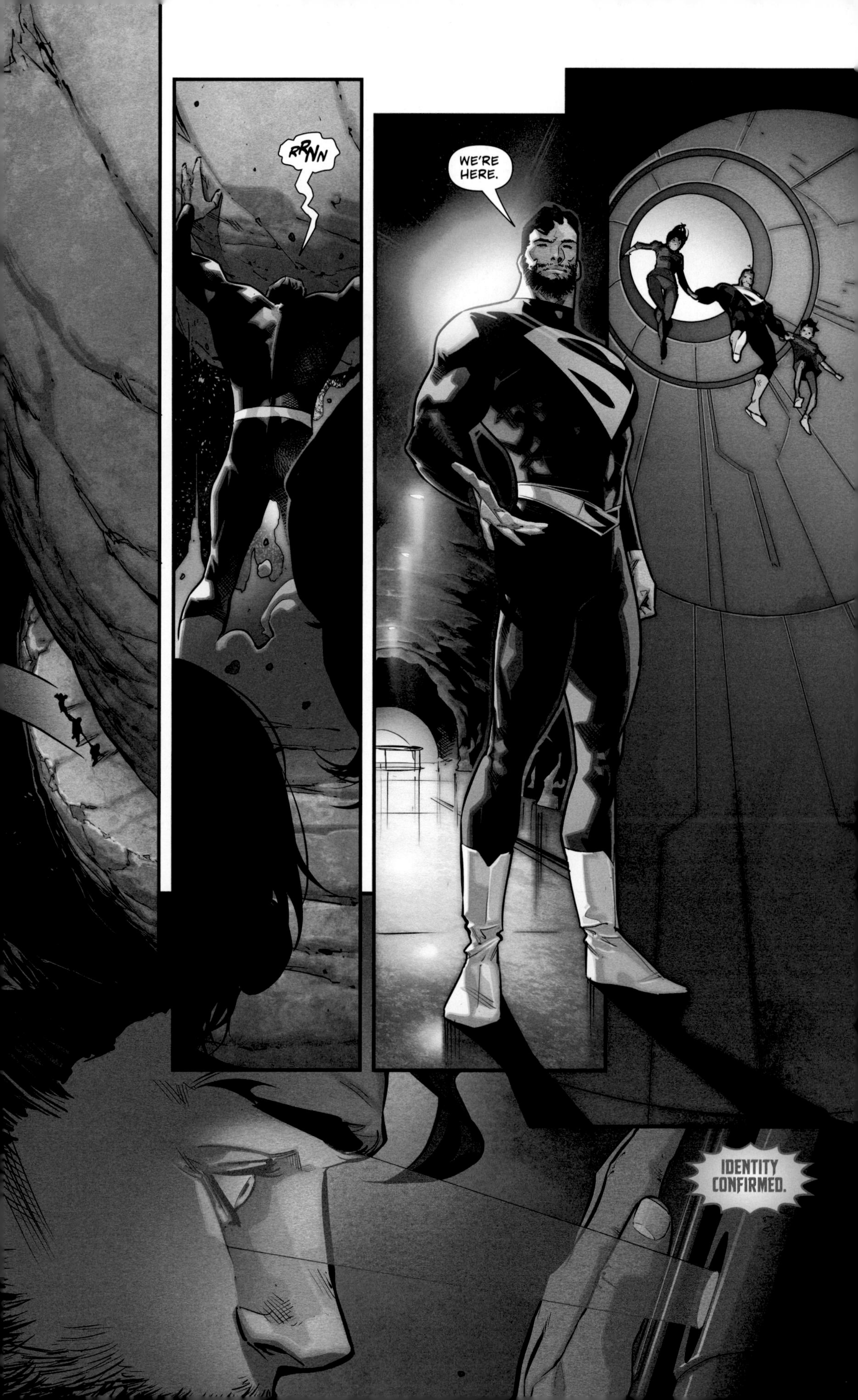
RRNN
WE'RE HERE.
IDENTITY CONFIRMED.

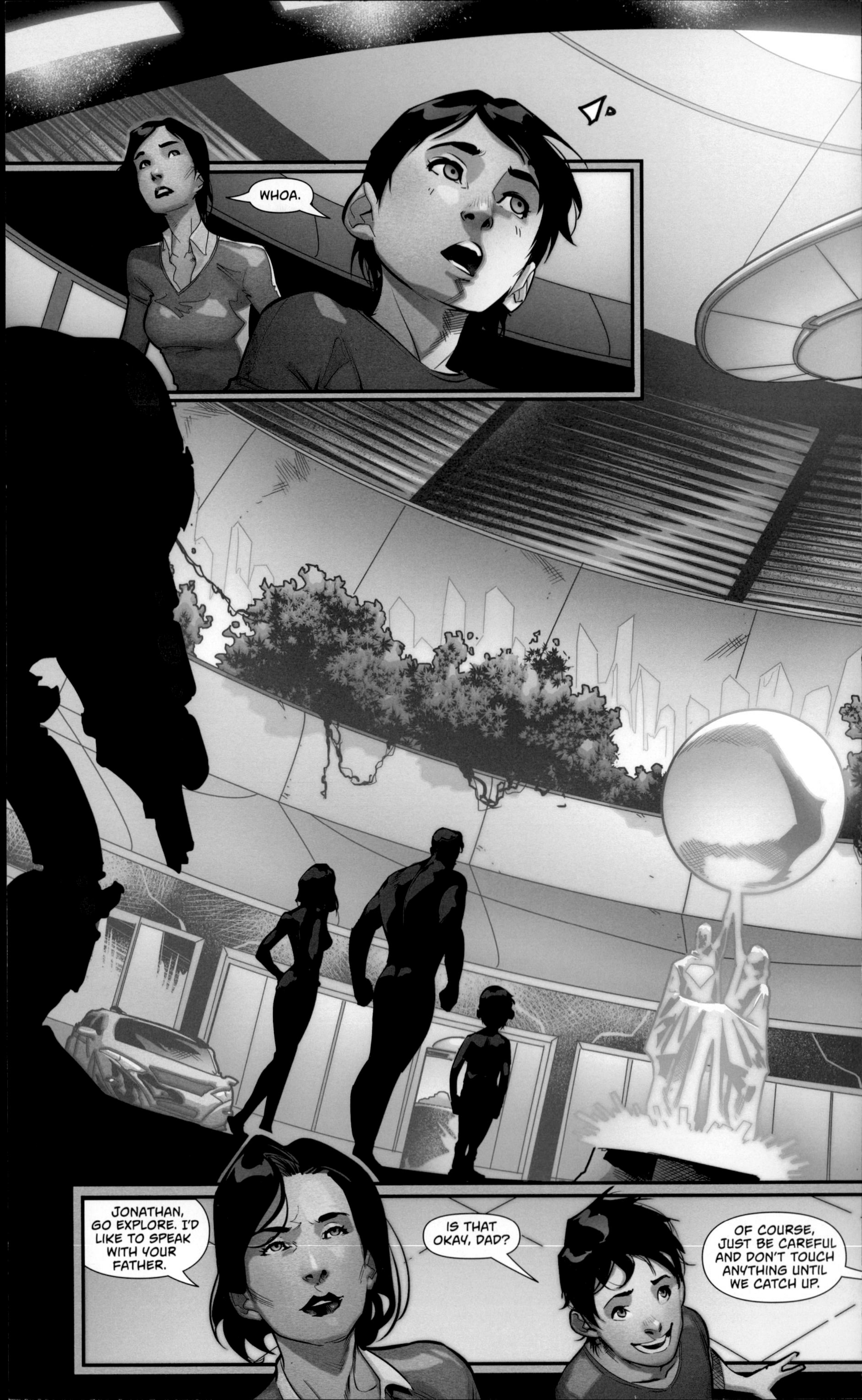
WHOA.
JONATHAN, GO EXPLORE. I'D LIKE TO SPEAK WITH YOUR FATHER.
IS THAT OKAY, DAD?
OF COURSE, JUST BE CAREFUL AND DON'T TOUCH ANYTHING UNTIL WE CATCH UP.

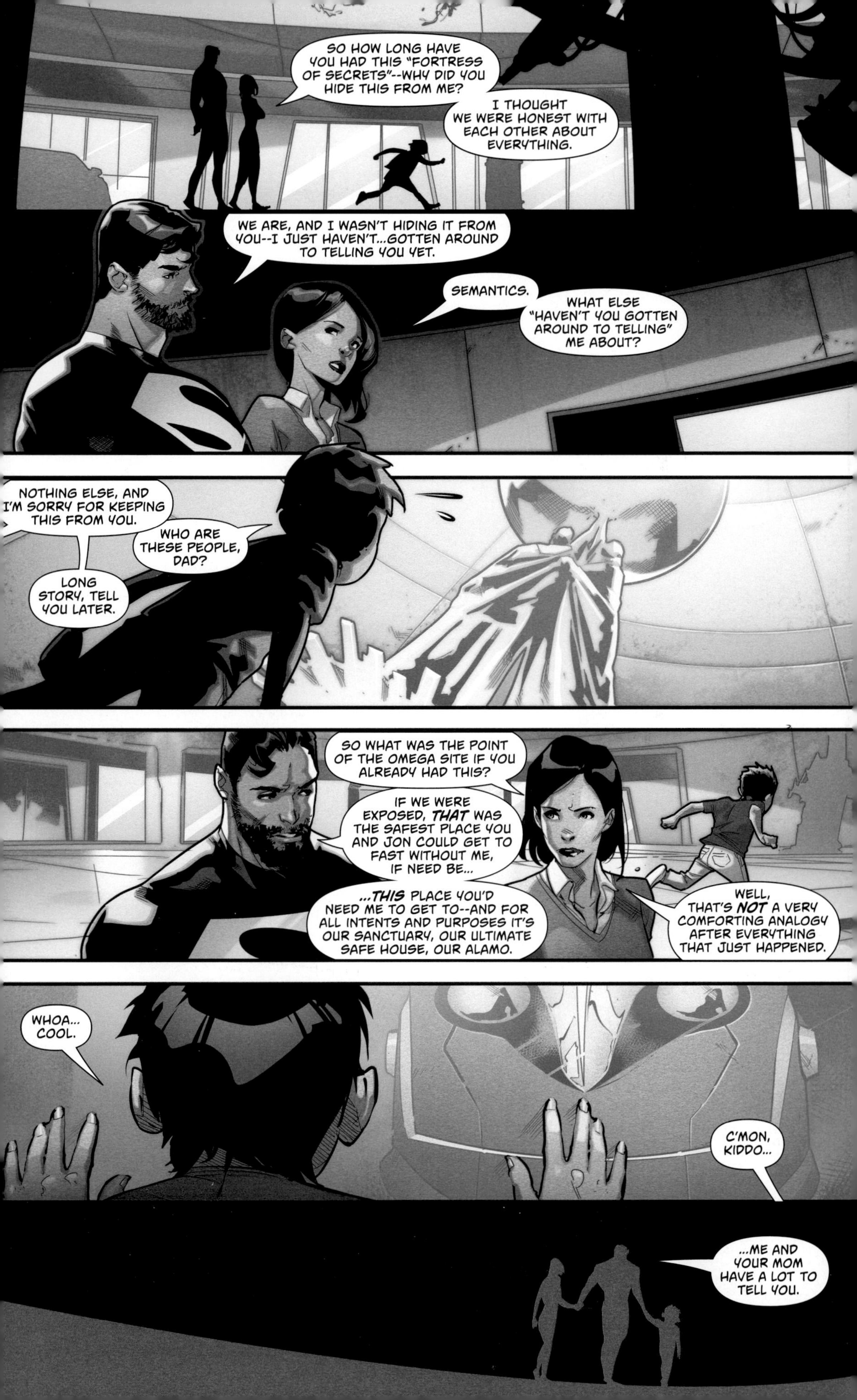
SO HOW LONG HAVE YOU HAD THIS "FORTRESS OF SECRETS"--WHY DID YOU HIDE THIS FROM ME?
I THOUGHT WE WERE HONEST WITH EACH OTHER ABOUT EVERYTHING.
WE ARE, AND I WASN'T HIDING IT FROM YOU--I JUST HAVEN'T...GOTTEN AROUND TO TELLING YOU YET.
SEMANTICS.
WHAT ELSE "HAVEN'T YOU GOTTEN AROUND TO TELLING" ME ABOUT?
NOTHING ELSE, AND I'M SORRY FOR KEEPING THIS FROM YOU.
WHO ARE THESE PEOPLE, DAD?
LONG STORY, TELL YOU LATER.
SO WHAT WAS THE POINT OF THE OMEGA SITE IF YOU ALREADY HAD THIS?
IF WE WERE EXPOSED, *THAT* WAS THE SAFEST PLACE YOU AND JON COULD GET TO FAST WITHOUT ME, IF NEED BE...
...*THIS* PLACE YOU'D NEED ME TO GET TO--AND FOR ALL INTENTS AND PURPOSES IT'S OUR SANCTUARY, OUR ULTIMATE SAFE HOUSE, OUR ALAMO.
WELL, THAT'S *NOT* A VERY COMFORTING ANALOGY AFTER EVERYTHING THAT JUST HAPPENED.
WHOA... COOL.
C'MON, KIDDO...
...ME AND YOUR MOM HAVE A LOT TO TELL YOU.

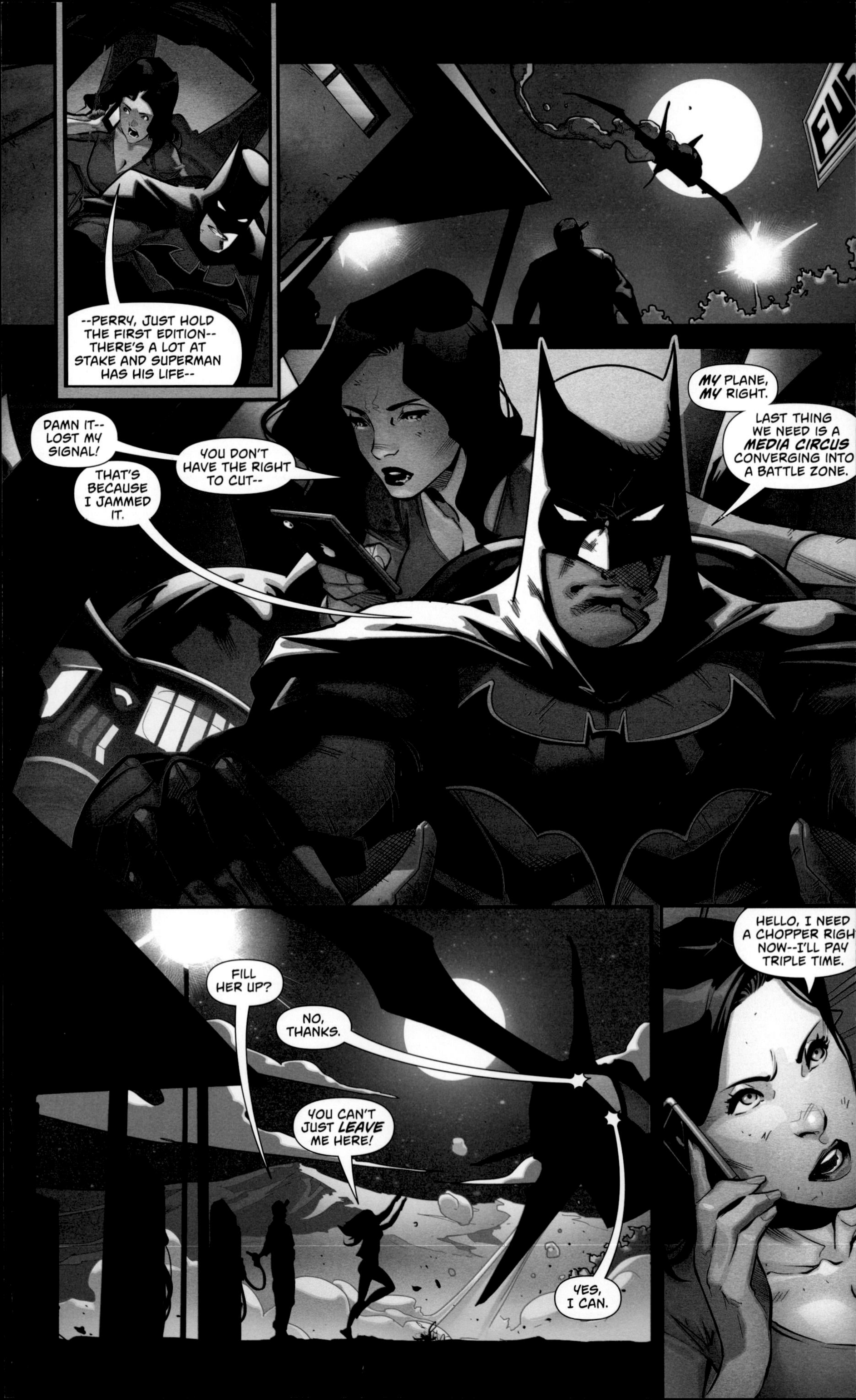

--PERRY, JUST HOLD THE FIRST EDITION--THERE'S A LOT AT STAKE AND SUPERMAN HAS HIS LIFE--
DAMN IT--LOST MY SIGNAL!
YOU DON'T HAVE THE RIGHT TO CUT--
THAT'S BECAUSE I JAMMED IT.
MY PLANE, MY RIGHT.
LAST THING WE NEED IS A MEDIA CIRCUS CONVERGING INTO A BATTLE ZONE.
FILL HER UP?
NO, THANKS.
YOU CAN'T JUST LEAVE ME HERE!
YES, I CAN.
HELLO, I NEED A CHOPPER RIGH NOW--I'LL PAY TRIPLE TIME.

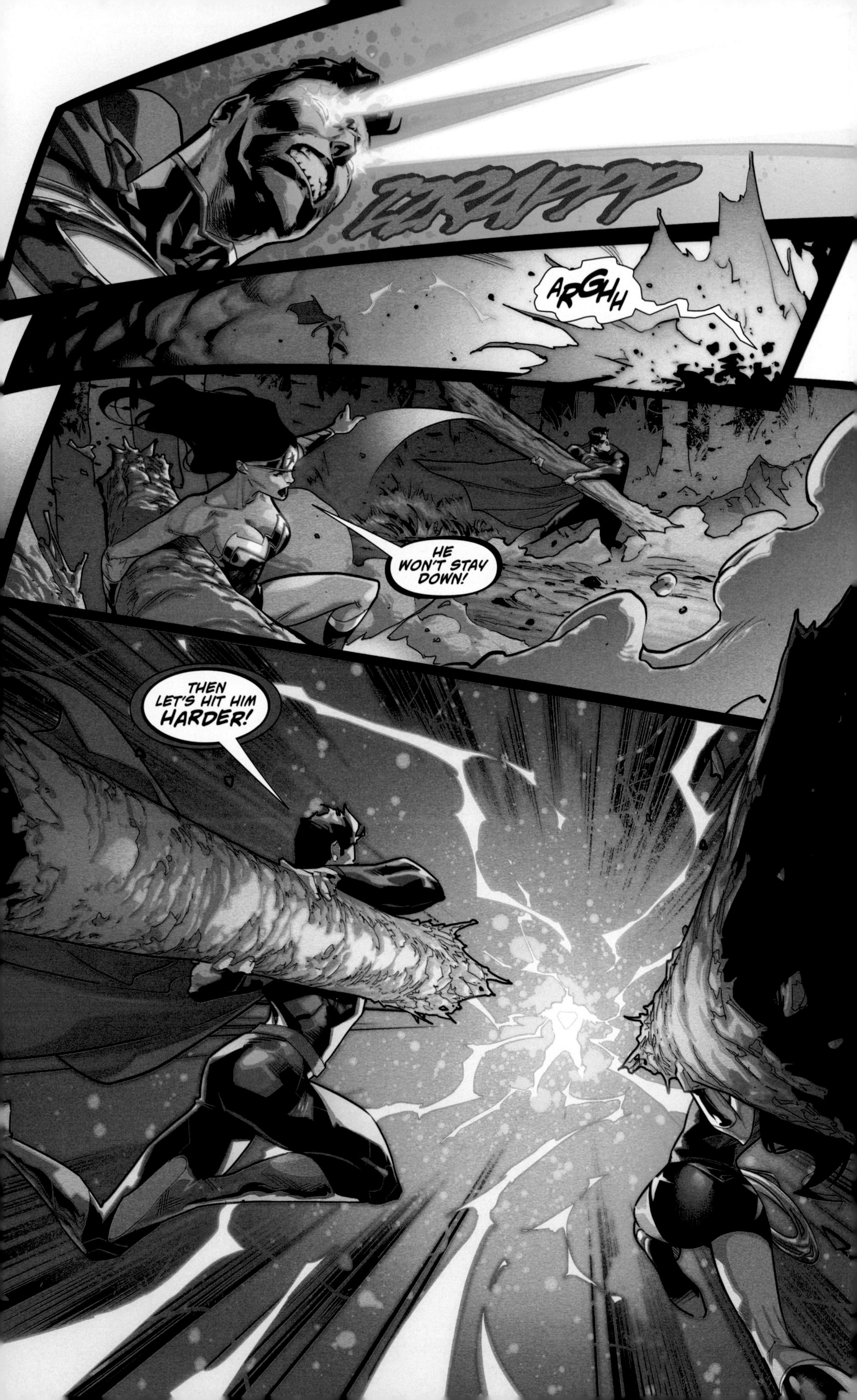
ZZRAPPP
ARGHH
HE WON'T STAY DOWN!
THEN LET'S HIT HIM HARDER!

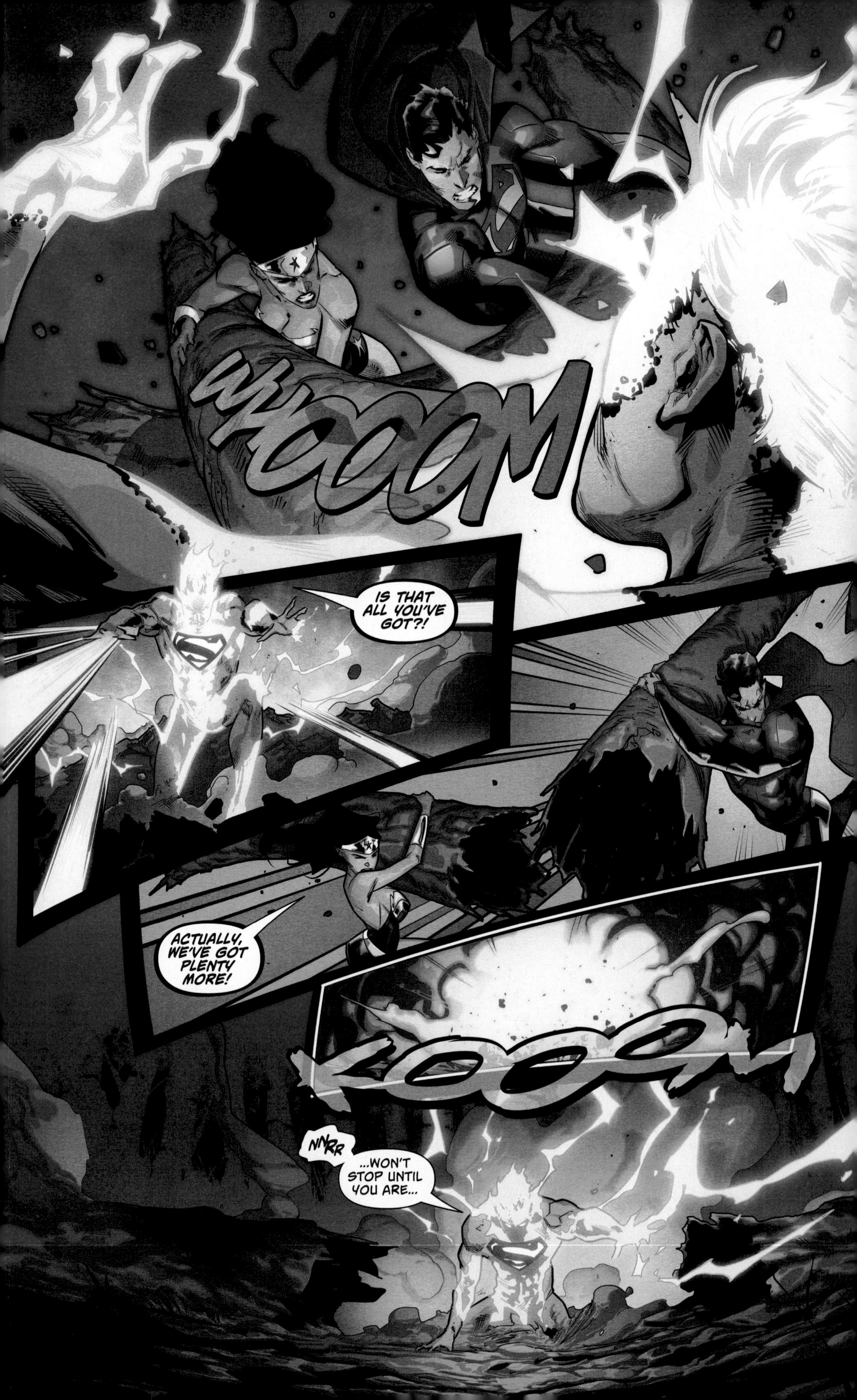
WHOOOM
IS THAT ALL YOU'VE GOT?!
ACTUALLY, WE'VE GOT PLENTY MORE!
KOOOM
NNRR
...WON'T STOP UNTIL YOU ARE...

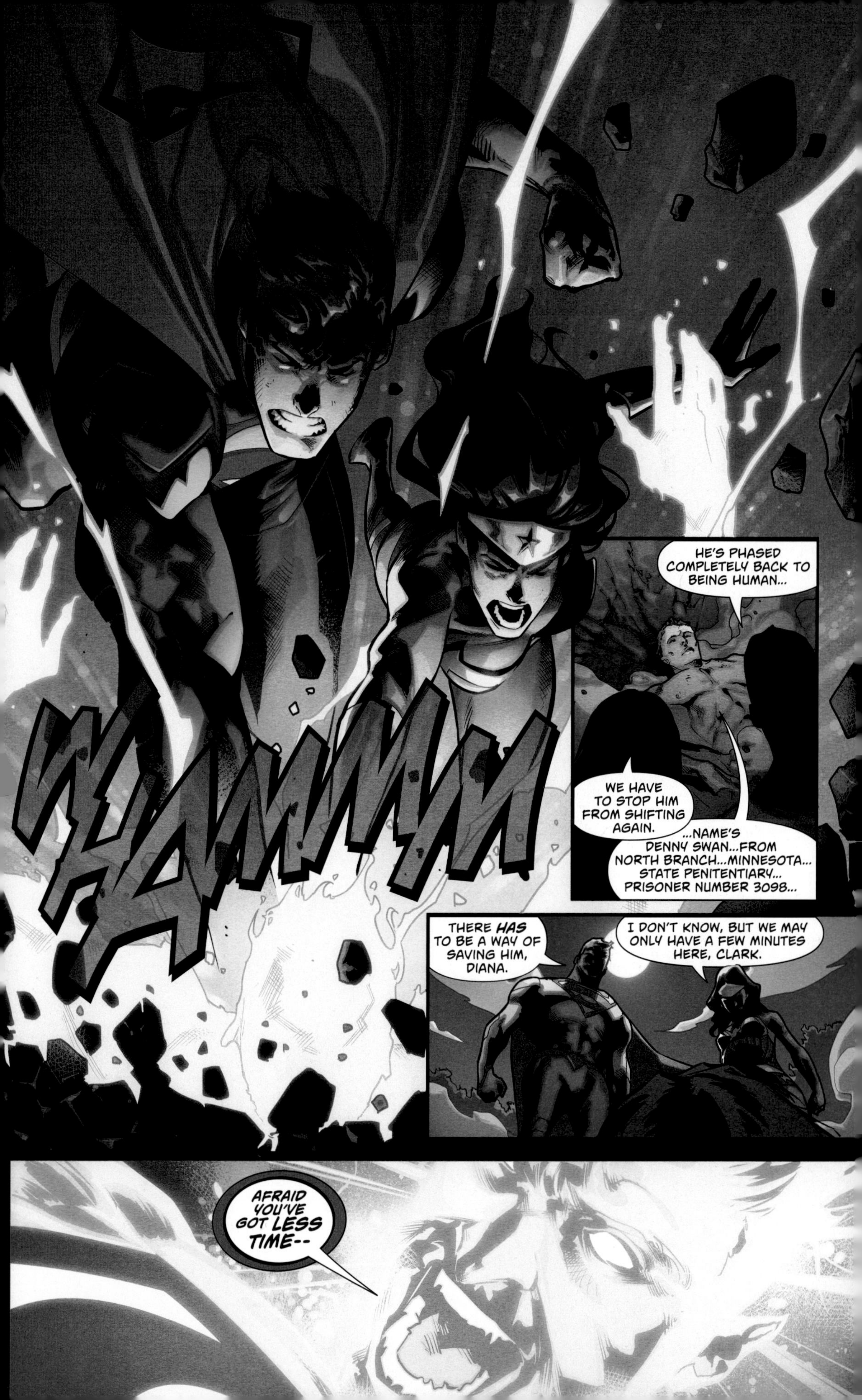
WHAMMM
HE'S PHASED COMPLETELY BACK TO BEING HUMAN...
WE HAVE TO STOP HIM FROM SHIFTING AGAIN.
...NAME'S DENNY SWAN...FROM NORTH BRANCH...MINNESOTA... STATE PENITENTIARY... PRISONER NUMBER 3098...
THERE HAS TO BE A WAY OF SAVING HIM, DIANA.
I DON'T KNOW, BUT WE MAY ONLY HAVE A FEW MINUTES HERE, CLARK.
AFRAID YOU'VE GOT LESS TIME--

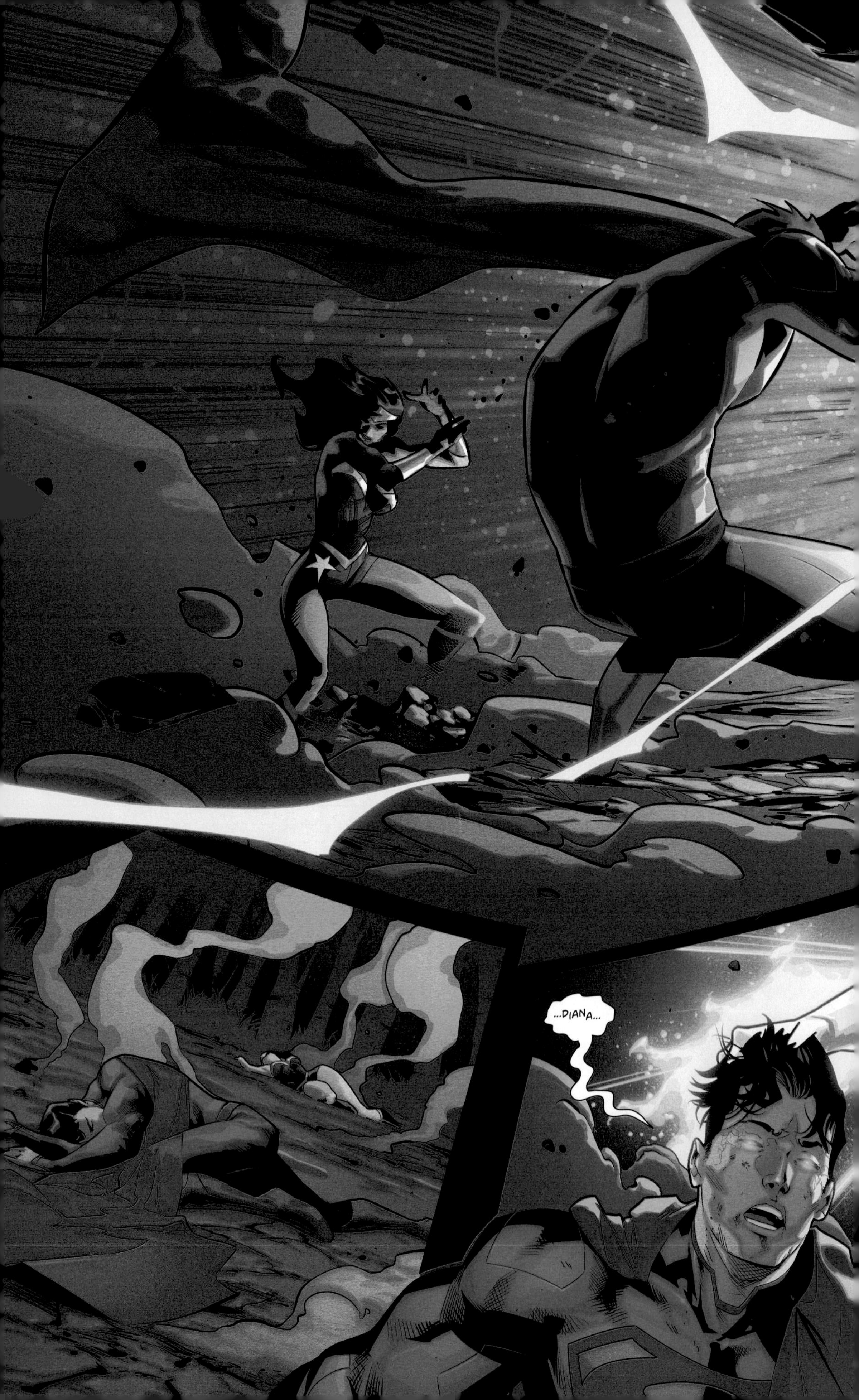
...DIANA...

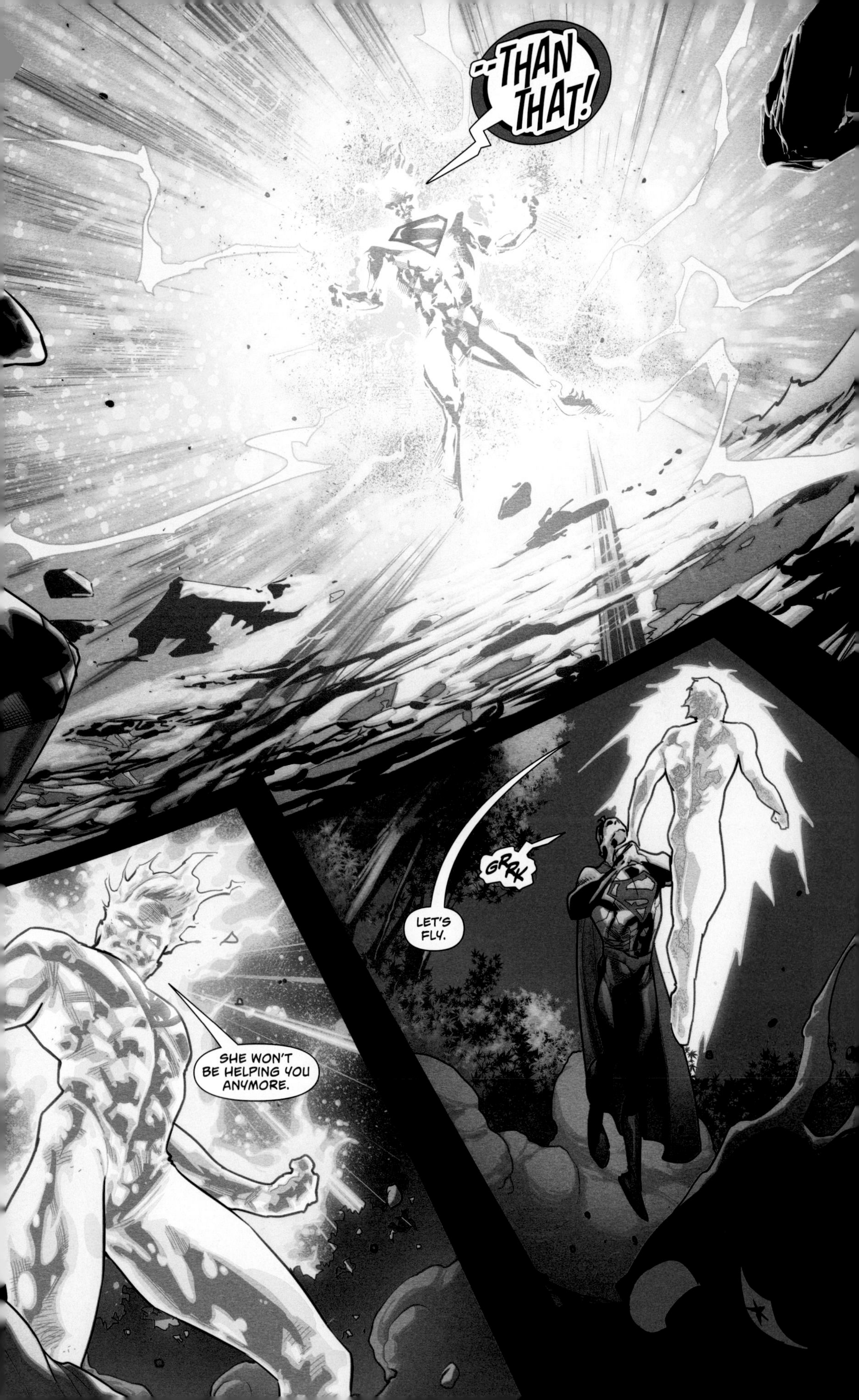

--THAN THAT!
SHE WON'T BE HELPING YOU ANYMORE.
LET'S FLY.
GRRK

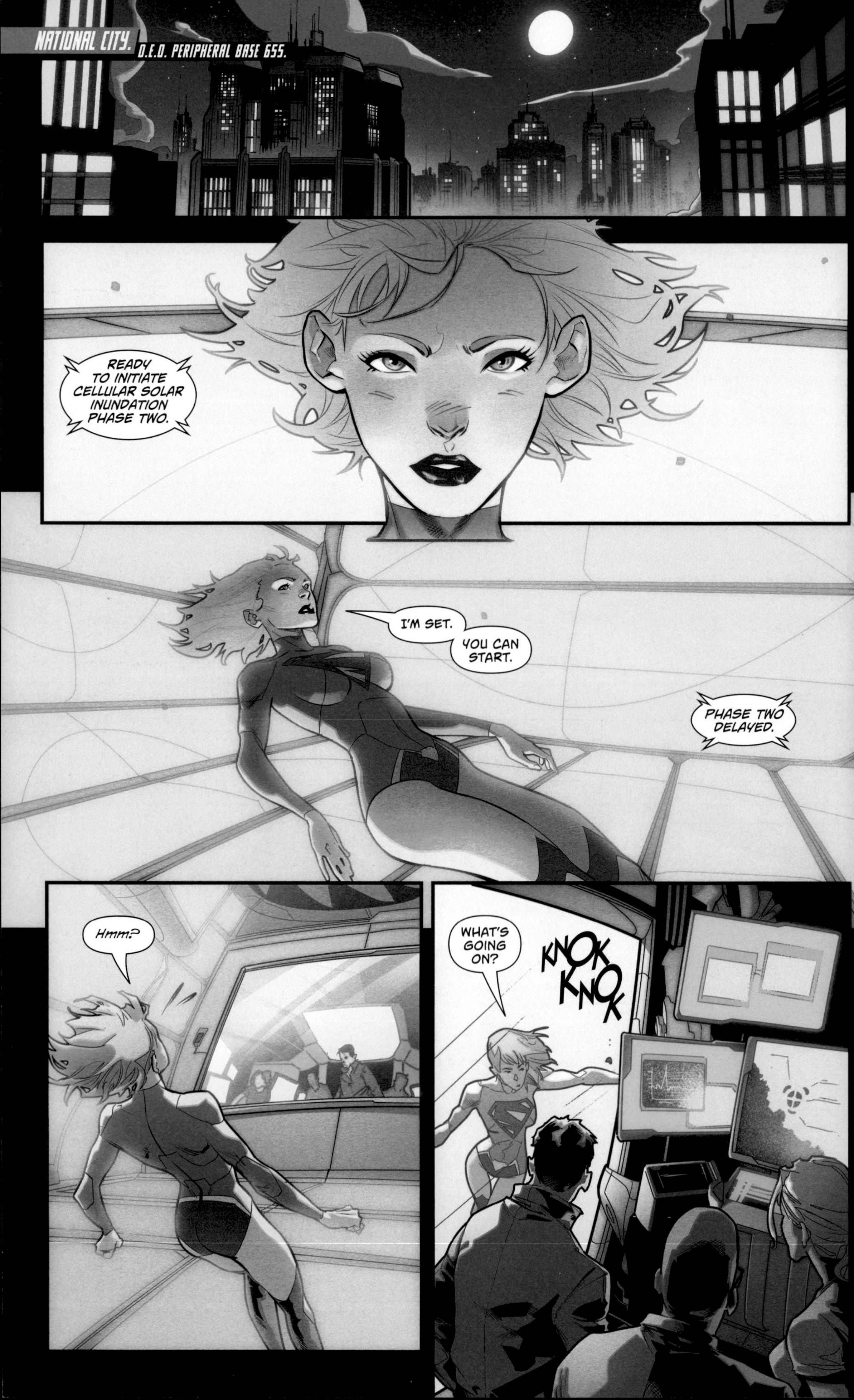
NATIONAL CITY.
D.E.O. PERIPHERAL BASE 655.
READY TO INITIATE CELLULAR SOLAR INUNDATION PHASE TWO.
I'M SET.
YOU CAN START.
PHASE TWO DELAYED.
Hmm?
WHAT'S GOING ON?
KNOK KNOK

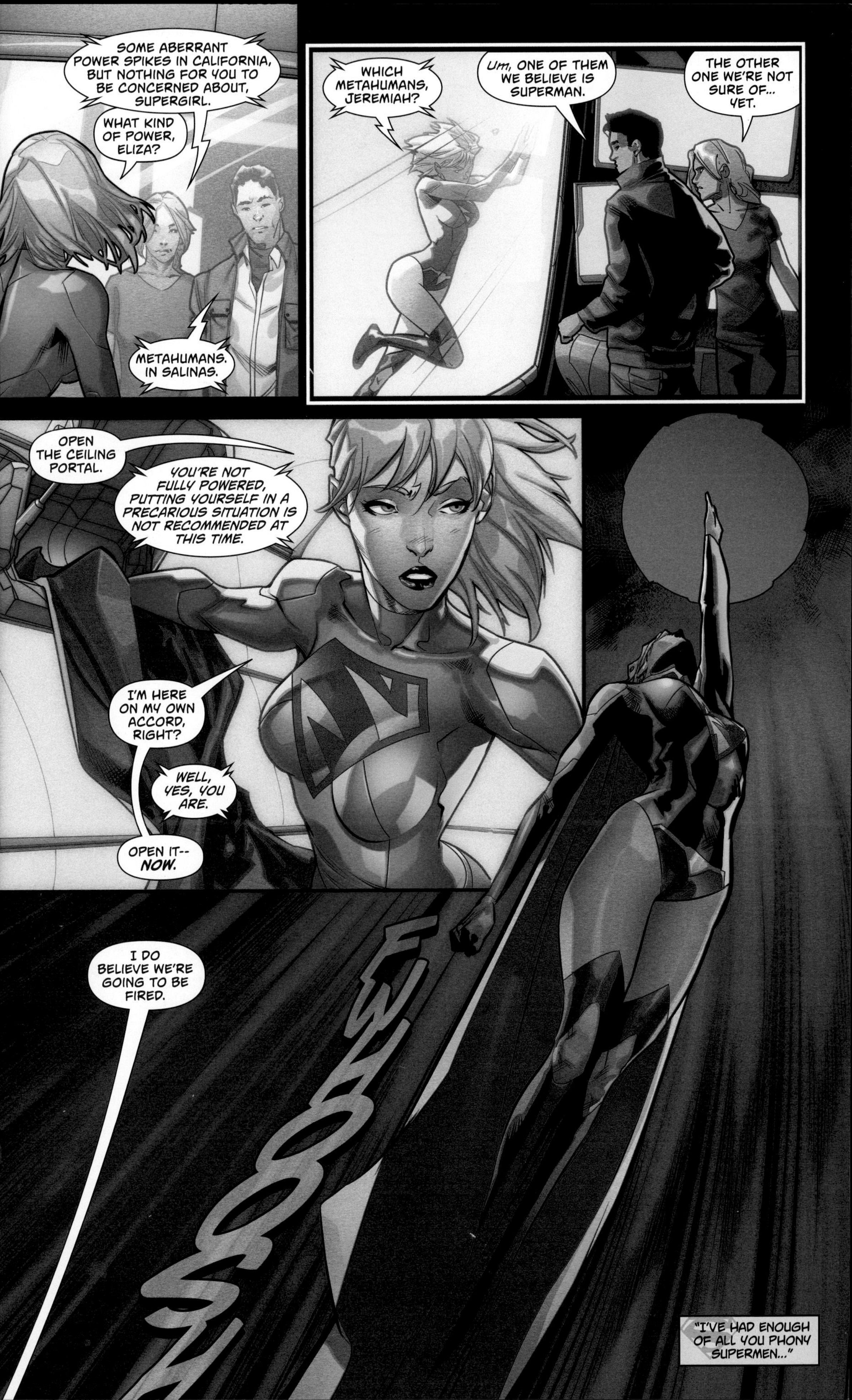

SOME ABERRANT POWER SPIKES IN CALIFORNIA, BUT NOTHING FOR YOU TO BE CONCERNED ABOUT, SUPERGIRL.
WHAT KIND OF POWER, ELIZA?
METAHUMANS. IN SALINAS.
WHICH METAHUMANS, JEREMIAH?
UM, ONE OF THEM WE BELIEVE IS SUPERMAN.
THE OTHER ONE WE'RE NOT SURE OF... YET.
OPEN THE CEILING PORTAL.
YOU'RE NOT FULLY POWERED, PUTTING YOURSELF IN A PRECARIOUS SITUATION IS NOT RECOMMENDED AT THIS TIME.
I'M HERE ON MY OWN ACCORD, RIGHT?
WELL, YES, YOU ARE.
OPEN IT-- NOW.
I DO BELIEVE WE'RE GOING TO BE FIRED.
FWHOOOOSH
"I'VE HAD ENOUGH OF ALL YOU PHONY SUPERMEN..."

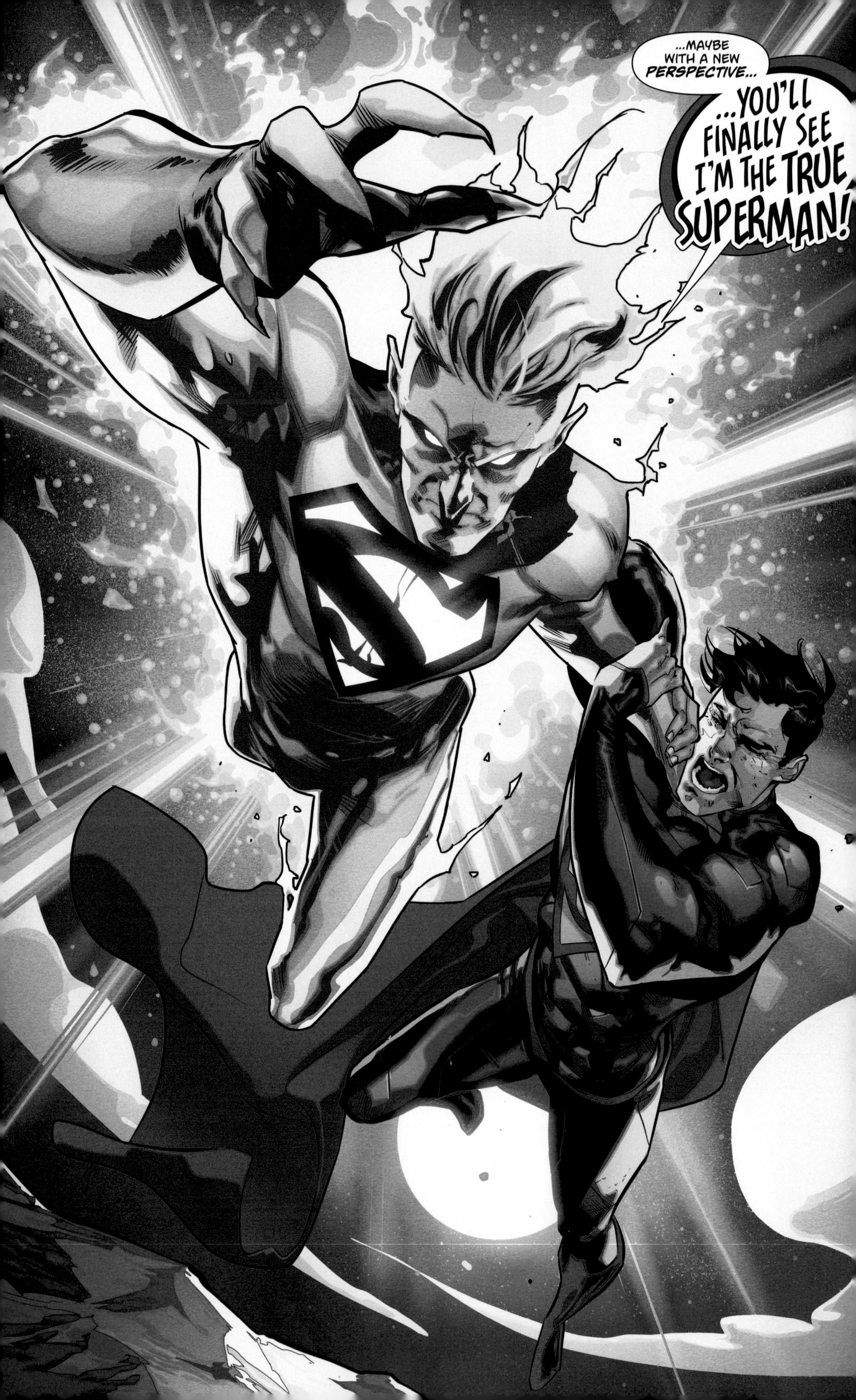
...MAYBE WITH A NEW PERSPECTIVE...
...YOU'LL FINALLY SEE I'M THE TRUE SUPERMAN!

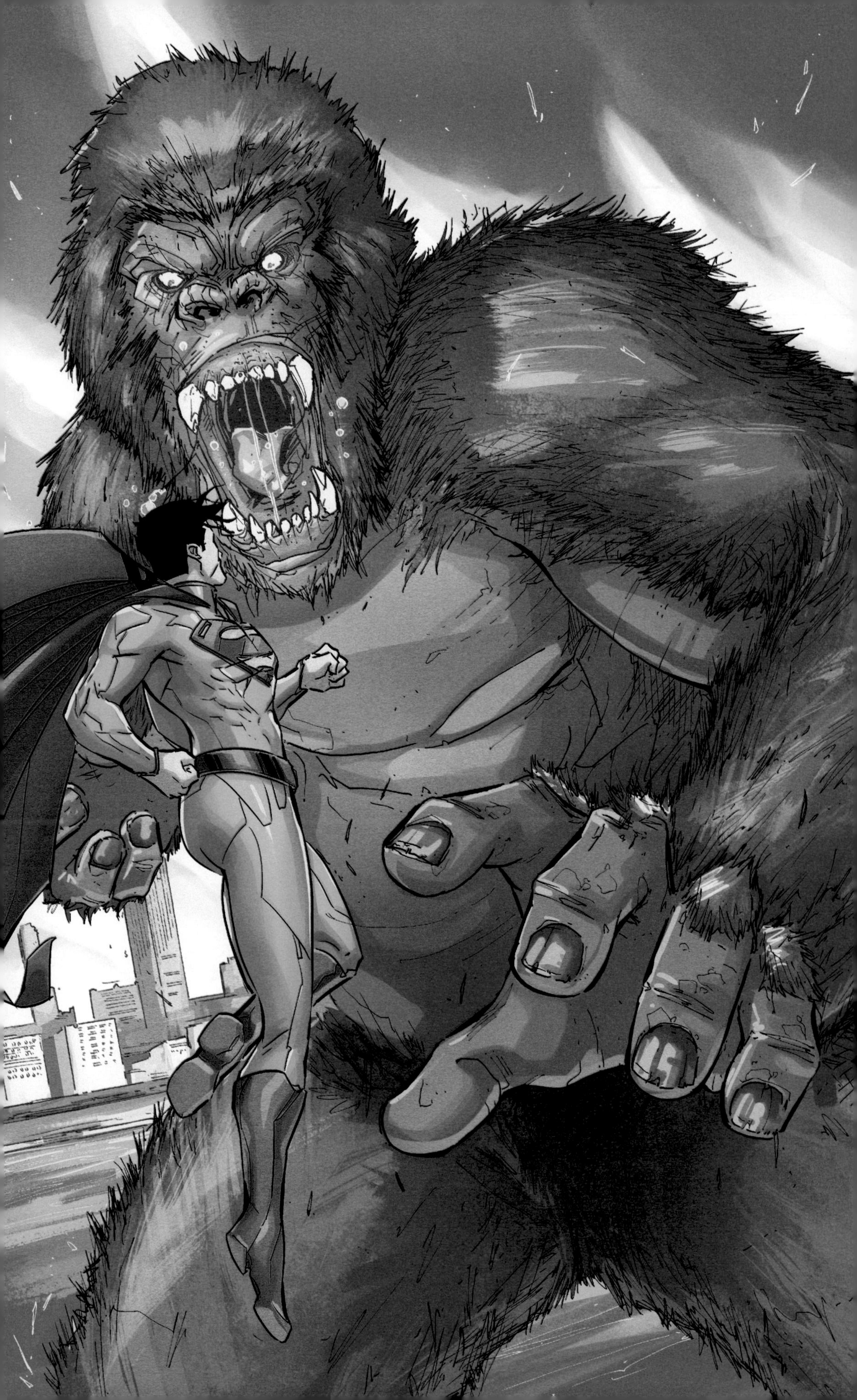

GRIEF

BRIAN BUCCELLATO writer **GIUSEPPE CAFARO** artist **HI-FI** colorist **TRAVIS LANHAM** letterer

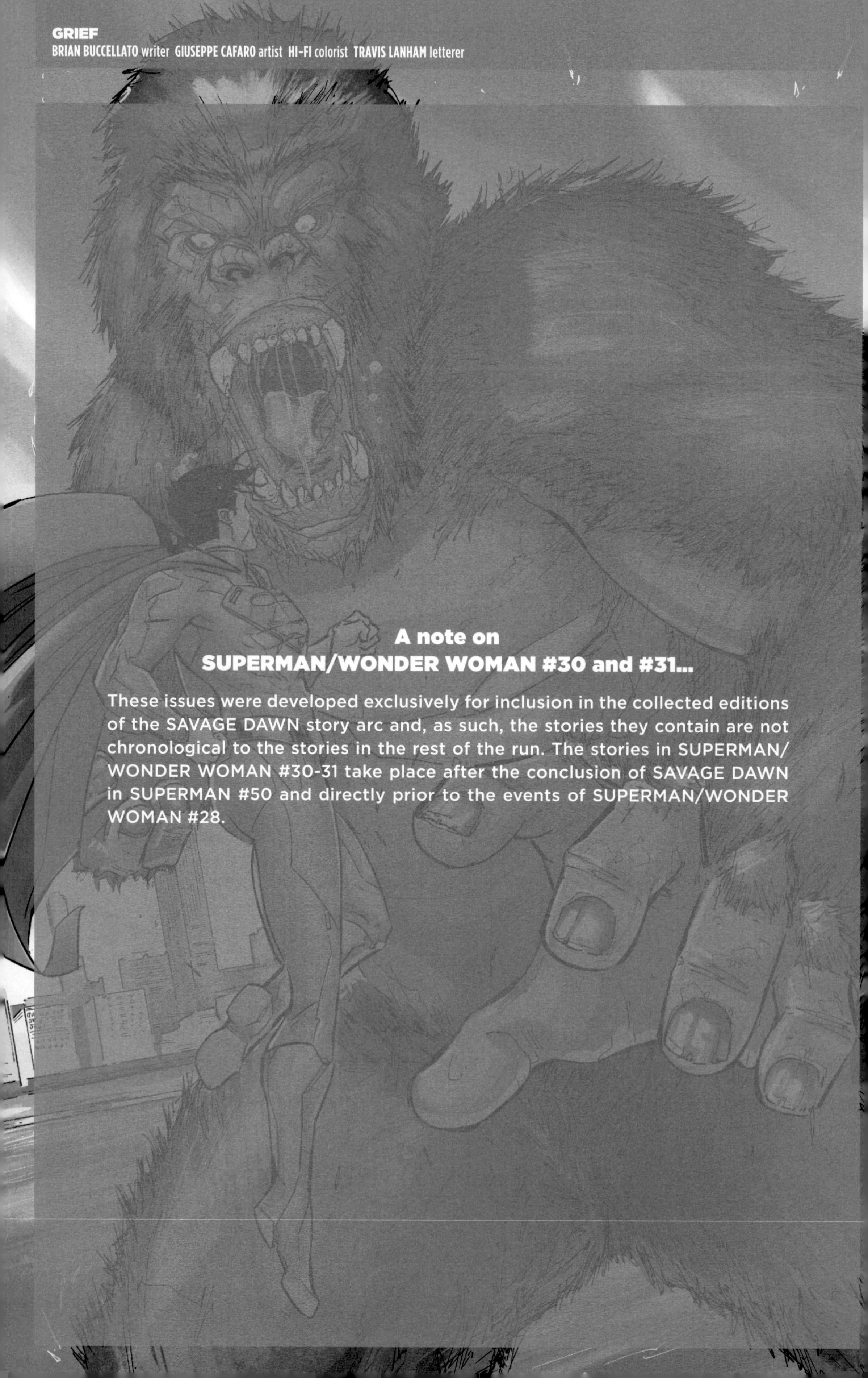

A note on SUPERMAN/WONDER WOMAN #30 and #31...

These issues were developed exclusively for inclusion in the collected editions of the SAVAGE DAWN story arc and, as such, the stories they contain are not chronological to the stories in the rest of the run. The stories in SUPERMAN/WONDER WOMAN #30-31 take place after the conclusion of SAVAGE DAWN in SUPERMAN #50 and directly prior to the events of SUPERMAN/WONDER WOMAN #28.

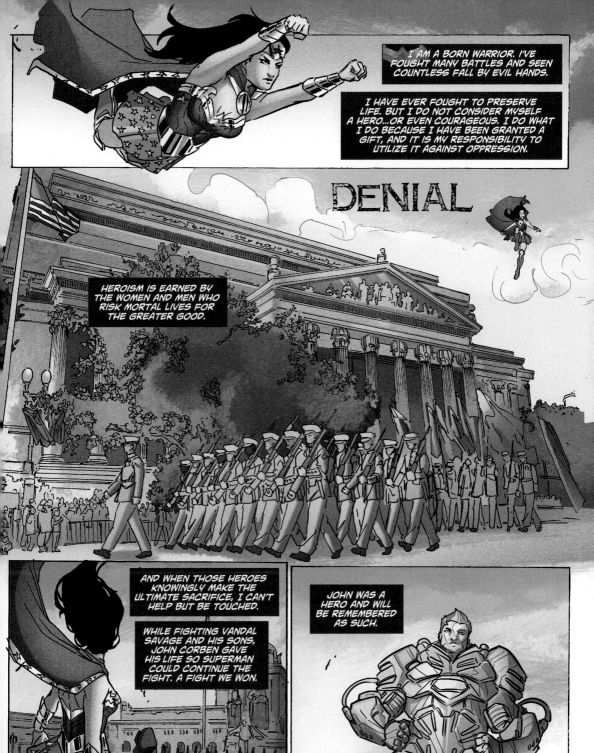

I AM A BORN WARRIOR. I'VE FOUGHT MANY BATTLES AND SEEN COUNTLESS FALL BY EVIL HANDS.

I HAVE EVER FOUGHT TO PRESERVE LIFE. BUT I DO NOT CONSIDER MYSELF A HERO...OR EVEN COURAGEOUS. I DO WHAT I DO BECAUSE I HAVE BEEN GRANTED A GIFT, AND IT IS MY RESPONSIBILITY TO UTILIZE IT AGAINST OPPRESSION.

DENIAL

HEROISM IS EARNED BY THE WOMEN AND MEN WHO RISK MORTAL LIVES FOR THE GREATER GOOD.

AND WHEN THOSE HEROES KNOWINGLY MAKE THE ULTIMATE SACRIFICE, I CAN'T HELP BUT BE TOUCHED.

WHILE FIGHTING VANDAL SAVAGE AND HIS SONS, JOHN CORBEN GAVE HIS LIFE SO SUPERMAN COULD CONTINUE THE FIGHT. A FIGHT WE WON.

JOHN WAS A HERO AND WILL BE REMEMBERED AS SUCH.

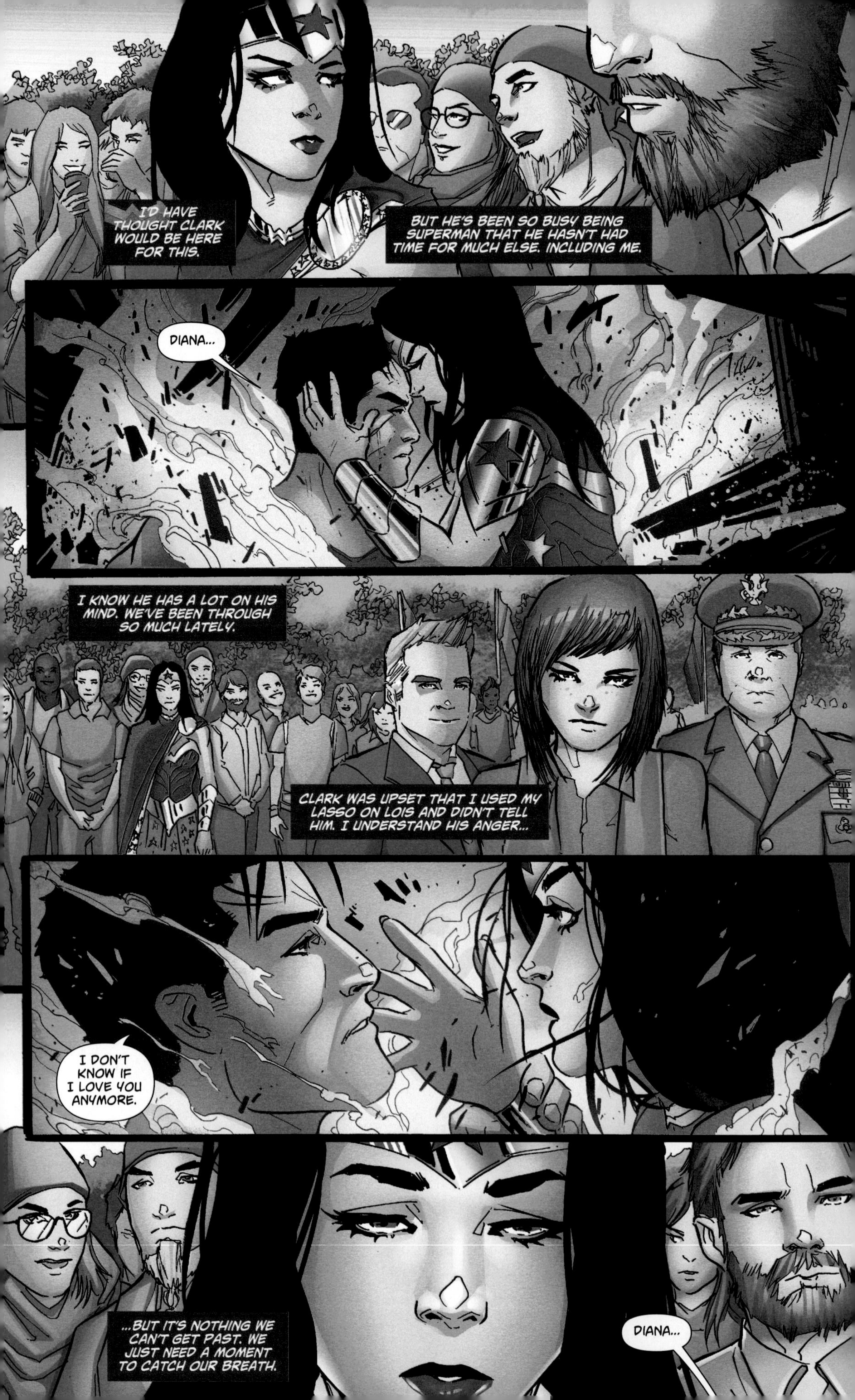
I'D HAVE THOUGHT CLARK WOULD BE HERE FOR THIS.
BUT HE'S BEEN SO BUSY BEING SUPERMAN THAT HE HASN'T HAD TIME FOR MUCH ELSE. INCLUDING ME.
DIANA...
I KNOW HE HAS A LOT ON HIS MIND. WE'VE BEEN THROUGH SO MUCH LATELY.
CLARK WAS UPSET THAT I USED MY LASSO ON LOIS AND DIDN'T TELL HIM. I UNDERSTAND HIS ANGER...
I DON'T KNOW IF I LOVE YOU ANYMORE.
...BUT IT'S NOTHING WE CAN'T GET PAST. WE JUST NEED A MOMENT TO CATCH OUR BREATH.
DIANA...

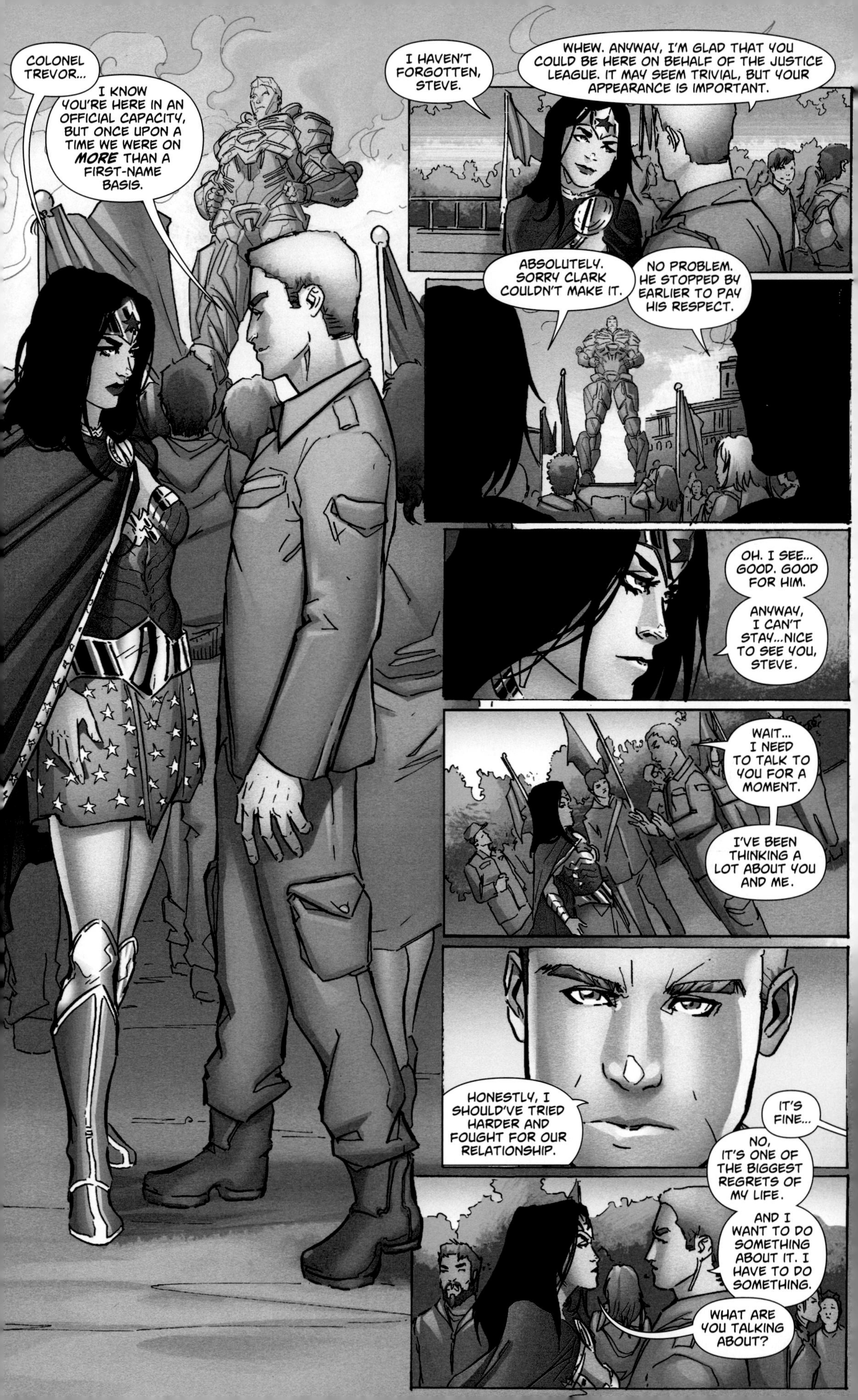
COLONEL TREVOR...
I KNOW YOU'RE HERE IN AN OFFICIAL CAPACITY, BUT ONCE UPON A TIME WE WERE ON MORE THAN A FIRST-NAME BASIS.
I HAVEN'T FORGOTTEN, STEVE.
WHEW. ANYWAY, I'M GLAD THAT YOU COULD BE HERE ON BEHALF OF THE JUSTICE LEAGUE. IT MAY SEEM TRIVIAL, BUT YOUR APPEARANCE IS IMPORTANT.
ABSOLUTELY. SORRY CLARK COULDN'T MAKE IT.
NO PROBLEM. HE STOPPED BY EARLIER TO PAY HIS RESPECT.
OH. I SEE... GOOD. GOOD FOR HIM.
ANYWAY, I CAN'T STAY...NICE TO SEE YOU, STEVE.
WAIT... I NEED TO TALK TO YOU FOR A MOMENT.
I'VE BEEN THINKING A LOT ABOUT YOU AND ME.
HONESTLY, I SHOULD'VE TRIED HARDER AND FOUGHT FOR OUR RELATIONSHIP.
IT'S FINE...
NO, IT'S ONE OF THE BIGGEST REGRETS OF MY LIFE.
AND I WANT TO DO SOMETHING ABOUT IT. I HAVE TO DO SOMETHING.
WHAT ARE YOU TALKING ABOUT?

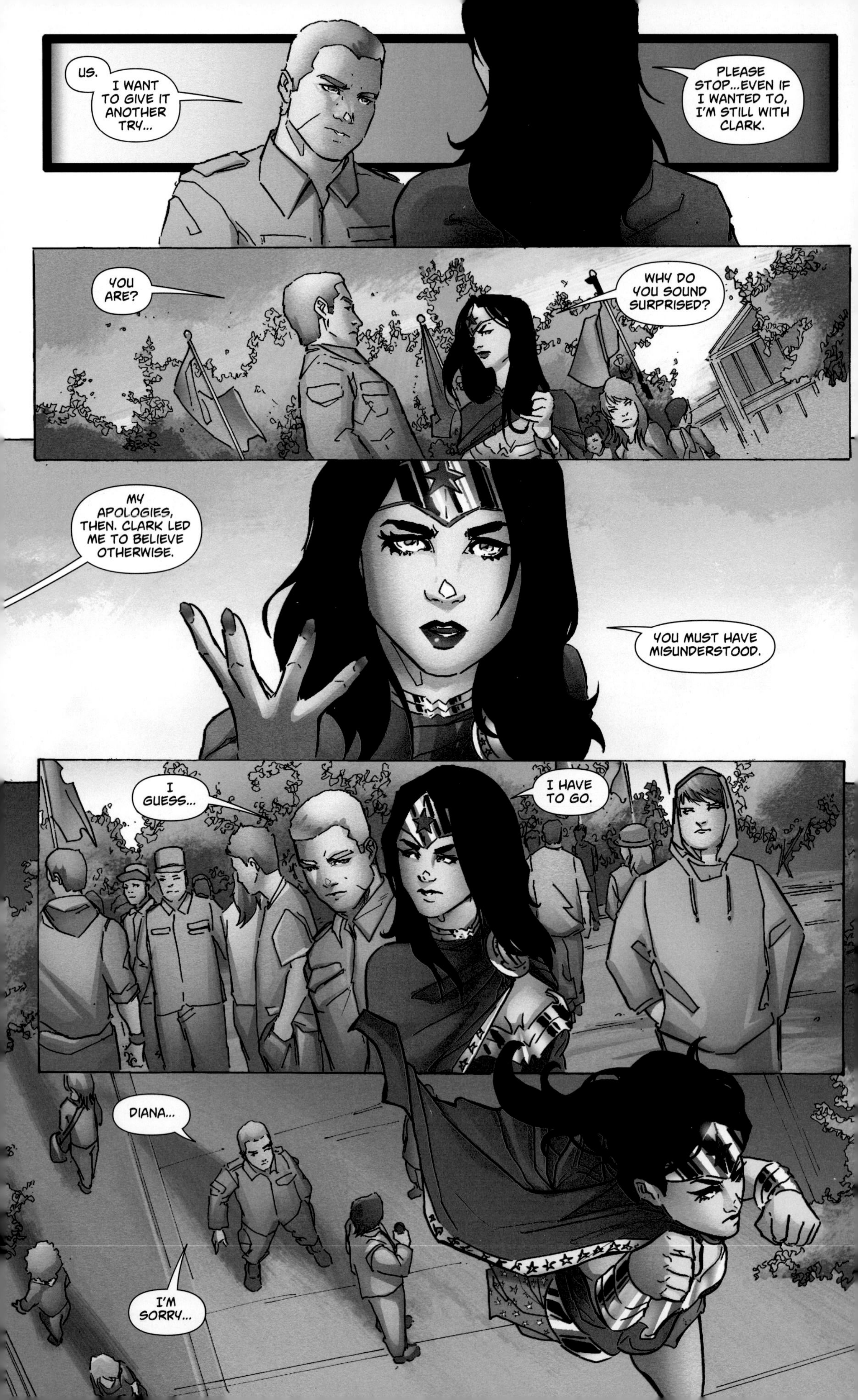
US.
I WANT TO GIVE IT ANOTHER TRY...
PLEASE STOP...EVEN IF I WANTED TO, I'M STILL WITH CLARK.
YOU ARE?
WHY DO YOU SOUND SURPRISED?
MY APOLOGIES, THEN. CLARK LED ME TO BELIEVE OTHERWISE.
YOU MUST HAVE MISUNDERSTOOD.
I GUESS...
I HAVE TO GO.
DIANA...
I'M SORRY...

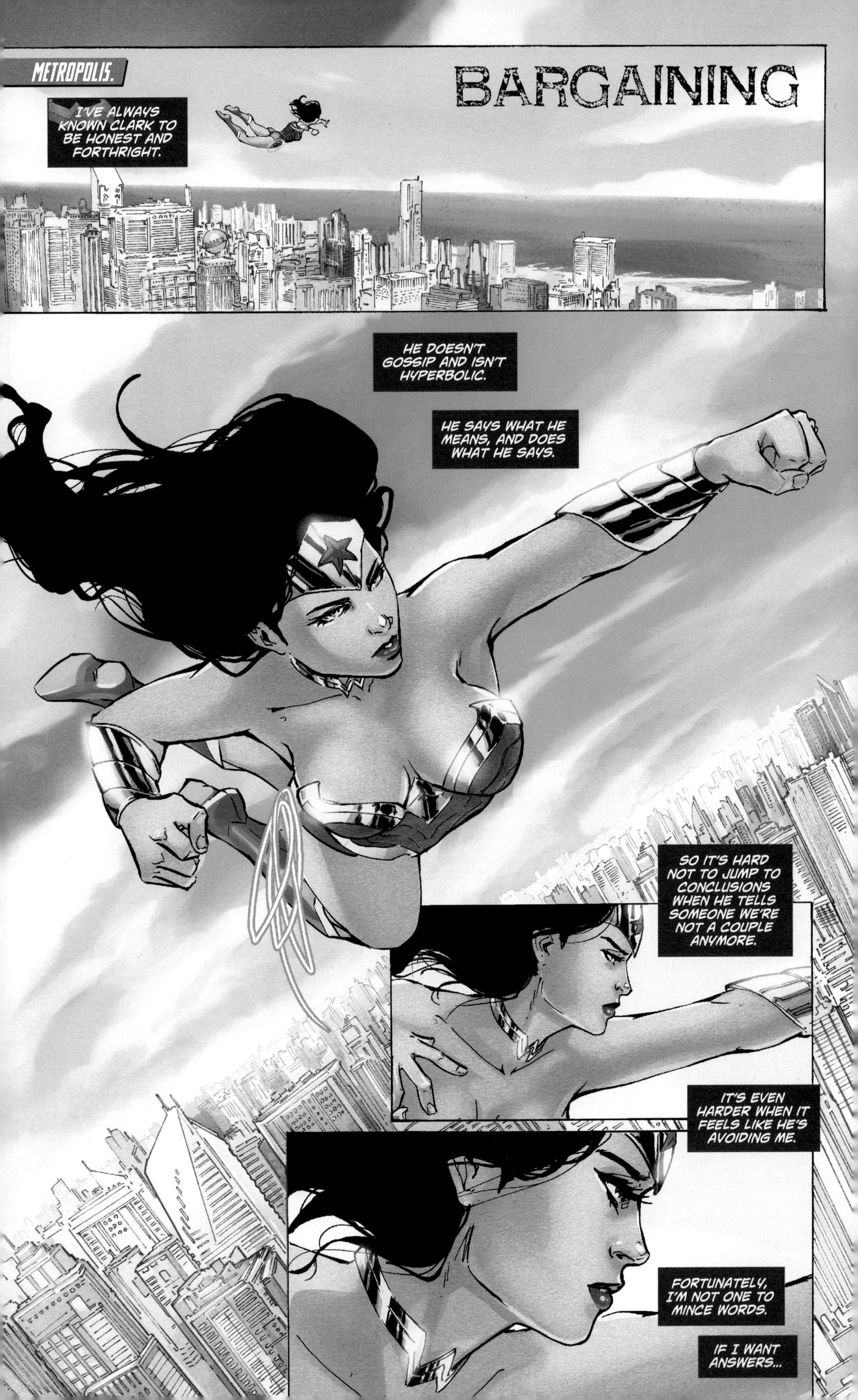
METROPOLIS.
BARGAINING
I'VE ALWAYS KNOWN CLARK TO BE HONEST AND FORTHRIGHT.
HE DOESN'T GOSSIP AND ISN'T HYPERBOLIC.
HE SAYS WHAT HE MEANS, AND DOES WHAT HE SAYS.
SO IT'S HARD NOT TO JUMP TO CONCLUSIONS WHEN HE TELLS SOMEONE WE'RE NOT A COUPLE ANYMORE.
IT'S EVEN HARDER WHEN IT FEELS LIKE HE'S AVOIDING ME.
FORTUNATELY, I'M NOT ONE TO MINCE WORDS.
IF I WANT ANSWERS...

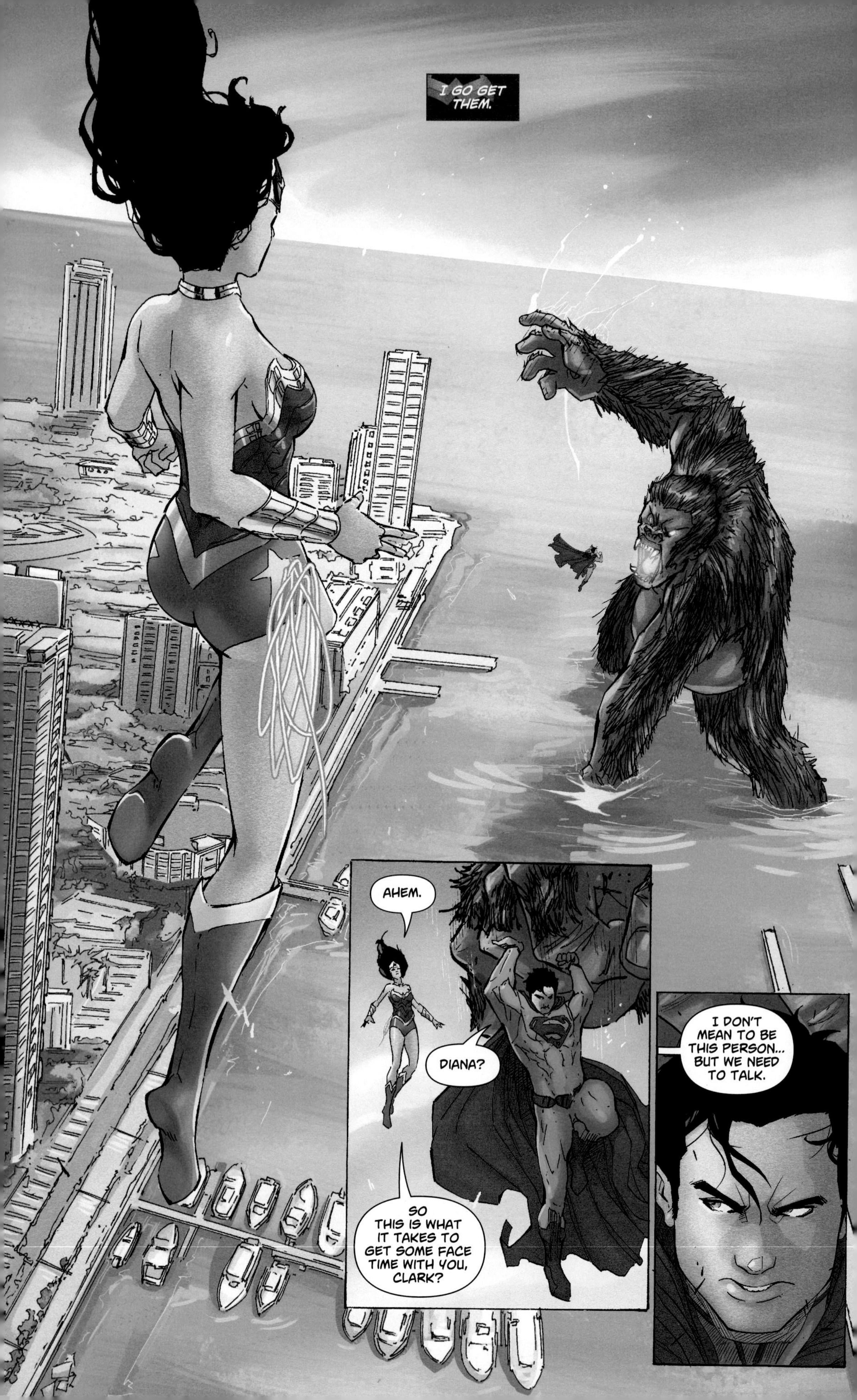
I GO GET THEM.
AHEM.
DIANA?
SO THIS IS WHAT IT TAKES TO GET SOME FACE TIME WITH YOU, CLARK?
I DON'T MEAN TO BE THIS PERSON... BUT WE NEED TO TALK.

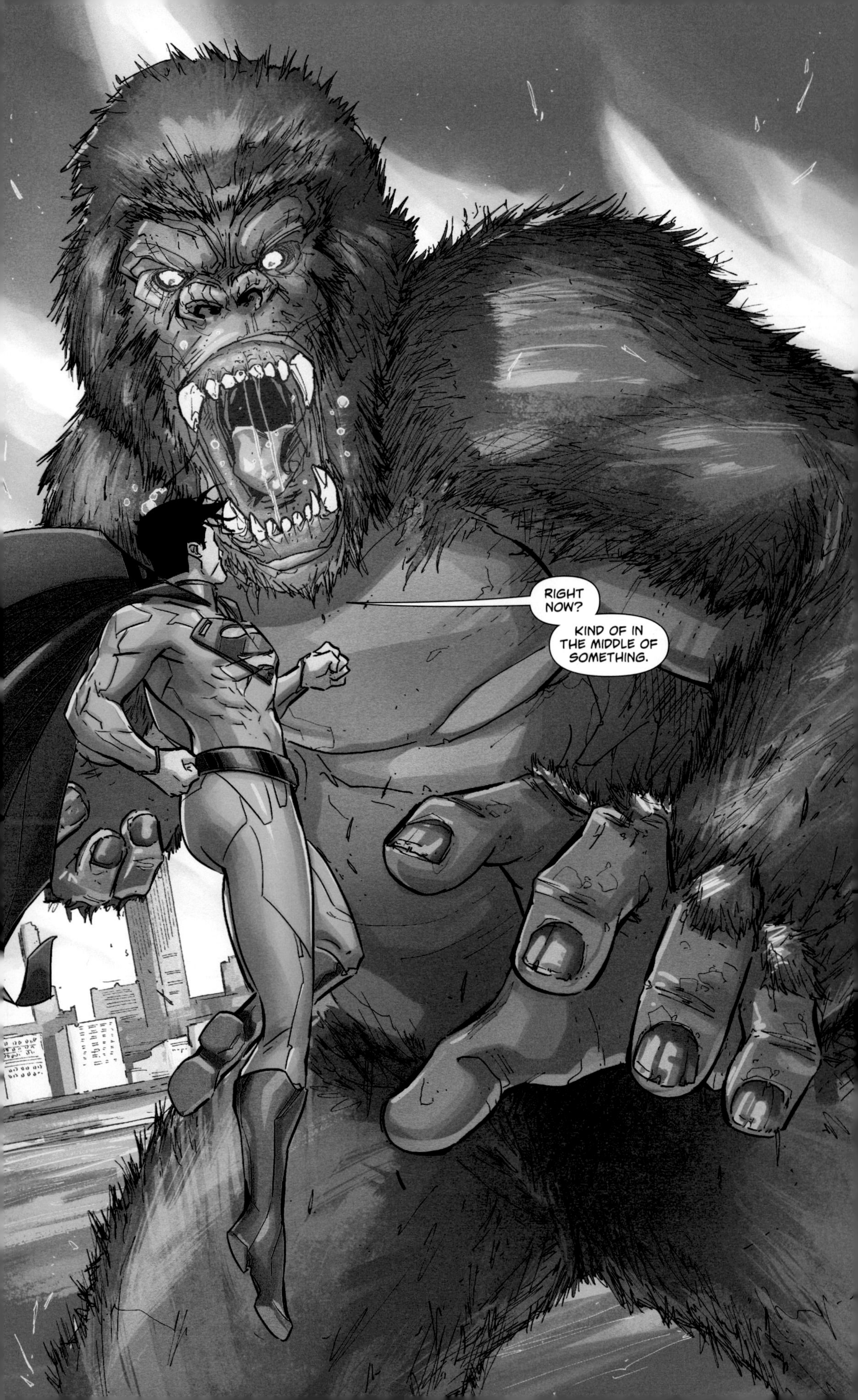
RIGHT NOW?
KIND OF IN THE MIDDLE OF SOMETHING.

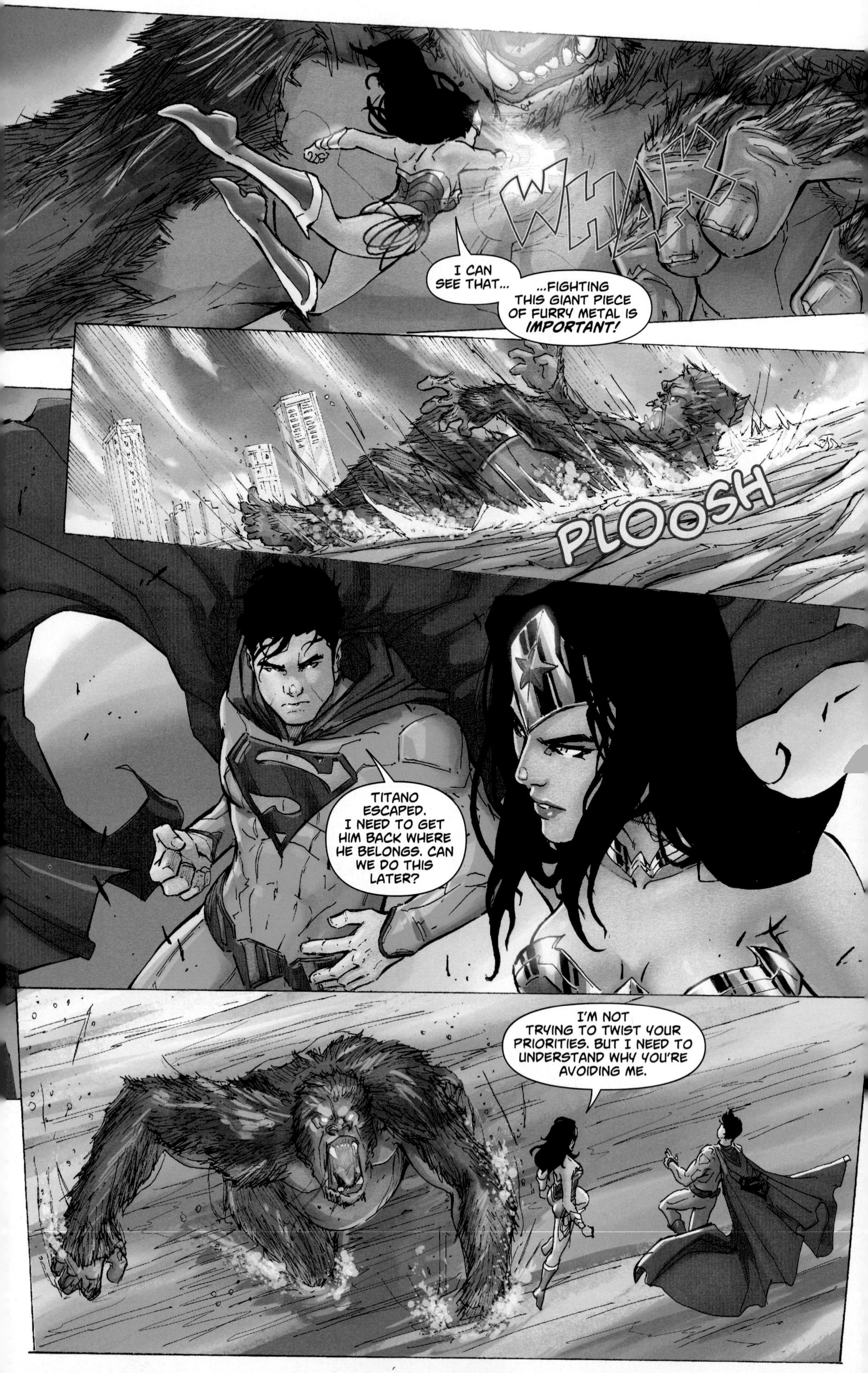
WHAK!
I CAN SEE THAT...
...FIGHTING THIS GIANT PIECE OF FURRY METAL IS *IMPORTANT!*
PLOOSH
TITANO ESCAPED. I NEED TO GET HIM BACK WHERE HE BELONGS. CAN WE DO THIS LATER?
I'M NOT TRYING TO TWIST YOUR PRIORITIES. BUT I NEED TO UNDERSTAND WHY YOU'RE AVOIDING ME.

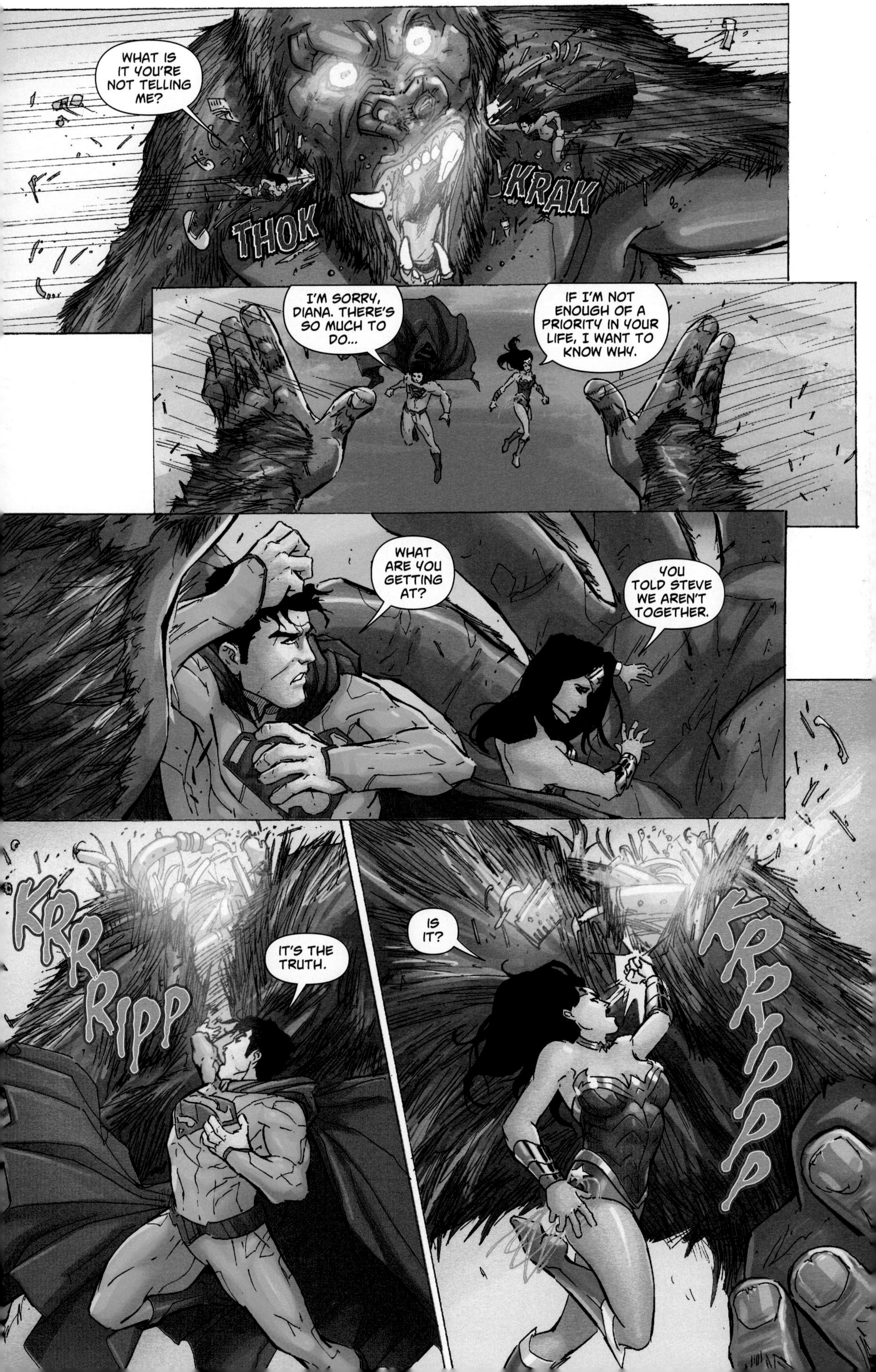
WHAT IS IT YOU'RE NOT TELLING ME?
THOK
KRAK
I'M SORRY, DIANA. THERE'S SO MUCH TO DO...
IF I'M NOT ENOUGH OF A PRIORITY IN YOUR LIFE, I WANT TO KNOW WHY.
WHAT ARE YOU GETTING AT?
YOU TOLD STEVE WE AREN'T TOGETHER.
KRRRIPP
IT'S THE TRUTH.
IS IT?
KRRIPPPP

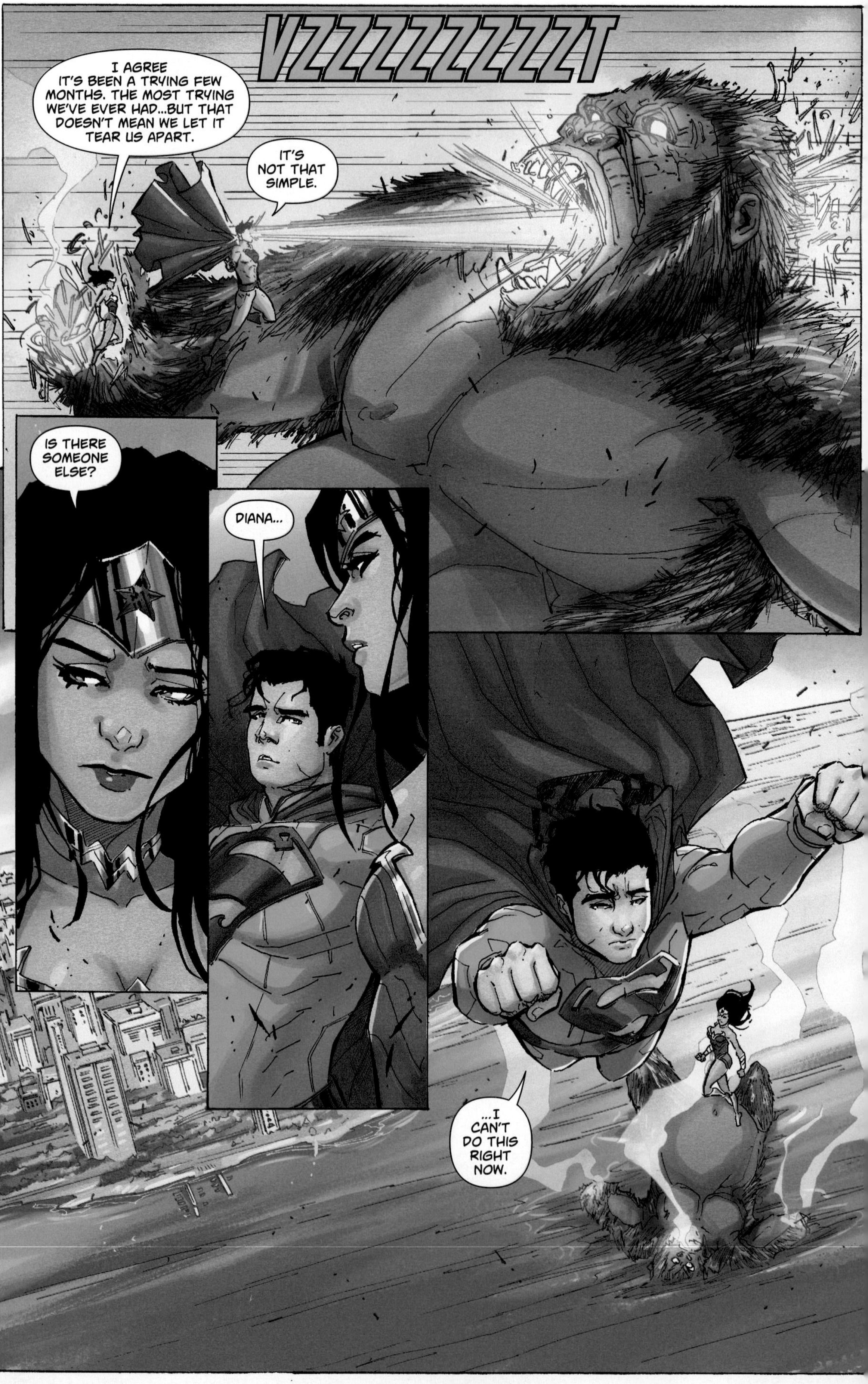
VZZZZZZZZZZT
I AGREE IT'S BEEN A TRYING FEW MONTHS. THE MOST TRYING WE'VE EVER HAD...BUT THAT DOESN'T MEAN WE LET IT TEAR US APART.
IT'S NOT THAT SIMPLE.
IS THERE SOMEONE ELSE?
DIANA...
...I CAN'T DO THIS RIGHT NOW.

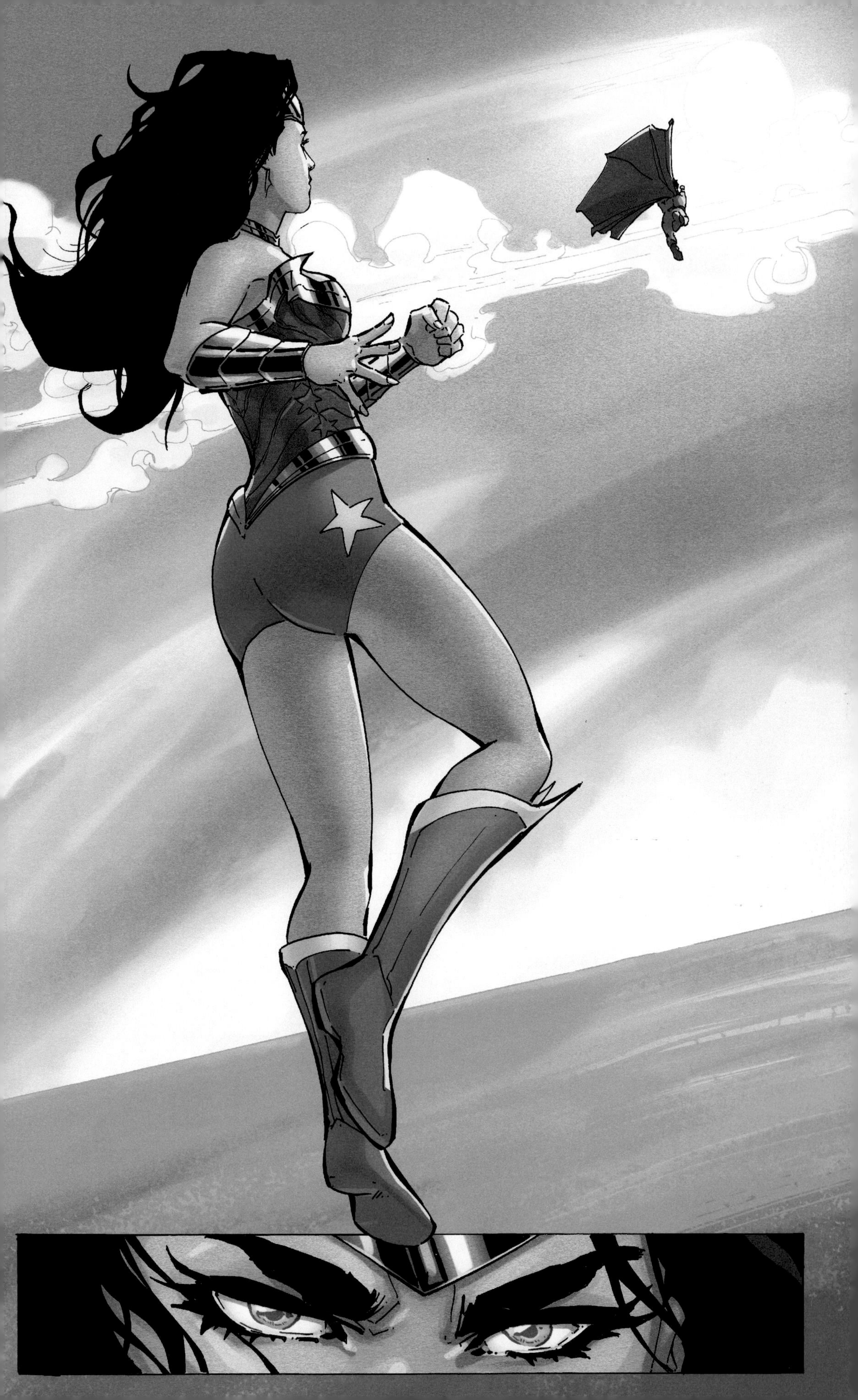

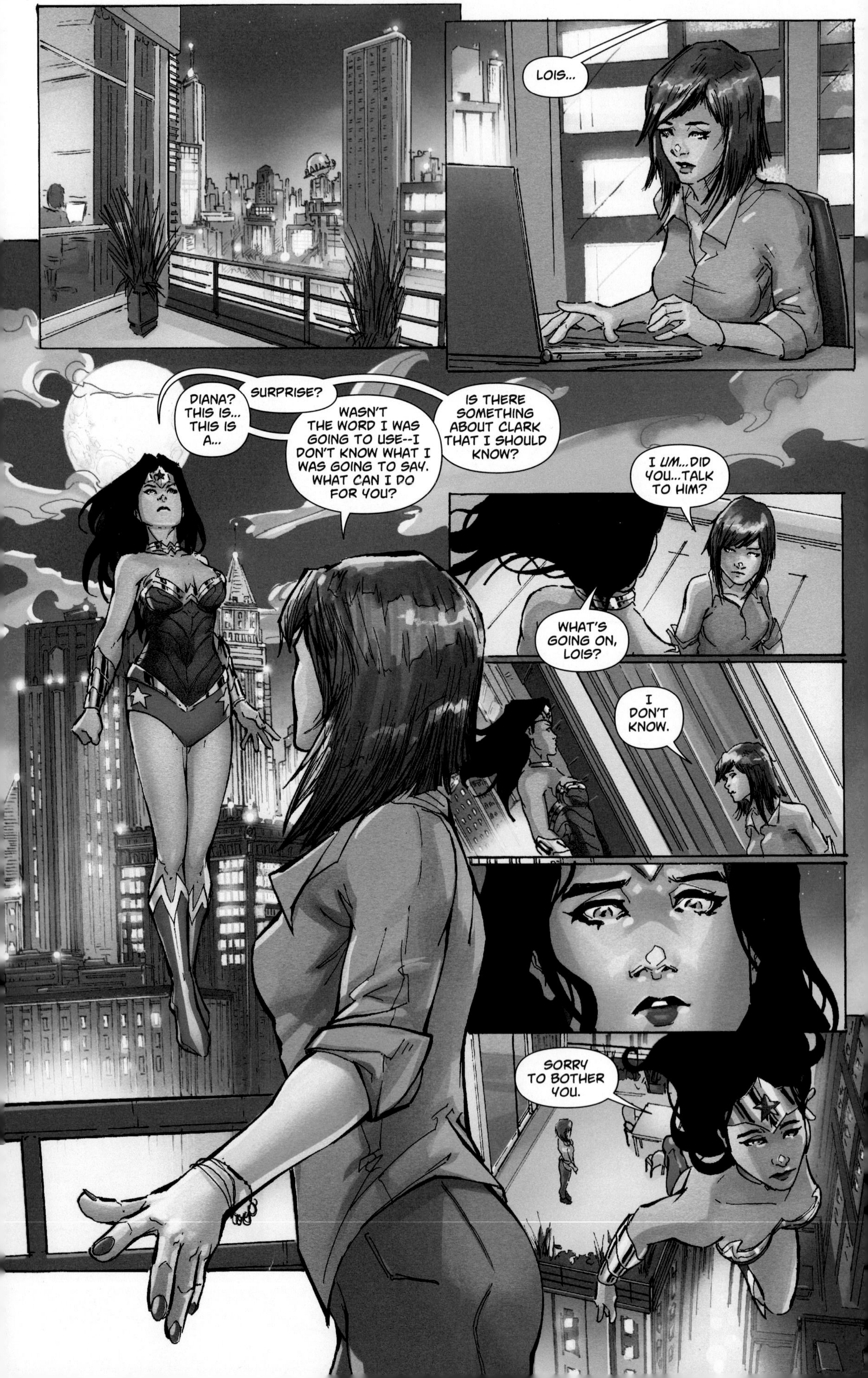
LOIS...
DIANA? THIS IS... THIS IS A...
SURPRISE?
WASN'T THE WORD I WAS GOING TO USE--I DON'T KNOW WHAT I WAS GOING TO SAY. WHAT CAN I DO FOR YOU?
IS THERE SOMETHING ABOUT CLARK THAT I SHOULD KNOW?
I UM...DID YOU...TALK TO HIM?
WHAT'S GOING ON, LOIS?
I DON'T KNOW.
SORRY TO BOTHER YOU.

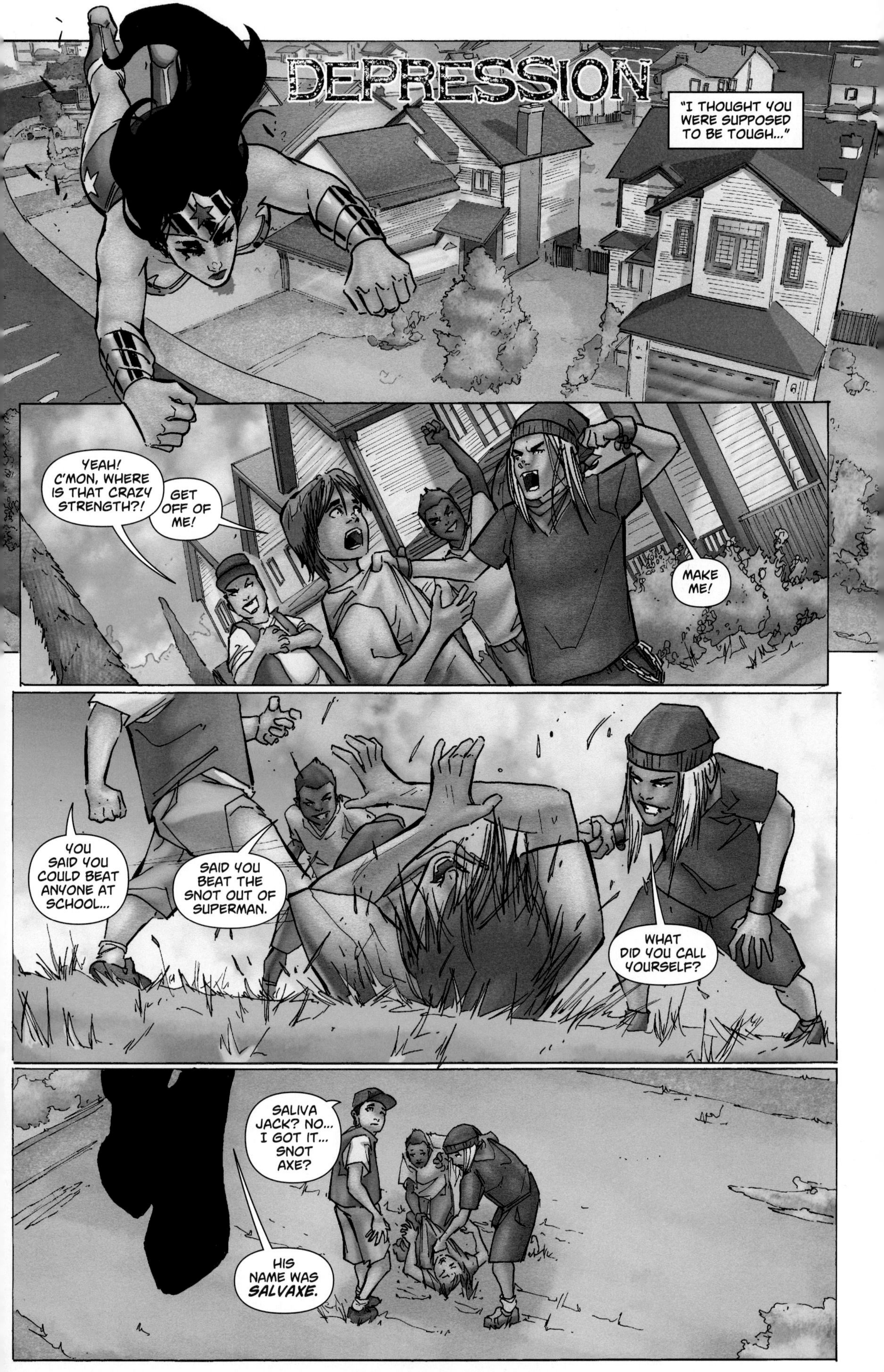
DEPRESSION
"I THOUGHT YOU WERE SUPPOSED TO BE TOUGH..."
YEAH! C'MON, WHERE IS THAT CRAZY STRENGTH?!
GET OFF OF ME!
MAKE ME!
YOU SAID YOU COULD BEAT ANYONE AT SCHOOL...
SAID YOU BEAT THE SNOT OUT OF SUPERMAN.
WHAT DID YOU CALL YOURSELF?
SALIVA JACK? NO... I GOT IT... SNOT AXE?
HIS NAME WAS SALVAXE.

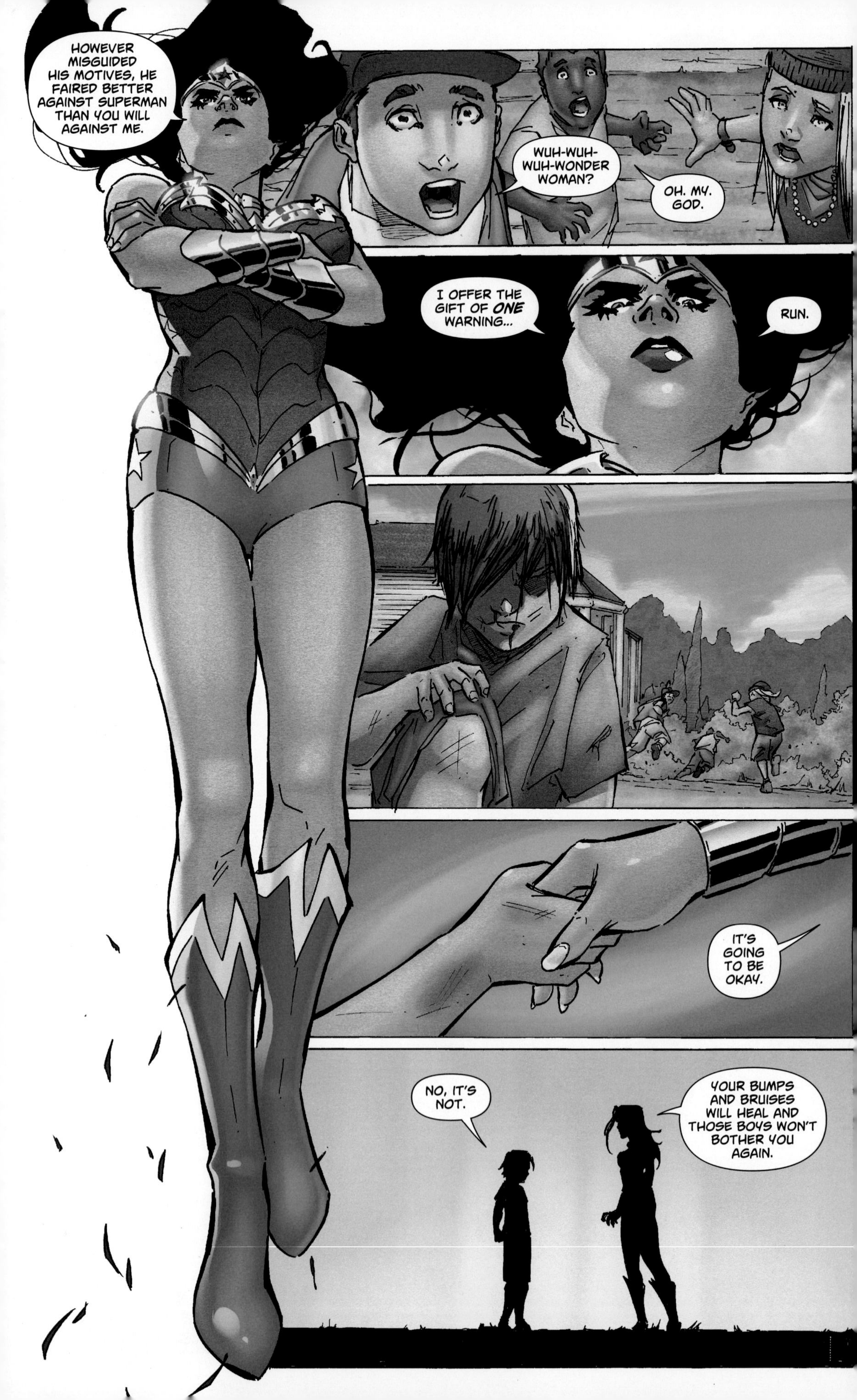
HOWEVER MISGUIDED HIS MOTIVES, HE FAIRED BETTER AGAINST SUPERMAN THAN YOU WILL AGAINST ME.
WUH-WUH-WUH-WONDER WOMAN?
OH. MY. GOD.
I OFFER THE GIFT OF ONE WARNING...
RUN.
IT'S GOING TO BE OKAY.
NO, IT'S NOT.
YOUR BUMPS AND BRUISES WILL HEAL AND THOSE BOYS WON'T BOTHER YOU AGAIN.

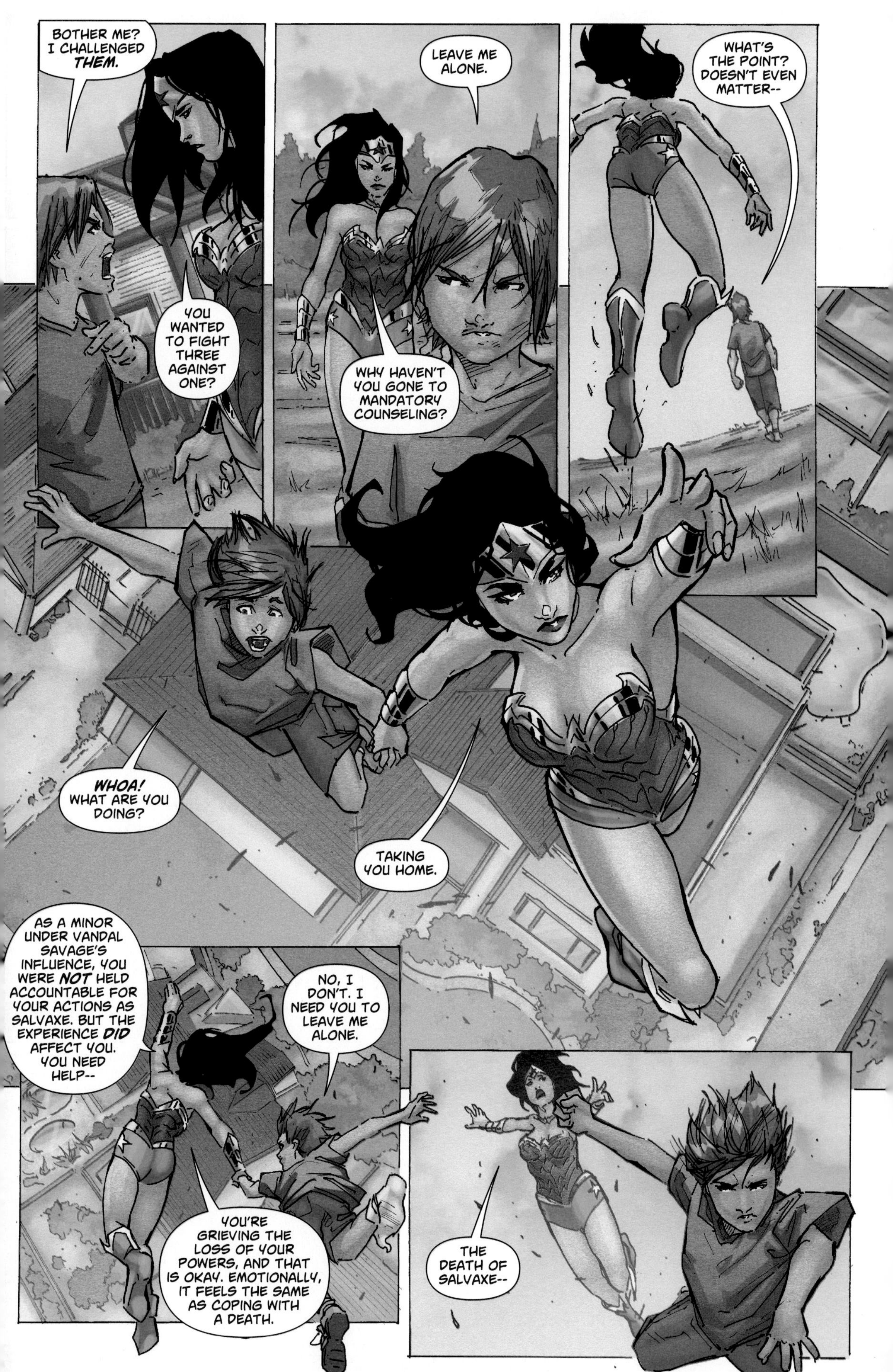

BOTHER ME? I CHALLENGED *THEM.*
YOU WANTED TO FIGHT THREE AGAINST ONE?
LEAVE ME ALONE.
WHY HAVEN'T YOU GONE TO MANDATORY COUNSELING?
WHAT'S THE POINT? DOESN'T EVEN MATTER--
WHOA! WHAT ARE YOU DOING?
TAKING YOU HOME.
AS A MINOR UNDER VANDAL SAVAGE'S INFLUENCE, YOU WERE *NOT* HELD ACCOUNTABLE FOR YOUR ACTIONS AS SALVAXE. BUT THE EXPERIENCE *DID* AFFECT YOU. YOU NEED HELP--
YOU'RE GRIEVING THE LOSS OF YOUR POWERS, AND THAT IS OKAY. EMOTIONALLY, IT FEELS THE SAME AS COPING WITH A DEATH.
NO, I DON'T. I NEED YOU TO LEAVE ME ALONE.
THE DEATH OF SALVAXE--

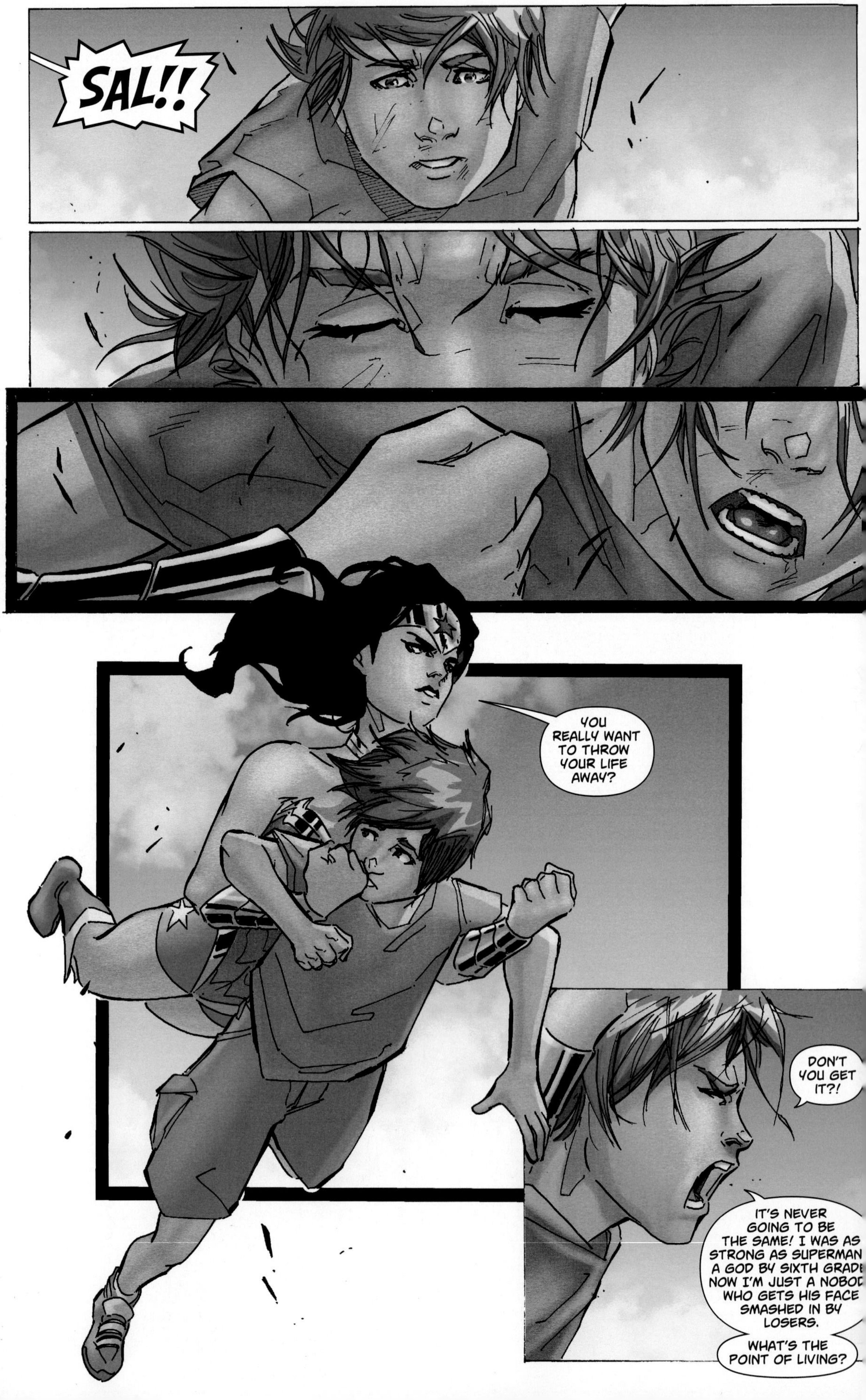
SAL!!
YOU REALLY WANT TO THROW YOUR LIFE AWAY?
DON'T YOU GET IT?!
IT'S NEVER GOING TO BE THE SAME! I WAS AS STRONG AS SUPERMAN A GOD BY SIXTH GRADE NOW I'M JUST A NOBOD WHO GETS HIS FACE SMASHED IN BY LOSERS.
WHAT'S THE POINT OF LIVING?

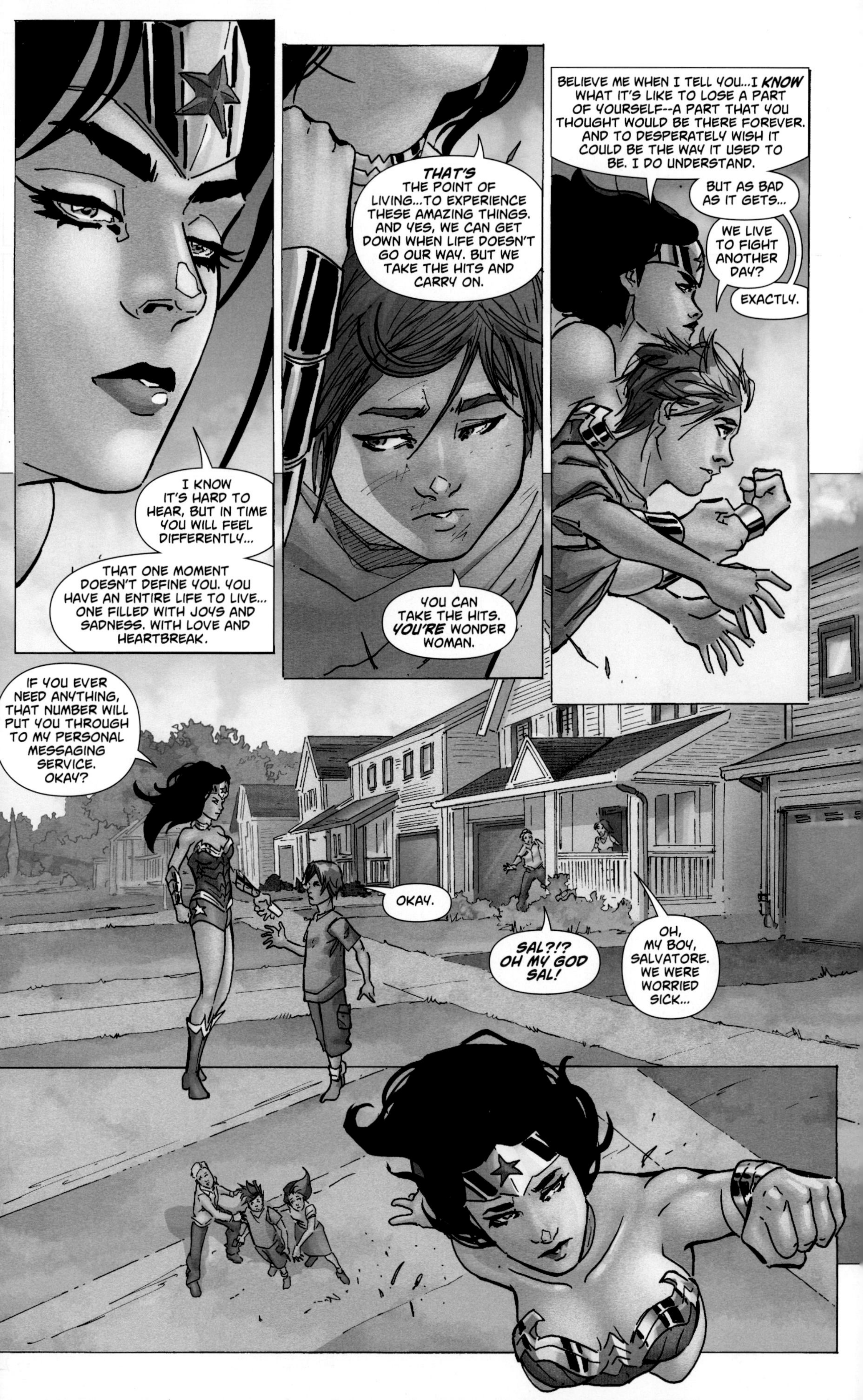
I KNOW IT'S HARD TO HEAR, BUT IN TIME YOU WILL FEEL DIFFERENTLY...
THAT ONE MOMENT DOESN'T DEFINE YOU. YOU HAVE AN ENTIRE LIFE TO LIVE... ONE FILLED WITH JOYS AND SADNESS. WITH LOVE AND HEARTBREAK.
THAT'S THE POINT OF LIVING...TO EXPERIENCE THESE AMAZING THINGS. AND YES, WE CAN GET DOWN WHEN LIFE DOESN'T GO OUR WAY. BUT WE TAKE THE HITS AND CARRY ON.
YOU CAN TAKE THE HITS. YOU'RE WONDER WOMAN.
BELIEVE ME WHEN I TELL YOU...I KNOW WHAT IT'S LIKE TO LOSE A PART OF YOURSELF--A PART THAT YOU THOUGHT WOULD BE THERE FOREVER. AND TO DESPERATELY WISH IT COULD BE THE WAY IT USED TO BE. I DO UNDERSTAND.
BUT AS BAD AS IT GETS...
WE LIVE TO FIGHT ANOTHER DAY?
EXACTLY.
IF YOU EVER NEED ANYTHING, THAT NUMBER WILL PUT YOU THROUGH TO MY PERSONAL MESSAGING SERVICE. OKAY?
OKAY.
SAL?!? OH MY GOD SAL!
OH, MY BOY, SALVATORE. WE WERE WORRIED SICK...

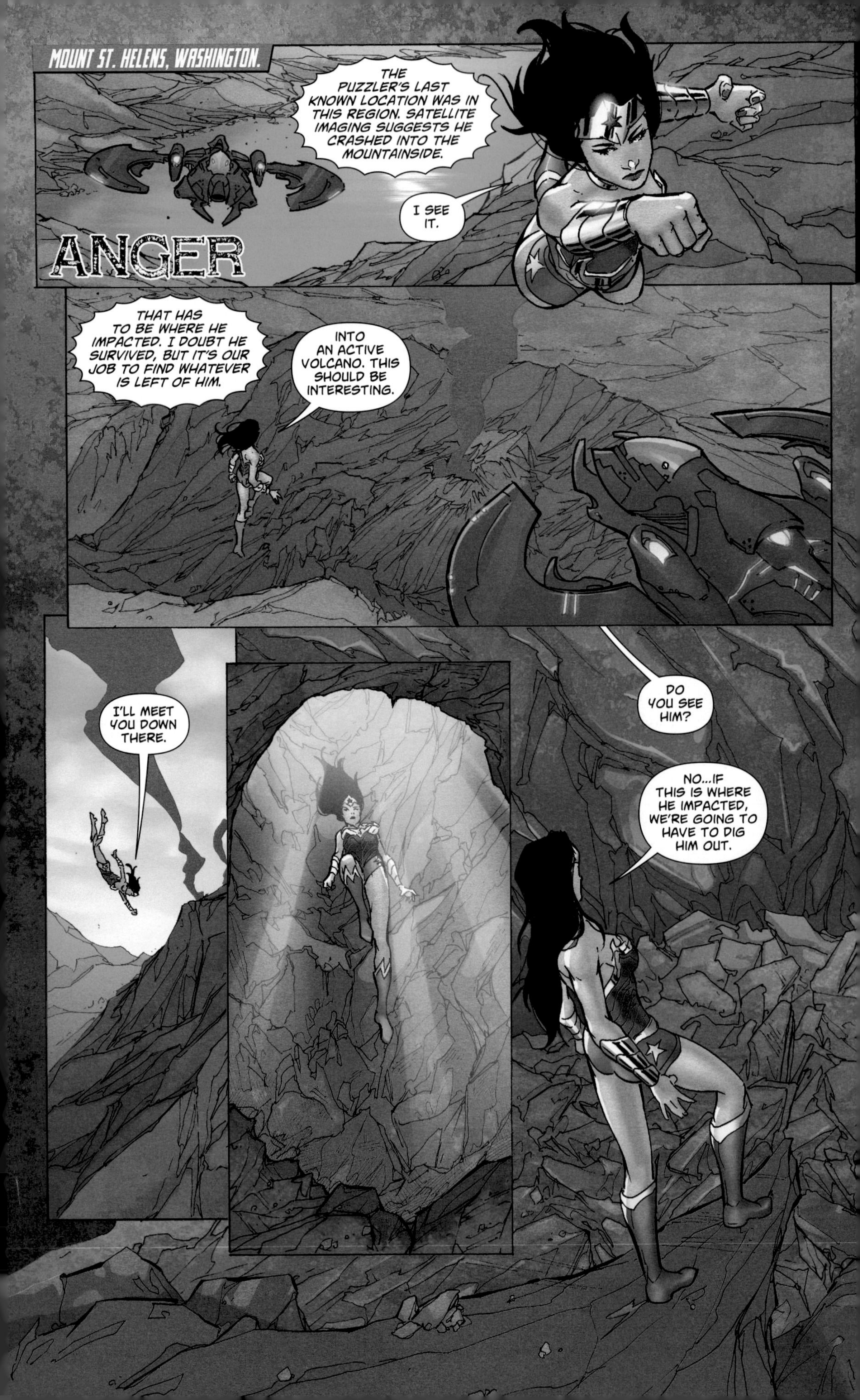
MOUNT ST. HELENS, WASHINGTON.
THE PUZZLER'S LAST KNOWN LOCATION WAS IN THIS REGION. SATELLITE IMAGING SUGGESTS HE CRASHED INTO THE MOUNTAINSIDE.
I SEE IT.
ANGER
THAT HAS TO BE WHERE HE IMPACTED. I DOUBT HE SURVIVED, BUT IT'S OUR JOB TO FIND WHATEVER IS LEFT OF HIM.
INTO AN ACTIVE VOLCANO. THIS SHOULD BE INTERESTING.
I'LL MEET YOU DOWN THERE.
DO YOU SEE HIM?
NO...IF THIS IS WHERE HE IMPACTED, WE'RE GOING TO HAVE TO DIG HIM OUT.

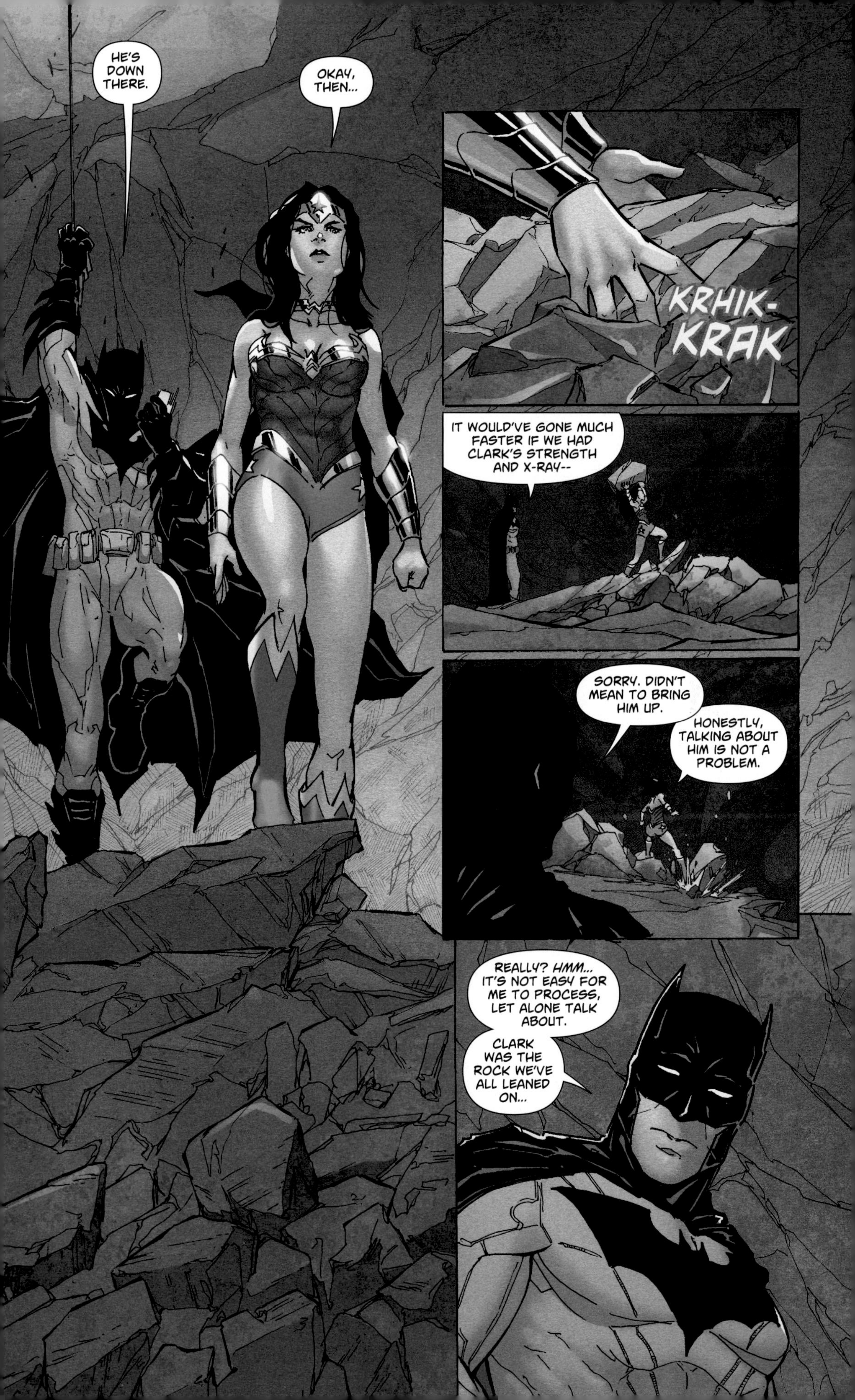
HE'S DOWN THERE.
OKAY, THEN...
KRHIK-KRAK
IT WOULD'VE GONE MUCH FASTER IF WE HAD CLARK'S STRENGTH AND X-RAY--
SORRY. DIDN'T MEAN TO BRING HIM UP.
HONESTLY, TALKING ABOUT HIM IS NOT A PROBLEM.
REALLY? HMM... IT'S NOT EASY FOR ME TO PROCESS, LET ALONE TALK ABOUT.
CLARK WAS THE ROCK WE'VE ALL LEANED ON...

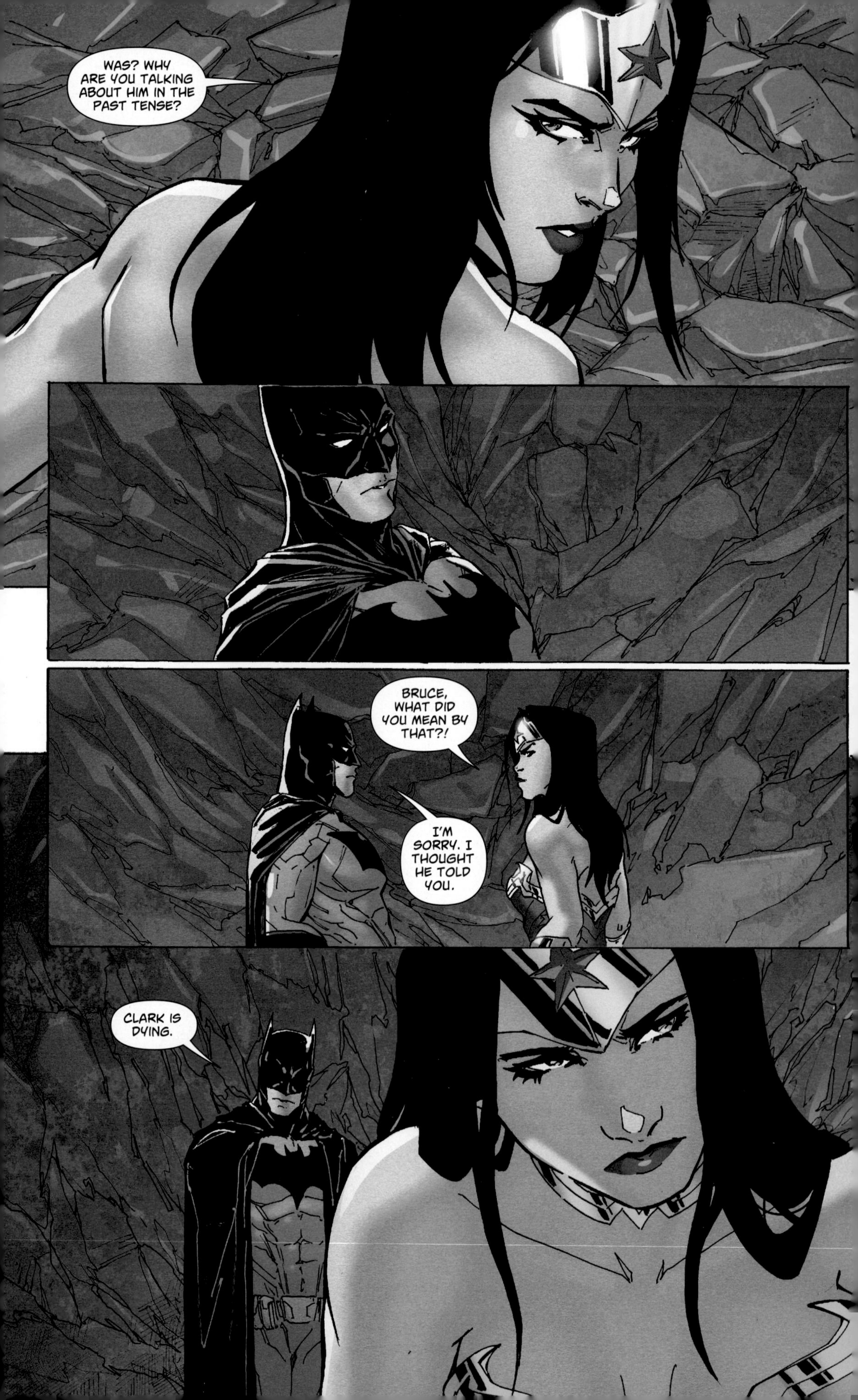
WAS? WHY ARE YOU TALKING ABOUT HIM IN THE PAST TENSE?
BRUCE, WHAT DID YOU MEAN BY THAT?!
I'M SORRY. I THOUGHT HE TOLD YOU.
CLARK IS DYING.

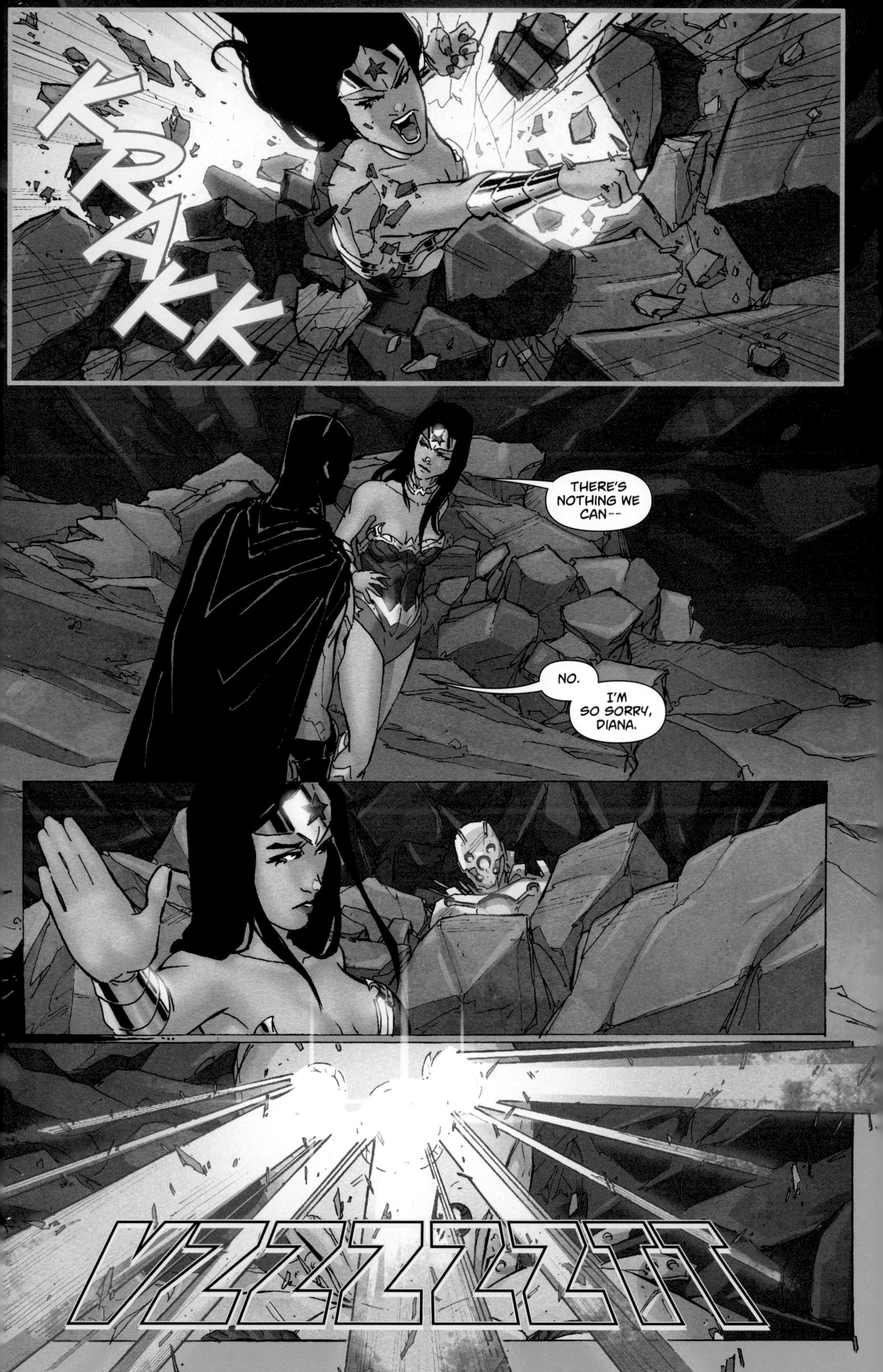
KRAKK
THERE'S NOTHING WE CAN--
NO.
I'M SO SORRY, DIANA.
VZZZZZIT

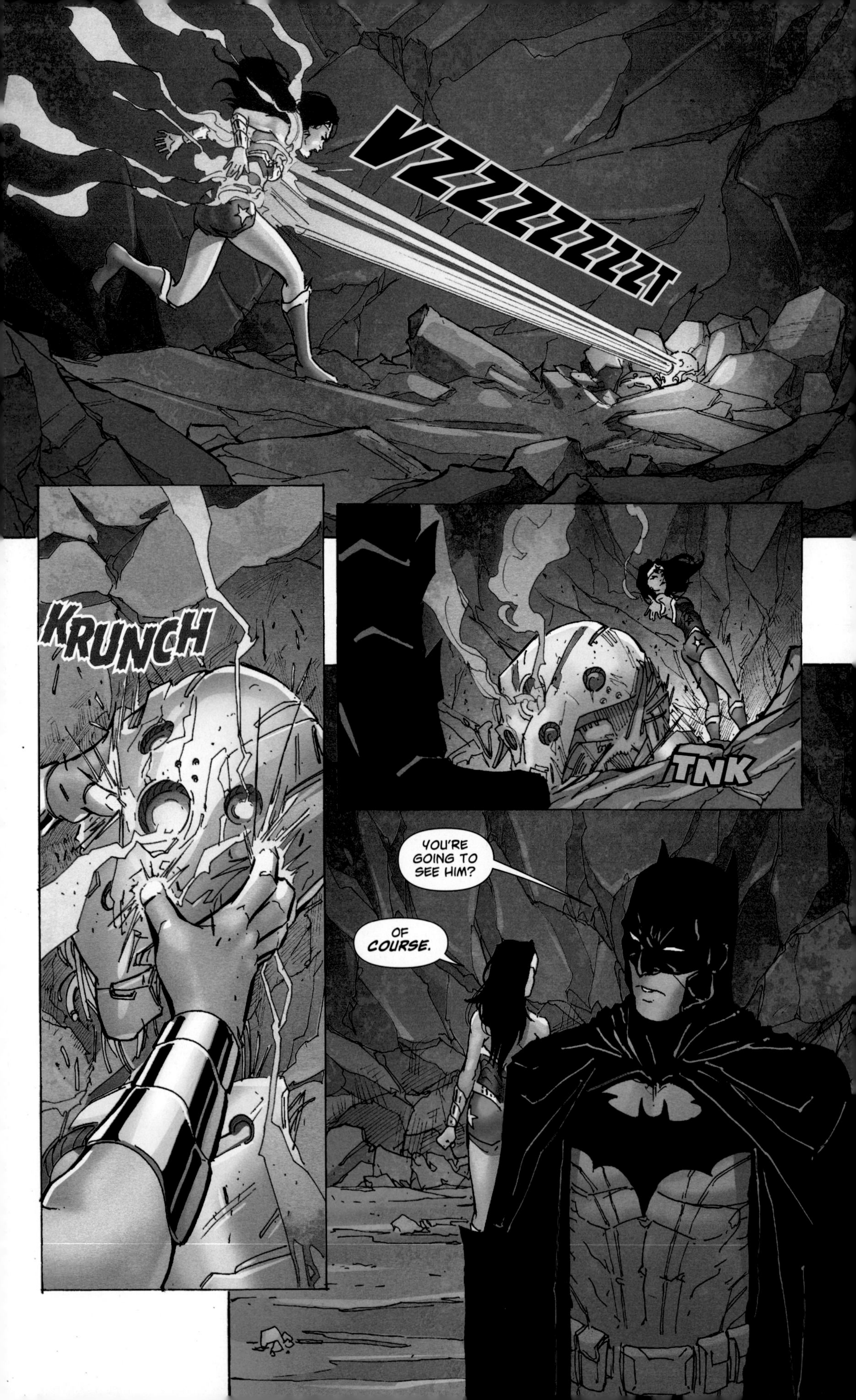
VZZZZZZZZT
KRUNCH
TNK
YOU'RE GOING TO SEE HIM?
OF COURSE.

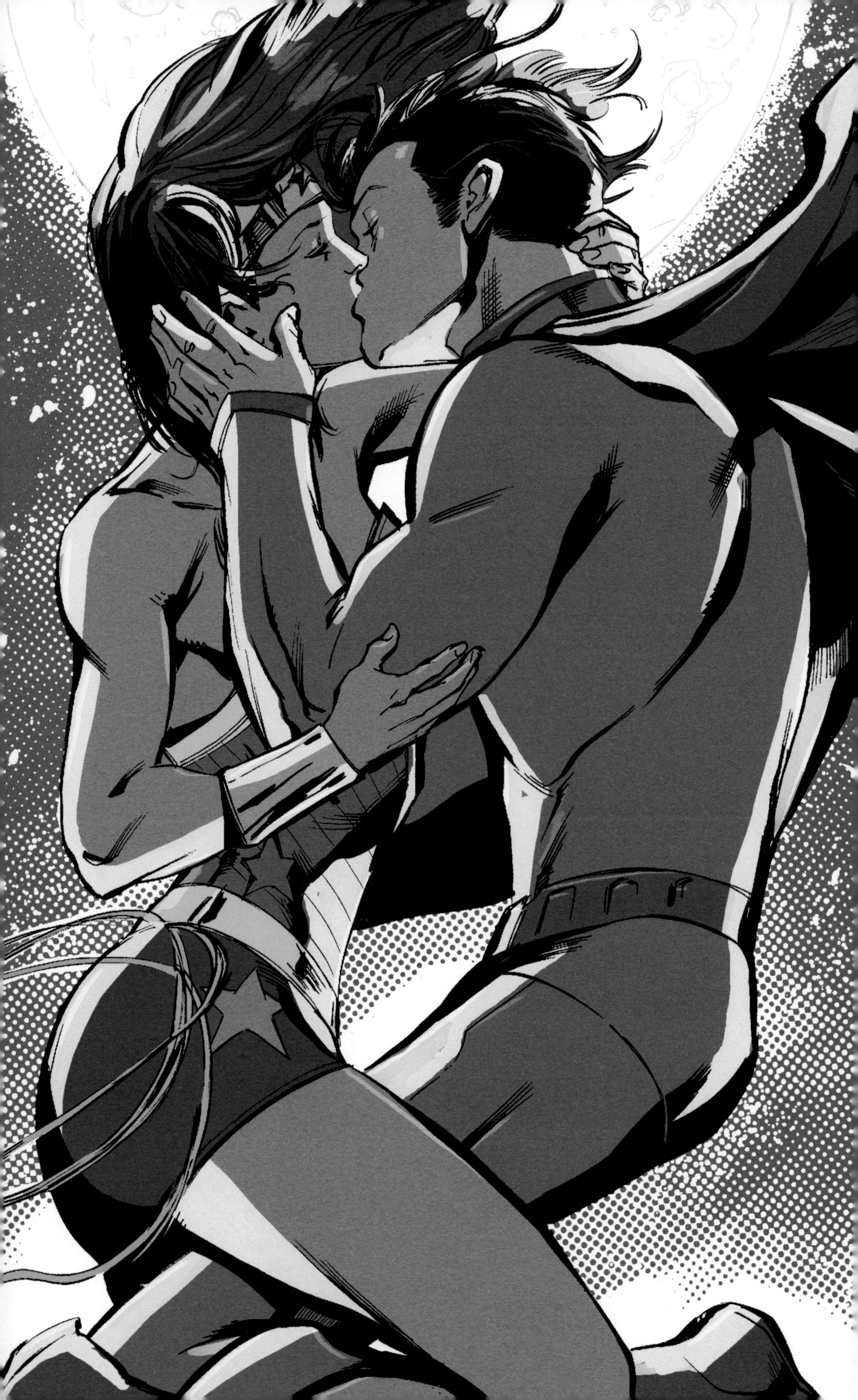

ACCEPTANCE

BRIAN BUCCELLATO writer **GIUSEPPE CAFARO, POP MHAN** artists **LEE LOUGHRIDGE** colorist **DAVID SHARPE** letterer

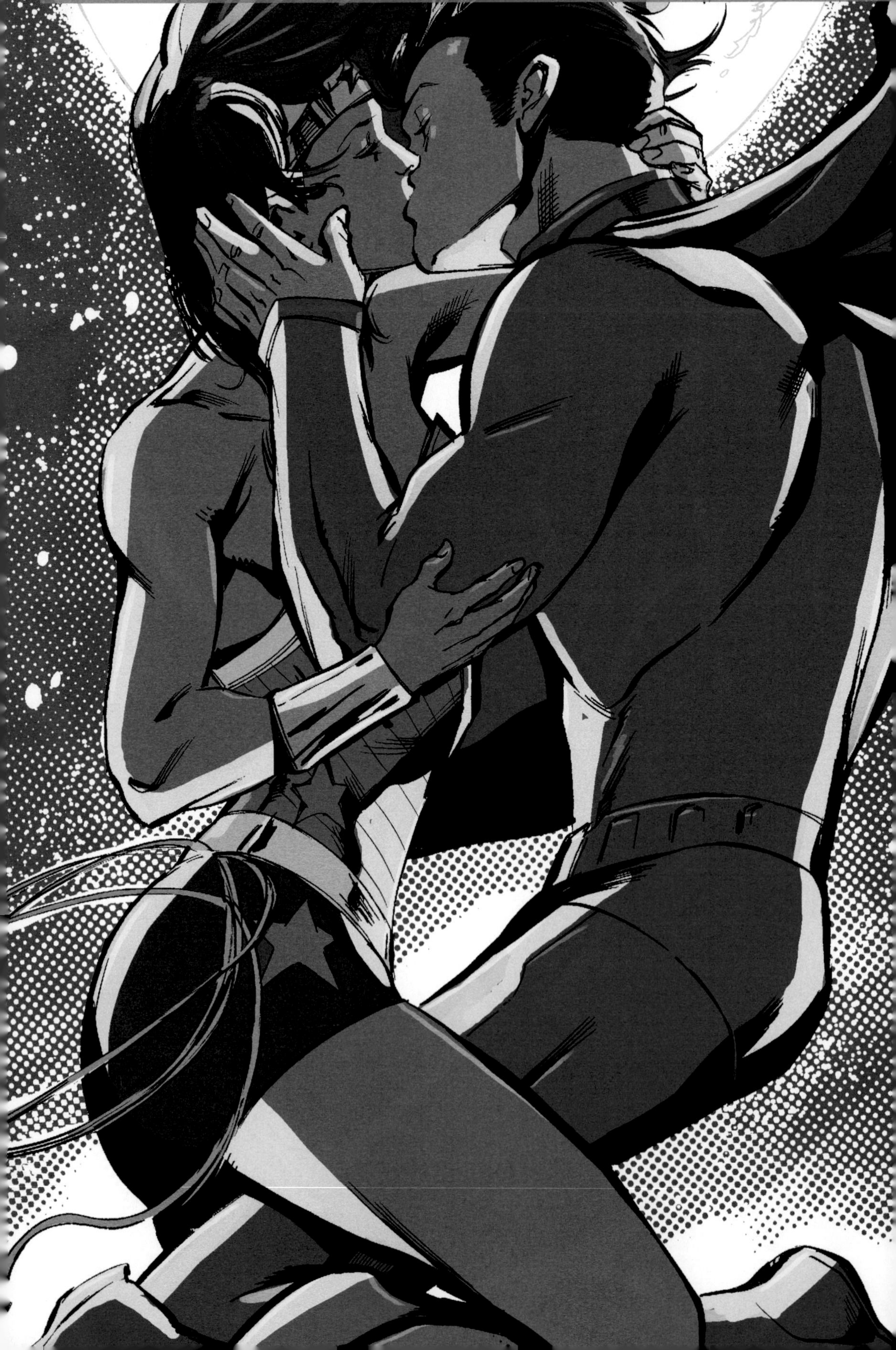

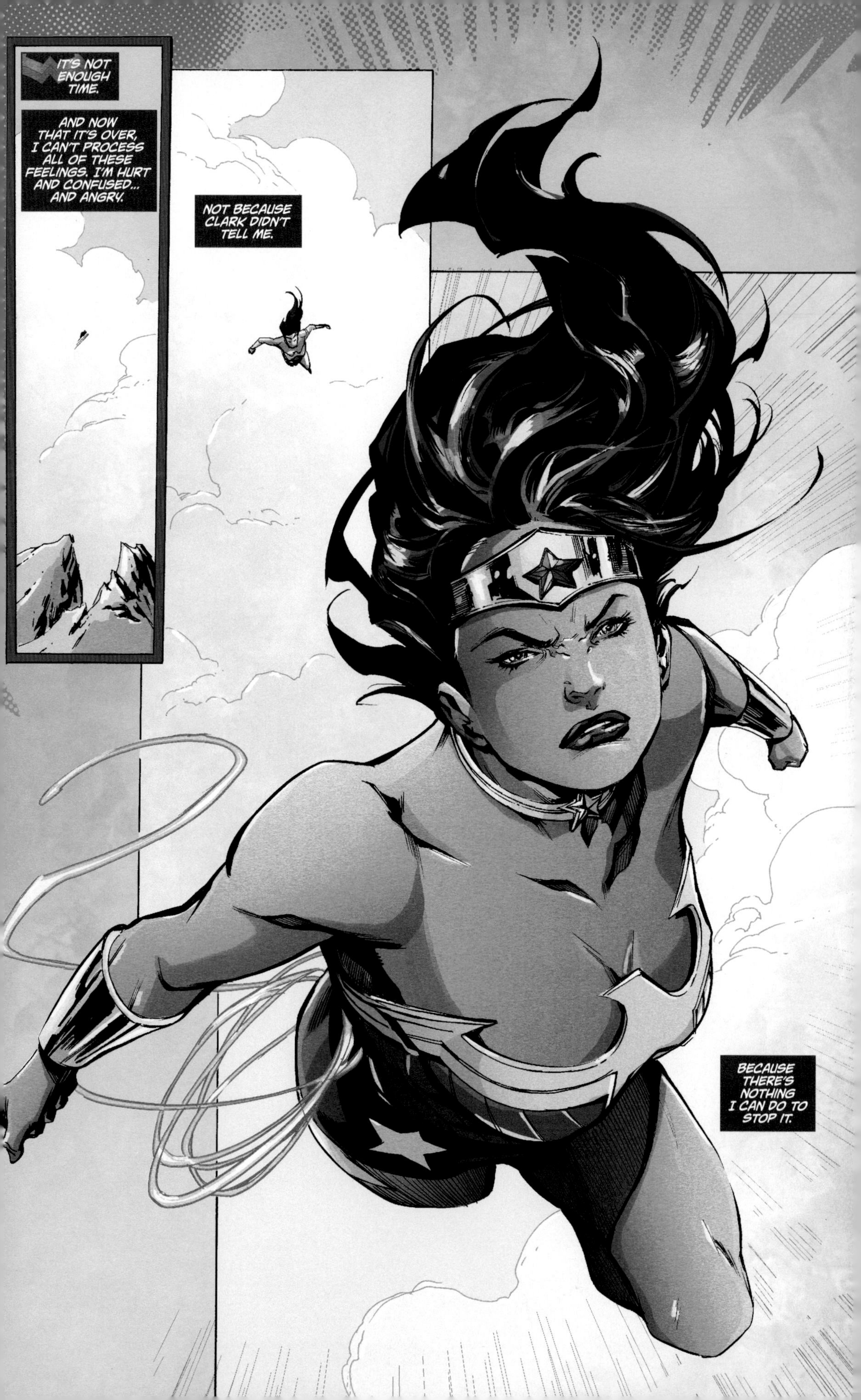
IT'S NOT ENOUGH TIME.
AND NOW THAT IT'S OVER, I CAN'T PROCESS ALL OF THESE FEELINGS. I'M HURT AND CONFUSED... AND ANGRY.
NOT BECAUSE CLARK DIDN'T TELL ME.
BECAUSE THERE'S NOTHING I CAN DO TO STOP IT.

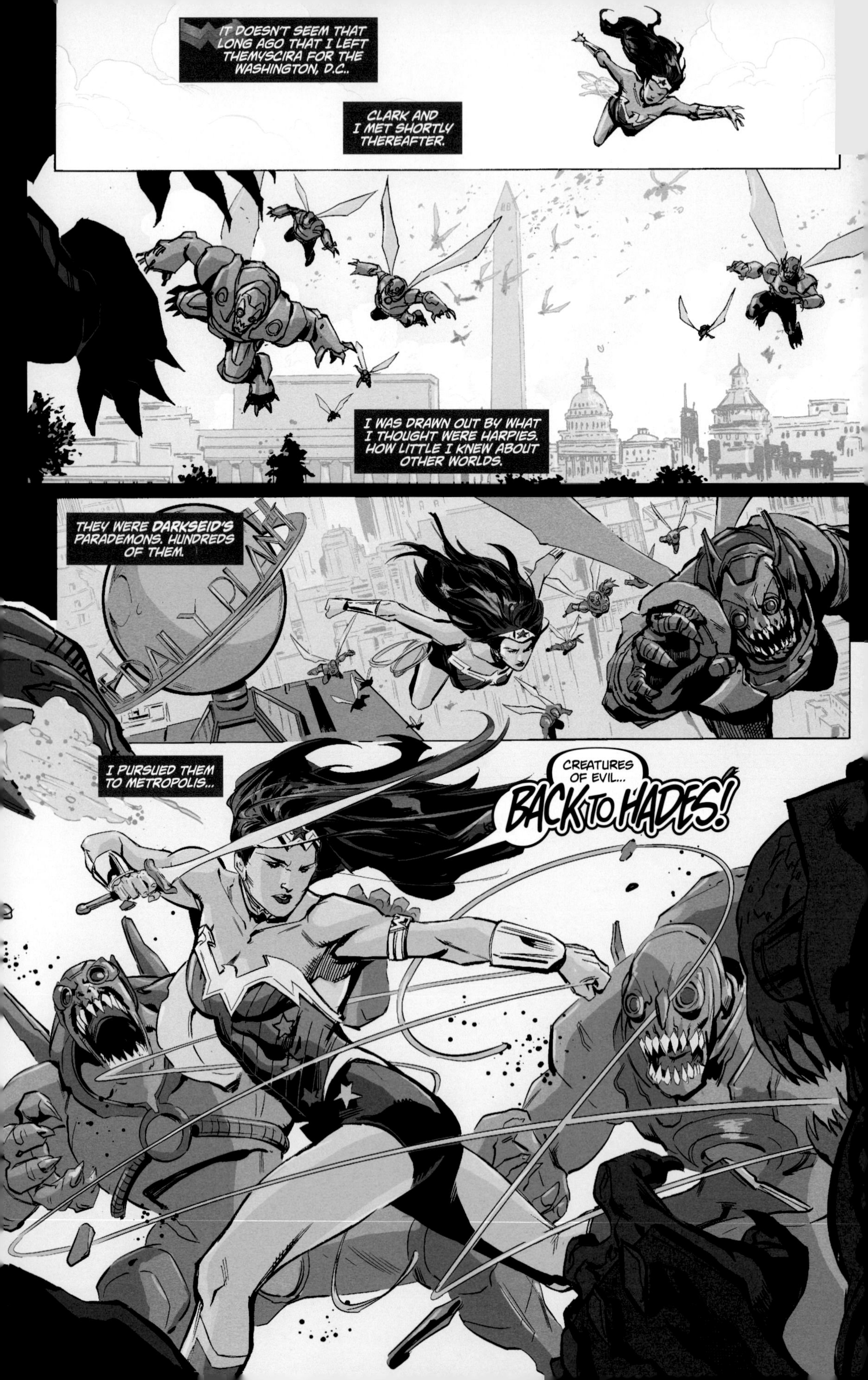
IT DOESN'T SEEM THAT LONG AGO THAT I LEFT THEMYSCIRA FOR THE WASHINGTON, D.C..
CLARK AND I MET SHORTLY THEREAFTER.
I WAS DRAWN OUT BY WHAT I THOUGHT WERE HARPIES. HOW LITTLE I KNEW ABOUT OTHER WORLDS.
THEY WERE DARKSEID'S PARADEMONS. HUNDREDS OF THEM.
I PURSUED THEM TO METROPOLIS...
CREATURES OF EVIL... BACK TO HADES!

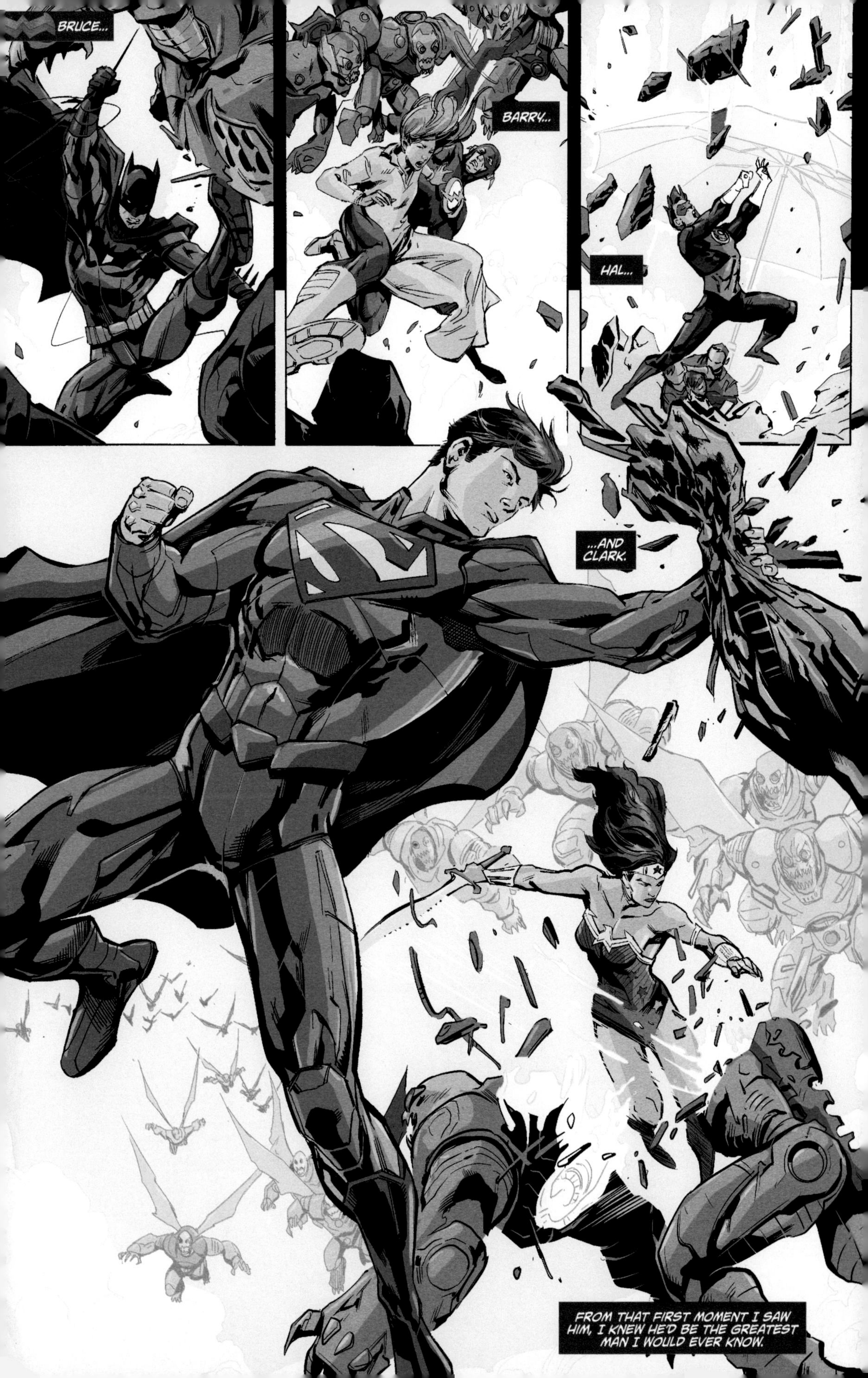
BRUCE...
BARRY...
HAL...
...AND CLARK.
FROM THAT FIRST MOMENT I SAW HIM, I KNEW HE'D BE THE GREATEST MAN I WOULD EVER KNOW.

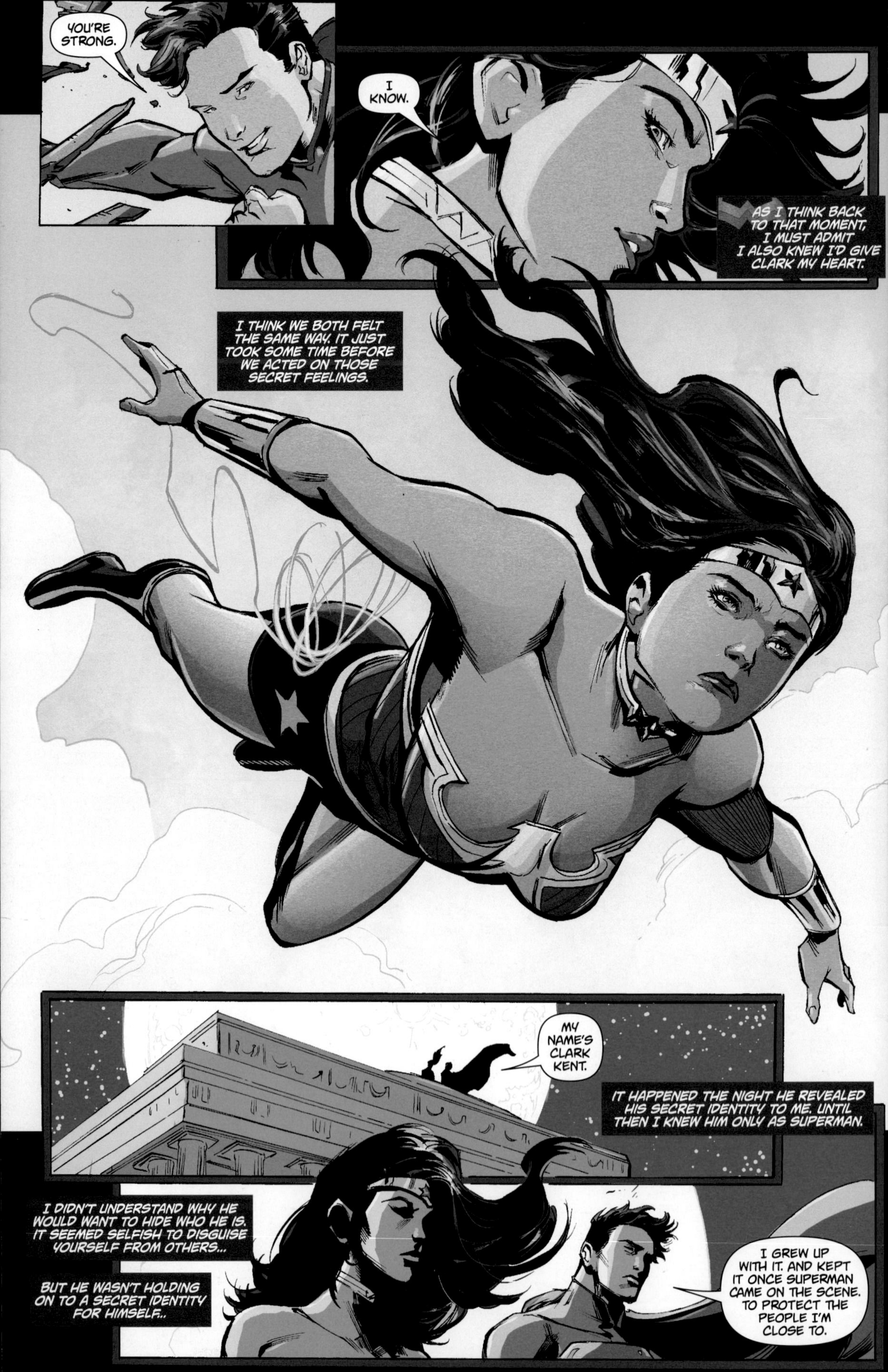
YOU'RE STRONG.
I KNOW.
AS I THINK BACK TO THAT MOMENT, I MUST ADMIT I ALSO KNEW I'D GIVE CLARK MY HEART.
I THINK WE BOTH FELT THE SAME WAY. IT JUST TOOK SOME TIME BEFORE WE ACTED ON THOSE SECRET FEELINGS.
MY NAME'S CLARK KENT.
IT HAPPENED THE NIGHT HE REVEALED HIS SECRET IDENTITY TO ME. UNTIL THEN I KNEW HIM ONLY AS SUPERMAN.
I DIDN'T UNDERSTAND WHY HE WOULD WANT TO HIDE WHO HE IS. IT SEEMED SELFISH TO DISGUISE YOURSELF FROM OTHERS...
BUT HE WASN'T HOLDING ON TO A SECRET IDENTITY FOR HIMSELF...
I GREW UP WITH IT. AND KEPT IT ONCE SUPERMAN CAME ON THE SCENE. TO PROTECT THE PEOPLE I'M CLOSE TO.

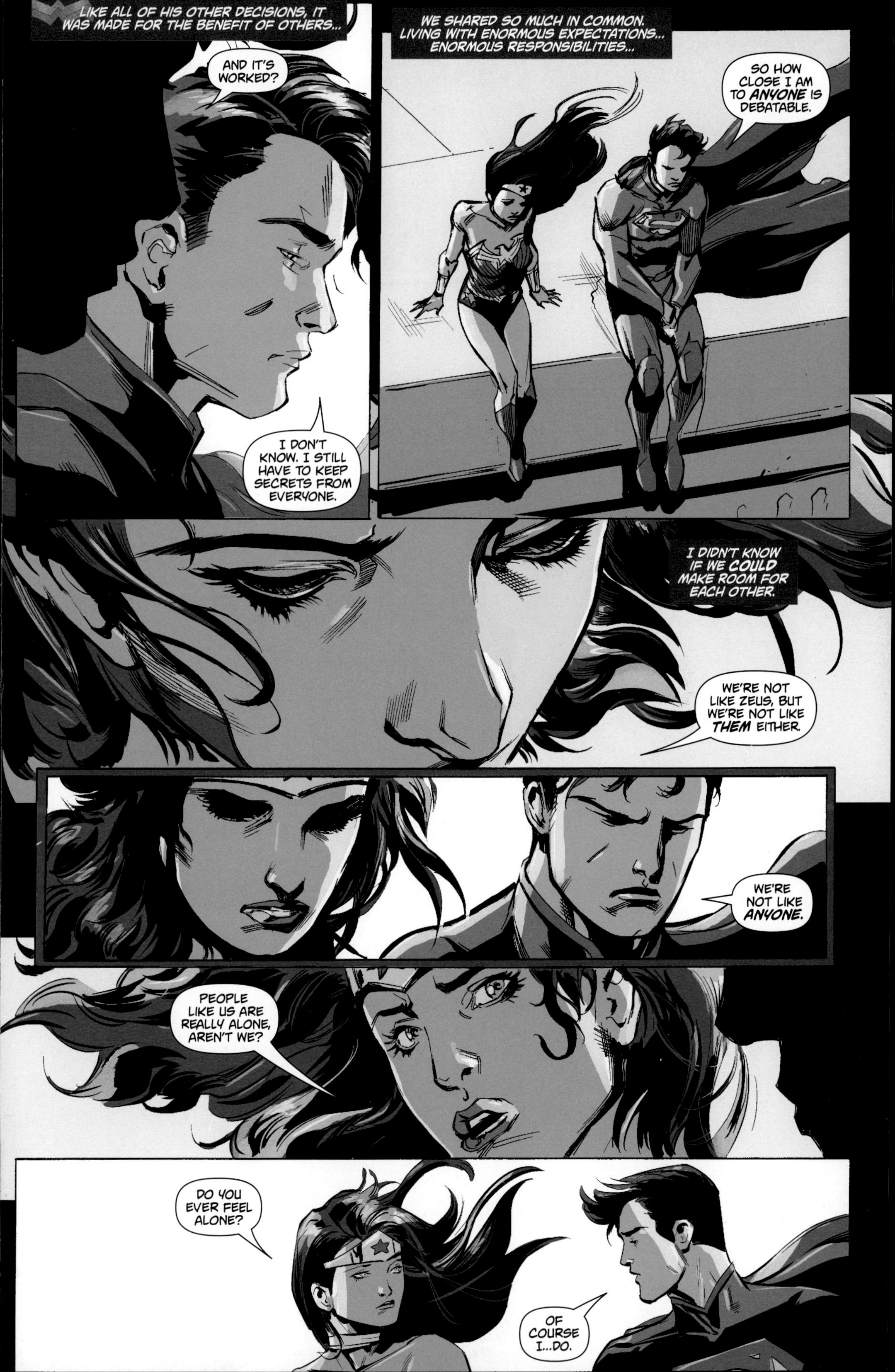
LIKE ALL OF HIS OTHER DECISIONS, IT WAS MADE FOR THE BENEFIT OF OTHERS...
AND IT'S WORKED?
I DON'T KNOW. I STILL HAVE TO KEEP SECRETS FROM EVERYONE.
WE SHARED SO MUCH IN COMMON. LIVING WITH ENORMOUS EXPECTATIONS... ENORMOUS RESPONSIBILITIES...
SO HOW CLOSE I AM TO ANYONE IS DEBATABLE.
I DIDN'T KNOW IF WE COULD MAKE ROOM FOR EACH OTHER.
WE'RE NOT LIKE ZEUS, BUT WE'RE NOT LIKE THEM EITHER.
WE'RE NOT LIKE ANYONE.
PEOPLE LIKE US ARE REALLY ALONE, AREN'T WE?
DO YOU EVER FEEL ALONE?
OF COURSE I...DO.

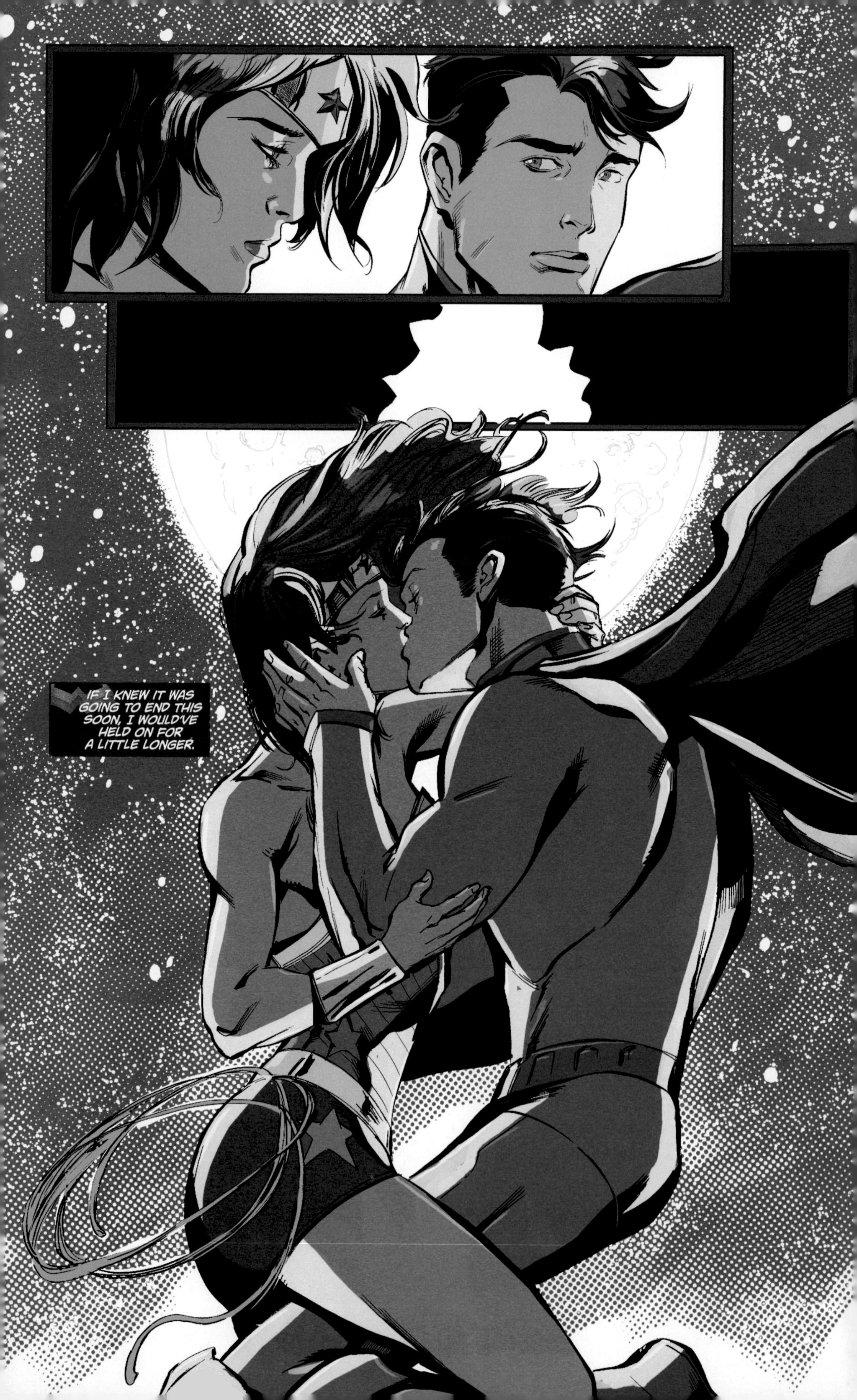
IF I KNEW IT WAS GOING TO END THIS SOON, I WOULD'VE HELD ON FOR A LITTLE LONGER.

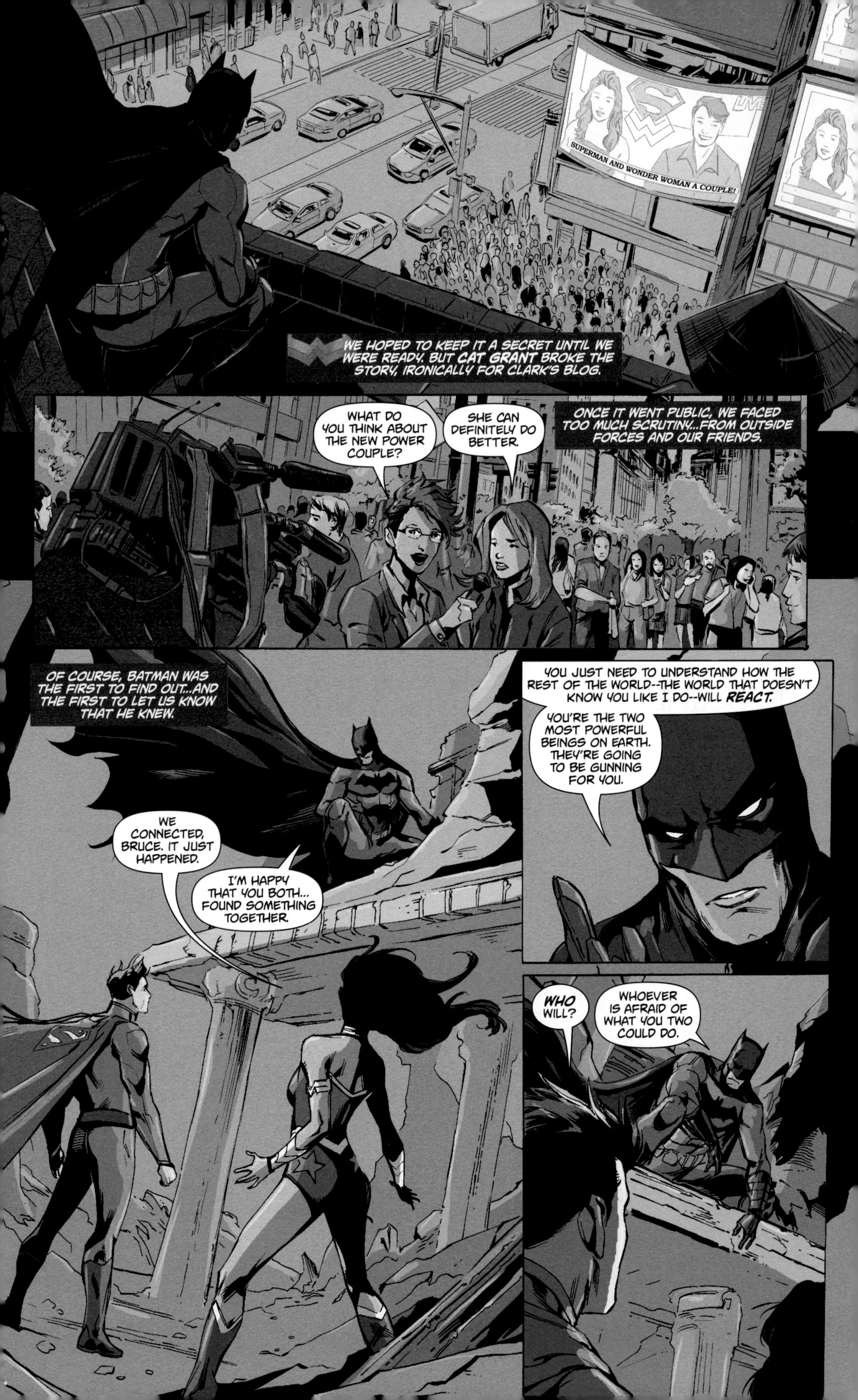

SUPERMAN AND WONDER WOMAN A COUPLE!
LIVE
WE HOPED TO KEEP IT A SECRET UNTIL WE WERE READY. BUT CAT GRANT BROKE THE STORY, IRONICALLY FOR CLARK'S BLOG.
WHAT DO YOU THINK ABOUT THE NEW POWER COUPLE?
SHE CAN DEFINITELY DO BETTER.
ONCE IT WENT PUBLIC, WE FACED TOO MUCH SCRUTINY...FROM OUTSIDE FORCES AND OUR FRIENDS.
OF COURSE, BATMAN WAS THE FIRST TO FIND OUT...AND THE FIRST TO LET US KNOW THAT HE KNEW.
WE CONNECTED, BRUCE. IT JUST HAPPENED.
I'M HAPPY THAT YOU BOTH... FOUND SOMETHING TOGETHER.
YOU JUST NEED TO UNDERSTAND HOW THE REST OF THE WORLD--THE WORLD THAT DOESN'T KNOW YOU LIKE I DO--WILL REACT.
YOU'RE THE TWO MOST POWERFUL BEINGS ON EARTH. THEY'RE GOING TO BE GUNNING FOR YOU.
WHO WILL?
WHOEVER IS AFRAID OF WHAT YOU TWO COULD DO.

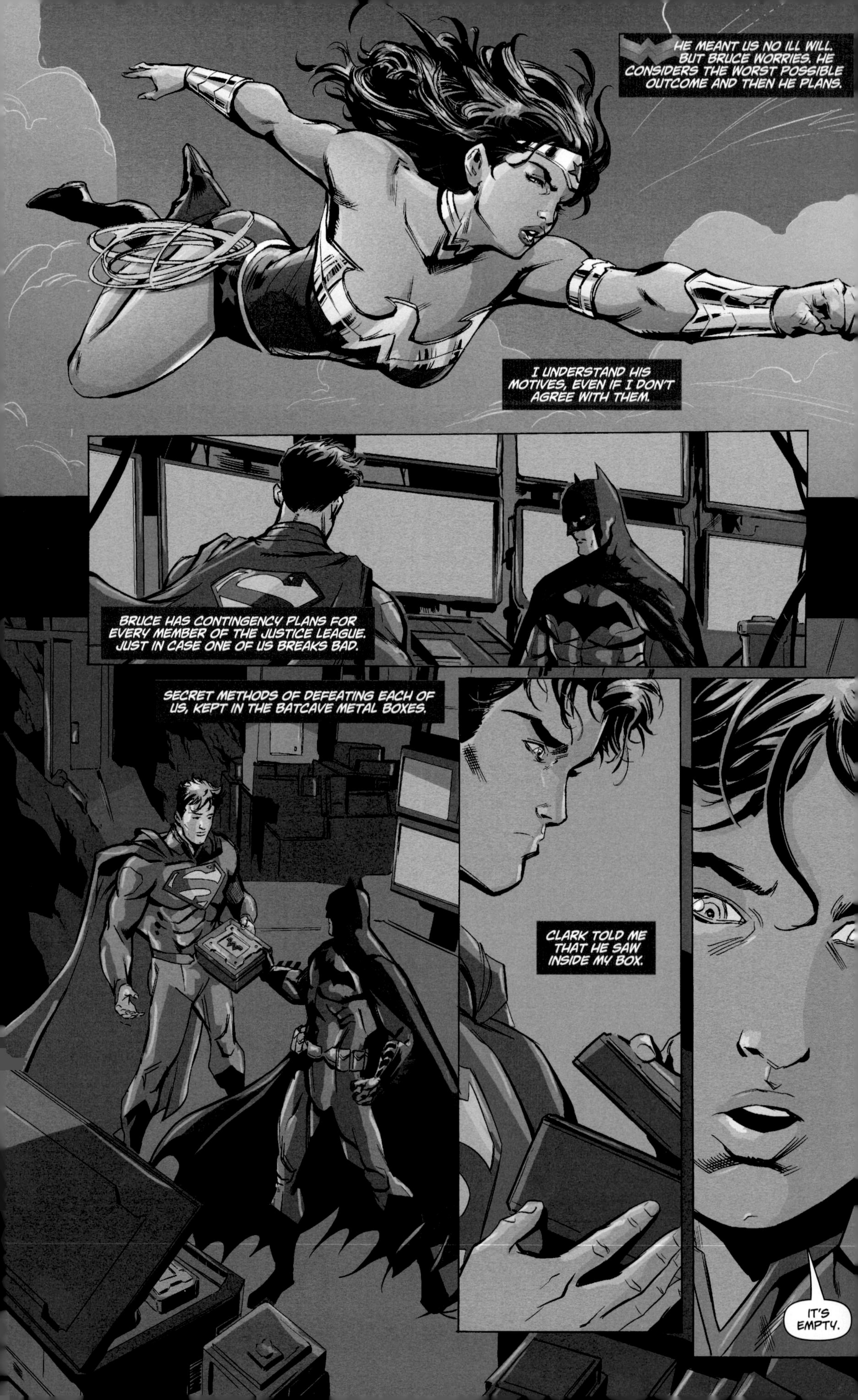
HE MEANT US NO ILL WILL. BUT BRUCE WORRIES. HE CONSIDERS THE WORST POSSIBLE OUTCOME AND THEN HE PLANS.
I UNDERSTAND HIS MOTIVES, EVEN IF I DON'T AGREE WITH THEM.
BRUCE HAS CONTINGENCY PLANS FOR EVERY MEMBER OF THE JUSTICE LEAGUE. JUST IN CASE ONE OF US BREAKS BAD.
SECRET METHODS OF DEFEATING EACH OF US, KEPT IN THE BATCAVE METAL BOXES.
CLARK TOLD ME THAT HE SAW INSIDE MY BOX.
IT'S EMPTY.

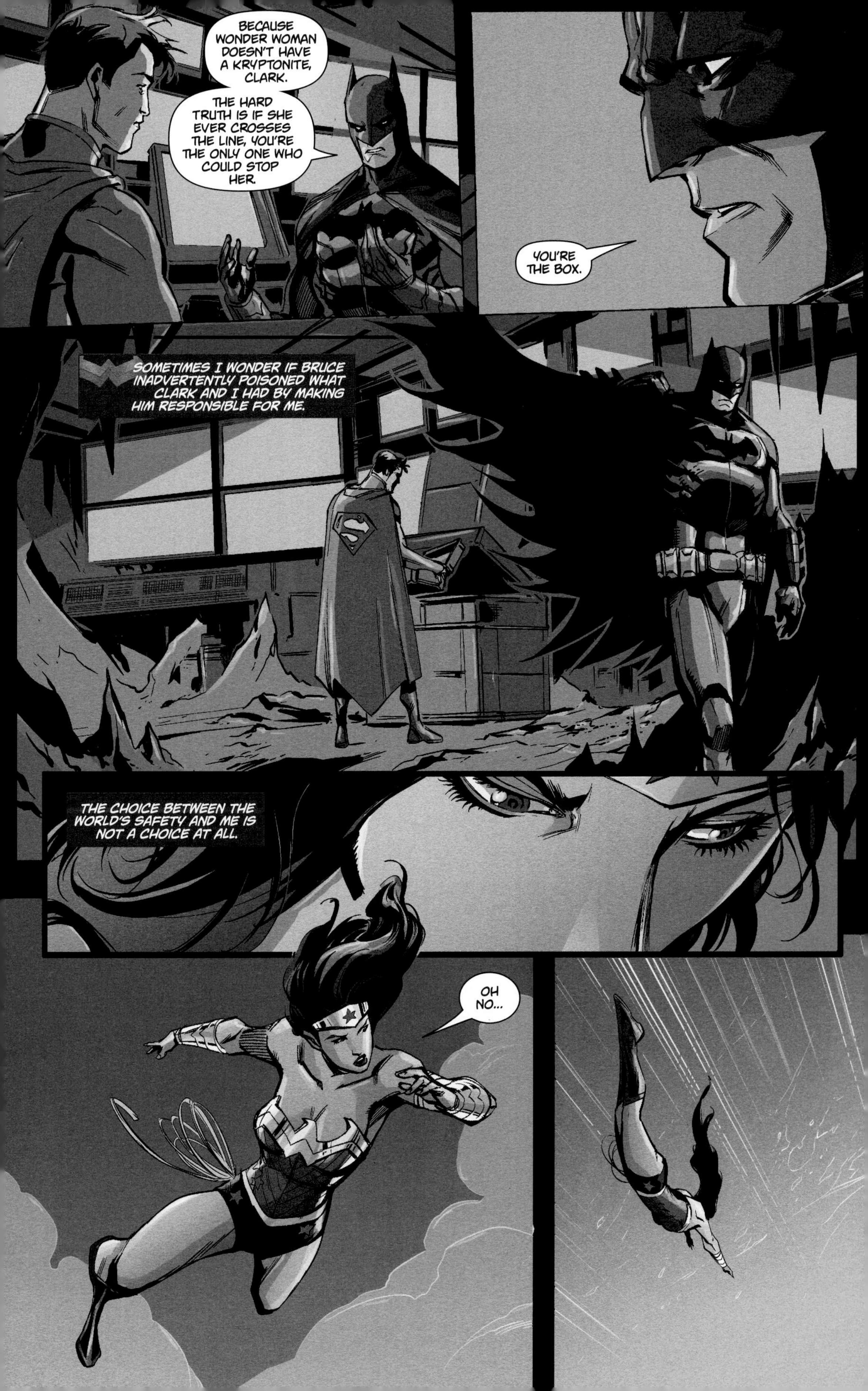
BECAUSE WONDER WOMAN DOESN'T HAVE A KRYPTONITE, CLARK.
THE HARD TRUTH IS IF SHE EVER CROSSES THE LINE, YOU'RE THE ONLY ONE WHO COULD STOP HER.
YOU'RE THE BOX.
SOMETIMES I WONDER IF BRUCE INADVERTENTLY POISONED WHAT CLARK AND I HAD BY MAKING HIM RESPONSIBLE FOR ME.
THE CHOICE BETWEEN THE WORLD'S SAFETY AND ME IS NOT A CHOICE AT ALL.
OH NO...

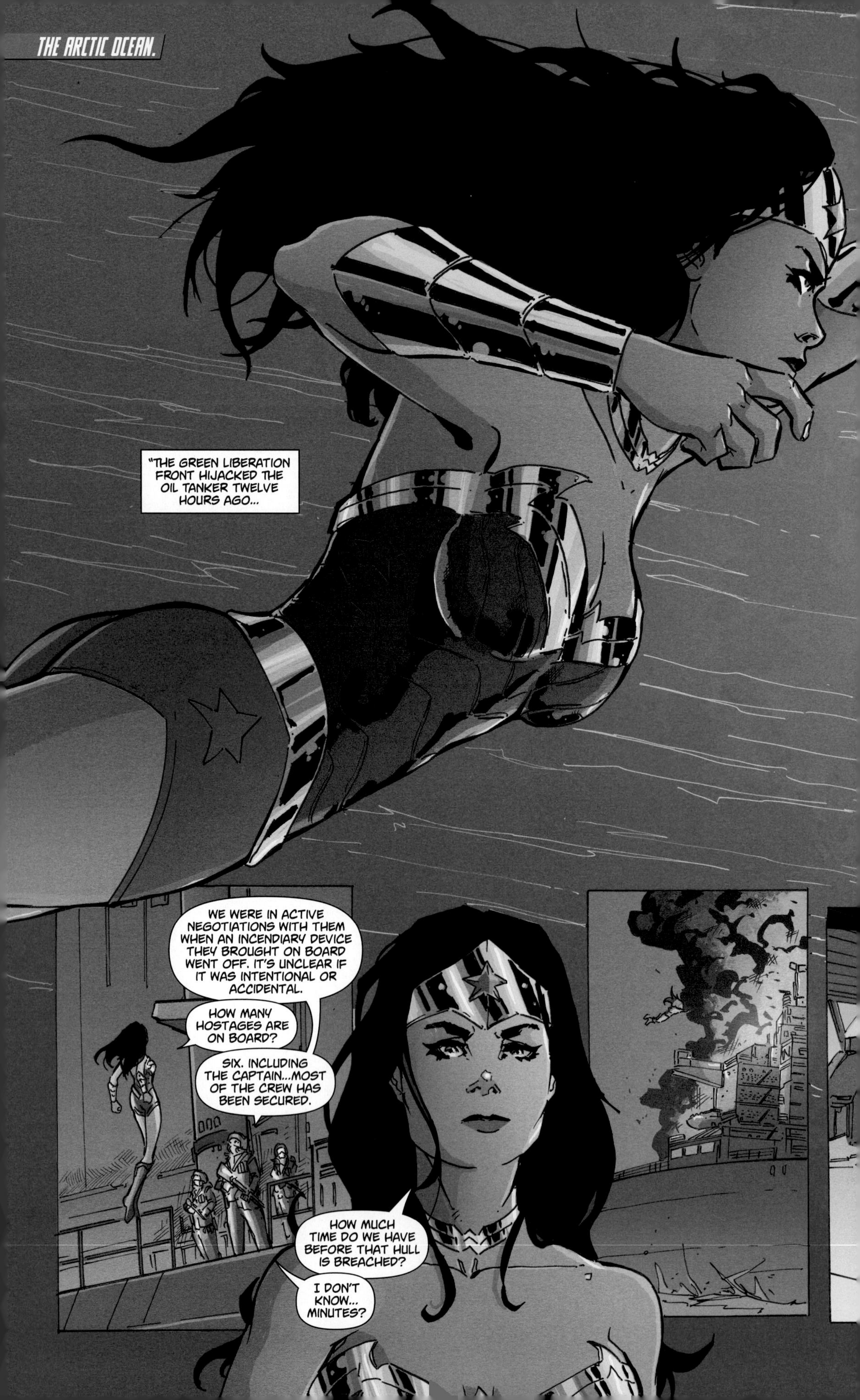
THE ARCTIC OCEAN.
"THE GREEN LIBERATION FRONT HIJACKED THE OIL TANKER TWELVE HOURS AGO...
WE WERE IN ACTIVE NEGOTIATIONS WITH THEM WHEN AN INCENDIARY DEVICE THEY BROUGHT ON BOARD WENT OFF. IT'S UNCLEAR IF IT WAS INTENTIONAL OR ACCIDENTAL.
HOW MANY HOSTAGES ARE ON BOARD?
SIX. INCLUDING THE CAPTAIN...MOST OF THE CREW HAS BEEN SECURED.
HOW MUCH TIME DO WE HAVE BEFORE THAT HULL IS BREACHED?
I DON'T KNOW... MINUTES?

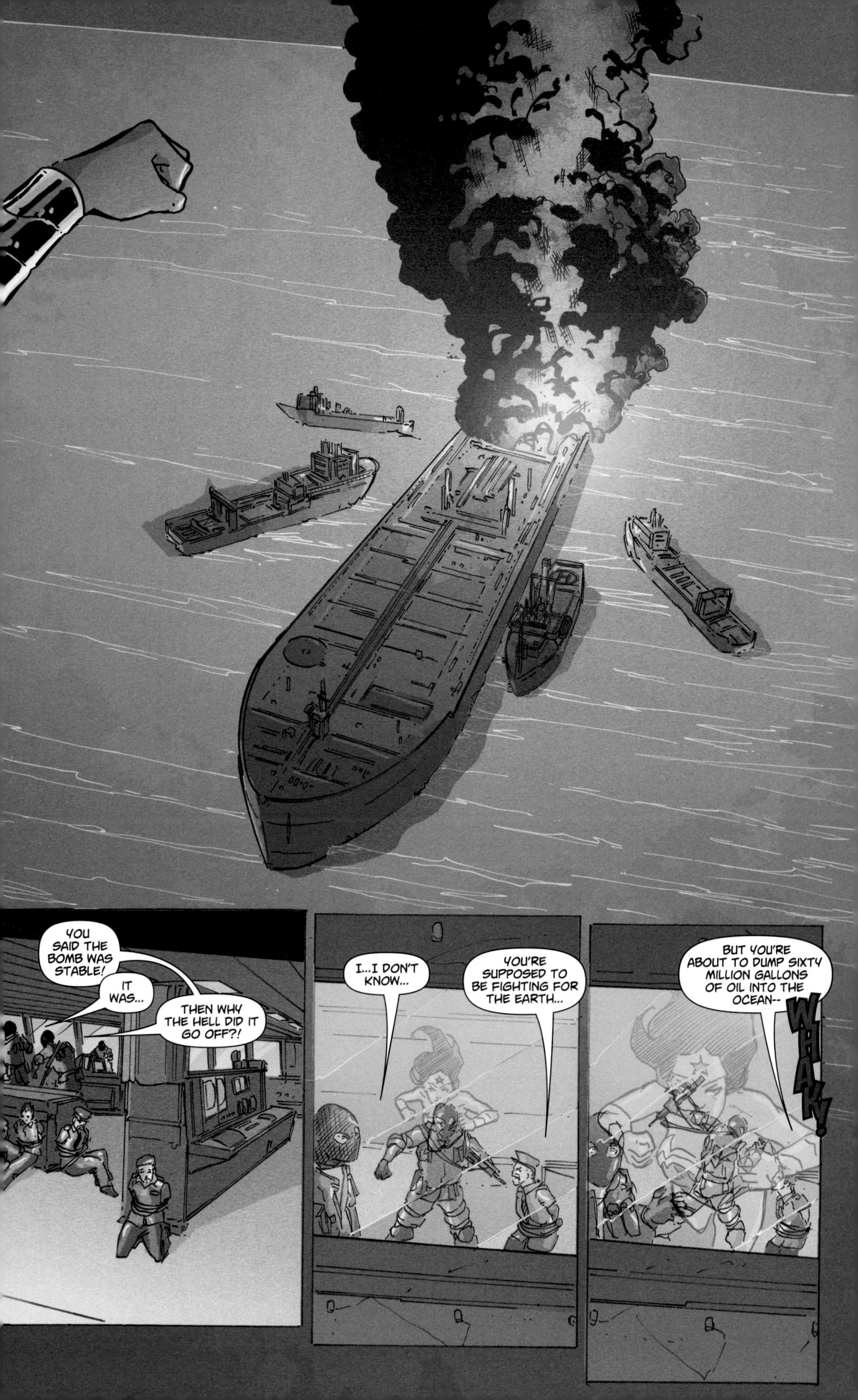
YOU SAID THE BOMB WAS STABLE!
IT WAS...
THEN WHY THE HELL DID IT GO OFF?!
I...I DON'T KNOW...
YOU'RE SUPPOSED TO BE FIGHTING FOR THE EARTH...
BUT YOU'RE ABOUT TO DUMP SIXTY MILLION GALLONS OF OIL INTO THE OCEAN--
WHAK!

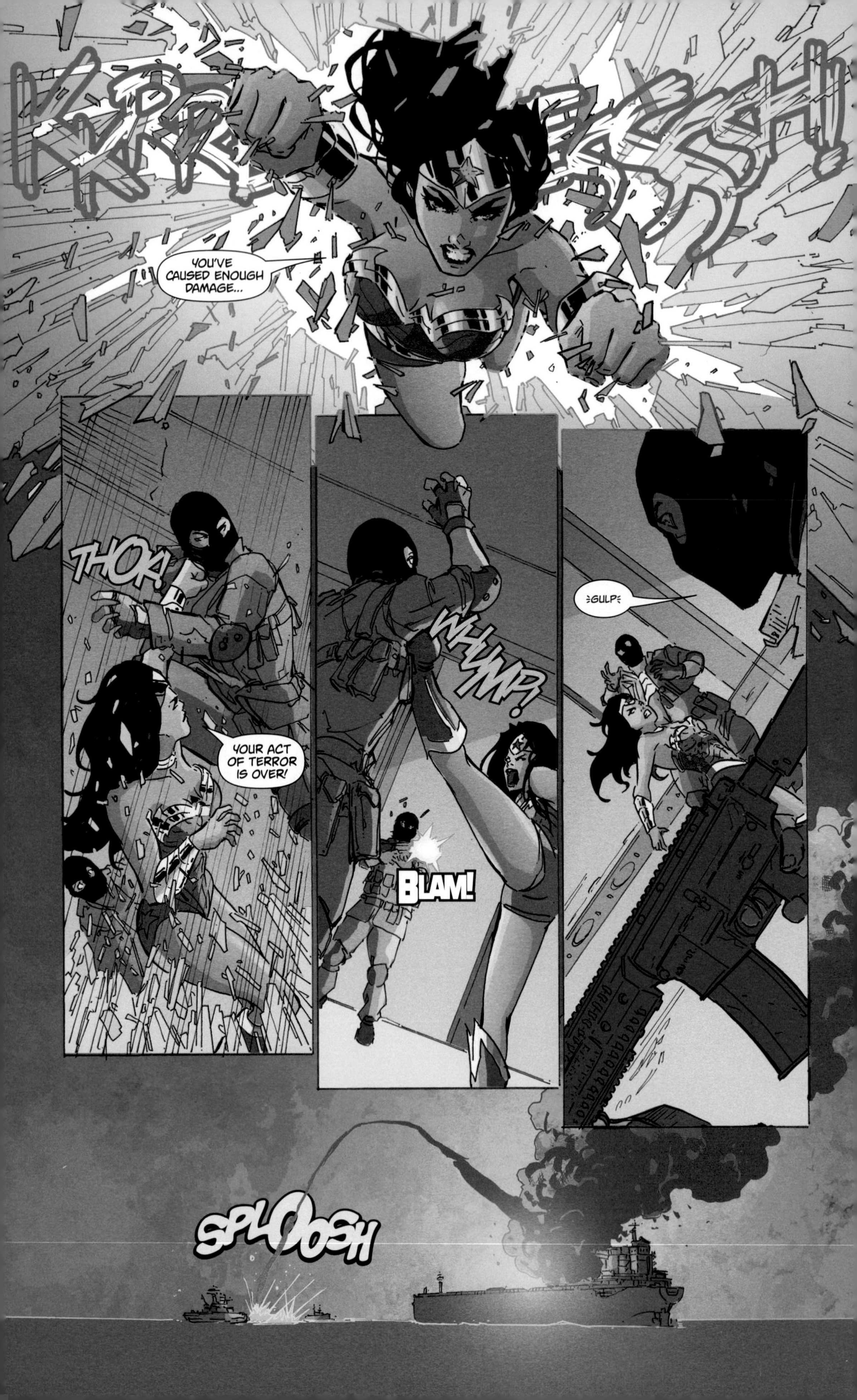
KRRAKKSSH!
YOU'VE CAUSED ENOUGH DAMAGE...
THOK!
YOUR ACT OF TERROR IS OVER!
WHUMP!
BLAM!
GULP
SPLOOSH

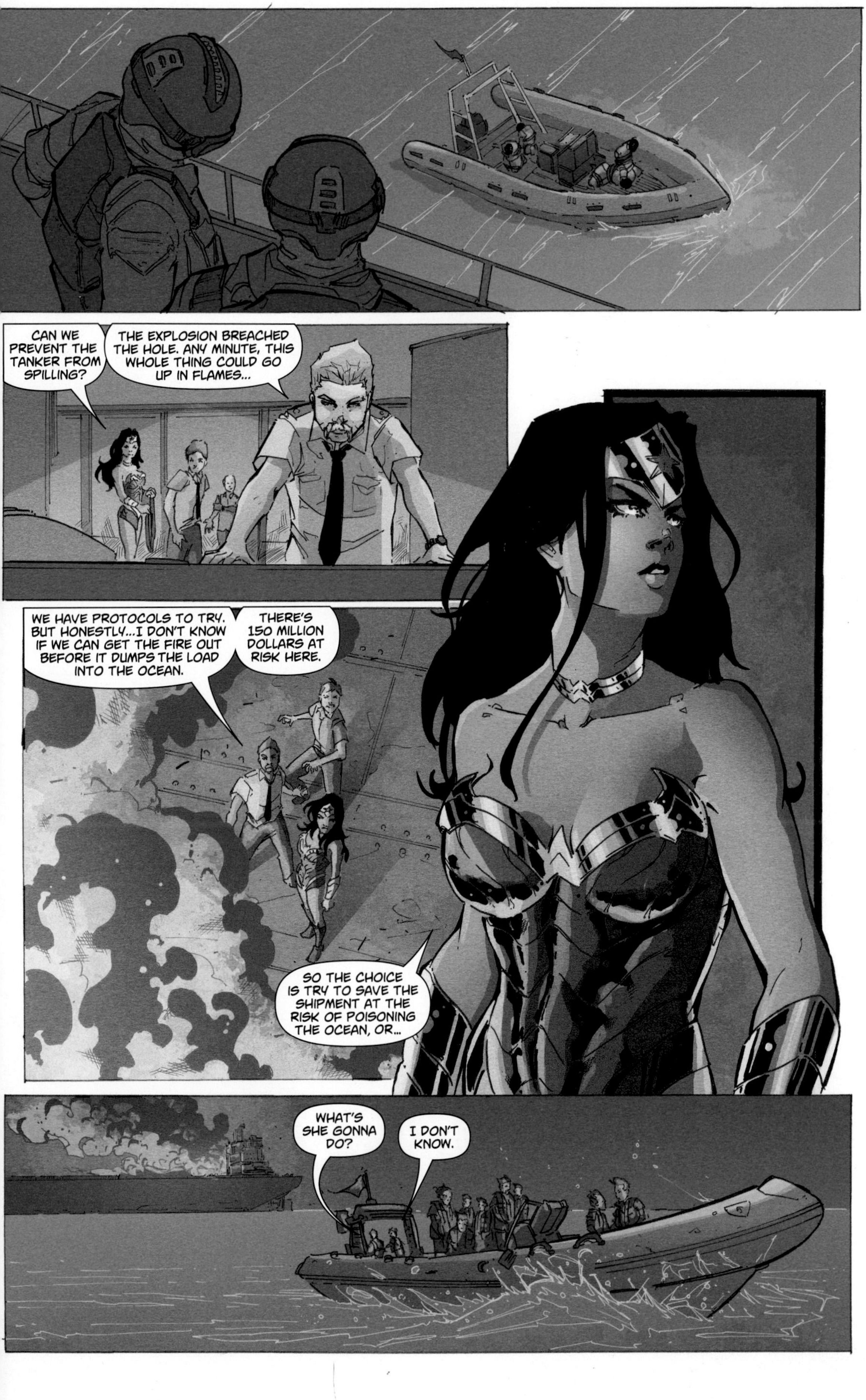
CAN WE PREVENT THE TANKER FROM SPILLING?
THE EXPLOSION BREACHED THE HOLE. ANY MINUTE, THIS WHOLE THING COULD GO UP IN FLAMES...
WE HAVE PROTOCOLS TO TRY. BUT HONESTLY...I DON'T KNOW IF WE CAN GET THE FIRE OUT BEFORE IT DUMPS THE LOAD INTO THE OCEAN.
THERE'S 150 MILLION DOLLARS AT RISK HERE.
SO THE CHOICE IS TRY TO SAVE THE SHIPMENT AT THE RISK OF POISONING THE OCEAN, OR...
WHAT'S SHE GONNA DO?
I DON'T KNOW.

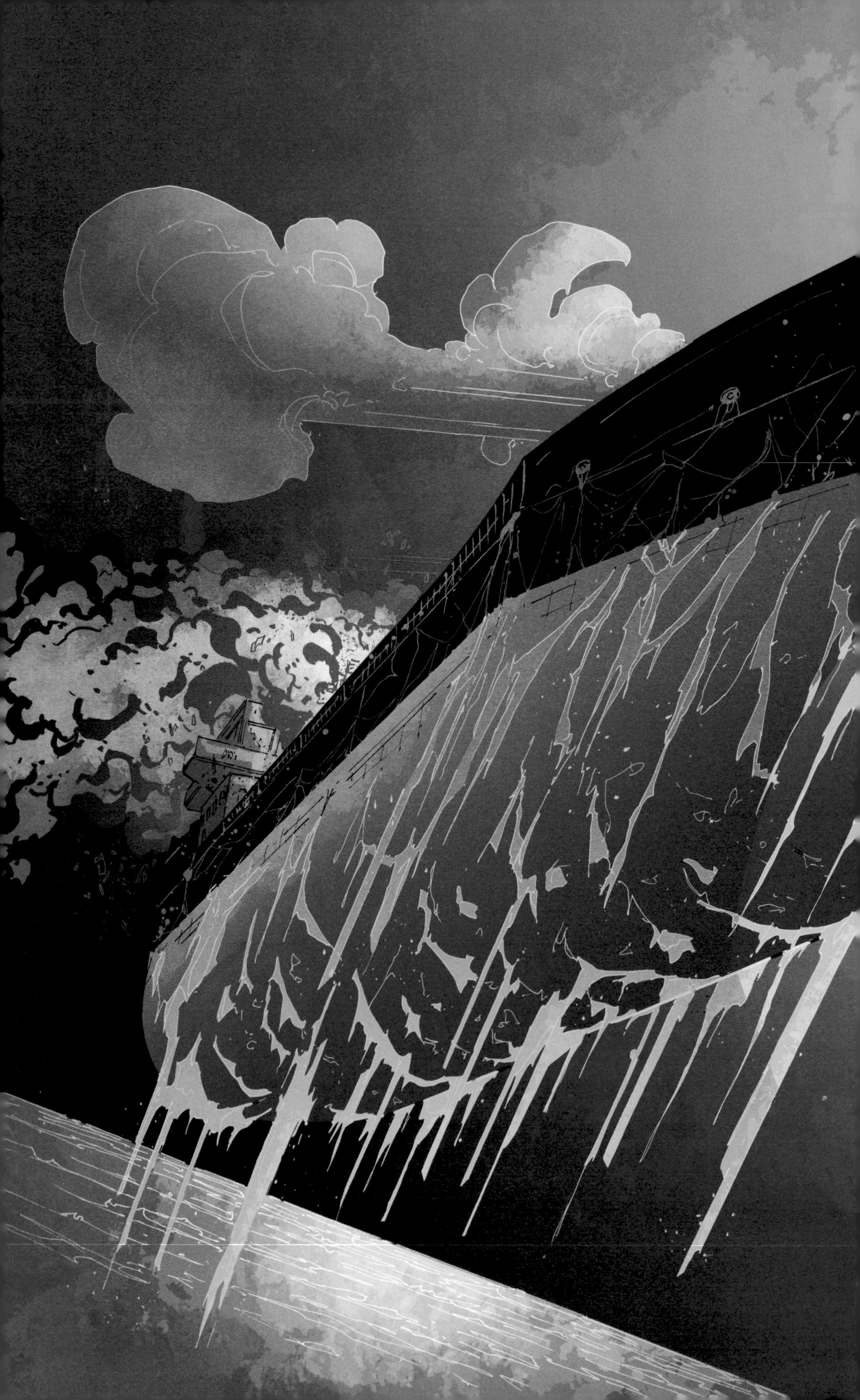

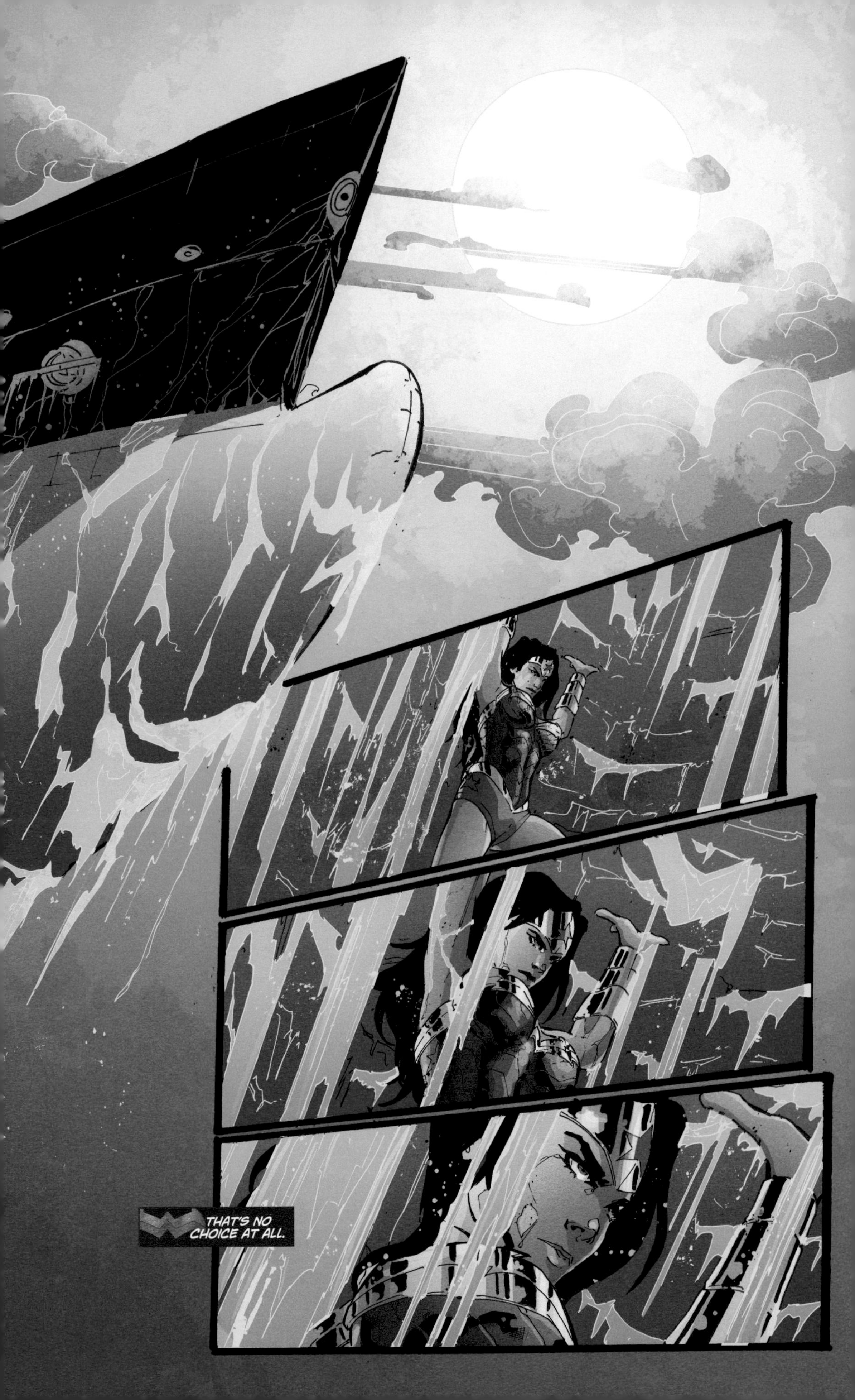
THAT'S NO
CHOICE AT ALL.

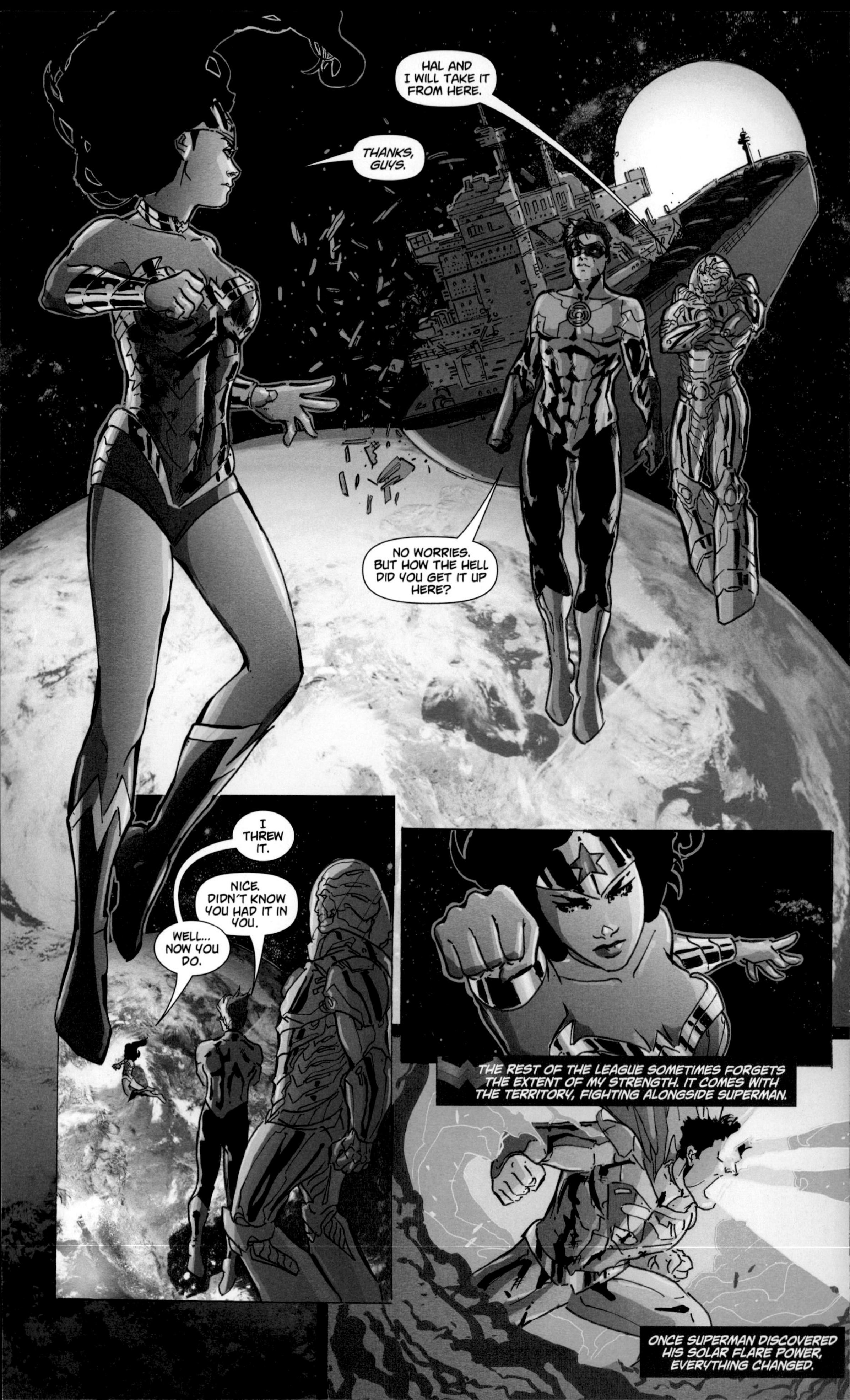
HAL AND I WILL TAKE IT FROM HERE.
THANKS, GUYS.
NO WORRIES. BUT HOW THE HELL DID YOU GET IT UP HERE?
I THREW IT.
NICE. DIDN'T KNOW YOU HAD IT IN YOU.
WELL... NOW YOU DO.
THE REST OF THE LEAGUE SOMETIMES FORGETS THE EXTENT OF MY STRENGTH. IT COMES WITH THE TERRITORY, FIGHTING ALONGSIDE SUPERMAN.
ONCE SUPERMAN DISCOVERED HIS SOLAR FLARE POWER, EVERYTHING CHANGED.

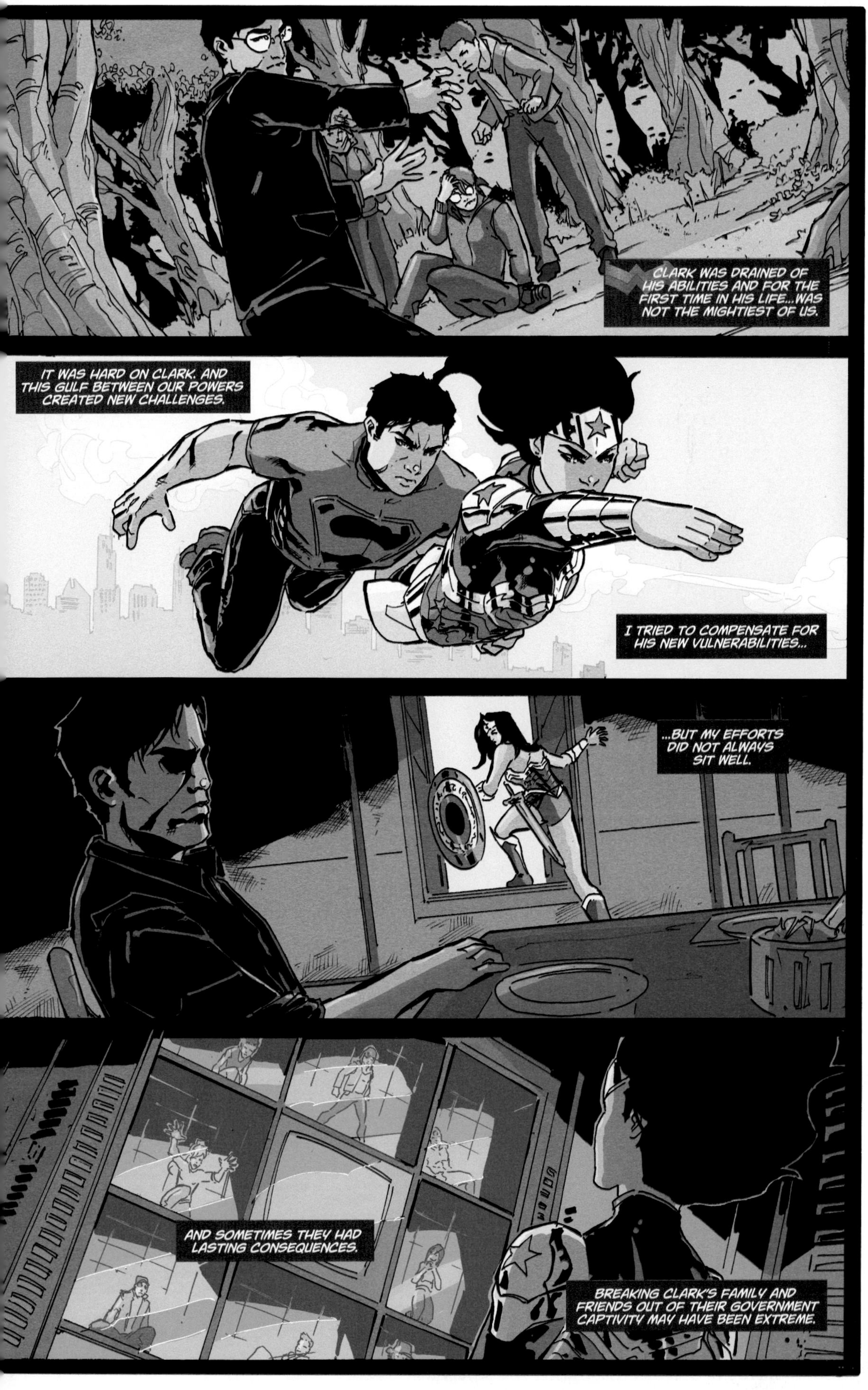
CLARK WAS DRAINED OF HIS ABILITIES AND FOR THE FIRST TIME IN HIS LIFE...WAS NOT THE MIGHTIEST OF US.
IT WAS HARD ON CLARK. AND THIS GULF BETWEEN OUR POWERS CREATED NEW CHALLENGES.
I TRIED TO COMPENSATE FOR HIS NEW VULNERABILITIES...
...BUT MY EFFORTS DID NOT ALWAYS SIT WELL.
AND SOMETIMES THEY HAD LASTING CONSEQUENCES.
BREAKING CLARK'S FAMILY AND FRIENDS OUT OF THEIR GOVERNMENT CAPTIVITY MAY HAVE BEEN EXTREME.

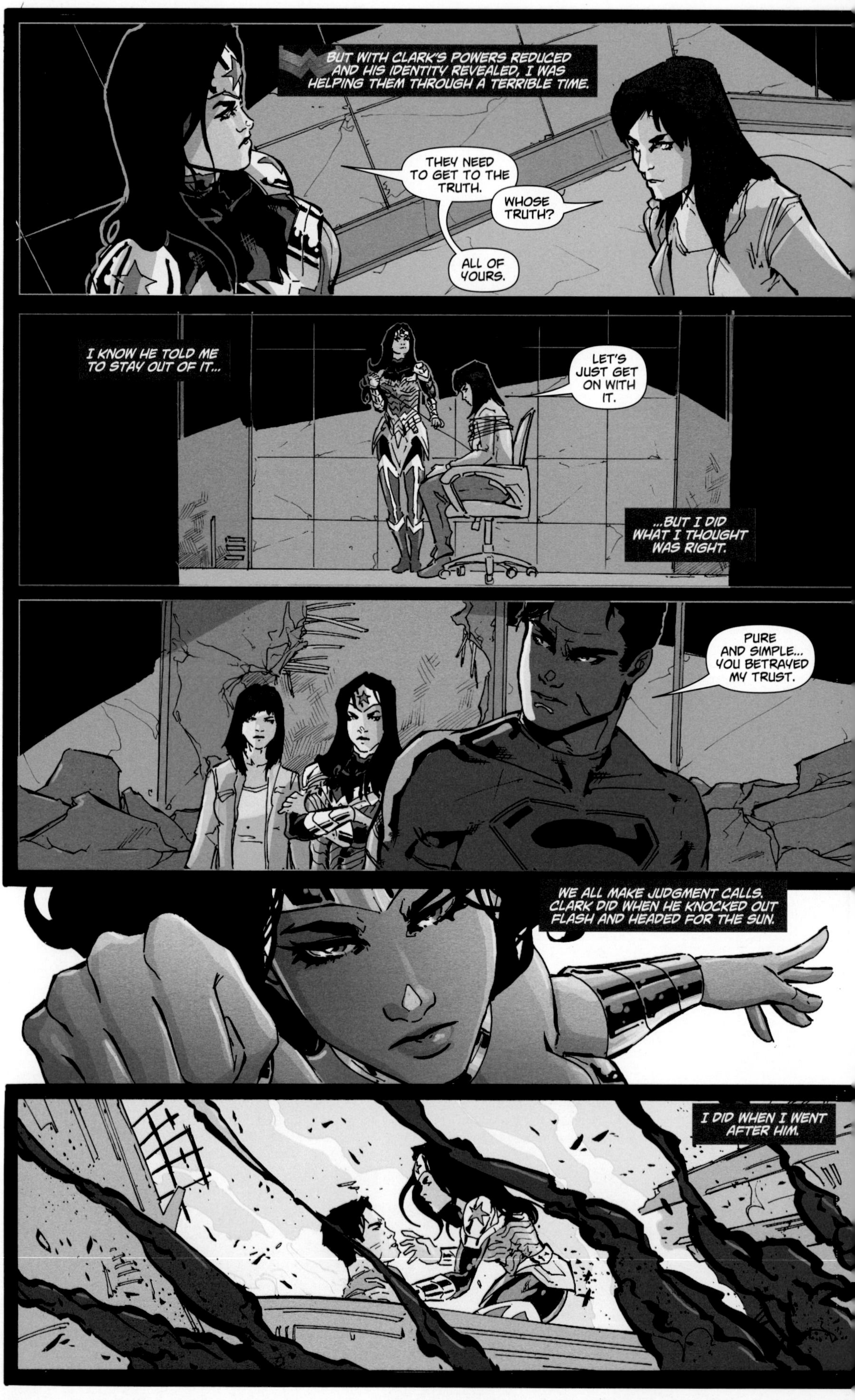
BUT WITH CLARK'S POWERS REDUCED AND HIS IDENTITY REVEALED, I WAS HELPING THEM THROUGH A TERRIBLE TIME.
THEY NEED TO GET TO THE TRUTH.
WHOSE TRUTH?
ALL OF YOURS.
I KNOW HE TOLD ME TO STAY OUT OF IT...
LET'S JUST GET ON WITH IT.
...BUT I DID WHAT I THOUGHT WAS RIGHT.
PURE AND SIMPLE... YOU BETRAYED MY TRUST.
WE ALL MAKE JUDGMENT CALLS. CLARK DID WHEN HE KNOCKED OUT FLASH AND HEADED FOR THE SUN.
I DID WHEN I WENT AFTER HIM.

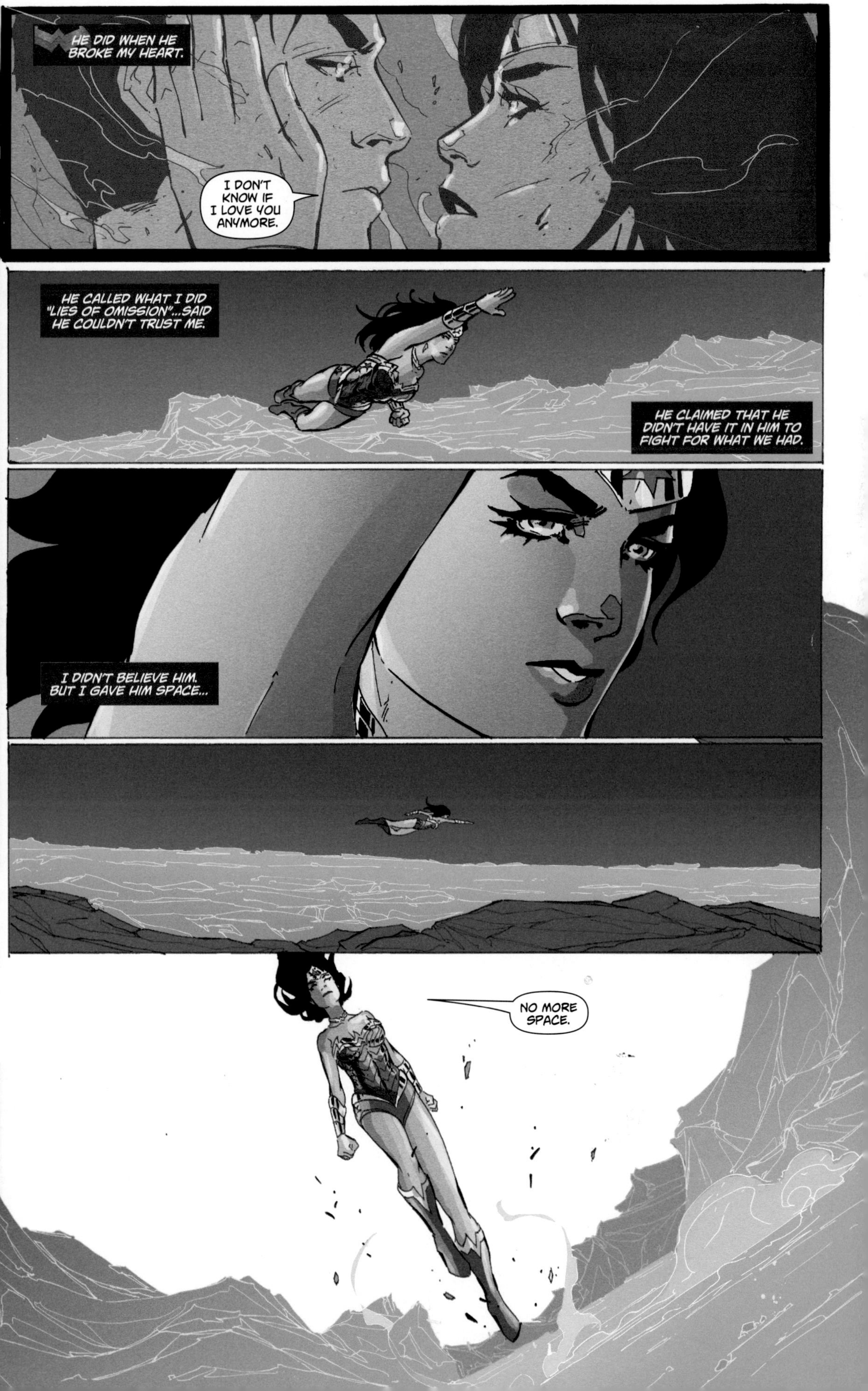
HE DID WHEN HE BROKE MY HEART.
I DON'T KNOW IF I LOVE YOU ANYMORE.
HE CALLED WHAT I DID "LIES OF OMISSION"...SAID HE COULDN'T TRUST ME.
HE CLAIMED THAT HE DIDN'T HAVE IT IN HIM TO FIGHT FOR WHAT WE HAD.
I DIDN'T BELIEVE HIM. BUT I GAVE HIM SPACE...
NO MORE SPACE.

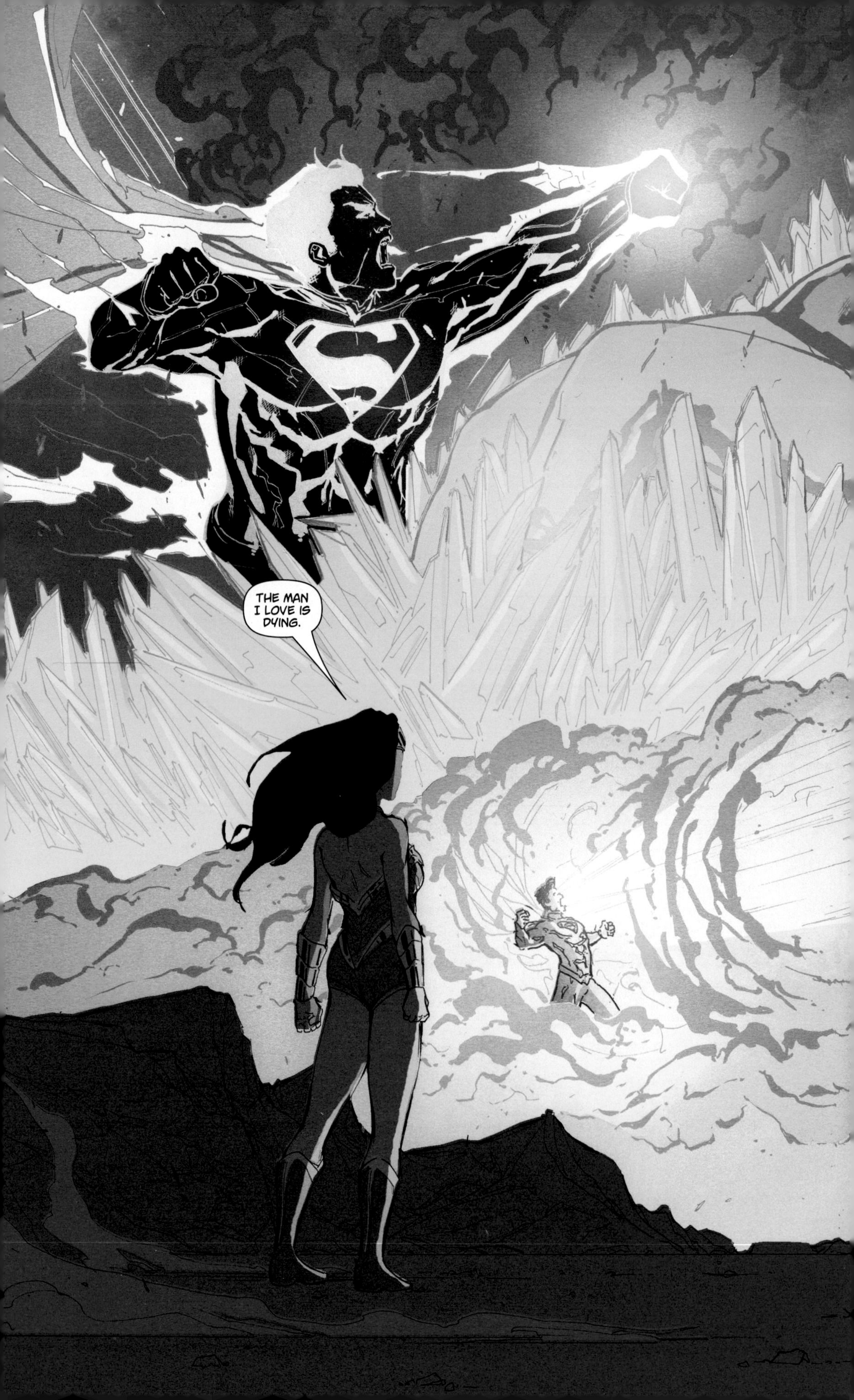
THE MAN I LOVE IS DYING.

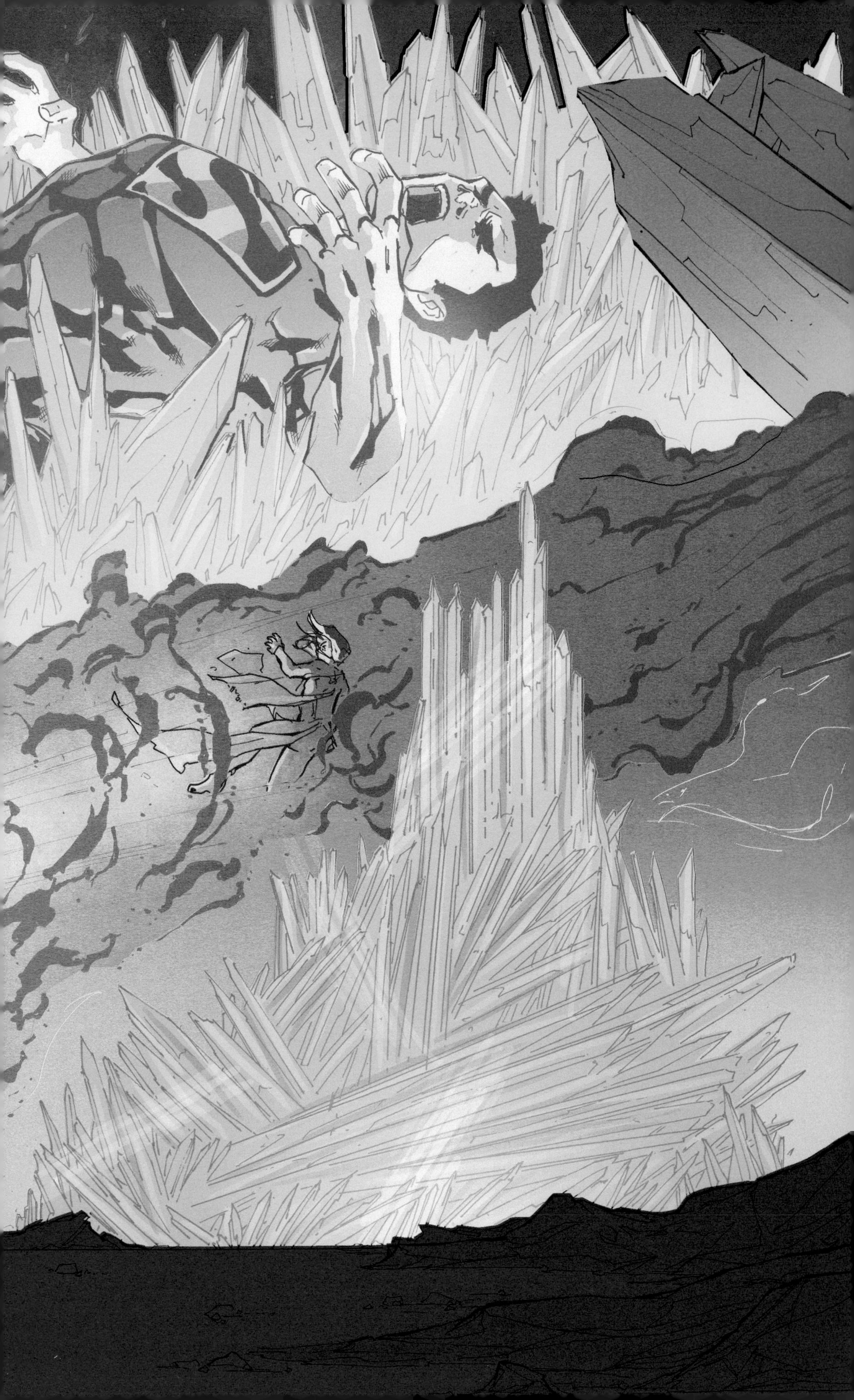

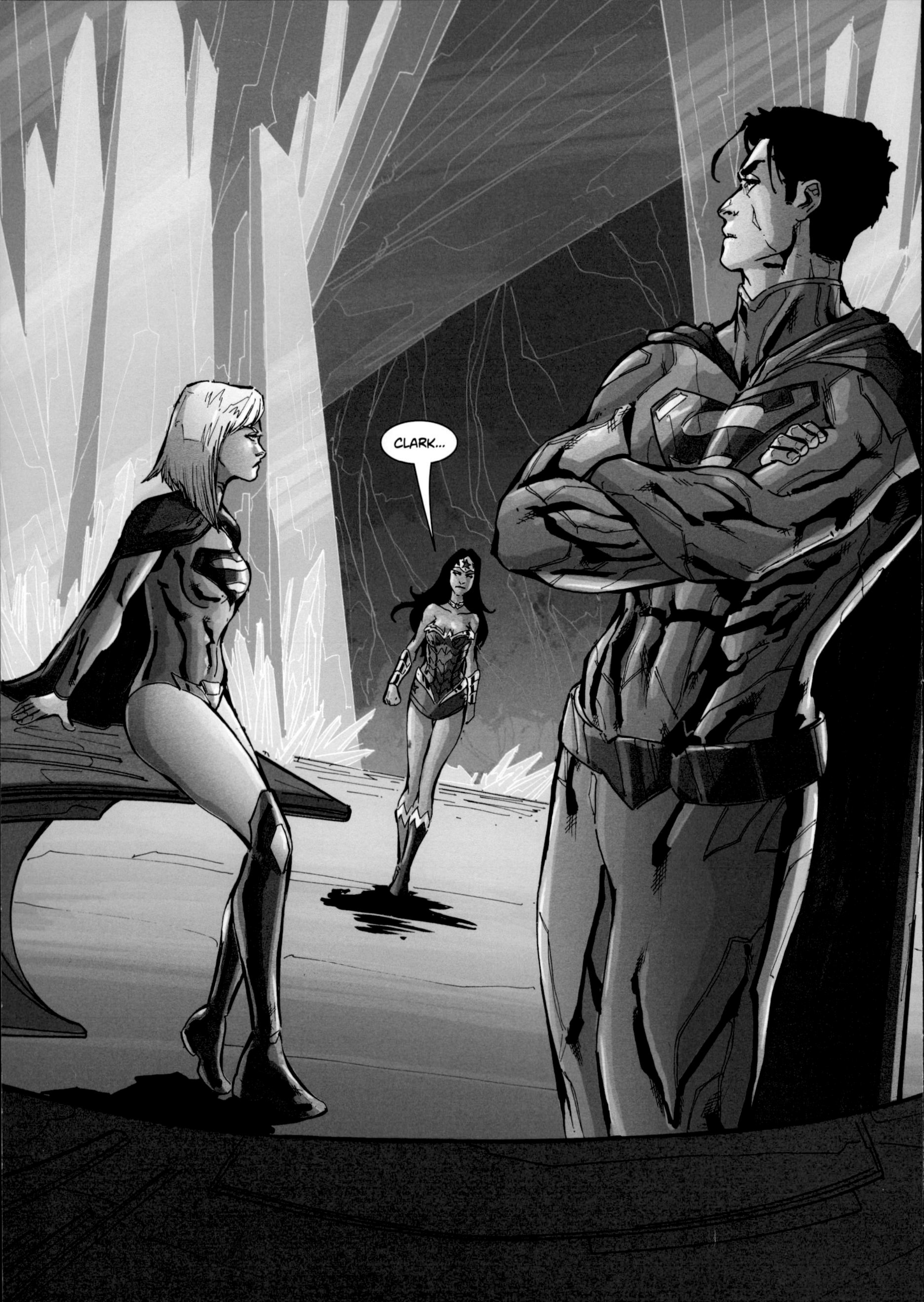
CLARK...

VARIANT COVER GALLERY

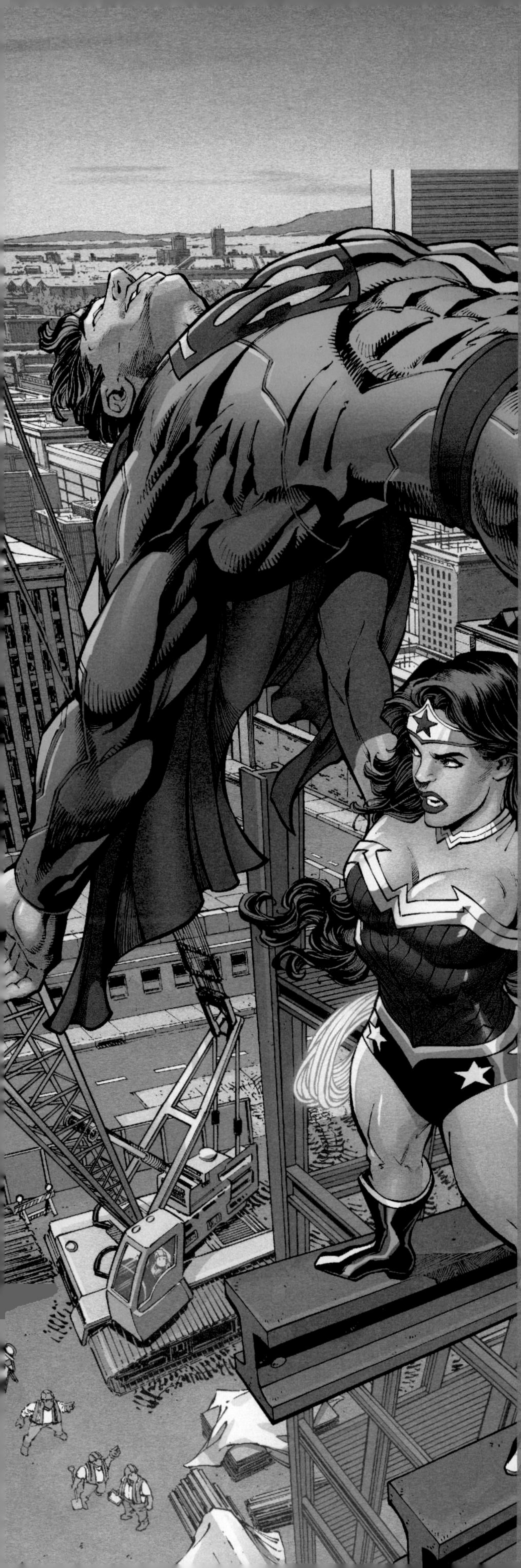

SUPERMAN/ WONDER WOMAN #25
ADULT COLORING BOOK
VARIANT BY AARON LOPRESTI

SUPERMAN/ WONDER WOMAN #26
NEAL ADAMS
VARIANT BY NEAL ADAMS
DANNY MIKI
HI-FI

SUPERMAN/ WONDER WOMAN #26
JUSTICE LEAGUE TRIPTYCH
VARIANT BY KIM JUNG GI
ALEX SINCLAIR

SUPERMAN/ WONDER WOMAN #27
BATMAN V SUPERMAN
VARIANT BY CHARLIE ADLARD
DAVE STEWART

SUPERMAN/ WONDER WOMAN #28
JOHN ROMITA JR.
VARIANT BY JOHN ROMITA JR.
SCOTT HANNA
LAURA MARTIN

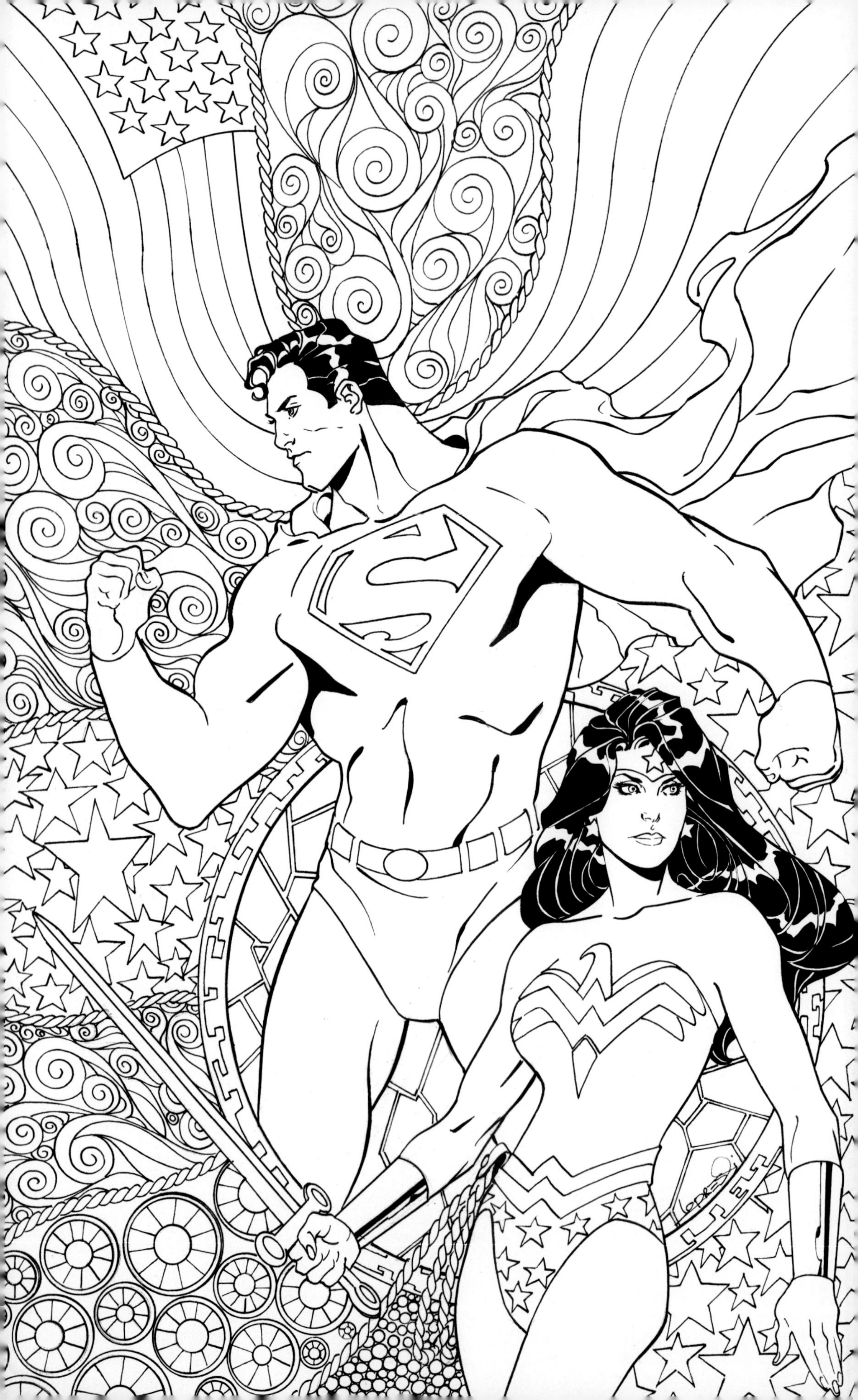

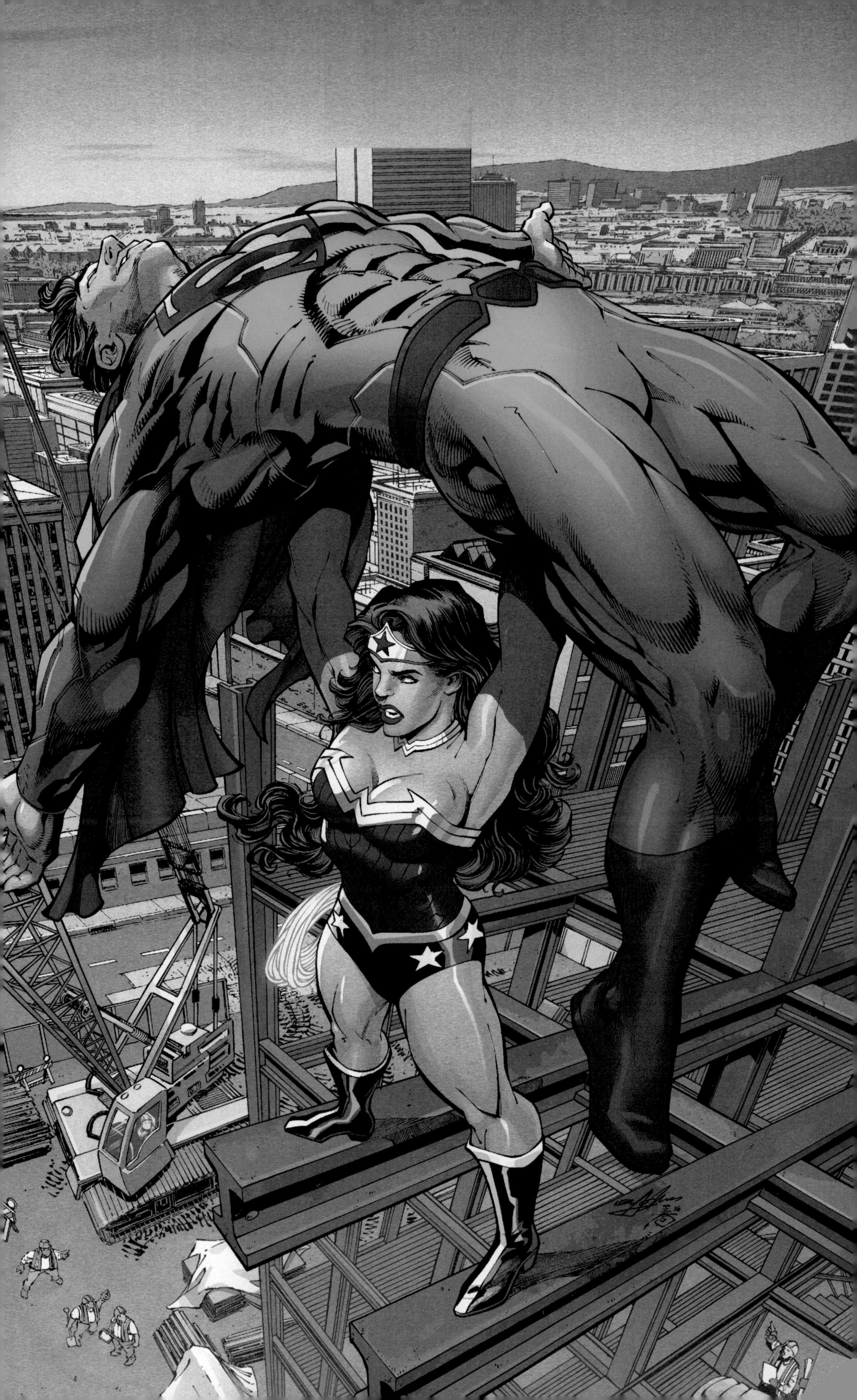

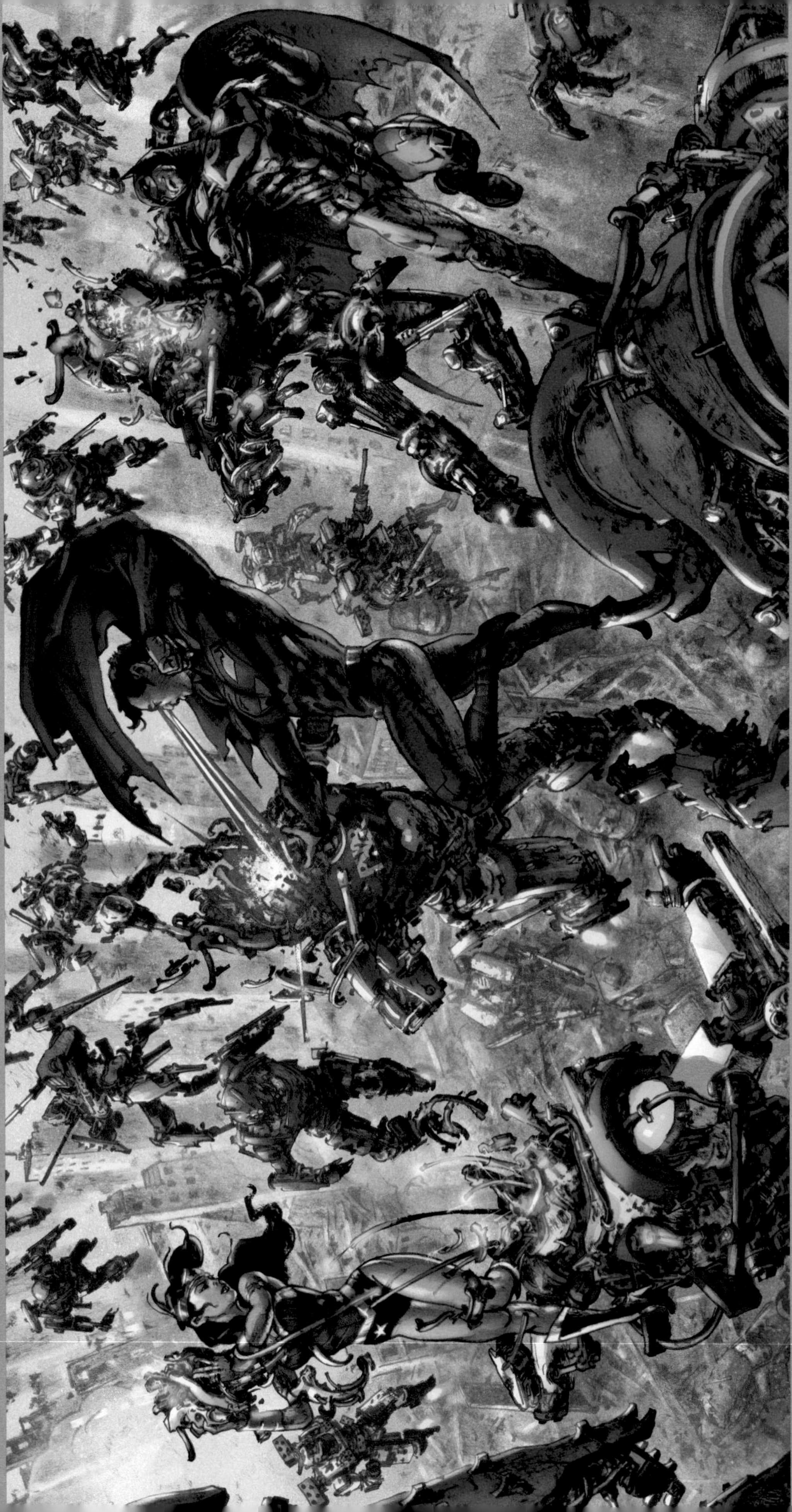

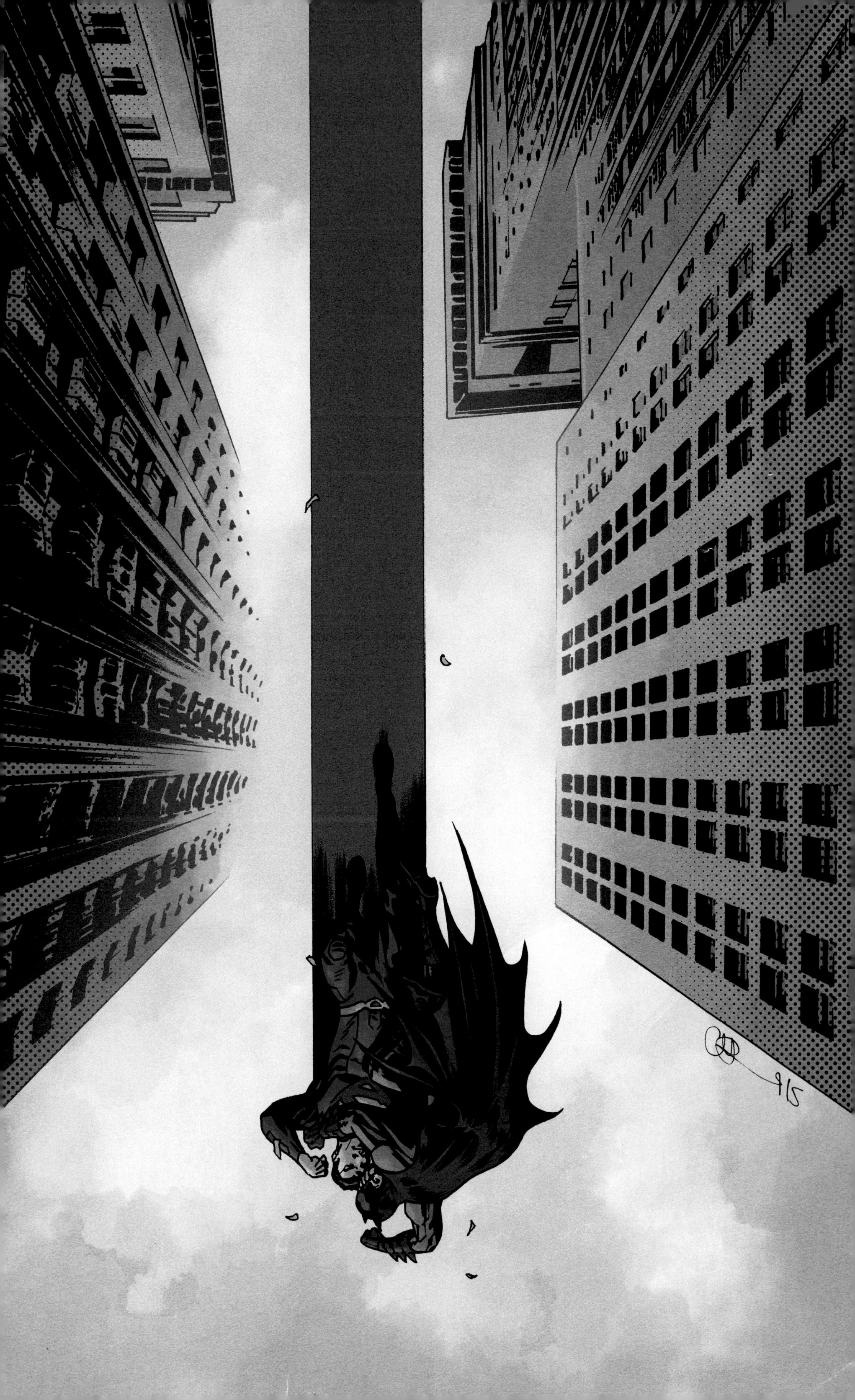

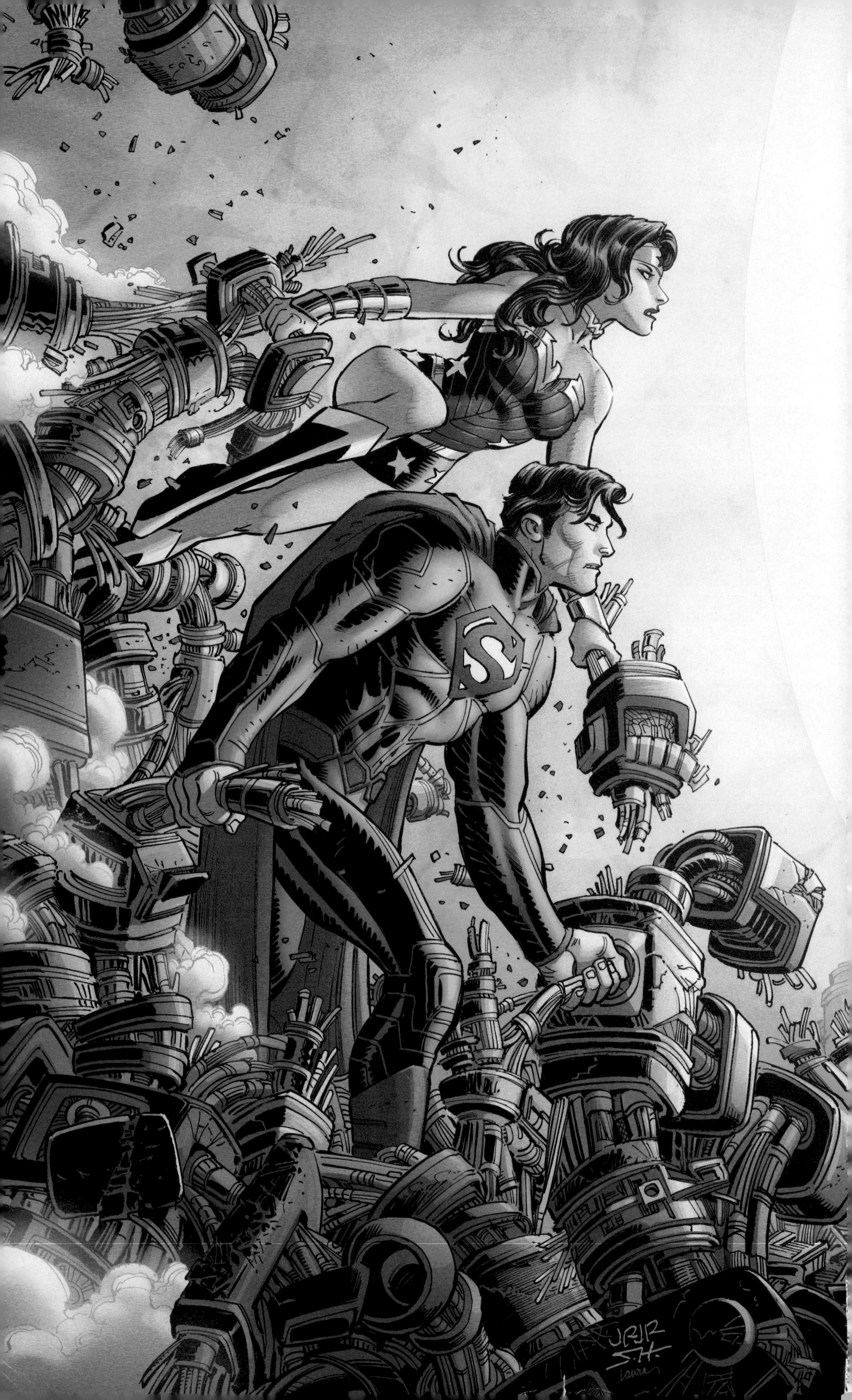
JRJR
S.H.
Laura